Getting Medieval

Edited by Michèle Aina Barale, Jonathan Goldberg,

Michael Moon, and Eve Kosofsky Sedgwick

Getting Medieval

Sexualities and Communities, Pre- and Postmodern

Carolyn Dinshaw

Duke University Press Durham and London

1999

Printed in the United States of America on acid-free paper ⊗

Designed by C. H. Westmoreland

Typeset in Monotype Fournier by Tseng Information Systems, Inc.

Library of Congress Cataloging-in-Publication Data appear on the last printed page of this book.

for Marget

We need history for life and action,
not as a convenient way to avoid life and action,
or to excuse a selfish life and cowardly or base deeds.

Nietzsche
The Use and Abuse of History

Contents

Acknowledgments

In imagining and writing this book I've been given lots of help from many people. I'd like to name several whose advice and encouragement over the years of my configuring and reconfiguring this project have proved crucial: Sue Schweik, Paul Strohm, David Hult, David Román, David Halperin, Sharon Marcus, Daniel Boyarin, Caren Kaplan, and Eric Smoodin. Several others read parts of the manuscript in various stages and offered welcome comments: Simon Gaunt, Steven Justice, Colleen Lye, Anne Middleton, Ruth Nissé Shklar, Rita Copeland, Ann Cvetkovich, Steven Kruger, and Ralph Hexter. Thanks go to Ralph Hexter as well for his guidance and hospitality as keeper of John Boswell's papers. Thanks too to Didier Eribon and to Robert Glück for invigorating conversations; to Anne Hudson for her willingness to answer a neophyte's questions; and to reviewers in the Berkeley English department for vigorous and stimulating remarks.

I have benefited enormously from presenting these materials to audiences—both receptive and challenging—and would like to thank many colleagues for gracious invitations: Peter Allen, Christopher Baswell, John Bowers, Gregory Bredbeck, Robert Burlin, James Cain, Michael Camille, Mary Carruthers, Jane Chance, Theresa Coletti, James Dean, Susan Dunn and Keith Baker, Richard Emmerson, Edward English, Louise Fradenburg, Carla Freccero, Dolores Frese and Katherine O'Brien O'Keeffe, Susanne Hafner and María Bullón-Fernández, Jill Havens, Martin Irvine, H. A. Kelly, Clare Lees, Mary Poovey, David Román, Francesca Canadé Sautman and Steven Kruger, Elizabeth Scala, R. A. Shoaf, Paul Strohm and James Schultz, Peggy McCracken, Karma Lochrie, and Karen Scott, in addition to the Medieval/Renaissance Studies Program at Wellesley College and the Gay and Lesbian Historical Society of Northern California. A special word of thanks is due my students at UC Berkeley over the years, both undergraduate and graduate, and at Stanford during the spring of 1997 for their daily willingness to engage and their provocations. I have been blessed by great graduate research assistants at Berkeley, including Claire Kageyama and Hilary Zaid, and especially Jim Hinch, Martha Rust, and Katie Vulić.

I'm very grateful for various grants of research support from UC Berkeley and particularly for a President's Fellowship from the University of California. And I am most thankful for the Martha Sutton Weeks Fellowship at the Stanford Humanities Center, where I spent a wonderfully productive year among the palm trees.

At Duke University Press, I'm happy to thank Ken Wissoker and Richard Morrison for their editorial care. Many thanks, too, go to the readers of the manuscript for the press, and to David Sullivan for the index.

Portions of chapter 2 and a few paragraphs of the introduction appeared in very early form in "Chaucer's Queer Touches/A Queer Touches Chaucer," *Exemplaria: A Journal of Theory in Medieval and Renaissance Studies* 7 (March 1995): 76–92; two paragraphs of "A Kiss Is Just a Kiss: Heterosexuality and Its Consolations in *Sir Gawain and the Green Knight*," *diacritics* 24.2–3 (1994): 205–26, represent an early version of an analysis in chapter 2. A previous version of the coda material appeared in "Getting Medieval: *Pulp Fiction*, Gawain, Foucault," in *The Book and the Body*, edited by Dolores Warwick Frese and Katherine O'Brien O'Keeffe, copyright 1997 by University of Notre Dame Press. Used by permission of publisher. I acknowledge permission to quote from *Pulp Fiction: A Quentin Tarantino Screenplay*, copyright 1994 by Quentin Tarantino, reprinted with permission by Hyperion.

At last, to my family goes my deep gratitude for their support. And to Marget Long, my ideal reader, go my never ending thanks for everything that made this book possible: touch, soul, color, spirit, love.

Getting Medieval

Introduction

Touching on the Past

"Tell me, Daddy. What is the use of history?"
Marc Bloch, *The Historian's Craft*

This book is about several interrelated groups, real and fictional, in late-fourteenth- and early-fifteenth-century England—groups that in particular had some contact with the tenets of the heretical Lollards.[1] It is about the ways these groups constituted themselves as communities, the phenomena they necessarily cast out in those constitutive processes, and the afterlives of those abjected phenomena. And it is about ways in which some people in the late-twentieth-century West make relations with those very phenomena from the past in constituting ourselves and our communities now.

The focus in the analyses that follow is sex: how do communities, then and now, form themselves in relation to sex? Sex is heterogeneous, multiple, and fundamentally indeterminate; such qualities have complicated, undermined, and frustrated not only critical efforts to define an object of study but also community efforts to build distinct and unified associations on the basis of sex. But those very slippery characteristics, I argue throughout this book, are the condition, not the failure, of historical analyses and of the formation of selves and communities. I pursue historical analyses that embrace the heterogeneity of sex. And I follow what I call a queer historical impulse, an impulse toward making connections across time between, on the one hand, lives, texts, and other cultural phenomena left out of sexual categories back then and, on the other, those left out of current sexual categories now. Such an impulse extends the resources for self- and community building into even the distant past.

The project of constructing queer histories that are constituted by such affective relations across time has led me to materials that are not usually associated with one another: I touch on traditional religious instruction for parish priests, ringing accusations of sodomy among heretics as well as among orthodox Christians, the possibly quite wily deposition of a male transvestite prostitute, the ostensibly heterosexual fellowship of Chaucer's Canterbury pilgrims, and the energetic verbal sparring of Margery Kempe, all in fourteenth- and fifteenth-century England, for example, alongside obscure archival work of Michel Foucault, the culture wars in the late twentieth century in the United States, and sodomy in the 1994 blockbuster movie *Pulp Fiction*. Exactly how these materials can be related to one another and exactly what we get by making them touch are among my principal concerns in this book. In this introductory chapter I shall lay out some of the empirical and theoretical problems.

I trace the contours of my wide-ranging project by discussing several prominent—or, better, prominently symptomatic—works in this chapter, late-medieval as well as late-twentieth-century texts. First I allude to the immense plasticity of terms for deviant sex in late-medieval England: I take up in particular a manual for priests written by John Mirk and suggest some of the consequences of this heterogeneity for queer historical projects. Since the insistence on the heterogeneous subject (in both senses of the word) of historical study links me with postmodern historiography, I turn next to postmodern discussions of writing history; looking particularly at Homi K. Bhabha's work, I demonstrate both its radical potential for contesting legitimating narratives of the past and its problematic totalizing of the distant past as well as essentializing of the present. I then turn to the problem of specifying what, precisely, the nature of these preferred relations with the past might be: I discuss the concern for community in John Boswell's historical work, which is pervasive and fundamental to his approach to the past, both exerting a limit on his own findings and also—perhaps surprisingly—inspiring more wide-ranging and radical approaches to history and community formation. I then look at such approaches that explode the categories of sameness, otherness, present, past, loss, pleasure. In the company of such revisions I suggest that my queer history is contingent history in the postmodern sense—its forms are intelligible but do not emerge out of teleological necessity—as well as in the etymological sense (Latin *com-* + *tangere*, to touch). In the final section of this introduction I want to exemplify a queer historical touch: I touch on the texts, early and late, of Roland Barthes, whose work displays across its variety a consistent impulse to make contact, even finally a desire for bodies to touch across time.

Murky Distinctions

In his *Instructions for Parish Priests*, a manual of basic religious instruction written in Shropshire sometime between the late-fourteenth and mid-fifteenth centuries, John Mirk advises unlearned priests on the care of their parishioners—on how they should preach to them, what they need to teach them, and how they themselves should behave.[2] In the course of this rhymed and generally plain-spoken treatise—reliant for its very conventional message on William of Pagula's early-fourteenth-century *Oculus sacerdotis*—Mirk, an Augustinian canon, discusses many concerns, from the doctrinal (belief in transubstantiation is to be fostered, for example; the Pater Noster and creed, articles of the faith, seven sacraments, and so on, are to be taught) to the more practical religious knowledge that should be imparted.[3] In the latter category, priests should teach that a pregnant woman, for example, when her time is near, should confess and take communion, "For drede of perele that may be-falle" (for fear of the peril that might happen [83; such was the teaching Margery Kempe should have heard and followed])—and if things indeed go bad, the midwife should be ready to cut open the mother if she dies so that the child might be saved and baptized (87–102).

My concern here is with a passage following that one. After a brief discussion of proper wedlock (the priest should inform his flock as to who can marry whom, what constitutes divorce, when the banns should be proclaimed, that lechery, as a deadly sin, should be avoided by both single men and single women, and so on), Mirk turns his attention to other modes of coupling:

> Also wryten wel .I. fynde,
> That of synne aȝeynes kynde
> Thow schalt thy paresch no þynge teche,
> Ny of that synne no thynge preche . . . (222–25)

Also I find indeed in writing
That concerning sin against nature
You shall teach your parish nothing,
Nor preach anything about that sin . . .

In the midst of a treatise that is all about what parishioners need to know, what priests must preach, how they must teach their flocks about religious matters, comes this admonition against any public divulgation whatsoever: about this topic you must not teach, you must not preach—lest, the fear conventionally runs, you give people ideas.[4]

But despite that admonition to say nothing the treatise does go on to suggest what *should* indeed be said on the subject:

But say þus by gode a-vys,
þat to gret synne forsoþe hyt ys,
For any mon þat bereth lyf
To forsake hys wedded wyf
And do hys kynde other way;
þat ys gret synne wyþowte nay.
But how and where he doth þat synne,
To hys schryffader he mote þat mynne. (226–33)

But say thus, by good advice,
That it is very great sin, indeed,
For any man that bears life
To forsake his wedded wife
And have sex in another way,
That is great sin, there is no gainsaying.
But how and where he does that sin,
To his confessor he must such things relate.

The mid-nineteenth-century editorial gloss on the text narrows—symptomatically—the topic in these latter lines, assuming that "adultery" alone is at issue. The lines clearly state that this sin takes place when a man forsakes his wife, so adultery might indeed be involved; but the structure of the whole passage (do not preach or teach, but say this advisedly, and let the specifics be confessed to the confessor) indicates that the above-(not) mentioned "synne aȝeyes kynde"—

on its face a more general term than "adultery"—is still the primary concern under consideration here.[5]

This editorial distortion as symptom—of a long history of purposely *not* talking about such sin, a history of which these lines themselves form a part—is only the most obvious of the complex problems involved in doing queer history that are highlighted by this passage. Ironies swirl around the lines: some sins "aȝeynes kynde" are defined by this unspeakability, as we shall see through the course of this book—they can be so thoroughly associated with unmentionability that the very Bible's speaking openly about them apparently needs to be defended—but the admonition not to teach or preach about such sin is in fact constant.[6] The passage is entirely conventional; Mirk finds it in fact already "wryten," presumably in William of Pagula, but in the more or less contemporary *Book of Vices and Virtues,* to take just one example, itself a translation of the late-thirteenth-century *Somme le roi,* there is a similar statement: the sin "is so foule and so hidous þat [it] scholde not be nempned [named], þat is synne aȝens kynde."[7] We can sense, in this explicitly traditional insistence not to speak, something of the productive nature of the taboo that Foucault makes the starting point of *The History of Sexuality,* volume 1. Thus if we want to begin to specify the problems raised for queer history here, our first question is therefore not the obvious "How can we trace something that has been deemed unspeakable?" but the subtler and more complex "How can we evaluate the insistent claim that this sin is unspeakable?" And in the specific contexts in which we find this judgment or admonition, we thus must ask: "What is the function of this claim of unmentionability here? How does this claim work to render some things intelligible, others unintelligible?"

But what is the sin of which we are not speaking? The difficulty of discerning the referent is tied up not only in the trope of unmentionability but also in the vagueness and polyvalence of the terms that are used—terms that strategically produce confusion as they are deployed in specific circumstances, as scholars such as Jonathan Goldberg and Mark D. Jordan maintain, following Foucault, and as I shall demonstrate specifically in chapter 1.[8] Note in the Mirk text that crucial phrase, "synne aȝeynes kynde." The complexities of the "natural" will emerge in chapter 2, so I shall not delineate exhaustively the uses of the Middle English "kynde" in my introductory discussion here; suffice it now to remark that "kynde," deriving from the Old English *cynd*, "nature," "kind," denotes innate or instinctual moral sense here, especially as that feeling draws on concepts of abstract Nature and the natural order of things as well as on concepts of origin, generation and generativity, birthright, natural bodily disposition and individual character, and a group with its commonalities.[9] Similarly, I shall simply note for the time being that in the project of understanding the meaning and function here of "aȝeynes kynde" it is important to determine what things, in realms other than the explicitly sexual, are deemed to be against nature: heresy, leprosy, treachery, for starters.[10] Mirk was writing in an unsettled climate in which Lollardy was feared; one major preoccupation of my book is to suggest ways in which discourses of heresy and of sexual irregularities are linked and mutually constitutive in England at this time.[11] That is part of the larger picture in which this passage operates.

At this introductory moment, though, I want just to glance at several uses of "aȝeynes kynde" and related phrases regarding sexual acts in fourteenth- and fifteenth-century English works, in order that we might begin to create a context for understanding this term and its use here.[12] In the *Book of Vices and Virtues*, the phrase is used to describe illicit acts with one's own wife: "Þe sixte [branch of lechery] is whan a man wiþ his owne wif doþ þing forboden and defended, aȝens kynde and aȝens þe ordre of wedloke" ("The sixth branch of lechery is when a man does a thing forbidden and prohibited with his own wife, against nature and against the order of marriage").[13] As Thomas Aquinas had set out, "part of the essence of animal sexual behavior" is "generative"; those sexual acts that are not directed to procreation are against nature, and thus heterosexual sex that avoids insemination is deemed unnatural; the author of the *Book* clearly concurs.[14] But when this author gets to the fourteenth and last branch of lechery, a sin against nature becomes *the* sin against nature; it is deemed unspeakable, unlike the others; it is taught by the devil to a man or a woman; it is unusually foul and shameful, and it is the reason that God destroyed the cities of Sodom and Gomorrah. The *Fasciculus morum*, similarly, uses the Latin *contra naturam* specifically for sodomy: "[Q]uinta et ultima species luxurie est illa diabolica contra naturam, que sodoma dicitur. Quam horrore accepto transeo, aliis relinquens exponendam" ("The fifth and last branch of lechery is the diabolical sin against nature called sodomy. I pass it over in horror and leave it to others to describe it"). Note that this fourteenth-century English Franciscan author links sodomy not only to the violation of nature but to diabolism, as did the *Book* author, yet another form of contrariness to God; he also performs the unspeakability of this sin that goes against nature: though sodomy is named it is not described but is traced a little further on to the people of Sodom and Gomorrah.[15] The late-fourteenth-century author of *Cleanness*, in his narrative of the cities, contrasts the "kynde crafte" of God-given male-female relations to the faulty sex of the Sodomites, males having sex in the manner of women with males and thus scorning "natwre [nature]": there, the sin of the Sodomites is very precisely male-male anal intercourse, and the scorning of nature seems to include scorning the proper gender order.[16]

The *Parson's Tale* in Chaucer's *Canterbury Tales* uses a wide-ranging category of the unnatural in its discussion of lechery, working from an assumption that whatever hinders the proper end of coitus is against nature: "Of Leccherie, as I seyde, sourden diverse speces, as fornicacioun, that is bitwixe man and womman that been nat maried, and this is deedly synne and agayns nature. / Al that is enemy and destruccioun to nature is agayns nature" ("From Lechery, as I said, arise various branches, such as fornication, that is between a man and a woman who are not married, and this is deadly sin and against nature. Everything that is enemy and destruction of nature is against nature").[17] So heterosexual fornication (fornication *simplex*, as Thomas Aquinas puts it) is among the sins against nature. Note that nonprocreativity in itself is not—or not the only—criterion of unnaturalness; acts that do not follow the proper position and form of intercourse, man on top performing vaginal penetration, are unnatural, and as Karma Lochrie stresses, these criteria of naturalness have everything to do with proper gender roles: "Worry about the procreative potential of specific sexual acts and positions is secondary to this primary cultural fear of the exchange of gender roles during sex."[18] But when the Parson gets to the fifth species of lechery that goes against nature, the unspeakability topos is invoked, and an allusion to male and female homoeroticism (perhaps among other deviations) thus seems to be made: "The fifthe spece is thilke abhomynable synne, of which that no man unnethe oghte speke ne write. . . . This cursednesse doon men and wommen in diverse entente and in diverse manere" ("The fifth branch is that abominable sin of which scarcely anyone [i.e., no one] should speak or write. . . . Men and women do this cursedness with diverse intent and in diverse manner" [10.909–10]). Variety among homoerotic acts may be indicated here. Moreover, the Lollard Bible uses the phrase "aȝens kynde" in its translation of Romans 1.26–27, a passage (as we shall see in chapter 1) that refers to male-male and female-female homosexual relations.[19] So there is plenty of contemporaneous late-medieval justification for reading the "synne aȝeynes kynde," in combination with the trope of the unnameable, as homosexual relations, which is sometimes equated with sodomy (the sin of the Sodomites); sodomy itself at this time ("sodomia," "sodomie") sometimes means male and female homosexual relations, and can sometimes specifically denote male-male anal intercourse. If we look a bit further afield in late-medieval confessional materials beyond specifically English ones, we see that sodomy also denotes mutual masturbation between males, according to Gerson, and unnatural intercourse with one's wife, according to Saint Antoninus of Florence.[20]

The precise act referred to in the Mirk poem cannot be discerned through the allusive and changeable phrase "synne aȝeynes kynde" alone. The precise act, in fact, is perhaps less important than the desire that propels it, disordered as all such desire is (according to Augustine's discussion, as we shall see)—and yet the pastoral context here would seem to require some specificity. The passage does seem to refer mainly to male-female nonprocreative adultery, and yet it deploys the unspeakability topos that associates the sin (as we've seen in other instances) with homoeroticism. Note, further, that while "kynde" seems to denote general concepts of abstract Nature, origin, and species, it takes on further meanings in its second appearance in this passage. It is a great sin, a preacher is allowed to say, for any man to forsake his wife "And do hys kynde other way" (230): this licit language suggests that a man's having sexual relations in any manner other than the married, procreative "missionary" norm is a problem ("kynde" is "sexual function" here, according to the gloss by Kristensson). But further, though that is the primary gloss of "kynde" here, there is a suggestion in the word of the very seed that is being wasted in such interaction.[21] The sense of the word "kynde" as "semen" definitely appears in the treatise later, in the priest's examination of a penitent on the seventh of the Ten Commandments:

Hast þou in synne I-lad þy lyf,
And put a-way þyn owne wyf?
Hast þou I-do þat ylke synne
To any of þy sybbe kynne?
Take also wel in mynde,
ȝef þou haue sched þyn owne kynde,
Slepynge or wakynge, nyȝt or day,
In what maner þow moste say. (929–36)

Have you led your life in sin,
And put away your own wife;
Have you done that same sin [i.e., committed adultery]
With any of your relatives?
Call to mind carefully also,
Whether you have spilled your own seed,
Sleeping or waking, night or day,
In what manner you must say.

So "kynde" itself is a notoriously shifting term, and though these variations may at first seem relatively inconsequential, different shades of its meaning blacken attempts to pin down what exactly goes "against" it. As in Gower's *Confessio amantis,* a text to which I shall turn in a moment, differing meanings (in Gower, even opposing ones) emerge in the space of a few lines, and thus even the opposition "natural/unnatural" may not hold.

Although the priest should not mention the sin against nature, the sinner is supposed to confess it duly to his confessor, according to Mirk's *Instructions.* But the priest is not instructed in any questions to ferret out this sin. Mirk's silence in this regard is imposed for the same reason as the public silence he earlier admonished, and it is a common one: not to introduce any ideas to those who might be receptive to such hints but would not have thought of them for themselves.[22] This sin against nature would seem to be something that can be learned, a dangerous knowledge to which some—or maybe all—people are vulnerable.

But nothing need be taught the unsuspecting *naifs* in the lines in

Instructions for Parish Priests that immediately precede the passage we have been considering. After priests are instructed in how to lead their parishioners to make a proper marriage—in particular, right after they are told to admonish their flocks to despise lechery in both single men and single women—Mirk adds another consideration:

Also thys mote ben hem sayde,
Boþe for knaue chyldere ⁊ for mayde,
That whenne þey passe seuen ȝere,
They schule no lengere lygge I-fere,
Leste they by-twynne hem brede
The lykynge of that fowle dede. (216–21)

Also this must be said to them,
Concerning both boy children and girls,
That when they pass seven years of age
They should no longer lie together,
Lest they breed between them
Pleasure in that foul deed.

Because of what precedes it, this passage would seem to proscribe boys and girls' sleeping with one another after they have reached the age of seven. But because of the syntax ("Boþe for knaue chyldere ⁊ for mayde," as if the two groups are to be considered separately) as well as what immediately follows in the poem ("of synne aȝeynes kynde"), the passage may indeed proscribe same-sex sleeping partners after age seven.[23] At the very least, children over seven seem to be poised here between sexual potentials, the deadly sin of simple fornication and the unnameable sin against nature, and the shared bed is feared as the breeding ground of desire.[24]

The shared bed is, indeed, the dangerous field on which Gower's Ovidian tale of Iphis and Iante unfolds, a tale in which natural and unnatural sexual inclinations are confusingly proximate. We might pause to consider the problems that this tale enunciates, since the *Confessio amantis* was written—if slightly earlier—in an anti-Lollard voice that makes a link to Mirk.[25] (I shall take up in some detail in chapter 2 the issues involved in relating a fictional text to an ostensibly nonfictional one.) Ten-year-old Iphis, a girl disguised in boy's clothing, is married as a boy to Iante, a playmate and peer, and they often sleep together, "sche and sche";[26] following the dictates of nature, one night they begin to have sex. Cupid, taking pity on their great love and hating that which is against nature, transforms Iphis into a male in accordance with nature, so that he can win the natural love of Iante. Since nature has constrained the two playmates toward sex in bed in the first place, while the "thing which stant *ayein* the lore / Of that nature in kinde hath sett" (thing which stands *against* the teaching / of what nature has set in innate morality [4.494–95, my emphasis]) is obviously erotic love between two females, the status of the natural here is very unclear: it seems hardly distinguishable from the unnatural.[27] But what *is* clear is that that desire did not need to be taught, no hints were needed, no knowledge enabled the two girls to desire sex: nature simply "[c]onstreigneth hem, so that thei use / Thing which to hem was al unknowe" ("constrains them, so that they practice / A thing which was completely unknown to them" [4.486–87]). And the same "thing" seems to be a problematic possibility in Mirk's *Instructions.* Desire for the foul deed is something bedfellows might discover together, without any instruction from priests. The deed is potentially attractive to any child past seven years of age, and consequently, they all must be protected from the pervasive threat of desire for same-sex relations.

We see here — and will see in much greater detail in chapter 1 — the contradicţory discourse about same-sex sexual relations that splits discussions of the issue, medieval and postmodern: desire for it is natural and presumably innate, but seems unnatural as well and can be taught, or even caught. Analysis of same-sex sexual relations, even as they cannot be clearly distinguished from opposite-sex sexual relations, implicates such relations in a larger confusion of the natural and the unnatural (that binome that would seem so clear in medieval discourse), and thus suggests that determinate oppositional structures are not going to hold very well in analyzing medieval sexual discourse. Such indeterminacies, contradictions, slippages in some major cultural phenomena in late-medieval England are the matter of this book, as are the ways we in the postmodern era in the West — indeterminate, contradictory, and slippery as we are — can make relations with those discourses, people, places, and things *in their very indeterminateness.*

This book, then, is about making relations with the past, relations that form parts of our subjectivities and communities; it is about making affective connections, that is, across time. Who, we who are doing queer history want finally to ask, were these boys and these girls, these men and these women, who might discover—and who must be prevented from so doing—unspeakable pleasures lying next to one another? How can we know them? And thinking we know them, what do we know?

New Times and Old, Old Stories

A hard-and-fast definition of "queer history" is neither the premise nor the goal of this book. Since I contend that queer histories are made of affective relations, I aim to make such histories manifest by juxtaposition, by making entities past and present touch.[28] But I shall make provisional definitional statements along the way, and here is the first: one thing that makes this history queer is its view that sex is heterogeneous and indeterminate—not the view that we can never know what really happened sexually in past cultures because their immediacy is lost, but the view that sex (sex acts, sexual desire, sexual identity, sexual subjectivity, sexuality, all of which I shall analyze as inflected by other cultural phenomena, and all of which, here for convenience only, I lump under the rubric "sex") is at least in part contingent on systems of representation, and, as such, is fissured and contradictory. Its meaning or significance cannot definitively be pinned down without exclusivity or reductiveness, and such meanings and significances shift, moreover, with shifts in context and location. Following a generation of feminist theorists such as Teresa de Lauretis, Barbara Johnson, Audre Lorde, and Hortense Spillers, and in the company of queer theorists—some of them medievalists—I understand sex to be heterogeneous and multiple, and thus I take it to be fundamentally indeterminate.[29]

To take a general example here: even the most orthodox formulations circulating in late-medieval England of normative heterosexual relations are not free of perversion. They are haunted by phenomena that have been marked as other to them; Saint Augustine early on and with continuing influence demonstrates the inessentiality of heterosexuality. In his *City of God*, book 14, Augustine famously analyzes normative, licit heterosexual relations that are nonetheless reenactments of original sin. After that first sin, lust began, and even the most rigorously dutiful procreative sex cites the Fall. Shame, as punishment, is the mark of the sinful in licit, married sex for procreation:

> Sic enim hoc recte factum ad sui notitiam lucem appetit animorum, ut tamen refugiat oculorum. Vnde hoc, nisi quia sic geritur quod deceat ex natura, ut etiam quod pudeat comitetur ex poena?
>
> This right action craves for recognition in the light of the mind's understanding, but it is equally concerned to escape the light of the eye's vision. What can be the reason for this, if it is not that something by nature right and proper is effected in such a way as to be accompanied by a feeling of shame, by way of punishment? [30]

The scholastic exegesis of the feminine as imperfect, as in some sense always already perverse, abets this understanding of heterosexual relations, as Karma Lochrie points out.[31] These are lasting conceptualizations that exert considerable power in daily lives in late-medieval England: we shall see the intertwining of the orthodox and the perverse in Lollard polemics, drawing on such an analysis of ever imperfect femininity, and we shall see Margery Kempe struggle with a spirituality that makes marriage a sacrament but maintains nonetheless that it is tainted. Such an understanding allows me to historicize the normative as well as the deviant, and to insist on their inextricability and even, at times, their indistinguishability. The inessentiality of heterosexuality is witnessed, further, in the fact that when any given normative model of heterosexual relations is transferred to a new context, it can have very nonnormative effects. This is true in fifteenth-century East Anglia, and it is true as well in present-day United States culture, as we'll see—in *The Book of Margery Kempe* and in the movie *Pulp Fiction;* and it is what I—following many others—call a queer view of heterosexuality.[32]

A *queer* history focuses on *sex* in particular as heterogeneous and indeterminate, even as it recognizes and pursues sex's irreducible interrelatedness with other cultural phenomena.[33] It thus draws on feminisms that have negotiated shifting relations between sex, gender, and other cultural phenomena. The indeterminacy of cultural phenomena in general is in fact crucial to my historical vision in this book. Such an attitude toward indeterminacy is not new to historians, especially after the "linguistic turn" of the discipline; it is, rather, a general tenet of antifoundational historical methods informed by postmodern theories of the sign.[34] Historian Joan W. Scott elaborates on procedures based on such a tenet: "The kind of reading I have in mind would not assume a direct correspondence between words and things, nor confine itself to single meanings, nor aim for the resolution of contradiction. It would not render process as linear, nor rest explanation on simple correlations or single variables."[35] With this tenet comes a concomitant sense of the discursivity of the historian's own approaches, perspectives, and knowledges, all contingent on systems of representation. At the same time, historians who have grappled with the epistemological implications have not completely abjured the idea of a "recoverable past," as Gabrielle M. Spiegel puts it. This paradoxical situation, characterized by "the simultaneity of the desire for history and the recognition of its irreparable loss," she writes, is "an irony that seems to me to be the very figure of history in the late twentieth century."[36] In a now classic article, Donna Haraway addresses such a postmodern condition of ironic simultaneity when she calls for "*simultaneously* an account of radical historical contingency for all knowledge claims and knowing subjects, a critical practice for recognizing our own 'semiotic technologies' for making meanings, *and* a no-nonsense commitment to faithful accounts of a 'real' world."[37] A queer history, not denying the desire for some sort of recoverable past, attempts to provide such an account of the production of knowledges that seeks as well to account faithfully for the "real." The queer history I develop here does so by means of what Haraway calls "partial connection"—"The knowing self is partial in all its guises, never finished, whole, simply there and original; it is always constructed and stitched together imperfectly, and *therefore* able to join with another, to see together without claiming to be another," she maintains—or what Foucault, much more allusively, as we shall see in chapter 2, calls a "vibration."[38]

Foucault's varied, complex, affective engagements with the past are in fact central motifs of this book. The poststructuralist historical tenets I mentioned above have been debated, elaborated, and demonstrated for years: Joan W. Scott, Dominick LaCapra, Michel de Certeau, and Roger Chartier, for example, have compellingly and relatively recently described for the West the production of knowledges both in the past and now, as well as interrelations and transferences between then and now—as have medievalists with varied theoretical allegiances and interests, such as Kathleen Biddick, Michael Camille, Umberto Eco, Louise O. Fradenburg, Aaron I. Gurevich, Brian Stock, Nicholas Watson, and Paul Zumthor.[39] But Foucault's work, from *Madness and Civilization* on, is perhaps the strongest current in the stream of poststructuralist historiography (though *Madness and Civilization* was itself critiqued by Derrida, whose work may be taken as another current).[40] Foucault's rejection of the "discourse of the continuous," his insistence on radical contingency, and his analyses of the constitutive interrelations of knowledge and power have been formative of poststructuralist historiographies, and it is of course Foucault's analysis in *The History of Sexuality,* volume 1, of the production of sex as the truth of the modern liberal subject that has broken the ground for many queer historical projects over the last twenty-five years. I am most interested, however, in the sometimes affective ways Foucault responds to the epistemological crisis of postmodern history. Thus I look in chapter 2 at Foucault in the archive, feeling a physical response to the documents he reads and concerned that he cannot reconstitute that intensity in an analysis. My concern in my coda with volume 1 of *The History of Sexuality* is not so much with Foucault's vision of modernity as it is with his Middle Ages: I shall look at the contradictory treatment of the medieval within his ruptured, nonlinear history. At first glance it seems merely nostalgic, idealized, totalized; I argue, however, that the nostalgia is tactical, that what I call Foucault's desire for the premodern is part of a serious ethical and political vision of a future that is not straitened by modern sexuality.

But even the *apparent* reductiveness of Foucault's postmodern medievalism is a warning sign for medievalists concerned about nuanced accounts of premodernity and the creeping implication that theoretical interventions are only made in relation to modernity or contemporaneity. If postmodern history has established that its objects are heterogeneous and multiple, it continues to be important to assert, however, *especially* to postmodern thinkers, the indeterminate nature of medieval cultural phenomena. In some very influential theoretical and critical work developing out of postmodernism, the

Middle Ages is still made the dense, unvarying, and eminently obvious monolith against which modernity and postmodernity groovily emerge.[41] It is important to assert medieval indeterminacy because such postmodern interventions are hampered by their binary blind spots; the point is not simply to claim that the medieval is postmodern *avant la lettre* but to argue that a more patient consideration of the Middle Ages would extend the range of their interventions and (I'll suggest) clarify their politics. I shall turn now to postmodern theoretical work that is not only widely read and taught in the United States but that intends to make a radical intervention in the ways we view history; it is potentially useful for furthering queer historical projects and, in fact, gestures into the arena of sexuality. I shall discuss this work in some detail because of the symptomatic way that its use of a reductive historiographic narrative intersects with its use of sexuality: what I see as its problems with alterity go hand in glove as the distant past is assumed to be too far away to have any relation to the present, while inversely the homosexual is not assumed to be different enough.

Let me take the postmodern postcolonial project of Homi K. Bhabha as an example, then, of a critical effort that has much to offer a queer historical project but whose treatment of the distant past reveals the limits of its revisionist clout. Bhabha's work understands that representation is a crucial—constitutive—cultural practice whose access is "unequal and uneven."[42] His analyses of political and cultural agency are informed by poststructuralist critiques of the sign and psychoanalytic critiques of identity: he describes colonialist power, for example, as ambivalent and fissured, achieved through a process of disavowal. Resistance is in fact enabled by this very ambivalence: "uncanny forces of race, sexuality, violence, cultural and even climatic differences . . . emerge in the colonial discourse as the mixed and split texts of hybridity."[43] Hybridity is one of Bhabha's major terms: the hybrid "breaks down the symmetry and duality of self/other, inside/outside."[44] A deconstruction of the Western liberal notion of the sovereign subject—and the attendant sovereign unities of language, narrative, nation—opens up "new times" and new locations, found in the very split of ambivalent signs, wherein other cultural meanings may be located, other histories found, and ultimately other modes of political and cultural agency sought.[45]

This drastic postmodern rethinking of subjectivity, time, and the writing of history in the context of a politics of social marginality is valuable to my development here of a queer history. Bhabha is interested in dismantling "each achieved symbol of cultural/political identity or synchronicity"—closed sentences of history, the closed narrative of nation, for example—finding a "temporal break in cultural synchronicity" where difference can be reinscribed and cultural meaning can be relocated.[46] He opposes, with Walter Benjamin before him, the "homogeneous, empty time" of continuist and teleological historical narratives; in his essay "DissemiNation" Bhabha invokes Benjamin's "Theses on the Philosophy of History" only allusively, via Benedict Anderson in *Imagined Communities,* but certainly shares not only Benjamin's interest in breaking up traditional historicism's temporal narrative but also his urgency.[47] Benjamin represents the past as a fleeting, instantaneous image to be "seize[d]" in another historical moment, "a moment of danger"; Bhabha seeks new kinds of time, other " 'times' of cultural meaning (retroactive, prefigurative), and other narrative spaces (phantasmic, metaphorical)" that can intervene in present forms of power.[48] He uncovers a "meanwhile" (a concept taken from conventional novelistic narrative, via Benedict Anderson) that opens a space for the voice of the people, within the narrative of the nation; he finds a "lag time" within the linguistic sign itself—its internal difference—wherein "new and hybrid agencies and articulations" may be elaborated.[49] Such new kinds of time in historical narrative and the "new forms of identification" that result may "confuse the continuity of historical temporalities, confound the ordering of cultural symbols, traumatize tradition . . . these moments contest the sententious 'conclusion.' "[50] These identifications recall Benjamin's suggestion of historical relations other than the duly causal connections posited by traditional historicism: "Historicism contents itself with establishing a causal connection between various moments in history. But no fact that is a cause is for that very reason historical. It became historical posthumously, as it were, through events that may be separated from it by thousands of years. A historian who takes this as his point of departure stops telling the sequence of events like the beads of a rosary. Instead, he grasps the constellation which his own era has formed with a definite earlier one."[51] Benjamin's brilliant image of the "constellation" revises any positivistic relation of past events to each other and to the present: its starry lights are emitted at different times even as they are perceived at once, together.

Bhabha, invoking Benjamin, describes a process of restructuring tradition, discovering other moments, finding new kinds of time in which other voices can be heard in official national historical narratives. Such a project has important implications for doing queer history. Bhabha's discussion of such a "meanwhile" can offer some suggestion of ways a queer history might proceed. Is there buried in some official representation, in gaps, repetitions, prefigurations, other weird narrative temporalities, some other sign to be read, some other voice to be heard? As I have argued elsewhere, the same-sex sexual potential in *Sir Gawain and the Green Knight* is adumbrated in the intricate interlace of two narrative lines, and that potential is itself refused and contained as the poem moves toward heterosexual closure.[52] As I shall argue here extensively in reference to Lollard polemics in chapter 1, the male transvestite prostitute John/Eleanor Rykener in chapter 2, and Margery Kempe in chapter 3, parodic repetitions—of accusations of sodomy—destabilize authoritative pronouncements and contribute to an atmosphere of unknowability in which heresy and orthodoxy, temporal and spiritual, even male and female are rendered indistinguishable and in which the voices of deviant desires may emerge.

But despite the fact that Bhabha explicitly intends to contest the sentence of traditional history, these "new times" emerge by contrast with paradigmatically "old times": the Middle Ages. His notion of the radical hybridity of postmodern identities is bought at the cost of the medieval. Bhabha develops all this (following Benedict Anderson) in contrast to what he calls "the sacral ontology of the medieval world and its overwhelming visual and aural imaginary": "By 'separating language from reality' (Anderson's formulation), the arbitrary signifier enables a national temporality. . . . Anderson historicizes the emergence of the arbitrary sign of language . . . as that which had to come before the narrative of the modern nation could begin. In decentring the prophetic visibility and simultaneity of medieval systems of dynastic representation, the homogeneous and horizontal community of modern society can emerge."[53] Bhabha reads Anderson as performing a mere back-formation in this historicization: if there is going to be a distinct modernity, the logic runs, then there has to have been a premodern with which that modern broke. And since semiotic arbitrariness is a hallmark of the modern, language could not have been separated from reality in the Middle Ages; therefore, there was no sense of the arbitrariness of the sign before the break of modernity: "dynastic representation" stands in as the only kind of representation in medieval culture here.[54] A postmodern theorist who, it seems, cannot do without totality but merely "displaces" it somewhere else (to use Paul Strohm's formulation regarding this phenomenon among other postmodern theorists), Bhabha has to have some totality against which the arbitrary modern can emerge; he thus produces via a convenient and simplified Anderson a binary narrative of history, the likes of which he routinely critiques in decrying "teleology and holism."[55] Though there are miles of crucial differences between them, this approach to history sounds a bit like that of the Republican congressmen I shall discuss in chapter 3 who sought to defund the National Endowment for the Humanities, citing as useless its sponsorship of projects about a clearly dead Middle Ages; it sounds, too, a bit like what Marsellus Wallace in *Pulp Fiction* intends when he threatens to "get Medieval" on the man who sodomized him, by which he means 'blow you away by means of unmediated violence'—I'll describe this totalizing use of the medieval in detail in my coda. By limiting the conceptualization of the Middle Ages, Bhabha thus limits the radicality of his remapping of the present: modernist historiography's crude periodization eliminates an immensely long stretch of time as a potentially productive site of new times, cultural locations, and identifications.[56] Heterogeneity, instability, arbitrariness, "here and there, a kind of refusal to be coded," as Paul Zumthor put it, are eliminated by such periodization—but they nonetheless haunt such closed narratives.[57] Further, Bhabha puts himself in problematic league with neoconservative politicians who would severely circumscribe the "relevant" past, and with a neoconservative film director and writer who would tell an old, homophobic story in slick new postmodern guise.

This problem with alterity—the Middle Ages are taken to be absolutely other but turn out to be only a refraction of the present—manifests itself in inverse form elsewhere as well in Bhabha's work. It is no mere coincidence that his treatment of the distant past intersects with his treatment of gayness. I refer specifically here to the opening of his essay, "Postcolonial Authority and Postmodern Guilt"; it features a passage from *The Pleasure of the Text* wherein Roland Barthes writes that he is sitting in a bar in Tangiers while listening and attempting " 'to enumerate the stereophony of [*sic*] languages within earshot.' " Bhabha writes appreciatively of the discontinuities and fragments that displace the "hierarchy and the subordinations of the sentence" as Barthes enacts "the affective language of cultural difference." Here is Barthes, quoted by Bhabha: " 'Through me passed words, tiny syntagms, bits of formulae and *no sentence formed* . . . It set up in me a definitive discontinuity: this *non-sentence* was in no way something that could not have acceded to the sentence, that might have been *before* the sentence: it was: *outside the sentence.*' " This is affective writing: "Writing aloud is the hybrid he proposes in language lined with flesh," Bhabha comments, "the metonymic art of the articulation of the body not as pure presence of Voice, but as a kind of affective writing, after the sumptuousness or suffering of the signifier." Such affective writing is becoming increasingly important, Bhabha notes, in "theoretical discourses that attempt to construct modes of political and cultural agency" where there has historically been "social, racial, and sexual discrimination."[58]

That last phrase points to the problem to which I alluded above. Bhabha specifies—as Barthes never does in this scene in *The Pleasure of the Text*—that the latter was "Sliding off his banquette in a *gay* bar in Tangiers" (my emphasis) when he "attempts 'to enumerate the stereophony of languages within earshot.' "[59] Bhabha outs Barthes in the first sentence of this essay, despite his subject's own complex, not to say "phobic," "relation to the act of gay self-nomination."[60] (In another essay that uses the same Barthesian material, but in which the bar in Tangiers remains sexually unmarked, Bhabha mentions "homosexuals" and "homophobia" as among the materials of a cultural studies whose methods must be rethought.)[61] Bhabha would name Barthes's location as "gay" in order to assimilate gayness into his concepts of hybridity and political agency; he would bring Barthes out into his community of the people, of the marginalized who seek to become political and cultural agents. But bringing out Roland Barthes is not as simple as throwing the word "gay" into a description and adding "sexual difference" and "sexual discrimination" to the list of relevant social marginalizations, as D. A. Miller has deftly demonstrated; as the posthumously published *Incidents* attests, interrelations among Barthes's sexuality and gender, class, race, and nation are complicated.[62] Sexuality is alluded to among the cultural differences and identifications Bhabha seeks to engage, even as he takes up the other differences of "gender, race or class,"[63] but his treatment is at this point insensitive to particular conditions and contexts, allusive at best, essentializing at worst.[64] Thus the distant past and sexuality are linked in a romanticized way across these essays by Bhabha. They are both blind spots in his deconstruction of colonial discourse; they are both treated as essentialized others, one (gayness) recuperated while the other (the medieval) is lost forever.

But Bhabha's concept of "affective writing" proves very fruitful for a queer project such as mine, especially as it sets up the possibility of contact between linguistic fragments across time. I shall look closely at Barthes's works in the last section of this introduction as I articulate what he might have to do with queer history—as I outline what I call his queer historical impulses. Like Bhabha, I want Barthes as a member of my community; his nonnormative sexuality is important to me as I seek to make a partial connection (not a full identification) with him across time. But I am hesitant to locate Barthes's resistance to dominant forms of association and the historical narratives they produce in a gay bar; I locate it rather in his desire—which I call queer, like mine—for partial, affective connection, for community, for even a touch across time.[65]

Problems with the Middle Ages lead us to other problems with difference and limit the range of this theorist's interventions. If we want to imagine, as does Bhabha, that the oppressed subject gains agency by means of identifications with others who elude resemblance,[66] let us imagine the widest possible usable field of others with whom to make such partial connections. Let us imagine a process that engages all kinds of differences, though not all in the same ways: racial, ethnic, national, sexual, gender, class, even historical/temporal. Thus—as we shall see in detail in this book—the medieval, as well as other dank stretches of time, becomes itself a resource for subject and community formation and materially engaged coalition building. By using this concept of making relations with the past we realize a temporal dimension of the self and of community.[67]

I have just argued, against even those who engage postmodern theories, that the medieval period should provide no exception to a view that sees cultural phenomena as fundamentally indeterminate. And I have argued that sex is among these indeterminate phenomena. Indeterminacy will thus coruscate off a queer history of the late Middle Ages in England. At the same time, I want to state in no uncertain terms that this kind of queer history can be usable history—usable to (among others, I hope) lesbians, gays, bisexuals, transgenders, queers forming selves and communities; to medievalists seeking to broaden the narratives of the field; to cultural theorists in search of new times. I want, in other words, to resist any invidious formulations that suggest that queer articulations of indeterminacy can't tell us a thing or have nothing to do with living in the "real world," past or present.

I am concerned in this book to demonstrate ways in which a historical past can and does provide material for queer subject and community formation now.[68] That term, "community," is taken most generally here to denote some sort of social grouping that is not a conventional kinship group; the term as I use it does not in itself imply unity or homogeneity, and the particulars and problematics of such formations will emerge throughout the course of this book. My use of the term draws on the concept of partial connection that I developed in regard to historical relations—thus I regard partial connections across time as constitutive of communities, and in chapter 3 I call today's coalitions, organized around single issues, postmodern communities—and in this way attempts to allow for the possibility of competing and shifting claims on individuals.[69] One still-prominent advocate of the necessity of history to what he called "gay community" is of course the late John Boswell, whose crucial *Christianity, Social Tolerance, and Homosexuality: Gay People in Western Europe from the Beginning of the Christian Era to the Fourteenth Century* brought the academic study of lesbian/gay history to widespread attention in 1980 and opened considerable—and seemingly interminable—debate about how to do gay history and about gay history's relationship to the constitution and political aims of "gay community." Boswell's own papers, kept now by his literary executor, Ralph

Hexter, are a rich resource of information about not only the scholarly but also the popular reception of the book; I looked in this archive to see how people talked about making use of this history. I found a range of responses to *Christianity, Social Tolerance, and Homosexuality,* from both those whose concern was integration into the cultural mainstream and those who used it as a foundation for gay community. I shall present them here, then analyze how Boswell's own concept of community shaped his history, and how that history has underwritten the present-day conservative agenda of "the gay community" on the national level; but it has, I'll argue, resonated perhaps surprisingly with a more radical vision of social organization, too.

In *Christianity, Social Tolerance, and Homosexuality* John Boswell undertook to tell a different narrative about the Catholic Church from the one that had theretofore been told. He wrote a story of relative tolerance among Christians toward homosexuality until about the mid-thirteenth century, providing new translations and interpretations of key scriptural passages to support this radically new scholarly view and developing a discussion of a vibrant, self-consciously gay urban subculture in the twelfth century in Western Europe. Boswell himself was "deeply religious," as Ralph Hexter memorialized him in an obituary, and his work has indeed proved immensely important not only to scholars ready to enrich the sparse histories of homosexuality but also to gay Christians seeking a place in the institution that other gays blamed for virtually causing "the anti-homosexuality taboo." [70] The book was immediately scrutinized and vigorously opposed in a collection of essays published by the Gay Academic Union entitled *Homosexuality, Intolerance, and Christianity: A Critical Examination of John Boswell's Work;* John Lauritsen there indicts Boswell for trying "to whitewash the crimes of the Christian Church." [71] There was immediate gay resistance to the project of recuperating Christianity.

But the desire for a place within the institution dominated the popular reception of *Christianity, Social Tolerance, and Homosexuality,* which was enormously positive. The book was an instant mainstream success upon its publication in July 1980, achieving a level of attention in the United States that was staggering—literally so to the book's publisher, the University of Chicago Press, which was immediately overwhelmed and couldn't keep the book available. To read the press's correspondence with the author is to witness a growing sense of excitement in the relatively quiet world of academic publishing. The hardcover volume went into five printings in less than a year—even at its steep price, which took it out of the range of many. In September *Newsweek* ran a review and article on the author (with a photo of the young professor, which proved crucial: he is pictured in his office, with *three* buttons of his shirt undone), and responses to this widely circulated coverage swelled a virtual flood of mail: Boswell claimed to have gotten between three hundred and five hundred letters a week ("fan mail," he called it) at the beginning of this media moment.[72] This figure may have been an exaggeration; the current archive of letters contains far fewer than that, but he may not have kept all of them; at any rate, I acknowledge that I'm working with a body of letters that was retained (perhaps selected) by the author, and so its representativity is certainly not guaranteed. That having been said, the letters do seem to have come from all over: Estonia, Ecuador, Belgium, Montana. They came from mostly male, but some female, correspondents. Within a year the book had won a major prize and high-profile recognition. It was eventually translated into French (a process Foucault facilitated), Italian, Spanish, and Japanese.

Boswell's name became a gay household word, as *The Advocate* put it in 1981.[73] But with its emphasis on "social tolerance" the book penetrated various mainstream institutions in the United States as well. The correspondence files are peppered with requests for interviews and articles in mainstream print media (while an energetic fan tried to get Boswell on talk shows with Phil Donahue and the like); a sympathetic reporter seeking an interview wrote, "[Y]our book is such a public act and America adores turning authors into media events."[74] The times were indeed right for this book to be perceived not only as a scholarly venture but as "a public act." True, an atmosphere of intolerance sat heavily on gays and lesbians: letters to Boswell mention Anita Bryant, Jerry Falwell, Reaganism, and "Moral Majorities" on the national scene as well as persecutions in schools on the local level. But at the same time there was considerable optimism, post-Stonewall and pre-AIDS: the letters witness an expanding gay public discourse and institutional presence in the United States. Letters from gay clergy (Catholic and Protestant) poured forth. One gay clergyman in the mental health professions, for example, wrote that he had gotten a copy of *Christianity, Social Tolerance, and Homosexuality* placed in the permanent library of a federal mental hospital.[75] A Christian counselor in the army wrote to say that he was shaken by the hypothesis of the book and needed clarification, since "in the military I have to counsel young people with all kinds of problems."[76] The staff member of a medical center's Institute of Religion attested to the power of the book: "Your work will assist me in setting my moral analyses within a better historical context."[77] A Houston lawyer wrote to say that the book "has given me some insights that may come into play from time to time when working with juries."[78] Professor Boswell was called upon almost immediately after the book's publication to give depositions in a sodomy case and in military discharge cases. Colorado's Amendment 2 came along near the end of his career; in his deposition for the winning side, he mentions that two authoritative translations of the New Testament "have recognized my arguments regarding the proper translation" of key passages.[79] These mainstream institutions (hospitals, the military, law courts, organized religions) were being touched from within by the book; reformation—the "social tolerance" of the book's title—is indeed what was sought by these various correspondents. The appeal of the book from this institutional point of view was not its argument that there was a distinct gay subculture in the high Middle Ages but that gayness was accepted in dominant ancient and medieval institutions that are still authoritative today. A large number of people in fact wrote before they had even read the book; they had only seen the *Newsweek* review. For some the very existence of *Christianity, Social Tolerance, and Homosexuality*, a chunky university press history book—read or unread—whose author taught at Yale, was enough to strengthen gay claims to cultural legitimacy. (The footnotes alone became something of a "fetish," as one correspondent put it, standing in for or at least signifying such legitimacy.)[80] In the eyes of many letter-writers, the assertion of a history—*some* kind of history—seemed fundamental to the mainstream acceptance of gay people now in the United States.

Just *how* that history would secure acceptance was a further question. Boswell was in fact contacted by two television production companies in 1982 about turning *Christianity, Social Tolerance, and Homosexuality* into a television mini-series—basing a PBS documentary on the book (and on further, modern materials)—and his discussions about the development of such a series reveal something about the function of history in a medium of United States cultural legitimation such as the Public Broadcasting System.[81] The starting assumption behind the development of such a series went something like this: if we gays have a real past, if in fact some of our gay forefathers were leaders of their societies and profound contributors to Western culture, we can be and should claim our *right* to be part of the culture of the present. "Our story is the story of Western civilization," Boswell stated in a conversation with one of the producers. He went on: "It is better not to think of gay people as either artistic or military or this or that . . . but to see that at the same time Aristotle is writing . . . there are gay generals and artists and people in other fields and that homosexuality, rather than being some strange thing, was the predominant influence on the leaders of Athenian society."[82] The series, in Boswell's mind, would show an integrated, holistic approach to gay lives past, not separating out homosexuality from other parts of Western culture but demonstrating the ways in which gays have participated in, have indeed shaped that culture. And thus a television series, showing the "sweep" (as he put it) of the gay cultural presence, would not only transmit foundational cultural values to people in the United States now but would defamiliarize and thus extend our notion of the mainstream. The fall PBS season in 1981 broadcast various programs transmitting Western cultural values—*Live from the Met, Masterpiece Theater,* Shakespeare plays—programs that were deemed appropriate context for the development of such a series on homosexuality in history.

But there were other programs on PBS in that fall 1981 season, documentaries whose very titles suggest not a liberal integration of homosexuals and an expansion of the mainstream but an objectifying gaze on an abjected other: "Whales That Wouldn't Die" was one such documentary, as was "The Human Face of China." The conversation between John Boswell and the producer in fact falls apart around the question of the relationship of past to present. Boswell proposed a six-part series that would move from the Greeks to the present, with the rise and times of Christianity at its center (as one would expect from his work); the producer liked the chronological divisions but favored more air time on the modern period. The historical continuum can get to be "terribly dull," he warned, and people would not be able to relate to it. "History" in his view remains something other—whale, Chinese, outer space (another favorite topic of PBS documentaries). It can be studied, but it remains a dull matter; it is cultural ballast, necessary to gay community assertion, yet is not living, not part of us now. But of course that abjected "other" turns out inevitably to be a version of "us" after all. The producer may here be revealing only that he has not thought very much about this, but his position, however unreflective, expresses a common assumption about the simultaneous necessity and irrelevance of history. (We shall see abundant examples of this assumption in chapter 3, in congressional discussions of the National History Standards for teaching high school United States and world history.) Both Boswell and the producer use history as a foundation for gays' assertion of a place in culture now; but while Boswell delineates how it might change the notion of what that culture is, the producer presumes only that history will reinforce the present. There was no doubt a variety of reasons that this television project didn't go forward, but I suspect that this difference may have been one of them; it pointed to limitations of the standard PBS-style documentary and the way it sought to guarantee legitimacy in an already established cultural field. Boswell's history sought "tolerance," an expansion of the mainstream, not a revolution—but it was going to require pushing beyond the reinforcement of present cultural categories, which is all the documentary producer could envision. As it turned out, even this reformation would not be televised.

The homosexualization of the mainstream such as Boswell proposed to broadcast was not the only concern of people who wrote fan mail to him. The letters also reveal the intense, personally enabling effects of *Christianity, Social Tolerance, and Homosexuality*, suggesting the importance of a gay community whose values include not only art and war and philosophy but also gay *sex*. Letters came from people who felt deeply isolated—one, indeed, wrote from a sex-offender program because of his involvement with a boy.[83] Married men, some over fifty, wrote narratives of long-hidden desires or of encounters in foreign countries (Lebanon, or Spain before the Civil War, for example); some of these letters, nominally concerning the book, provided the occasions of brief, private, supportive contact with another gay man, creating a tiny and temporary community of two.[84] Other letters were the medium of acting out fantasies, or newfound sexual boldness: several *Newsweek* readers were entranced by Boswell's picture and thus driven to write: "Do you have a boyfriend?" inquired one. "If so, do you see any immediate possibility of dumping him?" (Wrote another: "I see from the . . . photo that you are also very hot. Most academics aren't.")[85] A cartoon from *Christopher Street* made a related point about the way this gay history book fostered a separate gay culture: it featured two guys at a bar, one saying to the other: "How about coming back to my place for a little Christianity, Social Tolerance, and Homosexuality?" Occasionally there was the self-projection characteristic of fandom: "I'm . . . also 33," beamed one man; "I, too, have studied many languages," reflected another; while another remarked hopefully, "You will doubtlessly [have] noted by now a certain similarity in our names." [86] Fairly bald identification with Boswell seems to animate such phrases. But another correspondent, a young woman studying medieval history and literature, muses, "The reason I am writing to you is mysterious even to myself." Her letter, which attempts to explain her interest in the book (she had read the *Newsweek* review), nervously repeats this incomprehension—"I don't know why I am bothering you with this letter"—and further offers, "Perhaps a partial explanation stems from the fact that I am . . . taking a class in medieval literature." The letter is bursting with the unspoken; the mystery, in this context, seems very possibly to be the mystery of being gay, and the letter an extremely indirect coming out.[87] In yet another deeply felt response based this time on a close engagement with the book's argument, a philosophy professor reflects on the book's effect on him of creating something like a gay community across time: "Whereas I have often felt intellectual 'friendships' across the centuries—historical thinkers with whom I have felt such strong affinities that I feel I know them and that we speak for one another, I had never felt—until I read your book—that I had *gay* friends across the centuries." For this reader, history becomes a source—directly, itself—of gay community, a community of affinities, of friends, even perhaps (given this letter's impassioned tone) of lovers.[88]

This reader was not only impassioned but astute. Gay history and gay community are indeed tightly linked in Boswell's work. And this is where the issue of Boswell's apparent "essentialism" comes in. I want to turn now to consider how Boswell's concept of "the gay community" is related to his approach to history and how it shaped his findings. The subtitle of *Christianity, Social Tolerance, and Homosexuality, Gay People in Western Europe from the Beginning of the Christian Era to the Fourteenth Century,* is important, for Boswell suggested in a 1982 essay that the very possibility of "gay community" now might in fact depend on whether or not we can say there were indeed "gay people" back then. In an argument that reframed the current essentialism/social constructionism debate on homosexuality in the terms of the realist/nominalist philosophical debate on universals in the high Middle Ages, Boswell hypothesized in this article that the existence of a "real" phenomenon of homosexuality may be necessary to ground and justify homosexual community. He thus implies that if historically speaking one cannot say that there were people who "really" were "gay" or "homosexual" back then, the very concept of gay community now may be incoherent or unfounded: "Whether or not there are 'homosexual' and 'heterosexual' persons, as opposed to persons called 'homosexual' or 'heterosexual' by society, is obviously a matter of substantial import to the gay community, since it brings into question the nature and even the existence of such a community. . . . If the categories 'homosexual/heterosexual' and 'gay/straight' are the inventions of particular societies rather than real aspects of the human psyche, there is no gay history."[89] So a "real" category of homosexuality or gayness (the two mean the same thing here, I believe) is needed for both gay history and gay community. To Boswell, a gay history is a history of gay persons throughout temporal and cultural locations—people whom we would now call "gay," whether or not they called themselves that. His choice of the term was controversial—to his manuscript editor at the University of Chicago Press; to historians reviewing the book; even to sympathetic readers who wrote fan letters to him.[90] Simon Watney, in a review, noted that its "over-simplifying" was inconsistent with Boswell's own findings of historical variation.[91] But Boswell never swerved from his commitment to the term in premodern contexts. In a letter to his editor at Gallimard about the French translation of his book in 1984 he stated unequivocally, "[A]lthough it is not ideal, the word 'gay' is the only available term, in any language, for what I wish to convey."[92] Gay history, based on this "real" category of homosexual, may in fact be a necessity for gay community, for it may serve not only as a community resource but as proof of the community's conceptual justification, proof of its capacity to cohere at all. A current Internet website, *An Online Guide to Lesbian, Gay, Bisexual, and Trans* History,* maintained by Paul Halsall, is tellingly—polemically—entitled *People with a History:* it enters vigorously into this field of contestation over gay history and community.[93] For Boswell, who is featured prominently in this online resource, being a people—a community—without a history is not just a phobic threat or horror but might be simply impossible.

Boswell maintained that referring to a continuous phenomenon such as same-sex eroticism is not clearly "an 'essentialist' position." "Even if societies formulate or create 'sexualities' that are highly particular in some ways," he wrote, "it might happen that different societies would construct similar ones, as they often construct political or class structures similar enough to be subsumed under the same rubric (democracy, oligarchy, proletariat, aristocracy, etc.—all of which are both particular and general)."[94] There is merit to this position, and one of the important challenges to historians of the rupture is to acknowledge and account for such similarities.[95] But Boswell does seem to associate same-sex eroticism with something essential in humans,[96] and the troublesome potential distortions in the phrase "gay people" when used in premodern contexts are not avoided merely by making explicit statements about the analytical primacy of historical evidence, which seems to have been Boswell's mode of dismissing the problems. As I view Boswell's work, a specific gay essence grounds both community and history; and that essence looks very post-Stonewall. The gay relationships in Boswell's gay history resemble those of urban gay males in the United States (like that implied by the two men, both about the same age, in the *Christopher Street* cartoon): in particular, scholars commented on the problematic lack of distinction in *Christianity, Social Tolerance, and Homosexuality* between "institutionalised pederasty from what we nowadays call homosexuality," and made a similar criticism of *Same-Sex Unions*—a book published fourteen years later whose historical approach was effectively the same.[97] Turning to *Same-Sex Unions* for a moment: addressing the relation between premodern and current conventions of marriage, Boswell writes in the epilogue that the answer to the pressing question of "whether the Christian ceremony of same-sex union functioned in the past as a 'gay marriage ceremony' " is clearly yes, adding immediately that "the nature and purposes of every sort of marriage have varied widely over time."[98] But the premodern ceremony he is interested in is, as he presents it, gay marriage in the image of male gay marriages in the West today, between loving adult men; he elides consideration of the age dissonance in some of the documents he analyzes, as Randolph Trumbach contends, and with "the title of the book and the gender-neutral style of presentation," Bernadette J. Brooten points out, "Boswell masked the overwhelmingly masculine character of his material."[99] Earlier, in *Christianity, Social Tolerance, and Homosexuality,* as E. Ann Matter argued in 1982, Boswell oversimplified "the history of lesbian love" when he did not address "the differences that must have existed between the experiences of medieval lesbians and homosexual men."[100] (Thus we might read the comment of that young woman correspondent in her fan letter much more harshly than she appeared to mean it: "The reason I am writing to you is mysterious even to myself," because the place of the female in Boswell's work is hard to locate.) Despite his admirable desire that "gay" be understood as a broad category allowing for much historical and cultural variation, then, Boswell's actual historical work was constrained by an essentialism and a relatively narrow conceptualization of gay relationships (the dominant form of United States urban gay male relations in the 1970s and 1980s) from which that essence was derived.

This narrowness has had its consequences. True, the 1980 book was (in the words of the Gay Academic Union collection, *Homosexuality, Intolerance, and Christianity*) "a starting point for further scholarly investigation," which has proceeded apace.[101] The book opened up a whole field, lesbian/gay history; some works of lesbian/gay history had existed earlier, as Trumbach points out (by Jonathan Ned Katz, Jeffrey Weeks, and Trumbach himself), but in 1980 the field was not well known or even really established.[102] The book still sells about two thousand copies a year in the United States and has proved not only enabling of individuals but has helped move oppressive institutions toward reform: as Trumbach notes, it did not "have much of an impact on either the moral theologians or the church hierarchy,"[103] but, as I've suggested, it infiltrated church, military, courts, and schools on a more fundamental level—on the ground level. At the same time, it must be said that the book's popular reputation has lent legitimacy to a national gay agenda that, as Michael Warner argues, has abandoned the goals of a more radical gay activism to focus on reforming institutions such as marriage.[104] Boswell himself noted that "realism," with its transhistoricist tendency, has been viewed by nominalists "as conservative, if not reactionary, in its implicit recognition of the value and/or immutability of the status quo"—even as "nominalism," related to constructivism, has been viewed by realists as "an obscurantist radical ideology designed more to undercut and subvert human values than to clarify them."[105] Certainly we should resist the implication that a particular politics inheres in each of these approaches to history and hold, rather, that each can be deployed in particular political causes. But one might suggest that the fact that Larry Kramer cited Boswell as an authority on homosexuality in *Reports from the Holocaust*, his controversial 1989 rallying cry to gay men to cultivate "stable, responsible, mutually gratifying relationships" (which do not, therefore, differ much from heterosexual marriages), does indicate the usefulness of Boswell's approach to an argument that takes homosexuality as a transhistorical constant and would impose a single model on relationships gay or non gay.[106]

But I want to complicate this somewhat predictable assessment by turning to yet another sharp and appreciative reader of Boswell: Michel Foucault, whose "fan letter" about *Christianity, Social Tolerance, and Homosexuality* was among the correspondence Boswell preserved: addressed to Douglas Mitchell, Boswell's editor at the University of Chicago Press, and eventually smoothed out into a blurb on the book's jacket, Foucault's brief letter was written in rough English: "I receive John Boswell's work with thankfullness. I found through these proofs a very interesting matter: 'un vrai travail de pionnier' as we say over here. It makes appear unexplored phenomenons and this because of an erudition which seems infaillible."[107] Foucault wrote that in late 1979—well beyond publishing volume 1 of the *History of Sexuality* and as he was working on early Christianity: his course at the Collège de France for 1979–80 was "devoted to the procedures of soul-seeking and confession in early Christianity," according to the résumé.[108] In moving beyond his introductory volume he found he needed to shift his assumptions and reconceptualize the entire project of his *History*, as he writes in the beginning of volume 2.[109] In an interview in 1982, Foucault in fact stated that he took *Christianity, Social Tolerance, and Homosexuality* as a "guide" for his work on ancient Greeks:[110] in his book Boswell had drawn a distinction between "homosexual" persons ("of predominantly homosexual erotic interest," regardless of conscious preference) and "gay" persons ("who are conscious of erotic inclination toward their own gender as a distinguishing characteristic"),[111] and it was precisely that sense of self-consciousness that had a powerful influence on Foucault. He understood that such self-consciousness would imply a historically contingent sexual category, as he put it in another interview a "cultural phenomenon that changes in time while maintaining itself in its general formulation: a relation between individuals of the same sex that entails a mode of life in which the consciousness of being singular among others is present."[112] Later, however, in 1988 Boswell stated that he had shifted his position, eliminating that consciousness of same-sex inclination as a distinguishing characteristic of gayness and retaining same-sex eroticism only—and thus, it seems to me, increasing the problematic essentializing and anachronizing hazards of the term "gay."[113] But it is important—in these days in the late 1990s in which we may have tired of the essentialism/social constructionism "debate" but have hardly ceased to polarize the putative practitioners on each side—to attend to what Foucault said he got out of Boswell's *Christianity, Social Tolerance, and Homosexuality*. We need to reckon with the influence Boswell's work exerted on the direction of Foucault's late work: "Boswell's book has provided me with a guide for what to look for in the meaning people attached to their sexual behavior." A long statement by Foucault highlights what he sees as the methodological advance of the book:

> [Boswell's] introduction of the concept of "gay" (in the way he defines it) provides us both with a useful instrument of research and at the same time a better comprehension of how people actually conceive of themselves and their sexual behavior. . . . Sexual behavior is not, as is too often assumed, a superimposition of, on the one hand, desires which derive from natural instincts, and, on the other, of permissive or restrictive

laws which tell us what we should or shouldn't do. Sexual behavior is more than that. It is also the consciousness one has of what one is doing, what one makes of the experience, and the value one attaches to it.[114]

One can hear the Foucault of *The Use of Pleasure*—volume 2 of the *History of Sexuality*—in these lines even as he describes *Christianity, Social Tolerance, and Homosexuality*. He is not concerned with the elisions of Boswell's work (which have importantly been taken up by others, as I have intimated) but with that notion of self-consciousness. And as Didier Eribon has recently observed, a shift of emphasis in Foucault's final works—from the end of the 1970s to his death in 1984—was toward not only this concept of self-fashioning but *collective* self-fashioning, especially as he found it in the context of gay communities in the United States:[115] Foucault was interested in self-fashioning outside the bounds of identity but nonetheless in a collectivity—in precisely what could be called "queer community" today. A reckoning with the traces of Boswell in Foucault will expand our understanding of each historian as well as of the various possible social and political uses of their works. It will extend and complicate the relations that we trace as we hand down a history of researchers on sex in the Middle Ages. In tracing those relations, queer medievalists are not only doing history—our own—but also, as will become clear through the course of this book, constructing a community across time.

Many Histories of Sexuality

Thus our choices as queer historians are not limited simply to mimetic identification with the past or blanket alteritism, the two mutually exclusive positions that have come to be associated with Boswell and Foucault. Mark D. Jordan's work in *The Invention of Sodomy in Christian Theology* (1997) is concerned, as was John Boswell's, to deal with histories of sexuality in the context of Christian community today. Jordan, too, is religious—like Boswell, a gay Catholic—and wants to understand how gay and lesbian Christians can fully participate in the larger Christian community. In this way he can be seen to pick up where Boswell left off, though his focus—on theological argumentation—is more narrowly defined. But while Boswell was concerned to reread biblical and theological texts and traditions to discover that they were not univocally condemnatory of same-sex relations, as traditionally thought (retranslating the Bible, for example, or pointing to concessions in Aquinas's argumentation), Jordan's approach is not to assert that these texts did not say what tradition says they said but is rather to trace the ways they develop and deploy language for specific ideological purposes. He draws on poststructuralist tenets of nonteleological history, the instability of language, and the performative nature of texts, explicitly inspired as he is by Foucault, David M. Halperin, and Eve Kosofsky Sedgwick; his point is not to discover a continuous strain of gay-friendly moral theology or theologians (an effort he would find suspect from a historical and philosophical viewpoint) but to understand how moral theology has worked its oppressions in the past—and how to "appropriate moral theology's long and checkered past" for future use.[116]

Appropriation, misrecognition, disidentification: these terms that queer theory has highlighted all point to the alterity within mimesis itself, the never-perfect aspect of identification. And they suggest the desires that propel such engagements, the affects that drive relationality even across time: "To overstress the incommensurability of temporal or cultural difference," writes Louise Fradenburg, "prevents us from asking: how have I loved the other? how is the other *in* me, in the 'same'?"[117] Fradenburg and Freccero's ruminations on the force and effects of desire and pleasure in historiography open up the concepts of sameness and difference to reevaluation; they note that "[t]he opposition [between historiographical perspectives] . . . is itself highly ideological."[118] Pleasure can be taken in the assertion of historical difference as well as in the assertion of similarity, and any such pleasure should not be opposed to "truth": "What seems crucial to a queering of historiography is not the rejection of truth for pleasure—which would only repeat the myth of their opposition—but rather the recognition of their intimacy."[119]

Through this book I describe partial connections, queer relations between incommensurate lives and phenomena—relations that collapse the critical and theoretical oppositions between transhistorical and alteritist accounts, between truth and pleasure, between past and present, between self and other. As the just-quoted passages from

Fradenburg and Freccero suggest, palpable connections across time are not the only possible kinds of pleasures afforded by history, nor are they the only means whereby to break down these oppositions. Pleasure may be afforded by a break with the past, a rupture of historical identity, as well as by a touching across time, for example; the loss of the past might carry an erotic charge. I don't wish to deny or devalue such emotional investments by choosing to focus on partial connections; Fradenburg's work in particular suggests how moving they can be. My queer history is one model among various models that collectively can mount a powerful challenge to the received subject of history: I focus on the potentials for making pleasurable connections in a context of postmodern indeterminacy. Such relations are very much like the one Michael Camille forges with the late-medieval manuscript illuminator whom he calls Pierre Remiet. Both artist and scholar engage death: Remiet by obsessively painting it, Camille by aiming to "bring the dead to life," to describe the pictorial acts that make up this medieval artist.[120] Camille understands these "peculiar graphic acts" to constitute Remiet, and the scholar's process of recognizing the artist in these gestures is like the process of recognizing "the jaunty walk of an old friend in a crowd." History writing must attempt a "commun[ion]" with particular past entities, he contends, and in this process "images play an obviously crucial role . . . blurring the line between the past and the present, emphasizing not the chasm that separates the living from the dead but the shared space where the gazes of both can meet."[121] Camille's own book explores the intimacy of truth and pleasure as he subjectively, imaginatively, even sensation-ally joins Remiet in the dying artist's thoughts and final experiences. And he celebrates the "reality" of Remiet's art "traced within and from the body of a historical subject," in contrast to "the thousands of horrifyingly superficial, simulated deaths we see every day on television," thus suggesting to us perhaps a different responsiveness to the body in the future.[122]

I attempt in this book to contribute to just such history as these medievalists are writing, history that without implying simple identification challenges "legitimating narratives," seeks other ways of forming community, and is concerned, as Kwame Anthony Appiah puts it in a related context, "to avoid cruelty and pain."[123] This concern is the reason I argue that it is appropriate for medievalists as well as queers, and in coalition with each other, to intervene in "culture wars" and public policy.[124] In this position on medievalists and public policy I am not arguing anything new, however urgent our particular moment seems: in 1952, E. N. Johnson addressed the Mediaeval Academy in a joint session with the American Historical Association, urging: "[I]f we cannot justify our interests by some sort of contribution to the solution of major contemporary problems, then we shall be deserted for some system or some one who promises to do what we do not do."[125] The dark cultural context of Johnson's remarks—he mentions "thermo-nuclear research" and investigations into colleagues—gave particular force to their foreboding suggestion about a future if medievalists abandon any sense of social responsibility. And because of the increasingly conservative cultural climate in the United States now I cannot finally agree with the recent polemical characterization by Steven Justice of medieval historians as engaged at most in a "cultivation of the soul," pursuing our objects of study "from the safety of privilege and inconsequence."[126] We are not all safe, as Johnson's comments above make clear; in particular, while I am mindful of my privilege as a tenured professor at an elite university I know also that privilege does not guarantee my safety: I am a lesbian teacher of queer histories, and such teachers are extraordinarily vulnerable.[127]

My engagement with the Lollards throughout this book addresses this situation. It springs not from any simple identification with this persecuted minority; in fact my analysis complicates identifications with either the dissenters or the orthodox as it shows these two sides mutually contaminated and virtually indistinguishable on issues of gender. But such a complication of mimesis does not lead to a necessary sense of scholarly inconsequence, as Justice's argument would seem to imply, or to a phobic denial of identity-based community, as Stephen O. Murray might suggest.[128] My discussion reveals the pervasive interrelation of discourses of sodomy and heresy in late-medieval England, suggests shadowy threats to burn medieval English sodomites. This story fills in the received narrative of heresy in medieval England, heretofore assumed mysteriously to be relatively free of the sexual accusations common on the European continent. It furthers our understanding of the particular ways orthodoxy and deviation, normative and nonnormative, intermingle and at times are indistinguishable. It undermines the authority of claims that imply that persecutory discourses have ever been unequivocal, and thus contributes to an effort to delegitimate claims that religious and sexual discrimination now in the United States or the United Kingdom are based on simple historical precedents.[129] That effort is aimed at achieving the safety such an argument about scholarly inconsequence presumes historians already enjoy; it aims at developing the partial relations of community that break down sheer oppositions of truth and affect, self and other.

On a Tangent

In demonstrating the indeterminacy, heterogeneity, and arbitrariness within communities in late-medieval England, I go against their own explicit intentions.[130] Reductiveness and essentializing are not, of course, modern inventions. I expose their own essentializing gazes—the gaze of the Lollards as they seek to reform the true English church and extirpate the sodomy that is rife among the clergy (they say there is a "secret test" that proves whether a man "is one of those"); Chaucer's narrator's gaze in the General Prologue to the *Canterbury Tales*, especially those famous first eighteen lines, as he organizes and construes his fellow pilgrims to Canterbury as part of the natural, generative, and heterosexual order of things; the gaze of the hostile neighbors of Margery Kempe as they sneer at her queer devotional practices.

I want to highlight the various costs of that essentializing, to take up the leavings of normalizing categories, to recuperate the objects of the secret tests, to locate the kinds of desires such as those boys and girls imagined in Mirk's manual might be discovering, untutored, if allowed same-sex beds: the kinds of men who do not like women, as the Lollards put it; the weird Pardoner on the Canterbury pilgrimage, eunuch and/or sodomite, silenced and furious; the devotionally challenged, never-canonized Margery Kempe; John (AKA Eleanor) Rykener, a shadowy London figure whose identity (as male or female) apparently eluded many people with whom s/he had sexual contact. S/he was a transvestite prostitute arrested in the act of sex with a man (who had thought s/he was a woman) and interrogated in London in December of 1394. S/he was uncategorizable: no case seems to have been pursued, perhaps—as the editors of the document argue—because the authorities did not know what to make of him/her.[131] John/Eleanor's changeable, purchasable person haunts such essentializing efforts. And with these new pieces of history, I show that queers can make new relations, new identifications, new communities with past figures who elude resemblance to us but with whom we can be connected partially by virtue of shared marginality, queer positionality.

Such a queer history is contingent history. These new historical relations are not metaphorical: I don't seek to match or substitute one queer for another in history. As I shall detail in chapter 3, queerness, further, is not a hard and fast quality that I know in advance, but is a relation to a norm, and both the norm and the particular queer lack of fit will vary according to specific instances. But my queer history is contingent not only for these reasons—not only in the sense in which Benjamin understands materialist history; not only, either, in the sense on which Foucault insists ("We have to dig deeply to show how things have been historically contingent, for such and such reason intelligible but not necessary").[132] It is a history of displacements (of signs, of things, of people), of signifiers knocked loose and whose signifiers knock others loose, in turn: repeated accusations of sodomy displace the authoritative ground of knowing who's doing what; Margery Kempe's construction of a spiritual family displaces the community standard of earthly family. And Margery, as we shall see in chapter 3, wants to touch, literally, the divine. "The contingent," writes Bhabha, "is contiguity, metonymy, the touching of spatial boundaries at a tangent, and, at the same time, the contingent is the temporality of the indeterminate and the undecidable."[133] Related to metonymy (Carlo Ginzburg notes this about the use of clues), my queer history works sensibly.[134] It is a history of things touching: contingent < L. *com-* + *tangere*, to touch. Beyond the basic understanding that a queer history will be about the body because it is about sex, my queer history has a relation to the tactile.

This book turns out to be in many ways about touch: about who can touch the body of Christ, for example: a central issue in the eucharistic controversies of Lollard polemic. About whether one can discern the sex of someone by touching him: an issue in the deposition of the transvestite prostitute. About why Margery Kempe thinks Christ's saying "Noli me tangere" to Mary Magdalene is so cruel. About whence proceeds the "vibration" Foucault feels from documents such as those of Pierre Rivière, or Herculine Barbin, or the collected fragments of the lives of infamous men. About how nineteenth-century French historian Jules Michelet reenacts history in such a bodily way, as Roland Barthes describes him. And about how Barthes performs his own caress, across time, of—and from—the dead.

The Song of Roland

Roland Barthes's work provides an unusually sharp focus on the historicist and humanist concerns of a quintessential postmodernist. I turn to it, finally, not solely for methodological guidance in this book but also, and mostly, as it provides an example of an impulse toward queer history; I turn to it as sometime guide and as inspiration. Though the linking of lives across time is our shared preoccupation, the varied means by which Barthes accomplished this are not always the same as mine; the phenomenological turn at the end of his career, for example, is not one I take. But I discuss Barthes's works in considerable detail here because of their demonstration of a fully, if variously, formulated queer historical impulse. Barthes's concerns were not always in concert with a queer history, let alone a medievalist's view of such a history—I shall begin by looking at the breezily anachronistic use of the Middle Ages in that poststructuralist work, *S/Z*—yet his celebration of fragmentation did not preclude a profound desire for connectedness that was often a desire for touching across time. This introductory chapter will draw to a close as I raise questions stimulated by Barthes's projects that I shall address in the chapters to follow.

S/Z has always held out to me the promise that it might articulate a queer relation to the past, maybe even to the medieval. It is preoccupied with *Sarrasine*, Balzac's novella about a castrato on the nineteenth-century Roman stage, and I read that work as bearing an interesting thematic relation to a key moment in Chaucer's *Canterbury Tales*. I look at this moment in detail in chapter 2: it occurs when the Pardoner—perhaps a eunuch, certainly sexually odd—interrupts the Wife of Bath's autobiographical disquisition on the road to Canterbury. I argue that in this moment, the eunuch or eunuch-like figure, already having been marked as queer by the pilgrim narrator, reveals the Wife (theretofore represented as perfectly naturally robust and [hetero]sexual), to be herself unnatural, a construction. Similarly, and drastically, La Zambinella, the castrato in *Sarrasine,* destroys the very concept of a natural woman for his/her would-be lover: when the disenchanted sculptor Sarrasine learns that La Zambinella is not a woman but a castrato, he cries out to the terrified singer: " 'Your feeble hand has destroyed my happiness. . . . You have dragged me down to your level. *To love, to be loved!* are henceforth meaningless words for me, as they are for you. I shall forever think of this imaginary woman when I see a real woman.' He indicated the statue [which he has made of the castrato] with a gesture of despair. 'I shall always have the memory of a celestial harpy who thrusts its talons into all my manly feelings, and who will stamp all other women with a seal of imperfection! Monster! You who can give life to nothing. For me, you have wiped women from the earth.' "[135] My intent is not to prove that Barthes, or Balzac, had been reading Chaucer or literature of the Middle Ages: there is no such positivistic relation to the medieval here. I shall explore reasons for such shared textual preoccupations in chapters 2 and 3 when I treat the issue of queerness as a relation to a norm, a relation that can be historicized *and* traced across time. Here, moving beyond Bhabha's analysis of Barthes's "affective writing," and laying the groundwork of my own connections with medieval lives—as well as with the fragmentary textual lives of Barthes and of Foucault—I want to see how Roland Barthes links "new times" with a queer body, and how, therefore, his historicist impulses might themselves be queer.

Barthes lavishes critical attention on *Sarrasine*'s climactic denouement, from the moment of the sculptor's first encounter with the castrato to his devastating discovery and beyond. *Sarrasine "represents,"* he writes, "a generalized collapse of economies: the economy of language . . . of genders . . . of the body . . . of money" (215 [221]). Because "[t]he symbolic field is occupied by a single object from which it derives its unity," "the human body" (214–15 [220]), a transgression of that bodily unity in the act of castration can eliminate the conditions of meaning altogether. Neither male nor female, the castrato is "beyond life or death [*en deçà de toute vie et de toute mort*], *outside all classification*," transgressing "the very existence of difference which generates life and meaning" (197 [202]): "it is at the level of the body that the bar of opposition must burst apart and that the two *inconciliabilia* of the Antithesis (outside and inside, cold and heat, death and life) are brought together, are made to touch, to mingle in the most amazing of figures in a composite substance (without *holding together*)."[136] The collapse of "the wall of the Antithesis" thus occurs even as the "opposition of the sexes" (215 [221]) is breached and as the body's unity is shattered. The form of this collapse is of "an unrestrained metonymy," and its consequences are drastic: "it is no longer possible to *represent*, to make things *representative*, individuated, separate, assigned" (216 [221–22]). "Itself metonymic," castration nonetheless "jams [*bloque*] all metonymy" as it interrupts any replication, "aesthetic or biological" (202 [208]).

Catastrophic, yes, and fundamentally so, but this is not a crime or disaster to fear or dread. This disruption of representation enacted by the figure of the castrato is, rather, a poststructuralist version of literature itself, what Barthes was dedicated to; it is writing, what he calls the "writerly" (*scriptible*) in an otherwise "readerly" (*lisible*) text: "*Sarrasine* represents the very confusion [*le trouble même*] of representation, the unbridled [*déréglée*] (pandemic) circulation of signs, of sexes, of fortunes" (216 [222]). This unbridled circulation is the operation of the plural in the classical text with its plurality of entrees; "Only writing, by assuming the largest possible plural in its own task, can oppose without appeal to force the imperialism of each language" (206 [212]). In the writerly, plural text, contesting languages (codes) are engaged in a play of meaning, a game of meaning (177; 155 [182–83; 160]) wherein there is no hierarchy of codes (206 [211–12]), no single code that founds or underwrites the meaning of the others.

Barthes's own ludic writing here itself collapses distinctions between subject and object, reader and writer; that "generalized collapse of economies" is in fact what Barthes values most. Leslie Hill writes that Barthes in *S/Z* values as the "priceless *scriptible*" in Balzac's narrative "that moment where subject and object, Sarrasine and castrato, male and female, narrator and narratee, narration and plot, frame and intrigue, reader and writer, BartheS and BalZac, fuse together in a circuit of mutual contagion."[137] That "moment" is the whole denouement of the narrative, from the first contact of Sarrasine and the castrato, especially their kiss, to Sarrasine's being disabused and killed, to Sarrasine's story's meeting the frame-tale and its failure to seduce its listener, only infecting her in turn. To Hill's list of mutually contaminated pairs we might add readers and characters, copy and model, author and text.[138]

And medieval and modern. Describing the interchange between the deliriously wine-soaked, love-intoxicated Sarrasine and the reserved Zambinella—at their first meeting, when he carries her off to a boudoir and tries to ravish her—Barthes invokes the concept of "the 'scene,'" "the endless confrontation of two different codes communicating solely through their interlockings [*leurs emboîtements*], the adjustment of their limits (dual replication, stychomythia). A society aware of the—in some sense—linguistic nature of the world, as was medieval society with its Trivium of the arts of speech, believing that it is not the truth which brings an end to the confrontation of languages, but merely the force of one of them, can then, in a ludic spirit, attempt to encode this force, to endow it with a protocol of results: this is the *disputatio*."[139] At the very moment in the narrative that Sarrasine could find out the male inside the female, Barthes breaks in to note that this exchange of words is modeled on a kind of purely linguistic confrontation that was current in the Middle Ages. Further, "medieval society" resembles our contemporary one in its recognition of the "linguistic nature of the world" and its "ludic spirit."[140] So what crucially characterizes the valorized writerly—the ludic—is witnessed in medieval society as well as the modern day. Medieval and modern are fused in this moment as are female and male, reader and writer, object and subject in the ensuing narrative contagion. A plurality of codes opens up, without any master that would keep binary oppositions closed and in place: the modern is not characterized as simply different from the medieval but is touched by the medieval, and the medieval is touched by the modern; the absolute opposition cannot hold, the past cannot be used simply to ground the present.

Barthes seems thus to have seen what forms a blind spot in Bhabha's "DissemiNation": the fact that a postmodern view of history and causality will entail a breakdown of any binary opposition between medieval and modern. This deconstructive view of these relations means that historical difference enters into a whole field of difference, a whole world of the ne-uter, where no concept or phenomenon is purely or simply itself but is inhabited by an other. We need to complicate any positivistic understanding of causality when we think of the relations between medieval and modern, to open up more possibilities for understanding "new times." Benjamin alludes to such a treatment of past and present generally in his image of the constellation; Barthes begins that process of opening potentials here. And he pursues it, as we shall see in a moment, in *Camera Lucida*, where past and future touch in a photograph that has a corporeal impact on him—a man awaiting his execution: "By giving me the absolute past of the pose (aorist), the photograph tells me death in the future. What *pricks* me [*me point*] is the discovery of this equivalence."[141]

But first we must ask: doesn't this deconstructive view *really* mean only that the medieval is made over in the modern's image? That Barthes's seeing a playful, plural society of the Middle Ages that is as aware as he is of the apparently transhistorical "linguistic nature of the world" just means that he is reading modern selves into and covering over the medieval? That does seem to be the project that Barthes encourages in his short talk on teaching literature written in July 1969, at about the same time as he was working on *Sarrasine*. In proposing three provisional rectifications of classical (that is, traditional) instruction, he suggests first "to turn classicocentrism around and do the history of literature backward. Instead of considering the history of literature from a pseudo-genetic point of view, if we really want to do the history of literature we need to make ourselves its center, working backward from the great modern rupture and organizing history from the rupture. In this way, past literature would be spoken from a contemporary language and even from our contemporary language." Mere temporal precedence should not be valorized, and neither should continuities or causalities be assumed: Barthes's history of ruptures and discontinuities here resembles (as we shall see) Foucault's. "We would no longer see poor students forced to work first on the sixteenth century, whose language they barely understand, under the pretext that [it] comes *before* the seventeenth century, which is itself all bound up with religious disputes that have nothing to do with students' current situation."[142] A medievalist suspicion of historical asymmetry (such prominence accorded to the modern-postmodern) leads us to believe that the modern ludic model is being elaborated and the medieval is consequently disappeared—here and in *S/Z*. Similarly, a feminist concern with gender asymmetry makes us wary of the putative fusion of male and female we see in *S/Z;* we suspect rather that a male model is being extended.[143] And just as the loss of the feminine might lead one to conclude—famously—that "there is no sexual relation," so the loss of the medieval in this particular way suggests that moderns, sunk in "that rancid solipsistic pit" of (post)romanticism, will lose any possibility of a real relation to the past, exemplified here by the medieval.[144]

But Barthes's emphases shift and change; they are not always the same through his vastly varied oeuvre. And though he does advocate the translation and preemption of the premodern by the modern in this lecture, narcissism is not the only motive for relations to the past in Barthes's works.[145] The deconstructive view in *S/Z* points to other kinds of time, other functions of the past. Granted, discontinuity, fragmentation, isolation are the valorized terms of Barthes's poststructuralism: "*Society of the Friends of the Text:* its members would have nothing in common (for there is no necessary agreement on the texts of pleasure) but their enemies."[146] In Barthes, the writer is isolated, *writing* is isolation: "We allow people to be different (that is our master stroke), but not unusual. We accept types, but not individuals. . . . But what about the person who is absolutely alone? Who isn't a Breton, a Corsican, a woman, a homosexual, a madman, an Arab, etc.? Somebody who doesn't *even belong* to a minority? Literature is his voice."[147] And thus the prospect of community is very unclear. "*Ourselves writing*" ("*Nous en train d'écrire*" [*S/Z*, 5 (11)]) is the promise of the breakdown between subject and object that is the writerly—that *nous* in the act *is* the writerly, that perpetual present, according to *S/Z*—but as Michael Holland also observes, that *nous*—that something like community, connected across the differences—is very hard to realize.[148]

Yet despite this emphasis on the "absolutely alone," relations between lives, between entirely contingent and profoundly singular lives, were indeed a concern throughout the long and otherwise uneven span of Barthes's texts. Patrizia Lombardo comments that "history emerges as the deep obsession of one of the founders of French structuralism, which has been perceived as non-historical or antihistorical."[149] "His work is not anti-historical (at least, so he intends), but always, persistently, antigenetic," Barthes writes in *Roland Barthes*, "for Origin is a pernicious figure of Nature (of Physis): by an abusive interest, the *Doxa* 'crushes' Origin and Truth together, in order to make them into a single proof."[150] For Barthes, the historical is separate from the coercive natural; history is profoundly embodied and deeply desirous. Barthes's fascination with the ways historical writing engages the body past and present may be one reason the Middle Ages erupt seismically, in *S/Z*, at the moment that a body is about to be revealed to its would-be lover. Indeed, for this reason, perhaps, Barthes was drawn, very early in his career, to the nineteenth-century French historian Jules Michelet, that singularly somatic historical writer; Barthes commented in regard to the writer to whom he continually returned in his long career, that "it would be better to say the historical body, as Michelet sees it," than "the human body."[151]

Let me turn now to Michelet, "the author on whom Barthes had written the most—many articles and the 1954 book," as Lombardo notes.[152] The "themes," to use Barthes's own critical term, of past, present, bodies, sexuality, and gender in that book, *Michelet*, are not hard to find. And because Barthes's Michelet's history uses the body in unusual, nonnormative ways, in order to make loving relations across time, it provides interesting ideas for thinking about queer history. "Michelet conceived of History as love's Protest," Barthes states in *Camera Lucida*, love's protest against its apparently inevitable loss: History sustains, protects, enables, enacts love.[153]

The whole historical enterprise, massive as it was for Michelet, is somatic, as Barthes analyzes it: "In this vast amorous combat between Justice and Grace, the historian-as-priest cannot remain impartial. Objective, i.e., obedient to the object of history, yes, and Michelet has always claimed to be so. He could not endure being called a poet more than a historian. But where is the real stake of historical labor? Is it to rediscover a Pointillist order of details, as Taine and the scientific school would have it? or else the plenitude, the vast unctuosity of the past? For Michelet the historical mass is not a puzzle to reconstitute, it is a body to embrace. The historian exists only to recognize a warmth."[154] Documents are produced by that warmth; "a kind of residual memory [*une rémanence*] of past bodies" clings to them (81

[73]). Since "[t]he corruption of bodies is a pledge of their resurrection," "the goal of history is to rediscover in each piece of the past's flesh [*dans chaque chair du passé*] the corruptible element par excellence, not the skeleton but the tissue" (87 [78])—and Michelet can sum up a man of the past in a single adjective which "accounts for a touch, for an ideal palpation which has found out the body's elemental substance" (90 [82]).

The historian manages thus, by writing, to "touch" bodies across time. Resurrection is the aim of his history, unreached but nonetheless signaled: "Thierry saw a *narration* there and M. Guizot an *analysis*. I have called it *resurrection* and that name will remain with it."[155] If this resuscitation is an unreachable goal, if tactile contact between historian and past bodies is a metaphor, Michelet's corporeal responses to the historical phenomena about which he writes are not, Barthes maintains: "The historical being has virtually no psychology; rather, he is reduced to a sole substance, and if he is condemned, it is not by the judgment of his motives or his actions, but by virtue of the quality of attraction or repulsion attached to his flesh. . . . Michelet condemns by virtue of his nauseas, not of his principles" (92 [86]). Michelet's own body becomes the relay point or surface of historical convergence, according to Barthes: he suffers terrible headaches while writing of the terrors of the past: "[A] kind of surprising symbiosis is established between the historian and History. Fits of nausea, dizziness, oppression do not come only from the seasons, from the weather; it is the very horror of narrated history which provokes them: Michelet has 'historical' migraines. . . . September 1792, the beginnings of the Convention, the Terror, so many immediate diseases, concrete as toothaches."[156] Michelet's body is "the site," as Leslie Hill writes, "of an imaginary identification between the process of utterance and the object of that utterance"—in other words, Michelet the nineteenth-century historian ("the writing subject") is connected to the eighteenth-century phenomena ("the object of writing") "not on the plane of historical fact, but on the level of the utterance, the inscription, the writing of that history."[157]

Subject and object, past and present touch in Michelet's body in the act of writing. As do male and female. "I am a complete man, having both sexes of the mind [*Je suis un homme complet, ayant les deux sexes de l'esprit*]," Barthes quotes him as writing (182 [157]). Barthes finds double-sexedness in Michelet's heroes and heroines and in their chronicler. Feminine characteristics are displayed not only in the mind of the historian, however: Michelet's very morphology is feminine, "until the age of fifty, a thin, tense, pale figure (he looked like his wife, he would say), then, in old age, the fleshy face of a matron and a seeress" (182 [158]). This historian exploits that femininity, turning himself "into a woman, mother, nurse, the bride's companion" (153) in a writing act that demonstrates what Barthes calls "Michelet's lesbianism" (152 [136]). Further breaking down oppositions, Barthes claims that "[t]he ideal movement of love is not, for Michelet, penetration but juxtaposition [*élongement*]. . . . [T]o protect Woman, to cover her, to envelop her, to 'follow' her entire surface, is to do away with any discontinuity of substance. The ideal figure of the lover is ultimately the garment" (153 [136]). History, as "love's Protest," nurtures and protects love, and love works here metonymically, juxtaposing, touching. It is less "Michelet's lesbianism"—a rather limited concept based on a sororal model—that makes Barthes's Michelet's history queer; more fundamentally, Michelet's history links the fusing of past and present to the fusing of male and female. And it resolves surface/depth oppositions into sheer surfaces, following them, juxtaposing them, loving them. As is clear already, it is not only Michelet who thus caresses his historical subjects; Barthes caresses Michelet just so.

Barthes created his own queer relation to Michelet by "living with" him. In his various ideas of " 'lived' textuality" and theatricalization—what queer theory has now promoted as performance and performativity—Barthes addressed the ways in which "the opposition between book and life, practice and speculation" could be abolished.[158] In the Preface to *Sade, Fourier, Loyola,* for example, he interprets "the index of the pleasure of the Text" as "when we are able to live with Fourier, with Sade. To live with an author does not necessarily mean to achieve in our life the program that author has traced in his books. . . . [It] is a matter of bringing into our daily life the fragments of the unintelligible ('formulae') that emanate from a text we admire. . . . [Our] daily life then itself becomes a theater whose scenery is our own social habitat."[159] The Text is open, a collection of fragments, but fragments that do not remain unsituated in time or space; in our reading, taking up and "receiving from the text a kind of fantasmatic order" (8 [13]) we "spea[k] this text," cite it, and such citation theatricalizes our lives in turn, empties them of the impossible function of mere expressivity (of a soul, of a depth) and renders them capable of further *touching*—other lives, other texts.

Barthes thus "lived with" Michelet: first by in some sense ventriloquizing Michelet's voice (in *Michelet par lui-même*), later by publishing *Roland Barthes* in "Écrivains de toujours," the same series at Seuil as *Michelet par lui-même* many years earlier.[160] He describes his own body as individuated by migraines and sensuality (*Roland Barthes*, 60 [63]), the very phenomena that (at least arguably) individuate Barthes's Michelet. And though he protests, "So different from Michelet's migraines, 'amalgams of bewilderment and nausea,' my migraines are matte" (125 [114]), his repetition of what he perceives as Michelet's gestures in his own is explicit: "R.B. does exactly what he says Michelet does," in reference to a certain kind of pseudocausal reasoning (151–52 [134]); earlier, "if he speaks of Michelet, he does with Michelet what he claims Michelet has done with historical substance: he functions by sliding over the entire surface, he caresses [*il opère par glissement total, il caresse*]" (58 [61]). Reading Michelet is to caress him even as it is to imitate him.

And Barthes, in turn, would extend that touch to future readers of his own texts. Apropos of Sade, Fourier, and Loyola—fragmented, dispersed subjects of their texts the reader can nontheless love—Barthes happily projects: "[W]ere I a writer, and dead, how I would love it if my life, through the pains of some friendly and detached biographer [*un biographe amical et désinvolte*], were to reduce itself to a few details, a few preferences, a few inflections, let us say: to 'biographemes' whose distinction and mobility might go beyond any fate and come to touch, like Epicurean atoms, some future body, destined to the same dispersion" (9 [14]). The biographeme, Barthes writes later in *Roland Barthes*, is what "I lend to the author I love."[161] Such touching is accomplished through the citation, in another, later life, by yet another body, of those peculiar "details," "preferences," "inflections" of his life. It is what D. A. Miller performs in his text, *Bringing Out Roland Barthes*, responding to "a handful of names, phrases, images, themes (whether or not strictly written by Barthes, all inscribed in his *text*)" that are just such details, preferences, inflections: "What I most sought, or what I most seek now, in the evidence of Roland Barthes's gayness is the opportunity it affords for staging this imaginary relation between us, between those lines on which we each in writing them may be thought to have put our bodies—for fashioning thus an intimacy with the writer whom (above all when it comes to writing) I otherwise can't touch." That textual intimacy, that touching, Miller suggests, can be an act of community, as it is an act "between us."[162] That touching, that repetition, that reenactment, is, I argue, a particularly Barthesian act of queer history. It is what I attempt here as I pull out this strain in Barthes's work and lovingly cite it as it motivates my own work.

This act is queerly historical because it creates a relation across time that has an affective or an erotic component. A similar relation between artist and audience can be instantiated, Barthes argues, by hearing the grain of the voice, that something which is the "body" "beyond (or before) the meaning of the words."[163] Even when the phenomenon is not necessarily one which crosses time—as here, with hearing a voice singing—Barthes's presentation emphasizes historical distance: in this case, he contrasts one singer who is no longer listened to with one who dominates the present vocal culture, and argues that it is the earlier one who has the grain.

> The "grain" is the body in the voice as it sings. . . . If I perceive the "grain" in a piece of music and accord this "grain" a theoretical value . . . , I inevitably set up a new scheme of evaluation which will certainly be individual—I am determined to listen to my relation with the body of the man or woman singing or playing and that relation is erotic—but in no way "subjective" (it is not the psychological "subject" in me who is listening; the climactic pleasure hoped for is not going to reinforce—to express—that subject but, on the contrary, to lose it). . . . Thus I shall freely extol such and such a performer, little-known, minor, forgotten, dead perhaps.[164]

According to a fairly standard poststructuralist conception (which I treat apropos of Foucault in my coda), the loss of subjectivity here provides the opportunity for using the body in new ways and in making new kinds of bodily relations with others. What I find particularly provocative for queer history is Barthes's emphasis on the cross-temporality of these relations.

The deep desire physically to cross or span temporal divides, a desire that itself crosses into mourning for a lost body, drives the last work published in Barthes's own lifetime. Barthes visited not the archive materials of the Bastille (as did Foucault, in a similar queer historical impulse that I discuss in chapter 2) but the photographic archive of his own family in *Camera Lucida*. This last work is queer in a number of respects: it insists on the achieved somatic relation between bodies enabled by the technology of photography, thus finding the fulfillment of queer historical desire that impelled Barthes through his whole career; it abandons (oddly, queerly, according to some critics) the deconstruction of the subject that earlier enabled his queer history, operating instead according to phenomenological precepts; and it is driven by a desire to recover again his lost, dead mother, which relation itself might be marked as gay, queer.[165] What interests me in *Camera Lucida* is not its phenomenological assertions themselves, and neither is it the precise psychological value of the mourning that is enacted in the work; what interests me is the physicality of the historical contact that Barthes asserts as achieved in looking at a photograph, and that seems a likely culmination of a critical career whose first major publication was *Michelet*.[166]

At points, then, *Camera Lucida* echoes those bodily concerns and familiar deconstructive methods of earlier work. A photograph can delight: repeating the Preface to *Sade, Fourier, Loyola* Barthes suggests, "I like certain biographical features which, in a writer's life, delight me as much as certain photographs; I have called these features 'biographemes.' "[167] But the photographic detail, the fragment (what he calls the *punctum*), can wound the spectator, too, and such a somatic response to the contingent detail of the photograph is the greater concern of this work. Barthes is at pains to distinguish photography from writing in *Camera Lucida;* modern technology distinguishes photography from the written text. A photograph can convey a core knowledge (a *noeme*)—the certainty that *that has been*—that cannot be conveyed by the shifty linguistic signifier, empty and wayward, that Barthes earlier described and tracked with such gusto. "[T]he *noeme* 'That-has-been' was possible only on the day when a scientific circumstance (the discovery that silver halogens were sensitive to light) made it possible to recover and print directly the luminous rays emitted by a variously lighted object. The photograph is literally an emanation of the referent. From a real body, which was there, proceed radiations which ultimately touch me, who am here; the duration of the transmission is insignificant; the photograph of the missing being, as Sontag says, will touch me like the delayed rays of a star" (80–81 [126]). With this last metaphor, we might recall Benjamin's image of the constellation in his discussion of properly materialist historical relations.[168] Barthes reads the photograph as a proof of a "somehow experiential order": it is not inductive but rather is "the proof-according-to-St.-Thomas-seeking-to-touch-the-resurrected-Christ" (79–80 [125]). "[T]he thing of the past . . . has really touched the surface which in its turn my gaze will touch" (81 [127]). The photograph offers the fulfillment of Barthes's desire for a tactile history, his long-expressed desire for contact across time, across death. And it can draw on "new times," different kinds of time: as he views the photo of a man awaiting execution, Barthes contends that "the photograph tells me death in the future": it assures him "*this has been*" (the man was there, waiting) even as it depicts that "*[t]his will be*" (the man will die). The photo pricks Barthes with this equation of past and future: new times are scored on the desiring body.[169]

With *Camera Lucida* Barthes confronted and proposed a phenomenological resolution to the problem of discursive relations to the real that he deferred when, say, celebrating the death of the author and his reappearance as one among other textualities. In the Preface to *Sade, Fourier, Loyola,* for example, the author returns as a textual component of his text; his life is best reduced to a few choice textualities, "biographemes"; in the world of the pleasure of the Text, there is a smooth exchange, a transmigration between "the 'literary' text (the Book)" and "our daily lives."[170] A symptomatic moment occurs in this preface (not unnoted, of course, by Barthes) when a fictional character in a book is taken to function in the same way as a real reader of a book.

Barthes had even earlier configured the issue in "Historical Discourse" (1967) in such a way as similarly to focus not on reality but on the reality effect: "What is the place of 'reality' in the structure of discourse?" he asks, and answers, "[H]istorical discourse does not follow reality, it only signifies it; it asserts at every moment: *this happened*, but the meaning conveyed is only that someone is making the assertion." "[W]e can say that historical discourse is a fake performative [*un discours performatif truqué*], in which what claims to be the descriptive element is in fact merely the expression of the authoritarian nature of that particular speech-act." Barthes goes on to list various other deployments of the reality effect, emphasizing above all "the massive development of photography." A dozen years before *Camera Lucida* Barthes thus performed an ideological critique of the photograph's assertion that "the event portrayed *really* happened": "once we achieve the insight that reality is nothing but a meaning (*signifié*), and so can be changed to meet the needs of history," analyzing such effects as the reality effect can work toward subverting "the foundations of civilization 'as we know it.' "[171] (Similar, if less grandiose, claims have been made for the performative—citation, reenactment—in more recent queer theory.)

But in the later text Barthes was to note that history and photography function differently (*Camera Lucida* 93 [146]).[172] In *Camera Lucida* Barthes writes that photography's "force is . . . superior to everything the human mind can or can have conceived to assure us of reality" (87 [135]), that the photograph *is* "an emanation of *past reality*" (88 [138]), no mere effect. His goal is Micheletist after all: resurrection.[173] That emanation is of course controlled: just how much light reaches the film, just how that past reality meets that surface, is the mediating province of photographer and camera. But "the most precise technology can give its products a magical value," as Benjamin had suggested earlier; the viewer "feels an irresistible urge to search such a picture for the tiny spark of contingency, of the Here and Now, with which reality has so to speak seared the subject."[174] The human's relation to the real over time, in particular relations between human bodies across time, remained a live and poignant preoccupation from the beginning for Barthes.

If we are to take inspiration for our queer historical projects from this oeuvre, however, a host of questions and problems bursts forth. What importance do social, cultural, economic, and political constraints and hierarchies have if we speak so blithely of "reenactment," "citation," "living with" a figure from the past?[175] Where does awareness of particular locations go in such discussions? What kind of community is it, exactly, that consists of two people? How can we avoid triviality and idiosyncracy as we discuss community formations?[176]

In the analyses that follow here, I attempt to address such issues. For my main medieval materials I have chosen works written in London and East Anglia from the mid-1390s to the mid-1430s; by limiting the range of my discussion I make it possible to specify at least some particular functions of and constraints on the sexual discourses that are my focus. When I move to modern and postmodern appropriations of these medieval texts and concepts, I attempt to address gender, sexuality, and racial inequities (in George Lyman Kittredge's reading of the Pardoner and the Wife of Bath; in Robert Glück's use of Margery Kempe; in Quentin Tarantino's delineation of the abjects of current Los Angeles culture; and in Foucault's delineations of sexual acts and institutions of subjectivation in the Middle Ages, for some examples). I address the problem of effective community building as I analyze queer community and coalition building in relation to the "culture wars" in the United States today.

My project, finally, is not just for medievalists and queers, even less just for queer medievalists, though my ostensible focus would suggest as much. I want to demonstrate the ways in which aspects of cultural studies more broadly can be altered by a queer medievalist's touch. Medievalists have particular things to contribute to the discipline of cultural studies—a very long attention span and an insistence on long views of cultural phenomena—and a queer medievalist's discussion here can point out crucial links between ideologies that are usually kept quite separate: between the politics that support academic freedom at all educational levels in the culture wars, for example, and the ones that would preserve the National Endowment for the Humanities, and the ones that undergird queer history. As I suggest in chapter 3, medieval studies, history, postcolonial studies, queer scholarship, the fight for preservation of funding for the humanities, the defense of open inquiry in education—none will be the same once an articulation of one with another has taken place. The process of touching, of making partial connections between incommensurate entities—between, say, twentieth-century lives and the boys and the girls who Mirk counsels need to be kept in separate beds, or between various individuals now in coalitions, those postmodern communities gathered in the United States today around specific causes like academic freedom—that process I finally call, in the coda, getting medieval.

Chapter One

It Takes One to Know One: Lollards, Sodomites, and Their Accusers

It was necessary for there to be heresy,
so that something would be written that had no reason to be.
Jacques Rancière, *The Names of History*

At the end of the brash and polemical manifesto known as the *Twelve Conclusions of the Lollards,* posted on the doors of Westminster Hall during the 1395 Parliament session and (according to other sources) on the doors of Saint Paul's as well, there appeared a short poem in Latin.

Plangant Anglorum gentes crimen Sodomorum;
Paulus fert, horum sunt idola causa malorum.
Surgunt ingrati Giazitae, Simone nati,
Nomine praelati, hoc defensare parati.
Qui reges estis, populis quicunque praeestis,
Qualiter hiis gestis gladiis prohibere potestis?

The English people bewail the crime of Sodom.
Paul says that idols are the cause of these ills.
The ingrate Giezites, born of Simon, rise up,

Prelates by name, ready to defend this crime.
You who are kings, and whosoever preside over the people,
How might you be able to prevent such goings-on with force?[1]

We don't know much for sure about the *Twelve Conclusions* themselves, since (for one thing) they come down to us in mediated form: they are extant only because orthodox opponents of these heretics collected and preserved them. Thus we do not even know, for example, the original language of the document: were the *Conclusions* originally composed in Latin or in English? It is hard to tell from the extant versions.[2] We know even less, however, about the poem. It is not mentioned by the Dominican friar Roger Dymmok in his immense formal reply to the *Conclusions*—a response that notes that a text was posted at Parliament, repeats the *Conclusions* in both English and Latin, and proceeds to address each conclusion at great length in scholastic Latin.[3] Was the poem indeed, as sources claim, posted along with the manifesto? Perhaps the verses were simply beneath the Dominican Dymmok's notice, so he did not reproduce them—or perhaps they were not posted along with the *Conclusions* at all, but were linked by chroniclers of the events of that Parliament session: Thomas Walsingham, the monastic chronicler at Saint Albans who was no friend of the Lollard cause, includes a paragraph in his *Annales Ricardi Secundi* that very explicitly connects the contents of the two documents.[4] John Bale, one and a half centuries later and on the side of the heretics—who were seen by this time as heroic proto-Protestants—prints the Latin verses, provides an English translation, and suggests that the poem was used in a sort of Lollard guerilla action against particularly egregious clerical offenders, once the *Conclusions* themselves had failed to provoke reform: "[W]hen the Conclusions themselves would not help towards any reformation, but were laughed to scorn of the bishops, then were these verses copied out by divers men, and set upon their windows, gates, and doors, which were then known for obstinate hypocrites and fleshly livers, and this made the prelates mad."[5] Supposedly posted at Westminster, maybe plastered on suspected sodomites' doors—how are we to take this poem? Is its charge of sodomy serious—the charge is allegedly made by a group of heretics, and heretics, after all, were the ones usually so accused—or is it just a standard, needling insult of clerics, an irritating but minor smear?[6]

The shifting politics of this poem and of response to it is precisely the preoccupation of this chapter. The six Lollard lines might have been preserved by the orthodox not only because they seemed pointedly to sum things up but also because they offered something useful in orthodox efforts to discredit these heretics—who were proving tenacious, ubiquitous, and bold, as this aggressive action of publicizing their manifesto startlingly demonstrated.[7] The verses, I argue, do not just sling empty insults; they bring forward a concern that is both explicit in and a persistent shadow of Lollard discourse *and* of its orthodox opposition. That tenebrous element blurs any conviction that reform is in fact possible, darkens any clear opposition between catholic and heretic, makes the "other" hard to pin down—and frustrates any desires we might have to identify simply with these dissenters.

Lollard Nation

Not all Lollards thought alike—they were a heterogeneous lot, from a wide range of society at least at the beginning, and the term "the Lollards" might itself mislead us into a reductive view. Granted this caveat, there "is a coherence in the Lollard creed despite differences of emphasis and of declared inclusiveness," as Anne Hudson maintains, and the *Twelve Conclusions* provide a good guide to such a creed.[8] The Lollard vision, outlined there, of "þe reformaciun of holi chirche of Yngelond" (Hudson, *Selections*, 24) would eliminate clerical privilege and hypocrisy, which Lollards claimed were overburdening and oppressing the English people; the *Conclusions* in their entirety detail a number of complex and multifarious charges against the "blynde and leprouse" church. Just to mention the topics here: the twelve Conclusions oppose church endowments and the church's spiritually deathly practice of "appropriation" that frequently leaves parishioners without pastoral care (First Conclusion); the entire earthly priesthood itself, which is not ordained by Christ (Second); required vows of clerical celibacy, since such vows brought sodomy into the church (Third); transubstantiation, which conduces to idolatry—worshiping a piece of bread (Fourth); exorcisms and false blessings, which are really necromancy and not theologically sound (Fifth); the holding of secular office by spiritual leaders, which effects an improper mixing or double estate rather like a hermaphrodite or person who takes payment from both sides (Sixth); special prayers for dead men's souls, which are motivated by gifts and therefore not far from simony (Seventh); pilgrimages, prayers, and offerings to images and crosses, which, again, are akin to idolatry (Eighth); auricular confession, since with the feigned power of absolution it enhances priests' pride and gives them opportunity for secret dalliances (Ninth); manslaughter in battle or punishment, which is expressly contrary to the New Testament (Tenth); vows of celibacy for nuns and widows, since they might be performing nonprocreative sex acts as a result (Eleventh); and arts such as goldsmithy, armoury, and other crafts that are deemed unnecessary and thus sinfully wasteful, curious, and engaged with ornamentation (Twelfth). This list witnesses the theological, social, and political range of Lollard reformist commitments. From the voice of the *Conclusions* it seems clear that Lollard groups conceived of themselves as communities and sought to remedy the ills of secular as well as ecclesiastical society: "We pore men" denounce the proud prelacy and private religion "þe qwich is multiplied to a gret charge and onerous [to] puple her in Yngelonde" ("which is multiplied into a heavy burden and onerous to people here in England").[9]

The six Latin hexametric lines that conclude the manifesto in several sources allude to key issues that had come to be associated with followers of Wyclif by the mid-1390s and that are treated in the *Conclusions* themselves. In fact, John Bale called the verses "a brefe conclusyon sommarye of the unyversall contentes therof." [10] The poetic lines are animated by a well-established Lollard disgust with corrupt clergy, especially those who engage in the buying and selling of spiritual things. The Lollard desire for accessibility of the Holy Scriptures to all believers, further, is perhaps hinted at in the direct reference to "Paulus." Lollard opposition to images is audible as idolatry is cited as the cause of clerical ills. And that call to secular leaders for reform in the last lines links up with ambitions for the nation indicated in the first line: these Lollards are the true Englishmen, seeking to (re)create and reform a true national church. The argument here implies an energetic antihierocratic view of lay monarchy and supports the nation-reforming aspirations of the Lollards.[11]

But why is sodomy used in the poem, first and foremost, to characterize the rift between the reforming true Christian Englishmen and false, hypocritical prelates? What is it about the vice, mentioned by name in one conclusion and probably alluded to in another, that might make it a likely choice for a concluding riff on all the *Conclusions*? Lollard complaints against simony and idolatry are common; in comparison, their accusations of sodomy are not all that frequent. But if relatively infrequent, they are nonetheless persistent, as we shall see, and such persistency itself argues that these attacks are deeply significant in some way. If the Lollards are trying to reform the national community, as the first line suggests, their desired goal is a nation without sodomy: "Anglorum gentes" bewail this "crimen Sodomorum."[12] As Steven F. Kruger puts it, in the very naming of this sex act there might be "an attempt to make sexual difference ethnic or racial, to fortify the casting out of sexual 'perversity' by conflation with a morally charged geopolitical differentiation."[13] Thus this term lends itself to a group trying to reform a nation by extirpating other kinds of people—ironically, since many anti-Lollard polemics and statutes call for the extirpation of Lollardy. And if a call for the elimination of sodomy signals the possibility of peace and even a kind of protodemocracy in the reformed nation, we must nonetheless attend to the first line's echoing rhyme of "Angl*orum*" in "Sodom*orum*": sodomy, as we will see, is not so easy to eradicate.

"Crimen Sodomorum" in fact specifically engages two areas of acute Lollard concern, and I want to turn to these areas to see how the term might provide a powerful rhetorical condensation or means of articulating and controlling a complex polemical field. First, idolatry, identified as the general form of sinfulness in a long discussion in the General Prologue to the Wycliffite Bible (written at about the time of the *Conclusions*).[14] Most Lollards persistently refused to swear any oaths by created things, and resistance to swearing had come to characterize Lollards by the 1390s: think of Chaucer's Parson, who bristles at Harry Bailley's oaths in the epilogue to the *Man of Law's Tale* and whom Harry taunts as a Lollard.[15] This refusal to swear by created things is explained in the Lollard treatise *The Lanterne of Liȝt* in terms of idolatry: he who swears on a created thing makes a false god.[16] Idolatry is explicated at length in the *Conclusions* themselves in relation to the Eucharist—the charge is that innocent people are led into worshiping a little bread as God's body—and in relation to pilgrimages, prayers, and offerings "to blynde rodys and to deue ymages of tre and of ston" ("to blind crosses and to deaf images of wood and of stone" [Hudson, *Selections*, 27]). An idolater, in the Augustinian scheme that informs both Lollard and orthodox theologies, *enjoys* something that he should rather *use* in order ultimately to enjoy the Creator, the only entity that should be enjoyed in himself.

I shall explore the relationship in particular between the Eucharist and idolatry later in this chapter, and will as well get to the persistent carnal desire that poses a general problem for this Augustinian scheme. But at the moment I want to highlight the fact that the reference to idolatry cited by the Latin poem is quite specific: Saint Paul in his letter to the Romans explains that because the gentiles worshiped idols instead of the incorruptible God he delivered them up to their own uncleanness. Idolatry has led to relations "aȝens kynde," as the Lollard Bible renders Paul's words; it has led to homosexual relations between females and between males:

> And thei chaungiden the glorie of God vncorruptible in to the licnesse of an ymage of a deedli [mortal] man, and of briddis [birds], and of foure footid beestis, and of serpentis. For which thing God bitook hem in to the desiris of her herte, in to vnclennesse, that thei punysche with wrongis her [their] bodies in hem silf [themselves]. The whiche chaungiden the treuthe of God in to leesyng [lying], and herieden and serueden [praised and served] a creature rathere than to the creatoure, that is blessid in to worldis of worldis. Amen. Therfor God bitook hem in to passiouns of schenschipe [ignominious passions]. For the wymmen of hem chaungiden the kyndli vss [use] in to that vss that is aȝens kynde. Also the men forsoken the kyndli vss of womman, and brenneden [burned] in her desiris togidere, and men in to men wrouȝten filthehed, and resseyueden in to hem silf the meede that bihofte of her errour [received in themselves the fit recompense of their error].[17]

The Latin Lollard poem follows Paul in blaming idolatry for the very negative "crimen Sodomorum," same-sex sexual relations. Sodomy itself can be seen as an idolatrous practice that is the result of idolatry, the fitting wage paid in their bodies for this sin: sodomites are idolaters because (to use that Augustinian formulation) they *enjoy* bodies that should rather be *used* in procreating, in increasing and multiplying the faithful.[18]

So the first two lines of the Lollard poem bewail same-sex sexual acts—most likely among male clergy and among male private religious, since "prelates" in the next lines are said to be defenders of this sin. And they lament sodomy in a way that links it to a specific doctrinal concern: idolatry. In the next lines there is a shift toward what Wyclif called *spiritual* sodomy: simony, the sin of trading in spiritual things.[19] This is the second area of Lollard concern, and it is a broad one. A specific—and quite peculiar—genealogy is constructed in lines 3 and 4 of the poem, as the "crimen Sodomorum" is linked with Gehazi and Simon Magus, the prototypical seller of church offices and the buyer in such transactions: prelates are said in the poem to be ingrate Giezites, born of Simon, rising up and ready to defend this crime of sodomy. Gehazi, we recall from 2 Kings 5, is the servant of the prophet Elisha, who cured the Aramaean army commander Naaman of leprosy; when his master Elisha refused any token of gratitude from the cured man, Gehazi ran after Naaman and asked him for two talents of silver and two changes of clothing—which he received and promptly hid for himself. (The prophet Elisha was aware of this transaction and stated to Gehazi that Naaman's leprosy would fasten onto him and his descendants forever; the servant indeed left the prophet's presence covered with disease.) While Gehazi became the symbol of the seller, Simon Magus became the enduring symbol of the buyer of spiritual things: Simon was the magician who in Acts 8 saw that the apostles imparted the Holy Spirit by a laying-on of hands, and wanted to purchase this power for himself.

Those perennial objects of Lollard attack, friars, were often imaged by these figures.[20] Distinguishing the two biblical characters, Jan Hus explains in a 1408 letter that Simon is the exemplar of those who demand money *before* the sacrament is performed, and Gehazi those who take money *after*. Both, however, deserve the epithet "simoniac," Hus insists, quoting Peter Lombard, and such reasoning might explain the poem's strange genealogy, might be the reason the Giezites (descendants of the far earlier Old Testament figure) are said in this poem to be born of Simon.[21]

In Wyclif's *De simonia* the concept of simony "extended far beyond the usual bounds," as Williell R. Thomson comments; "it served him as a vehicle for assaulting almost every perceived excess in the church."[22] The crux of the matter for Wyclif was that the church had no fundamental right to possess property, so that it was entirely inevitable that ecclesiastical officials would be simoniacs.[23] But simony is related in specific ways, too, to the perversion that is sodomy. Wyclif, following William Peraldus, explains the relationship between these sins.

> Sicut enim in corporali sodomia contra naturam semen perditur, ex quo individuum humani generis formaretur, sic in illa sodomia semen verbi dei deicitur, per quod in Christo Jesu spiritualis generacio crearetur. Et sicut sodomia fuit tempore legis nature contra ipsam naturam unum de peccatis gravissimis, sic symonia est tempore legis gracie contra ipsam graciam gravissimum peccatorum. Et cum gravius peccant membra diaboli tempore legis gracie, quam tempore legis nature peccaverant, signanter dicit Christus symoniacis Matth. 10, quod tollerabilius erit terre Sodomorum in die iudicii quam populo eicienti dignos prepositos.
>
> For just as in carnal sodomy contrary to nature the seed is lost by which an individual human being would be formed, so in this sodomy the seed of God's word is cast aside with which a spiritual generation in Christ Jesus would be created. And just as sodomy in the time of the law of nature was one of the most serious sins against nature, so simony in the time of the law of grace is one of the most serious sins against grace. And since the devil's adherents sin more seriously in the time of the law of grace than they had sinned in the time of the law of nature, Christ expressly says to the simoniacs in Matthew 10:15 that it will be more tolerable for the land of Sodom on judgment day than for a people who reject worthy rulers.[24]

Sodomy is understood as something like murder here, while simony causes spiritual death. The General Prologue to the Wycliffite Bible rehearses this analysis in English, accusing clergy of "symonie with portenauncis [appurtenances] thereof," in fact "myche worse and more abomynable than bodily sodomye."[25] Sodomy in this General Prologue is linked to murder, too, and the murder that is sodomy is clearly not figurative: "[W]hether Oxunford drinke blood and birlith [pours out] blood, bi sleeinge of quyke mēn, and bi doinge of sodomye, in leesinge a part of mannis blood, wherbi a chijld myte be fourmed, deme thei that knowen."[26]

Literally, sodomy is murder; and figuratively, sodomy is simony. Simony, in turn, is seen as crucially corporeal as well: in Lollard polemic simony is repeatedly referred to as selling God's body.[27] And the question of who has power in regard to God's body is connected to another critical doctrinal question, the struggle over the doctrine of transubstantiation—which doctrine was the specific locus of Wycliffite heresy. Wyclif's language in *De simonia* clearly connects simony with Christ's body and the Eucharist.[28] Wyclif, further, opens his treatise on simony by discussing simony itself as a species of heresy, then hastens to a treatment of the sin since it "sit lepra quam ex natura morbi et induracione eius continua impossibile est nisi per insolitum dei miraculum quod sanetur" ("is a leprosy that, because of the nature of the disease and its stubborn duration, cannot be cured except by a miracle which God does not often perform these days").[29] Nothing, he contends,

> plus destruit contractus et regna, ymmo ipsum Christianismum, quam heresis symoniaca, quia tollit graciam spiritus sancti, per quam continuarentur membra ad invicem et cum Christo. . . . [E]t sic ve genti, ve loco et ve homini, qui nittitur in communitate seminare heresim symoniacam, defendere vel fovere.

> destroys alliances and kingdoms more, indeed Christianity itself, than simoniacal heresy because it takes away the grace of the Holy Spirit by which members are joined to one another and to Christ. . . . [W]oe to that nation, woe to that place, and woe to that man who strives to spread the seed of simony's heresy in a community, to defend or nurture it.[30]

Murder-sodomy-simony-leprosy-heresy: this clustering locates the perpetrators as deviants within community, nation (*gens*), and Christianity.[31] The concatenation is well in place and fully operant in the Wycliffite context on the European continent: Hus, for example, whose own vernacular treatise on simony takes Wyclif's work as a starting point and sometimes quotes it verbatim, inveighs against John XXIII, just deposed at the Council of Constance, as "a base murderer, a sodomite, a simoniac, and a heretic."[32]

And this configuration is fully operant in the context of Lollard polemic in England, as we see in that minor but telling Latin poem.[33] This clustering is not merely "rhetorical"—that is, these accusations are not only figurative, and their connections are not merely abstract philosophical constructions. Though sodomy does operate in a figurative register in this poem, and though leprosy in the *Conclusions* that precede is clearly figurative, I argue that sodomy, simony, and idolatry here refer to literal transgressions as well that preoccupy Lollards. Anxiety about the sin of sodomy applies pressure at the center of Lollard beliefs, as I shall demonstrate in this chapter: such anxiety informs Lollard concern with clerical corruptions, with idolatry, with the doctrine of transubstantiation. In fact, it is in the context of such clustering that sodomitical acts and anxieties—otherwise deemed unspeakable and nature-defying, as we have seen in the introduction—can emerge into view, as Alan Bray and Jonathan Goldberg have argued in a later context.[34]

So "crimen Sodomorum," with its long tradition in scripture and association with idolatry, its implication in other aberrations such as simony, heresy, leprosy, and murder, and its stereotypical link with clerics and with fraternal organizations which live and conduct themselves separately and in private (a late Lollard text states, "ȝour freres ben taken alle day with wymmen & wifes, / Bot of ȝour priuey sodomye speke I not here"),[35] may be used in this Lollard poem as a means of gathering all these associations under one rubric, of wresting semantic and rhetorical control of a complex web of cultural phenomena, and of indicting a whole range of deviations, imbalances, and faulty allegiances perpetrated in late-medieval English clerical culture.[36] That could be one way of answering the question, "Why sodomy here?"

But a complication arises. If sodomitical associations energize Lollard discourse against orthodoxy, working away at the center of specific Lollard beliefs, an accusation of sodomy hits the Lollards, in turn, full in the face. A line-for-line rejoinder to the short poem at the end of the *Conclusions* appeared with the original sometime after 1395—perhaps, the nineteenth-century editor, Thomas Wright, guesses, during "the reign of Henry V." In the manuscript known as Cotton Vespasian D. ix, following the six-line stanza we've been considering, appear these lines:

Gens Lollardorum gens est vilis Sodomorum,
Errores eorum sunt in mundo causa dolorum.
Hii sunt ingrati, maledicti, daemone nati,
Quos vos, praelati, sitis damnare parati;
Qui pugiles estis fidei populisque praeestis,
Non horum gestis ignes prohibere potestis.

The race of the Lollards is the vile race of Sodom,
Their errors are the cause of the world's troubles.
They are ingrates, cursed, demon-born,
Whom you, prelates, should be prepared to condemn.
You who are fighters of the faith and preside over the people,
You cannot withhold fires from their actions.[37]

Not much is known about this pendant; neither Dymmok, who did not mention the first poem, nor the *Fasciculi zizaniorum*, nor Walsingham alludes it. Cotton Vespasian D. ix is a manuscript of eighteen miscellaneous items "copied (and some printed) in different periods and gathered together from originally separate sources," as Alan J. Fletcher observes. It seems that these two Latin poems were in fact copied by the scribe William Mede, a Carthusian monk of Sheen Charterhouse in London (ordained in 1417, died 1472 or 1473). As Fletcher notes, the Carthusians were active in busily promoting the anti-Lollard literature in London that was circulating in the late fourteenth and fifteenth centuries.[38]

Indeed, this pendant poem might have been composed sooner after the 1395 original than Thomas Wright supposes. The last line urges that the Lollards be burned: could this be a reference to the 1401 English statute *De heretico comburendo* that legislated for the first time that the penalty for recidivist heretics was burning?[39] The *terminus a quo* for this poem might then be 1401. Or, given that the first Lollard was burned before the passage of the statute in March 1401, the date could be earlier still.[40] Of even greater interest to me is the further suggestion that might be inferred from the syntax: that Lollards be burned *because they are sodomites*—or, less causally: that Lollards, who are sodomites, should be burned. This poem may indeed provide a suggestion that the burning of sodomites in England—of which there is no extant record, though such a punishment was prescribed by *Britton*—could have taken place under the 1401 statute for heresy, since these heretics were sodomites; at the least it might imply that some orthodox thought that the law should be applied in this way.[41]

Orthodox accusations of Lollard sodomy were not very common, even though (as I have mentioned) the concatenation of heresy and sexual perversity was well established.[42] Reginald Pecock, quite late (around 1449), alleges some Lollards to be lechers and adulterers, but even his is a rare accusation;[43] the specific accusation of sodomy against Lollards in this short poem is very unusual. But though the mutedness of the discourse in England is notable, it should not be taken to mean either that same-sex sexual relations did not occur in Lollard contexts, or that people did not worry about them *as sodomy.* It means, rather, that we need to read the evidence differently, not so positivistically—to find, for example, in a poem the suggestion that one statute might have been understood to apply to a number of ills, not always specified; or to see that rhetorical interrelations between documents (these two poems together, for example) may open onto a range of vague, hard-to-pin-down but pervasive and frightening cultural potentials. It means we may need to explore the cultural work, for another example, of parody.[44]

Because what can be noted here with certainty is the fact of parody, the reciprocal form of the second poem's echoing of the original's meter, rhyme scheme, and accusations. The fact of parody, of reciprocity, in itself is highlighted by the actual vagueness of the second poem: it exists to return insult and accusation, not to develop precise countercharges. If causality is engaged by the earlier poem in its statement, following Paul, that idolatry caused the sorrows of the Sodomites, so it is in the second, as it adduces the unspecified *errores* of the Lollards-Sodomites as the cause of all the world's woes. If ingrate Giezite supporters of the crime of Sodom are born of Simon, here the Lollards-Sodomites are not only ingrates but also cursed and born of an unnamed demon—the traditional association of sodomy and the devil that we observed in the introduction is engaged here. The *gesta* are even more ambiguous here than earlier: in the first poem they were most likely sodomitical acts as well as simoniacal ones and, by association, all the bad acts intimated in the verses; later they are the *errores,* theological as well as sexual, and perhaps also the posting of the *Conclusions* themselves.

The basic point of this metrical response is a point made by the orthodox about Lollards in general, that they are hypocrites: they accuse others of the things of which they themselves are guilty. In the words of that false preacher who also was sexually odd, caricatured in about 1395 by a writer who knew well how to manipulate discourses by and about Lollards: "Thus kan I preche agayn [against] that same vice / Which that I use."[45] I shall discuss the Pardoner at length in the next chapter; at present I want to remark that hypocrisy is central to the accusations clerics made of Lollards, on the one hand, and of accusations Lollards made of clerics, on the other.[46] But though such an explanation seems of course generally right about these poems, it does not get at the particular force of their coupling. I want to analyze further the workings of the interaction of these documents, the functions of what I shall call "reverse accusation": in a dynamic that we will see repeated again and again, on both sides—in the *Conclusions*, in Roger Dymmok's reply, in the *Rejoinder* to Friar Daw's *Reply* to *Jack Upland*—the accusation of sodomy is exactly reversed, thrown back at the accuser.[47] How do accusations of sodomy, in their persistence, perform important functions for both the orthodox and the heterodox? What happens when such a plastic, agglutinative accusation is thrown back onto its accusers? How does the rhetorical ploy of the reverse accusation work when unleashed in this particularly heated, polemical context of hunting and prosecuting secret sins? What does it teach us about the place of sodomy in such late-medieval English contexts?

The paired accusations here can certainly suggest that accusations of sodomy were used as general disparagement. The exact reversal tends in fact to drain the accusation of specificity and render it an all-purpose vilification; indeed, in the second poem, *gens Sodomorum* works much the way "faggots" does today, even if that term is generally unacceptable in polite American society while the former was an acceptable moral judgment—and they work similarly for historical reasons: faggots were bundles of wood with which heretics (among other things) were burnt.[48] Sodomites, faggots—everything bad sticks to these names, whether or not same-sex sexual relations are specifically or primarily denoted: simony, murder, heresy, every way of violating God-given order. But the reversal raises more fundamental questions: if Lollards say clerics are performing sodomy, and clerics say Lollards are guilty of sodomy, who really *is* doing the deed? And how can you tell? Who has the authority to accuse? And why are these accusations being made?

The suspicions such a reversal raises: that sodomy is everywhere, or sodomy is nowhere to be found—fingers are pointing but they don't rest anywhere. That you can't tell who's doing it: anyone can be accused, and there's no way of knowing. And that such accusations are being made for the purposes of power, not for the reformation of the true church. *Crimen Sodomorum* was not the worst sin to be accused of in and of itself; the Wycliffite Bible General Prologue offers contemporary local evidence of this sentiment. Lollards themselves, in the *Thirty-Seven Conclusions*, claim that men of Sodom and men of Gomorrah shall have less torment than prelates, lords, and commons who quench the gospel of Christ and persecute its preachers.[49] Simony, Wyclif maintains, is "more dangerous than sodomy."[50] In the Wycliffite *On the Seven Deadly Sins*, "þo synne of Sodome" is thought to be "more unkyndely þen any oþer lecchorye. . . . And among oþer synnes þis hatis God myche [much]"; yet the text moves immediately to the broader analysis: "Bot bisyde þis bodily lecchorye of men þere is gostly lecchorye, þat God chargis [weighs] more."[51] Simony or heresy were finally far more consequential accusations in themselves. But as I have been suggesting, the accusation of the sin of sodomy is not so distinct from these others, and it may unleash a pack of anxieties that its use by Lollards as a specific insult may have been trying to bring under control.

Sodomy: Proof by Reason

There is some evidence that the 1395 Parliament may have been remembered precisely because of the sodomy accusations ringing in the air. The General Prologue to the Wycliffite Bible, written between about 1395 and 1397, may itself attest to their power. Simony is said there to be worse than sodomy—but not before "bodily sodomye" is itself castigated, especially sodomy in Oxford among doctors of divinity: "[W]hether Oxunford drinke blood and birlith [pours out] blood, bi sleeinge of quyke men, and bi doinge of sodomye . . . deme thei iustly [justly], that seen it at iȝe [eye], and knowen bi experiens."

Sodomy is a horrible sin—sodomy, and the "strong mayntenaunce thereof, as it is knowen to many persones of the reume, and at the last parlement." "The last parlement" here refers to the 1395 Parliament posting of the Lollard *Conclusions;* their accusations must have caused quite a stir.[52]

The specific terms of the discussion of sodomy in the Lollard *Twelve Conclusions* will help us see exactly how accusations of sodomy not only provide a convenient (because traditional) means of discrediting clergy but work at the heart of Lollard reformist beliefs. Though the Latin poem most likely refers to male-male sex, same-sex sexual relations both between men and between women (both treated as sodomy in Thomas Aquinas, for example, as we have seen in the introduction) are treated in two of the *Twelve Conclusions,* the Third Conclusion (concerning male clerical relations) and the Eleventh (concerning relations between avowed female celibates—nuns and widows). Both Conclusions are aimed at the perceived problems caused by mandatory vows of celibacy, concern with which is part and parcel of Lollard plans for reform of the English church.

After the "general" First Conclusion—stating that faith, hope and charity have fled the church because of its absorption in material possessions and because of "appropriation," whereby parish churches remain uncared for while monasteries benefit from parish revenues—and after the more specifically antiprelatical Second Conclusion—in which the priesthood of the current church is denied as the true priesthood ordained by Christ—the manifesto turns to the vow of celibacy required by the priesthood:

> Þe thirdde conclusiun sorwful to here is þat þe lawe of continence annexyd to presthod, þat in preiudys of wimmen was first ordeynid, inducith sodomie in al holy chirche; but we excusin us be þe Bible for þe suspecte decre þat seyth we schulde not nemen it. Resun and experience prouit þis conclusiun. For delicious metis and drinkis of men of holi chirche welen han nedful purgaciun or werse. Experience for þe priue asay of syche men is, þat þe[i] like non wymmen; and whan þu prouist sich a man mark him wel for he is on of þo. Þe correlary of þis conclusiun is þat þe priuat religions, begynneris of þis synne, were most worthi to ben anullid. But God for his myth of priue synne sende opyn ueniaunce.[53]

The third conclusion, sorrowful to hear, is that the law of continence [chastity] annexed to the priesthood, that was first ordained against women, induces sodomy in all holy church; but we excuse ourselves [for naming it] by the Bible against the suspect decree that says we should not name it. Reason and observation prove this conclusion. [Reason,] for delicious foods and drinks of men of holy church will have necessary purgation or worse. Observation [proves this conclusion,] for the secret test of such men is, that they like no women; and when you prove such a man mark him well, for he is one of those. The corollary of this conclusion is that the private religions, beginners of this sin, are most worthy of being annulled. But God, for his might, send open vengeance on secret sin.

The Lollards state that the "lawe of continence" first concerned priests' sexual activity with women; it then produced illicit sexual relations between clerics. Wyclif, earlier, had accused friars of sodomy in similar terms: among the great number of denunciations of clerics in the *Opus evangelicum,* in book 1 of *De Antichristo,* Wyclif writes that vows of continence and enclaustration among men harm women. This is because potential husbands are sequestered in cloisters—where they are having sex with one another.[54] The Lollards, in their subordinate clause about the original "preiudys of wimmen" in this Conclusion, claim a position much like the Wife of Bath's as she maintains that clerical vituperations against women and thus admonitions of clerical chastity harm women. (Such an associative chain, from vows of celibacy to the harm of women and then to male-male sodomy, may help explain why the Wife of Bath is linked to the mare-like Pardoner in the *Canterbury Tales.*) The debate between pro- and antifeminist discourses must have been a live one in London in 1395 (the approximate date of Chaucer's Wife of Bath's *Prologue* as well as that of the *Conclusions*); here the Lollards seem to stake a profeminist claim—though Lollardy may have been associated in fact with both sides of the issue: earlier, in 1382 in Leicester (according to Knighton), the Lollard William Swinderby took to preaching against the stereotypical faults of women—and women of the town threatened to pelt him with stones.[55]

But in the *Conclusions* the really problematic result of enforced heterocelibacy is not the harm of women but male-male sex: an absence of women, brought on by vows of chastity, provoked the rise of sodomy in the church. According to the logical proof, the rational explanation ("resun"; *ratio*), lecherous sexual activity is the result of bodily processes; delicious foods eaten by men of holy church will necessarily need purgation, and sexual activity may be one avenue of such release. In its general outline of buildup and release, this *ratio* draws on the standard medical understanding of male sexual response, as Joan Cadden relates it: "the buildup of superfluities, the accumulation of spirit or windiness, the pleasure associated with expelling what needs to be expelled at the place natural for its evacuation, and the ensuing feeling of harmony." [56] This particular dietary problem is endemic in such communities, it seems;[57] delicacy-driven sex is a commonplace accusation among orthodox and reformers alike of monks and friars—Gower, for example, paints a vivid picture of the overly well-fed and thus randy private religious in book 4 of his *Vox clamantis*.[58]

But the specific sexual response here is a less common allegation—though it, too, must have been fairly popular, since it follows the exegetical tradition on Ezekiel 16.49.[59] The *Fasciculus morum* alludes to this tradition: the treatise includes a four-line Latin poem, a kind of mnemonic, specifying four kinds of gluttony, then explains that

> Tercia species est nimis ardenter et nimis avide comedere, sicut fecerunt Sodomite, quorum ruina ab ocio et nimi⟨a⟩ habundancia incepit. Unde ex hoc proprie accidit crapula, scilicet quando quis sumit plus quam possit bene et congrue digerere. Per quod contingit frequenter vomitum facere; Ysaie 28: "Omnes mense eorum replete sunt vomitu."

> The third branch is eating too eagerly and too avidly, as the Sodomites did, whose destruction began with their idleness and an overabundance of food. From this branch comes overindulgence, that is, taking more food than one can easily and naturally digest. This vice frequently leads to vomiting; Isaiah 28: "All their tables are full of vomit." [60]

Notably, even as the bodily conditions that provoke the sin (idleness, overindulgence) are clearly immoral, the Franciscan text derives the sin of the men of Sodom physiologically.

The Lollards seem to be following such a physiological analysis too, suggesting that the indulgence in delicious foods results in some kind of buildup whose remedy is "natural" (purging) or "worse" (sodomy). (The English text of the Conclusion muddies Walsingham's clarity regarding natural and bad purgation.)[61] A moral is implied here, since the urge to have sodomitical sex is associated with vomiting and purging; moreover, according to their own rules the men of private religion should not be indulging in such delicacies in the first place (though many clearly did), so this *ratio* packs a doubly moralizing punch as it implicates the private religious in hypocritical dietary conduct even as it explicitly convicts them of sodomitical fornication. But sodomy here is represented as a physical act operating according to physiological laws, like purging. Though it is opposed to "natural" purging, it still is here a natural physiological process, a biological consequence of eating rich foods; Peter of Abano, in an early-fourteenth-century natural-philosophical treatise, makes a similar distinction between two ways of construing "nature."[62] The Lollard emphasis here is finally unlike that of the discussion in the *Fasciculus morum*, which is embedded in an anatomy of lechery; it is unlike the treatment in *Piers Plowman*, too, which focuses on the lack of "mesure" in eating and drinking that caused "þe meschief and þe meschaunce amonges men of Sodome."[63] Their very willingness to name the sin puts them in opposition to the traditional interpretation (*suspectum decretum*) of Ephesians 5.3 we have seen in operation already—a tradition that would "dictate silence with regard to a certain class of sins against nature," in Mark Jordan's words, a tradition that would, that is, treat sodomy as morally and ethically a different kind of sin from other sins.[64]

The lightly moralizing, relatively naturalistic nature of this Lollard argument by *ratio* is reinforced by the argument by *experientia* (observation, discernment) that follows.[65] Observation, the Conclusion maintains, proves that it is not just that there are no women around to have sex with, but that some men "like non wymmen" (*non delectantur in mulieribus*); and this aversion can be demonstrated by testing ("priue asay," *secreta probatio*).[66] More on this secret test in a moment; here I want to note that this psychological explanation is in concert with the naturalistic tendency we noted above.[67] The whole Conclusion, as a result, tends to downplay the ancient philosophical or ethical arguments for celibacy; in fact, in the entire Conclusion, no philosophical or spiritual justification of celibacy is offered. There is no sense that struggle with and denial of desire can lead to transcendence, to the good, to closer communion with God; there is no sense, in fact, that self-restraint is possible at all. Delicacies inevitably will be indulged in, by hypocritical clerics at least, and indulgence will require release of some kind, good or bad, natural or worse. And sometimes sodomitical activity takes place in the absence of gluttony: whether by birth or long habit the Lollards don't specify, but some men are just like that. The consequences of this kind of thinking about human nature—via what might seem the virtual inevitability of sodomy among clergy held to heterocelibacy—for the possibility of any real reform are acute; thus the exasperated tone of the Lollard poem's last line, where a wish is expressed for literal weapons to be taken up because figurative ones cannot be prevented from rising: "Qualiter hiis gestis gladiis prohibere potestis?"[68]

The Secret Test

Experientia in fact complicates that rational picture of clerics, lacking women and eating lavishly, who have been driven to have sex with other men. And this complication reinforces the difficulty of really imagining the "reformation" of the English church at all. The Lollard Conclusion's representation of sodomy depicts not only a natural physical act, like purging, an act, furthermore, that has its equivalent in sex with women and that thus would seem (from a heteronormative point of view) to be a potential in every man,[69] but also suggests a rubric of identification of certain men who share certain desires (or, more precisely, who share a lack of certain desires): "[M]ark him wel for he is on of þo" ("[N]ota eum bene, quia ipse est unus ex illis" [175]). The representation of sodomy here draws on both polarities in the categories we have tended to rely on in analyses of sexualities in history, especially after Foucault and Sedgwick: sodomy is here represented as neither simply a physical act nor simply a determinant of identity; and it is neither entirely a universal potential nor entirely a fact about a small group of people. We've already seen the shifting inclusivity and exclusivity of sin "against nature" in the introduction; increasingly, scholars are demonstrating the inadequacy of these oppositions for understanding medieval sexualities. Mark Jordan, for example, charts the oscillations of Aquinas's treatment of the vice against nature between "a circumscribed self-indulgence and a radical denial of human purposes . . . at once minoritizing and universalizing." [70]

But while we recognize the inadequacy of strictly binary options, seeing even the natural/unnatural divide collapse in Gower's *Confessio amantis*, for example, a host of questions is raised as we try to follow out the logic of this passage. Reading this Conclusion, we cannot be certain who might engage in sodomy or be a sodomite: all men? a few bad men? What is the sodomite's relationship to women—he would like them if they were around? he does not like them at all? If private religions were abolished, as the corollary admonishes, would that do away with this sin? Or is it a potential of men in any circumstance where women are scarce? Does the material potential for active heterosexual relations eliminate sodomy? Or is it always a possibility, a persistent shadow of heterosexual relations, because some men are like that? Or because all men are like that?

Maybe these questions matter to us but not to the Lollards, at least at this polemical moment. Our distinctions may be too precise. There's a broadness in the strokes, a sweeping certainty about and control of the topic in this Conclusion—not just a will to know but a confident knowledge of human nature. Sodomy is secret—a "priue synne"—but it can be found out, and the sodomite put in his apparently well-known, established place: "he is on of þo." You ("þu") can tell; perhaps anyone (in the vernacularizing spirit of the Lollards) can tell. Maybe it is written all over the cleric's face: as Gower suggests, "no index of the mind can be more reliable than the face" when one is expressing oneself silently.[71] Whatever the "asay" is, it would seem to be widely available; reading the sodomitical cleric is rather like reading the Bible, according to, say, the General Prologue to the Wycliffite version: if you simply know your grammar, you do not need further years of training. (And grammar, as Alain de Lille made abundantly clear in his influential *De planctu Naturae*, is heterosexual.) [72]

In the Lollard imagination a key feature of sodomitical activity is not only privateness (separation from the common world, the primary denotation of Middle English "priuat") but privacy in the modern sense: it is a "priue synne," a secret sin. The term "priuat religions" in the context of the Third Conclusion engages both concepts of separateness and secrecy, which seem the very breeding ground of sodomy. Privateness and privacy of course breed many sins (as Dymmok in his reply hastens to point out); and sexuality after Augustine "is always charged with issues of privacy," power, and individual freedom, as Peter Brown asserts;[73] but this Conclusion associates privateness and privacy with sodomy in particular when it makes the striking allegation that the private religions are "begynneris of þis synne" (in the Latin, seeking more precision, "inceptores, seu origo"). Maybe the authors make this assertion because they are focusing on the beginning of church sodomy; still, the very name of the sin itself, as Dymmok commonsensically remarks, suggests that it has been around even in the church rather longer than private religions have been. The allegation, not picked up in other texts, in its blatant disregard for commonsensical facts seems polemical—or anxious about being able to fix an origin for this rampant problem—rather than merely declarative.

The private is the problem, but it seems that it is part of the solution, too. In the very language of certainty and discernment and origin—finding out the sodomite—there is an echo of the language used to describe sodomy itself. And as in the poems with which I began this chapter, this echo tends to disturb the ringing tones of sodomitical accusation and diffuse, if not reverse, the directionality of that accusation. "Priue synne" of "priuat religions" will be found out by a "priue asay." (The Latin vocabulary is more varied, if semantically similar: *peccatum occultum* of the *privatae religiones,* and the revealing *secreta probatio.*) If privateness and privacy do breed such bad acts, as the language of origin here suggests, then how can they reveal them, too? What kind of knowledge can this "priue asay" yield?

Let's imagine, since there is nothing solid to go by, that such a secret test could have consisted of the offering of a woman to an avowed celibate—a woman rather than a boy (although that kind of entrapment also can be imagined) because the resulting diagnosis specifies women: such men "like non wymmen." Let's also imagine that the celibate resists the woman. What does this tell the inquisitive mind? That he is, in fact, celibate? That he is "on of þo," that is, a sodomite?[74] Or that he is, in fact, a *Lollard*?

This latter possibility is raised by the case of William Smith, a Lollard chronicled by Knighton in his account of 1382. Knighton's treatment is notably hostile. William Smith, rejected by a young woman, thereafter undertakes severe abstinence from the embraces of women and from other kinds of worldly comforts. His Lollardy, Knighton suggests, actually results from this rejection by his intended:

> Willelmus Smit principalis colator ab artificio sic uocatus persona despicabilis et deformis. Qui cupiens ducere in uxorem iuuenticulam quandam set ab ea spretus, in tantam prorupit sanctitatis ostentacionem quod omnia mundi concupiscibilia despexit, muliebrem amplexum perpetuo abdicauit, lineis renunciauit, carnes et carnea, pisces et piscina nullatenus admisit, uinum et ceruisiam quasi uenenum recusauit, nudis pedibus per plures annos incedens, medio tempore abcedarium didicit et manu sua scribere fecit.

> William Smith, so called from his craft, was a leading promoter of that sect. Despicable and deformed in his person, he had once sought to marry a young woman, and when she spurned him he affected the outward forms of sanctity so extravagantly that he despised all earthly desires, renounced the embraces of women for ever, abandoned the use of linen, shunned meat and fish of all kinds, refused wine and beer as though they were poison, went barefoot for many years, and in the meantime taught himself the alphabet and the skill of writing.[75]

This accursed "persona despicabilis et deformis"—he is certainly marked as *something*—is joined in his chapel of John the Baptist, next to the leper house (even the chapel seems marked), by William Swinderby, who had earlier begun his spiritual career by preaching against the defects and pride of women. Not liking women (after liking one too much, perhaps) is what seems to have solidified William Smith's Lollard style, according to Knighton, and is what starts Swinderby out, too, at least discursively. Reading Knighton's account of 1382 side by side with the 1395 *Twelve Conclusions* can suggest that despite the certainty and absoluteness of the accusation, the results of any actual "priue asay" might not be so clear.

I tend to think that no real test is being alluded to at all. The discourse of testing and proof circulated with increasing urgency in regard to Saint Bridget's canonization in 1391; perhaps that context added to Lollard scepticism (following Wyclif) regarding postbiblical saints, expressed in the Eighth Conclusion: "For men ben canonizid, God wot how."[76] *Probationes* were perhaps in the air; but they were not secret ones. It seems to me that the secret test in the Lollard Third Conclusion may be simply the gaze of the accuser, discreet but probing, seeing what he in fact already expects to see. And that is why I want to insist on the relevance of the precise, destabilizing questions I formulated earlier—because they are consolingly precluded by the all-knowing, see-nothing gaze. But how *can* you be so sure about who's going to turn out to be a sodomite? It is instructive, and chilling, to note at this point that sodomy seems itself to have been conceptualized as that which is to be sought out, found out, proven: as H. A. Kelly notes, procedures of inquisition and investigation in canon law—procedures of "general inquisition" newly instituted in 1215 at Lateran IV, the Council that consolidated the marginalization and persecution of nonnormative groups and shaped later responses to sodomy—were modeled on God's approach to Sodom and Gomorrah after he has heard rumors: "I will go down and see whether they have done according to the cry that is come to me: or whether it be not so, that I may know" (Douay-Rheims; "Descendam, et videbo utrum clamorem qui venit ad me, opere compleverint: an non est ita, ut sciam" [Genesis 18.21]).[77] Sodomy is the prototype of rumored sins to be found and rooted out. The inquisitive Lollard, seeking sodomy, could find himself in turn the object of the same kind of gaze, mirrored in the sin that he is investigating.

The Lollard could find the accusations rebounding back upon him, not only because of the ready orthodox tradition that associates heretics with sodomites, but also because of the dusking effect of secrecy, the way in which what is done in secret can implicate the one who is there to find it out. "Plangant Anglorum gentes crimen Sodomorum" . . . "Gens Lollardorum gens est vilis Sodomorum": these assertions are not like the baiting question of Jack Upland, who accuses friars of buying precious clothes: "What betokeneth youre grete hood, your scaplerye, youre knotted girdel, and youre wyde cope?" William Woodford—writing a long Latin response to *Jack Upland* in the autumn of 1395—slaps back the question onto the Lollards themselves: "Item dico quod similiter potest quaeri a Lollardis: Quid significant eorum lata caputia furrata . . . ?" ("And I say that similarly it can be asked of Lollards: What signify their widefurred hoods . . . ?")[78] Such accusations about hypocritical dressing (preaching poverty, wearing expensive clothes) can be corroborated by open observation. But sodomy happens in private, and the test—the gaze on the putative sodomite—is kept secret, as is any gaze on the gazer. . . .

In the Lollard discourse we have been tracing clerical sodomy is known in a variety of sometimes conflicting ways: accusations of it form part of a broad system of abjection and disparagement; sodomy provides figurative language for apparently worse sins, even as it has a literal, identifiable place: the sodomite is "unus *ex illis*," "on *of þo*." And while the sodomite is one of that acknowledged group, sodomy seems to be understood in addition as a potential act of any man. While condemned, sodomy is nonetheless associated with the natural act of purging. For the Lollards in the Third Conclusion, sodomy seems an enactment on a wrong object of an originally licit desire; they do not seem to share the Pauline-Augustinian sense of sexual desire itself as fallen and sinful, and, apparently haunted by a sense that self-restraint is impossible, they thus urge the end of mandatory vows of celibacy.

But sodomy is at the same time figured as a bonding between men in a separate community, and that privateness and privacy of male clerical sodomy are indeed troublesome. The private religions may be irksome to the Lollards not only because of the deadly sins and heresy that allegedly are rife therein, but also and more generally because they are really different from the heterosexual community they know. Male sodomy may be not only understood here as a perverse desire that can be rerouted toward its correct goal—a consoling conception, to be sure—but feared as a potential outgrowth of a wholly different culture. It is notable that while women are explicitly absent and are themselves said not to be desired here, sodomites are not held to be acting like women in their stead. Such gender violation is operant in other well-known late-medieval cases against male sodomy, as we've seen, when the men of Sodom, for example, are accused by God in *Cleanness* of having sex like women, copulating "on femmalez wyse."[79] But sodomy is not always described as heterosexual relations *manqués*.[80] The Lollard Third Conclusion in fact may hint at masculine-masculine desire—these men like no women, but are not necessarily like women for that—which is not a perversion of a licit, heterosexual desire but something, coming from somewhere (this Conclusion attempts to fix an origin) that might be entirely, and fearsomely, different.

Body or Bread?

"Nota eum *bene*," "mark him *wel*." Mark him well so that you can recognize his kind; mark him well because we're scared of him. What is it, exactly, that marks the man who doesn't like women? What will the inquiring eye fix on? Is there something that desire leaves marked on the body? In William Smith's case, Knighton sneers that he is generally "persona despicabilis et deformis." In the Pardoner's case, there might be the peculiarities of hair, eyes, and voice to go by.[81] Robert Mannyng notes in *Handlyng Synne* that lechers can be discerned by their black faces.[82] But nothing is specified in the case of sodomitical clerics painted by the Lollards in their *Conclusions*, perhaps because their assertion of the efficacy of a test expresses more a wish for certainty than any means to achieve it.

Yet Lollard awareness that bodies are marked by desires and behaviors, by the individual's navigations of social institutions, is keen. It is manifested in the vivid corporeal images they use in the Sixth Conclusion, for example, to describe priests who hold both secular and ecclesiastical offices.

> [T]emperelte and spirituelte ben to partys of holi chirche, and þerfore he þat hath takin him to þe ton schulde nout medlin him with þe toþir, *quia nemo potest duobus dominis seruire*. Us thinkith þat hermofodrita or ambidexter were a god name to sich manere of men of duble astate.[83]

> Temporality and spirituality are two parts of holy church, and therefore he who has taken himself to the one should not mix himself with the other, "because no one can serve two masters." It seems to us that "hermaphrodite" or "ambidexter" would be a good name for such manner of men of double estate.

Once again, as in the poem with which I began this chapter, improper economic transactions are linked to sexual perversion: in addition to their general excoriation here of private control of the church and the concomitant detriment of the care of souls, the Lollards specifically associate "taking fees from both sides"—the then-current denotation of "ambidexter"—with the condition of the hermaphrodite, a being in which "is yfounde boþe [both] *sexus*, male and femele."[84] "Hermofodrita" may also carry here the late-medieval confusion with sodomite (as in Dante, *Purgatorio* 26); the context encourages double-sexedness as the primary meaning, but there might be a more general suggestion of sexual disorder or confusion as well.[85] "Ambidexter" hints at corporeality even in the figurative denotation of double dealing. Bad exchanges, excessive transactions mark the body in private yet, the Lollards insist, knowable ways.

The provocative, sarcastic tone of the *Conclusion*, this baiting Lollard assertion about clerical bodies that are ambiguous, may be working to deflect a certain anxiety about the discernment of bodies in general, however, just as that tone may have worked to deflect uncertainty about the discernment of sodomy among men. What touches all Lollards very deeply is, in fact, the question of knowing a body at all: when is something a body, after all, and when is it just "a litil bred" (Hudson, *Selections*, 25)—bread that, as in the Fourth Conclusion, conduces to idolatry, and, in the Latin poem, idolatry thus to sodomy?

Insisting on transubstantiation, orthodox Christians, according to the Lollards in the Fourth Conclusion, take a mere created object to be entirely and in essence the body of Christ:

> Þe ferthe conclusiun þat most harmith þe innocent puple is þis: þat þe feynid miracle of þe sacrament of bred inducith alle men but a fewe to ydolatrie, for þei wene þat Godis bodi, þat neuere schal out of heuene, be uertu of þe prestis wordis schulde ben closid essenciali in a litil bred þat þei schewe to þe puple.[86]
>
> The fourth conclusion that most harms the innocent people is this: that the feigned miracle of the sacrament of bread leads all men but a few to idolatry, for they believe that God's body, that shall never leave heaven, by virtue of the priest's words should be enclosed essentially in a little bread that they show to the people.

The doctrine of transubstantiation propounds that what appears to be bread is in fact Christ's body; the bread and wine disappear, their substances are replaced by the substance of Christ's body and blood, and they only appear to be bread and wine. What, then, if anything, marks the host as a body, and how can you know? John Burrell maintained in 1429 that since the sacrament does not have eyes, ears, mouth, hands, or feet, it cannot be the true body of Christ.[87] Arguing more pointedly against the priestly claim to have performed a miracle, the Fourth Conclusion holds that correct knowledge of the nature of God (expressed in Wyclif's words) disproves the putative miracle of transubstantiation: "Godis bodi . . . neuere schal out of heuene" (Hudson, *Selections*, 25). Reason, too, argues against any such miracle, since by the logic of transubstantiation any hen's egg's hatching is a miracle as great, a belief patently false according to these Wycliffites.

Not all Lollards agreed about the exact nature of the sacrament of the altar: Burrell insisted that the host is really a cake of bread made of wheat flour, while the Lollards here seem content with the notion of a spiritual body, invisible and consubstantial with material bread.[88] But the issue of discernment is central, as Dymmok in his refutation sees: against the putative assumption that the material bread remains because it looks unchanged, he argues back that "sacramental action constantly affirms and reveals the possibility of inward change without outward change." Nothing, he argues, marks the host as a body.

> For if this [Lollard] argument should thrive, all the sacraments of the church, all the oaths of kings, and all political exchange should be completely destroyed. . . . I ask, what sensible change do you see in a boy newly baptized, in a man who has confessed, in a boy or man who has been confirmed, in consecrated bread, in a man ordained into the priesthood, in marriageable persons betrothed or joined? All receive a new virtue, except the bread, which simply ceases to exist without any kind of sensible change, and is transubstantiated into the body of Christ. In what way also is the body of a king changed, when he is newly crowned, or anyone similarly advanced?[89]

What makes the transubstantiation claim unlike the other sacramental ones, and what Wyclif could not accept, is that the bread "simply ceases to exist," invisibly disappears; not making anything of this exceptionality (symptomatically, Paul Strohm argues), Dymmok dwells instead on the concept of invisible effects of acts—sacraments, but also other kinds of acts as well—on bodies. He highlights the fact of indeterminacy: whether someone has been married, or even if someone has been advanced, you can't tell, he argues, just by looking. And Dymmok maintains that crucial political and ecclesiastical phenomena depend on the presumption of invisible virtues, invisible effects.

But Lollards home in precisely on the disparity between the claims about other sacraments and about the Eucharist: "Þes foolis shulden undirstonde þat Baptist, when he was naked, holly ceesid not to be Jon, ne non oþer þing" ("These fools should understand that the Baptist, when he was naked, did not cease to be John, or any other thing").[90] Insisting on the material continuities of created things (as they do in the Fifth Conclusion as well), Lollards argue in a later text that a mouse can indeed tell bread when it sees it, even if a friar can't.[91] Since consecrated and unconsecrated bread are in fact indistinguishable, according to the author of *De blasphemia, contra fratres,* a friar cannot tell the difference any more than can an animal.[92] These fraternal blasphemers, he states, by insisting that the host is not in material fact bread, have undervalued the bodily sense of touch: "But gropynge þei marren by hor foly sentence; ffor no bodily þing we knowen more certeynly þen hardenesse and sofftenesse of þis holy bred" ("But they mar testing by feeling with their foolish doctrine, for no bodily thing do we know more certainly than the hardness and softness of this holy bread").[93]

Can you tell a body if (or when) you touch it? The debates on the doctrine of transubstantiation indeed focus on whether or not a priest handles a body or a "little bread" or some combination thereof. Nicholas Love, explicitly arguing *contra lollardos* (as the marginalia in this section of his *Mirror of the Blessed Life of Jesus Christ* point out), attempts to prove the blessed bodily presence in the host by describing the "delectable paradise" into which a certain parson is pitched when he is touched, by "þe touchere oure lord Jesu," with

> a ioy & likyng þat passeþ without comparison þe hiest likyng þat any creature may haue or fele as by wey of kynde in þis life, þorh þe which ioy & likyng'. alle þe membres of þe body bene enflaumede of so deletable & ioyful a hete þat him þenkeþ sensibly alle þe body as it were meltyng for ioy as waxe doþ anentes þe hote fire, so farforþ þat þe body miht not bere þat excellent likyng, bot þat it shold vtturly faile, nere

þe gracious kepyng & sustenyng of þe touchere oure lord Jesu aboue kynde.

A lorde Jesu in what delectable paradise is he for þat tyme þat þus feleþ þat blessede bodily presence of þe, in þat precious sacrament, þorh þe which he feleþ him sensibly with vnspekable ioy as he were ioynede body to body?[94]

a joy and pleasure that surpasses without comparison the highest pleasure that any creature may have or feel naturally in this life, through which joy and pleasure all the members of the body are inflamed of so delightful and joyful a heat that it seems to him sensibly that all the body is as it were melting for joy as wax does next to the hot fire, so much so that the body might not bear that excellent pleasure, but it should utterly fail if the gracious keeping and sustaining of the toucher our lord Jesus were not beyond nature.

Ah, lord Jesus, in what a delightful paradise is he for that time who thus feels the blessed bodily presence of you, in that precious sacrament, through which he feels sensibly with unspeakable joy as if he were joined body to body?

The erotic aura around celebration of the Eucharist clearly extends beyond the thirteenth-century women mystics Caroline Walker Bynum has famously studied.[95] Bynum discusses the ways in which an empowering female fusion with Christ in the Eucharist is achieved "through asceticism and through eroticism," sometimes themselves completely fused: the Eucharist provided "a moment of encounter with that *humanitas Christi* which was such a prominent theme of women's spirituality. For thirteenth-century women this humanity was, above all, Christ's physicality, his corporality, his being-in-the-body-ness."[96] And some male clerics, too, including the "one person [parson] þat I knowe now lyuyng [living] & perauenture þere bene many þat I knowe not," as Love mentions, felt themselves fused "body to body" with Christ in the celebration of the Eucharist. This fusion may indeed have been understood erotically.

Clerics in the high and late Middle Ages were plagued by persistent fears and anxieties about self-pollution surrounding their celebration of the Eucharist. Dyan Elliott, who has brilliantly documented and analyzed the contours of this phenomenon, mentions in particular the fifteenth-century Jean Gerson, who dedicated several treatises to the problem. *De praeparatione ad missam,* for example, begins forthrightly by addressing doubts among clergy "si quis nocturno pollutus somnio a celebrando missam cessare deberet" ("whether he who is polluted by a night dream ought to stop celebrating mass").[97] Gerson goes on to discuss the issue, in part by reworking a narrative of a dream of Celestine V — a dream Celestine had, occasioned by worries about "his own worthiness to celebrate the Eucharist after experiencing a pollution" — in order to explore the question put to him by certain priests.[98] Elliott suggests that such pollution fears finally pose a threat to clerical masculinity:

> The occasion of involuntary ejaculation, and its phantasmic accompaniments, opens the way to anxious acknowledgment of gender turmoils held at bay by original and inadequate acts of stabilization and exclusion. . . . Finally, the dissolution of the priest's gender identity in the course of demonic illusions elevates pollution fears surrounding the Eucharist to an entirely different plane by challenging not simply the purity of the clergy, but also its claims to unalloyed masculine ascendancy. This is a critical anxiety, since transubstantiation was fast becoming the central mystery of the faith, threatening to displace the Incarnation and its heterosexual core. For transubstantiation was based on the ineluctable stability of gender identity — a male cleric handling the body of a male God.[99]

Elliott's analysis revolves around the feminization with which nocturnal pollutions threaten clergy, and her final statement suggests that the male handling of the male body of the transubstantiated Eucharist will be unproblematic as long as clerical masculinity is unalloyed. That handling may become problematic — potentially sodomitical, perhaps — if priests' masculinity is undone. But even without feminization, male handling of male body can be problematic: the discussion of sodomy in the Lollard Third Conclusion, we recall, does not suggest gender violation.

My argument here — very speculative — is enabled by a conceptualization of the Eucharist as a broad and engaging cultural symbol which "ground[s] and sustain[s]" many different "meanings," "experiences," and a "vast field of action," such as Miri Rubin proposes.[100] It is furthered by preoccupations expressed even in unpolemical works such as *Cleanness,* which opens with a discussion of the sacrament of the altar in which priests are said to handle the body of Christ—they had better be clean, outside and in—and proceeds through its scriptural history narration, treating the filth of the Sodomites in great, disgusted detail.[101] It is advanced, too, by the popular legend of the incarnate Christ's radical antipathy to sodomy, a legend adapted by Mirk in his *Festial:*

> as Seynt Austeyne saythe: "When Cryst schuld be borne, þe world was so full of derknes of synful lyuyng, and nomely of syn of lechery, and of syn aȝeyne kynde, þat had nye to haue laft to haue ben yborne of mankynd." Wherfor þat nyght þat Cryst was borne, all þat doden synne aȝeyne kynd, deydyn sodenly þrogh all þe world, in schowyng how horrybly þat synne ys before Goddys een.[102]

> As Saint Augustine says: "When Christ was to be born, the world was so full of darkness of sinful living, and namely of the sin of lechery, and of the sin against nature, that he almost declined to be born of mankind." Therefore, that night that Christ was born, all those who engaged in the sin against nature died suddenly throughout the world, demonstrating how horrible that sin is before God's eyes.

The Lollard attack on the "crimen Sodomorum," adducing idolatry as the cause, may not only be a standard means to attack clergy but may in fact tie into an issue at the heart of Lollardy: the sacrament of the altar. Given the Lollard association of clerics with sodomy—particularly expressed in the Third Conclusion—sodomitical fears might attach, however vaguely, to the orthodox clerical performance of the Eucharist. Clerics might not only be suspected of performing sodomitical crimes in secret but might, in the very open celebration of the sacrament of the altar, be seen by Lollards in particular (since in Lollard eyes these clerics insist that they touch the substance of the body of Christ) to be implicated in a sodomitical touch.[103]

Could such a fear or suspicion form part of the context of William Colyn's strange testimony in his 1429 trial procedure for heresy in Norwich? The accusation against him runs,

> Item quod tu [William] asseruisti te malle videre secretum membrum mulieris quam sacramentum altaris. Ad istum articulum idem Willelmus dixit et fatebatur iudicialiter quod ipse dixit se velle libencius tangere secretum membrum mulieris quam sacramentum altaris.

> And that you [William] claimed to prefer to see the secret member of a woman than the sacrament of the altar. To this article the same William said and confessed judicially that he said that he would rather touch the secret member of a woman than the sacrament of the altar.[104]

The distinction between seeing and touching is paramount here: in orthodox terms, to which William may have been appealing, all eyes may and should see and adore the host, but only reverent and authorized hands may touch it. William Colyn was a skinner, not a cleric, and thus lacked such authorization. But might there have been something about touching the host that makes William's comparison to touching a woman's secret member especially apposite? Might the comparison even have been somewhat useful to William, as a convenient denial of male-male sodomy in the course of a trial for heresy?

Could such an association, similarly, have animated the vivid refutation of transubstantiation attributed to Margery Baxter in a deposition by Johanna Clyfland against her in heresy trial procedures about a year earlier?

> [S]i quodlibet tale sacramentum esset Deus et verum corpus Christi, infiniti sunt dii, quia mille sacerdotes et plures omni die conficiunt mille tales deos et postea tales deos comedunt et commestos emittunt per posteriora in sepibus turpiter fetentibus, ubi potestis tales deos sufficientes invenire si volueritis perscrutari.

> If that sacrament were God, the true body of Christ, there would be infinite gods, because a thousand priests and more every day make a thousand gods, and afterwards eat those gods, and once they are eaten discharge them through their hinder parts into the stinking latrine, where you can find plenty of such gods, if you cared to sift through it.[105]

Perhaps the intensity of Margery's bodily images, like that of William Colyn's striking asseverations, is fueled by an association of clerics with sodomy—and in this case, a particular association of purging with sodomy on which the Lollards themselves drew in the Third Conclusion itself. While later Lollardy tended to reduce the complexity of Wyclif's doctrine of consubstantiation (remanence) so that, for example, Margery Baxter (like John Burrell, as we saw above) claims that the host is nothing but bread, all these dissenters from the orthodoxy of transubstantiation were responding to the weakness in the philosophical system;[106] that weakness in the explanatory system regarding the body of Christ intersects with other weaknesses in the Christian system regarding the bodies of Christians and their apparently inevitable proclivities.

Issues of discernment, particularly concerning the bodily, are crucial in this overdetermined late-fourteenth-century English context of debates about transubstantiation, heresy trials, efforts at community building, and attempts at reforming the nation. Not only was there the orthodox problem of how to identify Lollards, a problem becoming increasingly urgent: Arundel's *Constitutions,* lists of questions, and other means sought to delineate the realm of the heretics clearly and eliminate the "grey area" that Hudson mentions "between clear orthodoxy and outright Lollardy," an area that despite these official attempts still persisted.[107] And not only was there the issue of Lollards' being able to identify one another as community members—by passwords and sartorial cues, for example.[108] But one of the central theological concerns itself features the discernment of a body and worries it at enormous and mortal length. When we consider that the groups of men touching this supposed body are themselves thought to include or to be sodomites inevitably, on the one hand, and are in turn accusing the Lollards of this sin, on the other, then the very existence of the pendant pair of poems with which I began this chapter seems not a minor rehearsal of tired insults that don't add up to anything but rather a performance of sodomitical fears that are always circulating, destabilizing and undermining efforts at building community and reforming a nation.

The Trouble with Girls

The *Twelve Conclusions* treat the problems generated by vows of celibacy not only for male clergy and private religious, but also for nuns and female religious. Lollard anxieties about the consequences of required vows for women religious are also deep and wide, but they are radically different from those we have just seen about male vows. The Eleventh Conclusion's treatment of female celibacy and its consequences suggests that female sexual perversion has an important function in Lollard belief. But the heretics' treatment shows that on this issue of female perversion they are virtually indistinguishable from the orthodox. Thus both male and female sexual deviance collapse distinctions between heretic and catholic, but they do so in very different ways.

The Conclusion's ostensible claim is the same, the sexes having been switched, as that of the Third Conclusion: absence of men, and sex with men, brought on by vows of celibacy, produces female perversion.

> Þe xi conclusiun is schamful for to speke, þat a uow of continence mad in oure chirche of wommen, þe qwiche ben fekil and vnperfyth in kynde, is cause of br[i]ngging of most horrible synne possible to mankynde. For þou sleyng of childrin or þei ben cristenid, aborcife and stroying of kynde be medicine ben ful sinful, ȝet knowing with hemself or irresonable beste or creature þat beris no lyf passith in worthinesse to ben punischid in peynis of helle. Þe correlary is þat widuis, and qwiche as han takin þe mantil and þe ryng deliciousliche fed, we wolde þei were weddid, for we can nout excusin hem fro priue synnis.[109]

> The eleventh conclusion is shameful to speak, that a vow of continence made in our church by women, who are fickle and imperfect by nature, is the cause of bringing the most horrible sin possible to mankind. For although slaying children before they have been christened, abortion, and contraception by medicine are very sinful, yet having sex with themselves or irrational beast or inanimate object surpasses those sins in worthiness to be punished by the pains of hell. The corollary is that we would that widows, and those who have taken the mantle and the ring deliciously fed, were wedded, because we cannot excuse them from secret sins.

Nuns and avowedly celibate widows, this conclusion implies, were already associated with the sinful practices of infanticide, abortion, and contraception: a long tradition witnessed in the Lollard version of the *Ancrene Riwle,* for example, undergirds this implication.[110] But they can be indicted for even worse perversions. Augustine himself had worried much earlier about sinful same-sex behavior in his influential letter about women's monastic life:

> [N]on autem carnalis sed spiritalis [*sic*] inter uos debet esse dilectio; nam quae faciunt pudoris inmemores etiam feminis feminae iocando

> turpiter et ludendo, non solum a uiduis et intactis ancillis Christi in sancto proposito constitutis sed omnino nec a mulieribus nuptis nec a uirginibus sunt facienda nupturis.
>
> The love which you bear to each other must be not carnal, but spiritual: for those things which are practiced by immodest women in shameful frolic and sporting with one another ought not even to be done by those of your sex who are married, or are intending to marry, and much more ought not to be done by widows or chaste virgins dedicated to be handmaids of Christ by a holy vow.[111]

And the *Ancrene Riwle* warns that nuns must not mess with the unmentionable sins of lechery, such unnameability linking these sins with vice against nature: "Þe scorpion of stynkande Leccherie nyl ich nouȝth nempny. for þe foule filþe of þe foule name for it miȝth done harme in to clene hertes" ("The scorpion of stinking Lechery I will not name for the foul filth of the foul name, for it might do harm to clean hearts").[112] But unlike this moral framing of the issue in the *Riwle* and in Augustine, hints of a physiological frame for sexual behavior are offered in the Eleventh Conclusion, as was the case in the Third: the nuns are "deliciousliche fed," and again there is no suggestion of self-restraint or intention toward transcendence. Pent up, deprived of men, and lavishly fed, such women cannot be assumed *not* to be having sex—privately, some way, somehow, with someone or something. "[A]fter wyn on Venus moste I thynke" ("After wine I am compelled to think of Venus" [3.464]), admits the Wife of Bath, and here the Lollards suggest a similar physiological reaction.

The physiological framing of female sexuality here extends to the whole range of sexual behaviors mentioned or implied, and this framing occurs through an emphasis on generation. Generativity or its deliberate negation is implied in the mention of contraceptive acts for which "celibate" women are apparently known as well as in the mention of nonprocreative sexual acts. These latter perversions—female sexual relations with one another, with beasts, and with sex toys—were traditionally associated with one another. Among the sins *contra naturam,* all of which hinder procreation (according to Thomas Aquinas), the *Summa theologica* (citing Romans 1.27) lists male-male and female-female homosexual relations and bestiality;[113] and a long, unbroken habit of thought (compellingly demonstrated by Bernadette Brooten) linked female same-sex relations with dildoes: from Seneca the Elder to Montaigne, women who have sex with women have been thought to use a device or to take advantage of abnormal anatomy, an enlarged clitoris.[114]

These acts—characterized by the Lollards as the worst, performed without men—are not only physiologically enabled but modeled on a phallic morphology: they require supplements of various sorts in order to supply the missing penetrative part (other women's enlargements, dildoes, perhaps animals). According to a traditional analysis deriving from Aristotle, the sex act takes place between an active and a passive partner; such a tradition supports this Conclusion's presumption of the necessity of phallic substitutions. If the women in the Eleventh Conclusion who have sex with men are active in seeking out the sex, desiring it and destroying the results, they nonetheless are assumed to play the passive role in generation itself, offering the passive matter to be impregnated by the man's active, form-bearing seed. In contrast, the woman penetrating is assuming that active function herself; as we saw in the introduction, violation of the proper gender role is what makes such sins so heinous.[115]

Exactly what women do with other women and how they manage it is ever unclear. Female sexual activity without men is incompletely imagined—and the Eleventh Conclusion's blurriness in this regard is no different from any other document that we have from the early Christian period onward.[116] Natalie Boymel Kampen has noted the strikingly unvisual quality of the extant evidence of such female activity; a late-thirteenth-century French statute makes this point inadvertently:

> 22. Cil qui sont sodomite prové doivent perdre les c . . . [*sic*]. Et se il le fet segonde foiz, il doit perdre menbre. Et se il le fet la tierce foiz, il doit estre ars.
>
> Feme qui le fet doit à chescune foiz perdre menbre, et la tierce doit estre arsse.

> He who has been proved to be a sodomite must lose his testicles. And if he does it a second time, he must lose his member. And if he does it a third time, he must be burned.
> A woman who does this shall lose her member each time, and on the third must be burned.[117]

Which "menbre"? Can it be lost twice? If the woman's anatomy is seen to be man's turned outside in, is the punishment really to cut out the member (a standard, indiscriminate term for body parts, be they organs or tissue) from inside?[118] Two times? It is doubtful that such a sentence was practically imagined. The language of the Eleventh Conclusion tends not to distinguish female homosexual acts from masturbation; such conflation (attested in various earlier texts Brooten finds as well) is conveyed here by the locution "communicatio cum seipsis," "knowing with hemself":[119] *seipsis*/"hemself" can refer to a group of women, among whom each has sex with herself, or to a group of women, among whom women are having sex with one another.[120]

The Eleventh Conclusion is in fact generally unexplanatory and allusive, compared to the Third. It lacks the dual proofs by reason and observation, and it lacks any clarifying historical remark (in the Third Conclusion, we recall, men are seen as substitutes for women, who were initially proscribed). Feminine desire here is activated by the phallus or its substitutes, and in this conclusion seems an undifferentiated urge for penetration. In contrast to the description in the Third Conclusion of men who do not like women, there is no suggestion of a shared proclivity or antipathy that would drive a woman into another woman's arms. The context of generativity in this conclusion further evacuates any consideration of a specific desire of females for females. The same women who drink potions or smother their babies may also be having sex with each other, with animals, and with things.

Women's wandering desires can be corrected by being properly directed, or redirected, toward men. The sins are again secret and separate here, and their cure is public—yet it is not the open and complete destruction recommended for male sodomites in the Third Conclusion but the public affirmation of marriage. No such recommendation appears in Third Conclusion, with its understanding that sodomitical ecclesiastics don't like women; there is no claim that marriage would be effective in turning sodomitical men straight so they could have the licit sex in marriage the Lollards advocate. Any possible recommendation for their treatment is elided by the Third Conclusion's return to the more general Lollard agenda item of dissolution of the "priuat religions" and that fierce statement of God's vengeance on these sinners. Male sodomy is thus not simply a perversion that can be safely turned around, though it is seen many times as just that; but it is also conceptualized or at least feared as a potential outgrowth of all-male communities, of homosocial bonding, something that might characterize a culture different from a heterosexual culture that at least tells itself that it is concerned with women. The same cannot be said of female same-sex relations; male-male sodomy may be feared, but female-female desire is unknown in an androcentric culture, the kind of culture inhabited by Lollards and orthodox alike.[121] The very proportions and energies of each of these two Lollard Conclusions indicate in little what is the case in orthodox discourse as well: although there is an awareness of female-female sexual activities, the bulk of discourse about same-sex sexual activity is about men, and female acts, when mentioned, are understood on male models. The place in late-medieval English culture of female desire, and of the woman who desires women, is very unstable: it is either so inconsequential or so deeply subversive as to be unrepresentable.[122] "We can nout excusin hem fro priue synnis," but we cannot prove the sins, either—at least no specific "priue asay" is mentioned.

This may be because women are, it seems, always already perverted. The cause of their sinful acts with each other, with beasts, and with inanimate objects is only circumstantially the avowed refusal of sex with men; it is really feminine nature itself. If the language of psychology is missing here, there is another language quite in evidence: working in tandem with the language of natural philosophy that we have observed is a language of morality. Women are immediately called "fekil and vnperfyth in kynde" ("mulieres, quae sunt fragiles et imperfectae in natura"). The discourse of Albertus Magnus and especially Thomas Aquinas resonates here; even if the Lollards deride the teachings of "frere Thomas" on transubstantiation, they are following the Angelic Doctor closely here on the issue of women. Thomas, following Albertus, elaborates minutely on the question of how God's creation could be perfect and yet woman could be imperfect; the solution depends on a distinction between universal nature and particular nature: though the generation of men and women in universal nature was willed by God and therefore perfect, the generation of individual women is a defect in the order of nature.[123] The fragility of women, deriving from their secondary creation, is one of Paul's main points when discussing marriage and proper social hierarchy in his first letter to the Corinthians. Lollards themselves routinely engage such traditional discourse, not only (according to Knighton) William Swinderby in 1382, in his cynical attempt to gain a following in Leicester, but also the author of Sermon 65:

> Þis gospel telliþ hou Crist apperide to Mary Maudelen, for Crist wolde þat womman kynde hadde þis priuylegie bifore man þat he shewide hym aftir his deþ raþere to womman þan to man, for wymmen ben freele as water and taken sunnere prynte of bileue.[124]
>
> The gospel tells how Christ appeared to Mary Magdalene, for Christ desired that womankind should have this privilege before man, that he showed himself after his death earlier to woman than to man, for women are frail as water and sooner take the imprint of belief.

Without the guidance and protection of men, avowed female religious engage in perverse acts that are potentials for all women, the Lollards contend in the Eleventh Conclusion. In absolute and extremely negative language (speaking of the "cause of br[i]ngging of most horrible synne possible to mankynde"), there's a hint of Eve, the original fragile creature. And though licit sexual relations in heterosexual marriage may be recommended as a cure for women's wayward nature here, the recommendation cannot solve the problem; it might just produce another: the potentially licentious relations between wife and husband. Thus in a move opposite to the Eleventh Conclusion's solution, a Wycliffite sermon advocates separation of the two sexes because it keeps men and women "fro lecherye."[125] But when those weak and fragile women get together, lechery may not be far behind.

Although Lollards "wished to express the radical spiritual equality of women and men," therefore, as Shannon McSheffrey has recently written, they wished to do so "without challenging the social hierarchy, also divinely ordained, which placed women under the authority of men and restricted their public activity."[126] Thus the claim, for example, held by a few Lollards, that women could be priests—"every man and every woman beyng in good lyf oute of synne is as good prest [priest] and hath [as] muche poar [power] of God in al thynges as ony prest ordred [ordained], be he pope or bisshop," as

Hawisia Moone put it—*and* the lack of evidence that any woman ever was a priest, at least in a conventional sense.[127] Women may not have been as powerful in or as enabled by Lollardy and Lollard communities as has been recently assumed; McSheffrey documents the extent to which women's participation and men's participation were vastly unequal, as men dominated conventicles, families, and marriages, and as the particular theological beliefs (especially Lollard opposition to the cult of saints and allied phenomena) "attacked precisely those aspects of late medieval Catholicism that most reflected popular creativity, and thus women's devotion."[128] The structure of Lollard communities was deeply androcentric. The gender dissymmetries I have noted in the Conclusions are small examples of a larger phenomenon of Lollard social conservatism with which we must reckon as we attempt to understand the limits of the social and cultural resistance Lollards exerted at various moments—as well as any late-twentieth-century desires to identify with these dissenters.[129]

It Takes One to Know One

The resistance in regard to gender and sexuality that Lollards offer in these Conclusions in fact seems finally inextricable from orthodox clerical positions that gave rise to it in the first place. Roger Dymmok's blast against the Conclusions argues point for point against the heretics, but his strategy of reverse accusation is more crucially functional in this context of propaganda and insult, I contend, than are his specific claims. For the reverse accusation erodes the very basis of distinctions Dymmok is invested in upholding.

Dymmok zeroes in on the Lollard emphasis on lack of self-restraint in the Conclusions. Distinctions between men and women—which at times he levels, at other times employs—seem less important than the main point Dymmok urges in his replies to both Conclusions: the Lollards are wrong about human nature. It is a debasement to suggest that coitus is necessary to the human condition, he maintains in his reply to the Third Conclusion. It is not only bad logic to suppose that men, lacking the consort of women and the desire for it, therefore are sodomites; it also suggests that Christ was ignorant of the human condition when he recommended chastity; and it reduces the human condition to something even lower than animals, since beasts do not commit sodomy.[130] In contrast to the natural philosophical discourse of the Lollards, Dymmok's argument is that sex is not implicated in the natural human processes of eating, drinking, and purging. According to him this is proved in Aristotle's *De animalibus* and in the lives of Christ and his apostles: they did not entirely abstain from food and drink, but that did not create in them the necessity in turn to have either natural or unnatural sexual relations. It is fully possible to live continently, Dymmok contends; the vow of chastity was instituted by the Virgin Mary and has been faithfully held by Christ, by his apostles and saints, and by holy people of the church. The chaste life is difficult, requiring vigilance; prayer is needed to calm especially vehement desires, and medicine may even be necessary to aid the body in quelling desire. But Christ would not have urged humans toward something beyond their capacities; if temptations do arise, Dymmok goes on in his reply to the Eleventh Conclusion, they still cannot be attributed to the vow itself, and they can be resisted, since God created all creatures free to sin or to act virtuously.

Echoing the Lollard Third Conclusion's proof by reason and observation, Dymmok uses not only logical argument against the logic of the Lollards, but also quotes Abbot Cherimon in Cassian's *Conferences* concerning proof by experiment and examination. The abbot holds that even something that looks contrary to nature, like getting sweet honey out of wheat, or smooth oil out of linseed, can nonetheless be proven to occur by the testimony of witnesses and by an exact rehearsal of the process in question. Disciplined study can reveal what really is necessary and inevitable in human nature, he maintains. And in a move that proves crucial to my analysis, Cherimon states—and Dymmok repeats—that there are those who would attribute to nature what are really their own sins: "[I]ntemperanciam suam ad necessitatem carnis, imo ad eius referunt Creatorem, proprias culpas ad nature infamiam transferentes" ("They attribute their intemperance to the necessity of the flesh, or even to its Creator, and transfer their own faults to the infamy of nature").[131] The guilty ones, the abbot alleges, blame their own sinfulness on human nature, transferring their sin to all others and maintaining that no one can keep vows.

The dynamics of reverse accusation—the sinners blame everyone and everything for the sin of which they are guilty—are in fact palpable in Dymmok's response to these Conclusions. After the long quotation from Abbot Cherimon, Dymmok repeats the same formula, indicating that the abbot's sentiment is in fact encapsulated by the idea that these false believers, even as they are aware of their own incontinence, believe nobody capable of being continent ("isti falsarii, proprie incontinencie conscii, neminem credant posse continere"). Further on in his discussion, Dymmok adjudicates the question, so problematic in the Third Conclusion, of how you can tell who's a sodomite by bringing to bear the reverse accusation: the Lollards, he claims, have no evidence of clerics' sodomy other than their own malice, their own sinfulness ("nec euidenciam ad hoc habuerunt nisi propriam maliciam").[132] It takes one to know one—or, at least, it takes one to blame one.

Dymmok keeps pounding away with this rhetorical hammer in his reply to the Eleventh Conclusion. Aware of their own shortcomings ("proprie fragilitatis conscii"), he contends immediately, the Lollards try to lead others into the very same. Such reverse accusations resound further on.[133] But I hope it is clear by now that to reverse the charge does not automatically get rid of suspicion of the phenomenon in one's own camp; in fact, the appearance of reversible accusations here points up the nearly overwhelming persistence of desire. Dymmok stresses the vigilance necessary to fulfill one's vows; he stresses, too, that taking a vow is not for everyone. He points out the many holy exemplars of chastity, and maintains that the vices of a few cannot taint the virtuous, or the ideal itself. But if the vow itself does not cause temptation, temptation—desire—nonetheless erupts in (or as) the occasions for sin that the vow allows.

Dymmok admits, in fact, that there are those who commit sodomy in orders. He names "sodomite, ydolatre, blasphemi uel heretici" to be found occasionally in the private religions (note once again the association of sodomites with other abjects). But they are rare, he insists, and they *can* be discerned, convicted, and punished according to the discipline of the order. Their existence should not serve to indict the private religions in themselves; it is not God's way, as is particularly exemplified in his words to Abraham about the Sodomites, to extirpate an entire people because of the sins of a few. Moreover, privateness, Dymmok argues, does not cause the sin, but merely provides an opportunity for it. It is ridiculous to contend that private religions began the sin of sodomy, he concludes, since sodomy is seen from the time of Abraham on.[134] Dymmok admits, too, in his response to the Eleventh Conclusion, that there are avowed women committing sexual improprieties. Persistent and apparently ineradicable, sexual deviance, and especially male-male sodomy, he nonetheless—anxiously—contends, seems manageable.

Sodomy charges are specifically poignant as well as always available, circulating, and reversible. They were telling constituents of the propagandistic atmosphere that surrounded the Lollards. The twists and turns of the strange case of Peter (or William) Pateshull, for example, become a bit more comprehensible and recognizable when we view them in such a context. In Walsingham's vivid (and doubtless exaggerated) account of 1387, Pateshull, an Augustinian friar, was appointed papal chaplain, after which he became a Wycliffite and began to preach against his former fellow Augustinians.[135] Followed by a hundred Lollards he went to preach about their evil ways at Saint Christopher's, London, whereupon a dozen incensed friars, hearing this, hastened to the place and were strongly moved in opposition against him. Pateshull's Lollard supporters attacked them, in turn, throwing them out of the church and threatening to destroy them and burn their houses, in a rage crying out, "Disperdamus homicidas, incendamus sodomitas, suspendamus Regis et Angliae proditores" ("Let us rout these murderers, burn these sodomites, hang these traitors to king and country"). The riot that ensued was only with difficulty put down by the intervention of friars and the sheriff. Pateshull then wrote down his accusations and nailed them to the doors of Saint Paul's, taking care that they should be believable: he accused the brothers of murdering their own and, moreover, of being sodomites and traitors.[136] Walsingham goes on to say that many knights, of Lollard leanings, believed and adopted these charges: the Lollard sodomy accusation against the friars, combined with accusations of murder and treachery, circulated even after the incident. If friars were accusing Lollards of sodomy, these same friars, turned Lollard, would accuse friars of sodomy. Fingers point everywhere, are believed to be pointing at oneself or one's peers; who has the authority to make such accusations, and why are they being made?

In the language of Sir Lewis Clifford, too, in his apparent recantation in 1402 of Lollard beliefs, may be heard the echoes of sodomitical accusation. Walsingham records a list of recanted Conclusions which was probably compiled from what people had heard or overheard Clifford saying around the royal court.[137] Clifford maintains that Lollards say marriage is the best and highest state, ordained by God, and that all religious should be married and should procreate, else they be murderers of potential offspring in their seed: his Second Conclusion rehearses Lollard warnings that those virgins, priests, and religious who do not marry or do not plan to marry "sunt homicidae, et destruunt sanctum semen unde consurgeret secunda Trinitas" ("are homicides, and destroy the holy seed whence a second Trinity would arise").[138] The language of destroying seed, not merely letting it go unused, echoes the rhetoric of sodomy as homicide.[139] And in his Fifth Conclusion, in addition to a statement of Lollard opposition to infant baptism that is radical in the sect but not without a rich context in Lollard belief,[140] we might hear a *double entendre* accusation of grabby pedophilic priests: "Item si haberent puerum modo natum, non baptizaretur per manus presbyterorum apud Ecclesiam; quia puer iste est secunda Trinitas, non contaminata peccato, et pejor esset si deveniret in manus eorundem" (Also if people have a newborn boy, he should not be baptized by the hands of priests at church; because that boy is a second Trinity, not contaminated by sin, and he would become worse if he were to fall into their hands).[141] Clifford might have recanted for reasons of convenience; or he may not have been prosecuted for these heresies at all. But in whatever politically charged context Clifford rehearses the beliefs of the Lollards and ends up echoing their sodomitical accusations. The uncertainty surrounding this "confession" magnifies the uncertainty of the subject and object of these echoed, allusive, accusatory strains: did he believe them formerly? Does he now (or is he swearing, as suggested by the tenets of later Lollards, to anything to save his life)? Who owns, as it were, these accusations? They inhere in Lollard language, bred from within a whole discourse, as I have been suggesting.[142] At the same time they are free-floating accusations, always available, ever ready to be tuned to answer a need. Who can detach them, then, from their discursive web and when and for what reasons?

Clifford's apparently solemn abjuration again raises the questions opened by the two poems that began this chapter. Sodomy rings, and rings, and rings in an echo chamber of accusations, ever useful in a propagandistic atmosphere such as envelops the Lollards in the last years of the fourteenth century and the early years of the fifteenth. Unlocatable and unstoppable, such accusations focus deep and destabilizing anxieties of both orthodox and heretic about bodies, pleasures, and knowledges. Bred from within, these uncertainties tend to collapse simple distinctions between catholic and heretic: the signal Wycliffite heresy, the denial of transubstantiation, for example, may in fact engage the same anxiety about male-male relations as dogs the orthodox; female sexual perversion points to the same gender hierarchies in both camps, and in fact suggests that licit and illicit sexual relations bear a certain resemblance, since some involve an always already perverse feminine nature. Discourses of orthodoxy and of dissent are not unalloyed, and neither can be the communities or reform strategies that such discourses foster; each is contaminated—always. Ever circulating, deviancy may slip its discursive bonds: thinking they can, *no one* can tell the sodomite for sure.

Because of their focus on literacy and their perceived proto-Protestantism, the Lollards have long been a favorite focus of identification for scholars, especially in the Anglo-American tradition, and their status as dissenters has rendered them appealing to a current generation eager to excavate buried pasts of the marginalized. My discussion here is intended to complicate any simple identification, but not because I have dug up dirty Lollard laundry that makes the heretics less savory as role models. Rather, I have suggested that certain issues—sexual deviance among men and among women—compromise the clear categorization of the resistant group to begin with. From the perspectives of creatures who deviate from the sexual norms of their communities, as we shall see, dissent and orthodoxy, resistance and power, can look remarkably alike. And it is with several such creatures, I'll suggest in the next chapter, that queers now might partially connect.

Chapter Two

Good Vibrations: John/Eleanor, Dame Alys, the Pardoner, and Foucault

A nightmare has pursued me since childhood: I have under my eyes a text that I can't read, or of which only a tiny part can be deciphered; I pretend to read it, but I know that I'm inventing.
Michel Foucault, "The Discourse of History"

The Real *Cook's Tale*?

One Sunday evening in December 1394 Eleanor Rykener walked the streets of Cheap Ward, a busy commercial district in London. It was no doubt cold that night, and Eleanor was no doubt bundled up. But she was still woman enough to catch the eye of John Britby as he traveled through the high road of Cheap; he approached her and asked her to have sex with him. Eleanor agreed, named her price, and the two withdrew to a stall in nearby Soper's Lane to do the deed.[1] It was then that the authorities of the city of London, waiting nearby, apprehended them and put them in prison, and it was sometime thereafter, in front of the mayor and aldermen in Guildhall, that her confession unfolded.

The confession, that is, of "*John* Rykener, calling [himself] Eleanor, having been detected in women's clothing" ("Johannes Rykener, se Elianoram nominans veste muliebri detectus").[2] In a separate examination, John Britby confessed that he thought Rykener was a woman, and, thinking thus, asked her to have sex. Maybe they hadn't really gotten started in that libidinous act, and so John Britby might not yet have been disabused when the two were apprehended. But by the time of his interrogation at the latest, Britby understands that Eleanor is a man, and the two are described as having committed "illud vitium detestabile, nephandum, et ignominiosum," as the recording scribe phrased it: "that detestable, unmentionable, and ignominious vice"—most likely sodomy, *the* unspeakable vice. Under interrogation, Rykener responded to questions about who taught him/her how to ply his/her trade, for how long, where, and with whom s/he had committed the act; s/he related a tale of unofficial apprenticeship in embroidery (with one Elizabeth Brouderer), tutelage in the act of having sex in the manner of a woman and getting paid for it, and many, many sexual contacts in various locales. In private houses as well as taverns, s/he had sex as a woman with clerics (who remunerated him/her well), and had sex as a man with women (nuns, wives, and unmarried women), whose monetary rewards, if any, Rykener didn't mention.

John/Eleanor Rykener's story, recorded in late 1394 in the London Plea and Memoranda Rolls—six or seven weeks before the Lollards posted their *Conclusions*—reads like a nightmare of the Lollard imagination. This cross-dressed prostitute who had sex with so many clerics s/he couldn't remember them all confirms the Lollards' lowest expectations of the prelacy. And further, as a male creature who is able to live, work, have sex, and pass as a woman s/he defies other Lollard certainties that I have discussed in the previous chapter—about who is "one of those"—and reveals those certainties to be but anxious desires for incontestable knowledge.

Yet John/Eleanor's tale reads not only like a Lollard nightmare but also like something less portentous—as if it could have been a model for the *Cook's Tale,* Chaucer's barely begun yet vivid and high-spirited narrative at the end of the *Canterbury Tales'* first fragment. In many respects, the Cook and his tale occupy just this world described by John/Eleanor. Chaucer, probably writing in the early to mid-1390s, seems indeed in that fragmentary narrative to have intended to portray the tale of a real London citizen, since he has the Cook identify himself as "Hogge of Ware," who addresses the Host in turn as "Herry Bailly" (1.4336, 4358); both names have been documented in London.[3] Specifically, Roger, a cook originally of Ware, shows up in a London ward presentment as having been accused, and pleading guilty, of being a "common nightwalker" — "one guilty of wandering the streets after curfew" consorting (frequently) with people of ill repute.[4] Such disorderly conduct charges might be pressed on the Cook in the Prologue to the *Manciple's Tale* (a problematic link in terms of narrative continuity—it proceeds later in the pilgrimage as if the Cook had never been asked to tell a tale in the First Fragment—but a clear continuation of character and theme): as the pilgrimage nears Harbledown, the Cook nods and seems in danger of falling off his horse. The Host asks him why: "Hastow had fleen [fleas] al nyght, or artow dronke? / Or hastow with som quene [whore] al nyght yswonke?" (9.17–18). The pilgrim apparently looks as if he might well have passed the night with a whore.

And tell a tale he does, when asked by the Host after hearing the *Reeve's Tale*, about a Cheapside victualler and his jolly, rotten apprentice Perkyn Revelour—who, upon dismissal, goes to live with a friend whose wife keeps a shop as a front while turning tricks for a living. Prostitution in the trades seems to have been a fact of London life: incidents of prostitution among female apprentices, a young and particularly vulnerable lot, in London have been well documented by Ruth Mazo Karras. In fact it appears that the same embroideress Elizabeth who took in Rykener was convicted of bawdry on the side nine years before his/her interrogation—convicted of taking on and then prostituting apprentice embroideresses.[5] The verisimilar *Cook's Tale*, sharing elements of John/Eleanor's milieu, offers a whiff of the London world of the trades that Chaucer does not otherwise portray—his guildsmen in the General Prologue are a pretentious bunch as they apparently angle to be aldermen, and bring along their own cook on the pilgrimage—and even here declines to elaborate.[6]

This Cook indeed stands somewhere in between aldermen and prostitute, the two sides of that 1394 interrogation. As narrator of the fragmentary *Tale*, the Cook modulates his tone between identification with Perkyn Revelour, on the one hand, and the master victualler his dissatisfied boss on the other, as V. A. Kolve has discerned.[7] But if the *Cook's Prologue* and *Tale* (and the *Manciple's Prologue*) read like documents of London life in the 1380s and 90s, Rykener's examination, in turn, reads like a *Canterbury Tale*. The very names of the principals fit nicely: "Brouderer" is most probably a by-name for Elizabeth the embroideress (whose surname seems to have been Moryng); "Eleanor," the name John Rykener apparently chose to go by, plays on his own alienness, his own otherness;[8] and "Rykener" seems particularly appropriate for a prostitute (who reckons—counts—money) telling (reckoning—recounting, narrating) a story. The emphasis on lascivious clergy hints at estates satire, and the voluminous enumeration of sexual partners has the makings of a good fabliau—not to mention the engagingly fabliau-like episode of clothes-stealing and blackmail, which is worthy of the *Shipman's Tale*.[9] The record by the court clerk (about which more later) piles up the erotic encounters, the deadpan legal language both refusing and attracting interpretation; and the fact that no further records exist leaves crucial questions open forever to interpretation. Indeed, in such a document of an otherwise obscure life there is "a certain equivocation of the fictitious and the real," Foucault writes in "The Life of Infamous Men," since in such documents the infamous (such as John/Eleanor) "do not have and will never ever have any existence except under the precarious shelter of these words. And thanks to the texts which speak of them, they come into our hands without bringing any more indices of reality than if they came from the *Golden Legend* or from an adventure novel."[10]

So John/Eleanor Rykener's existence has something of a textual nature. I want to explore further what such a textual nature might mean for a queer history later on; at the moment it is important to note that Rykener's narrative starts with a very specific premise that makes it unusual if not unique among English documents of practice and distances it as well from the Chaucerian fragment of the Cook. John/Eleanor Rykener is a man dressed as a woman, and his/her infraction seems not just to be prostitution—or maybe not prostitution at all, as Karras and Boyd suggest, since there is "no case extant from the medieval English ecclesiastical courts (or in fact from any other medieval courts, as far as we know) in which a man was accused, let alone convicted, of prostitution." Prostitution seems defined as a strictly female crime.[11] His/her infraction seems indeed to be sodomy, though sodomy was not technically under the jurisdiction of this court. And John/Eleanor's participation in this vice involves feminization: s/he is taught by women how to behave, indeed live, like a woman; s/he learns, as they apparently have previously, that femininity can be not only studied but exploited. S/he learns to solicit desires (I shall argue) that may in fact defy categorization. Chaucer indeed took up the kinds of issues Rykener's interrogation raises, starting in the fabliaux of the first fragment of the *Canterbury Tales* but elaborating them most fully, I would argue, in the confessional performances of Dame Alys (the Wife of Bath) and the Pardoner.[12]

I want to look more closely in this chapter at the complex issues John/Eleanor Rykener's interrogation raises. I then shall turn to Chaucer's queer character, the Pardoner, and his queering effects, which resonate with John/Eleanor's: the Pardoner, like John/Eleanor, appears sexually and gender-indeterminate, and he reveals, again like John/Eleanor, the unnaturalness of the behaviors and desires of those—like the Wife of Bath—around him.[13] Finally, I shall turn to an essay I have already mentioned, Foucault's 1977 piece, "The Life of Infamous Men," intended as a preface to a collection of the same title (only in 1982, and in collaboration with historian Arlette Farge, did a volume eventually appear, entitled *Le Désordre des familles*). Didier Eribon maintains that this short piece condenses all of what one could call Foucault's "philosophie profonde."[14] I shall discuss what kinds of knowledge we can derive from this critical act of considering such a record of an interrogation vis-à-vis the fictional narratives of the Pardoner and the Wife. In the context of queer history, the issues are particularly poignant: in what ways can we consider a document that is part of the late-fourteenth-century English legal apparatus side by side with fictional texts written by an aging late-medieval English civil servant for a diversely imagined audience? What might such a meeting of texts reveal? What implications for queer historical projects does such a "simple fact," as Foucault put it, make—that John/Eleanor existed and the Pardoner didn't?[15] I shall approach these questions by considering Foucault in the archive, sensing a "vibration" from the very documents he reads.

Unmentionable/Aforementioned

The paradoxical references to vice in this document focus some of the linguistic and rhetorical issues that arise in this deposition. The offending act during which John/Eleanor Rykener and John Britby are apprehended is initially denoted thus: "illud vitium detestabile, nephandum, et ignominiosum" ("that detestable, unmentionable, and ignominious vice" [461, 462]). Plenty of strong language is used in documents for acts of prostitution; one late-fifteenth-century ordinance banning prostitutes from London, for example, refers to it as "the stinking and horrible sin of lechery" practiced by strumpets.[16] But the adjective "nephandum," traditionally (after Saint Paul, as we have seen) used for same-sex sodomy, marks the unnamed vice as sodomy here, as Boyd and Karras also assert. As the interrogation proceeds, the document refers again and again, after its opening salvo, to such vice: unmentionable by nature, it nonetheless becomes "illud vitium antedictum" (462), the *aforementioned* unmentionable vice. This paradox neatly exemplifies Foucault's point about sexuality in general as it developed out of premodernity: the sexual act here is defined as unspeakable, yet it is spoken of voluminously. This sexual behavior constitutes the truth of the confession, the thing that is confessed, the knowledge which is pursued:[17] Rykener is asked "who had taught him to exercise this vice, and for how long and in what places and with what persons" ("quis ei docuit dictum vitium exercere et quanto tempore, in quibus locis, et cum quibus personis").

Whose language is this? How did John/Eleanor Rykener and John Britby themselves refer to what they were doing? What questions were asked in the interrogation of this crossed-dressed creature in Guildhall? Unless other texts come to light, we'll never know. The court proceedings were conducted in English; the clerk interpreted and recorded the proceedings in Latin, and these phrases—though they could be John/Eleanor Rykener's own, as Karras and Boyd suggest, learned in the confessional or in sermons (see the *Parson's Tale* for such language)—are necessarily also the clerk's interpretation of John/Eleanor's words.[18] The clerk chose to write a précis in Latin rather than a verbatim English confession (another option, exercised in other, perhaps specifically politically sensitive, cases);[19] but he nonetheless wrote a fairly detailed account, which suggests that he at least viewed the case as having some interest or revealing something about city life, privileges, and customs.[20] The emphasis on clerical offenses in the document might be the clerk's, in his recording; it might be the questioners'; or it might be Rykener's own, shaping his/her narrative to appeal to London officials' zeal to apprehend licentious clerics, on the one hand, and, on the other, to save his/her own life.[21] (After all, though no records of temporal laws against sodomy exist until the sixteenth century, the punishment for sodomy in legal textbooks was death.)[22] The intent to save his/her own life perhaps indeed shapes the confession; Rykener had already apparently proved him/herself compliant, agreeing at the outset of his/her testimony that everything happened just the way John Britby had said it had.

The appearance of this man brought into court "in veste muliebri" (461) must have been unusual indeed. Marjorie Garber contends in *Vested Interests* that the appearance in a text, whether historical or fictional, of a transvestite marks a crisis of categorization: "By 'category crisis' I mean a failure of definitional distinction, a borderline that becomes permeable, that permits of border crossings from one (apparently distinct) category to another. . . . The binarism male/female, one apparent ground of distinction (in contemporary eyes, at least) between 'this' and 'that,' 'him' and 'me,' is itself put in question or under erasure in transvestism, and a transvestite figure, or a transvestite mode, will always function as a sign of overdetermination—a mechanism of displacement from one blurred boundary to another."[23] I want to resist the tendency of this approach to efface the transvestite's own subjectivity: to look *at,* not *through,* the transvestite, as Garber insists we should, still privileges the interrogating eye.[24] My resistance will become clear later on; for the moment, the general hypothesis about category confusion is useful here on the legal stage of this Guildhall chamber, where the indeterminacy of gender categories intersects with the sexual-category confusion—the likes of which we observed in the last chapter—that is sodomy. Foucault's observation that sodomy is "that utterly confused category" is borne out in this short document:[25] whereas the traditional condemnatory language of male-male sodomy is used initially (by at least the clerk) to describe the vice the two men were caught performing, the interrogatory pursuit of this crime entails a questioning as to "with what persons, masculine or feminine, [he] had committed that libidinous and unspeakable act" ("cum quibus personis masculis sive feminis illud actum libidinosum et nephandum commisit" [461]), which results in a narrative of Rykener's many sexual contacts in the manner of a woman with men, and many other sexual exploits as a man with women. As we have seen, heterosexual relations can certainly be deviant, and sodomy can be among such male-female deviant acts. But the specificity of sexual behaviors, presumably of some interest in this court (a temporal court, which handled cases of prostitution but very rarely male-male sodomy), is blurred by this cross-dressed figure; perhaps s/he deploys, further, the confusing discourse of sodomy him/herself ("illud vitium detestabile") to try to produce effects such as we have seen around Parliament in the last chapter, especially to break down the threateningly oppositional relation between him/herself and the officials s/he faces in Guildhall. But further, as I suggested in the last chapter, even the basis for discernment, for knowledge—of a body, or orthodoxy, or sexual perversion—is undone by such discourse, and such undoing is signaled by the transvestite here.

Other language in the document, however, works hard against such confusion: it tries to hold the line between the sexes and preserve the distinct and proper sexual and gender binaries that sustain notions of normative heterosexuality. Heterosexual gender relations form a powerful structuring matrix through which the events seem to have been presented (by the participants) and a lens through which this incident is seen (by the arresting officials, by the clerk).[26] Male-male sex is here clearly modeled heterosexually, as it so often was in medieval discourse: an unambiguous example of this modeling is found in *Cleanness*, a text I have mentioned earlier, written probably within a decade of Rykener's interrogation.[27] In the language of the apprehended John Britby, we hear the force of binary heterosexual organization: the gender of the pronouns shifts from masculine to feminine when Britby's words at the time are indirectly quoted, reinforcing his testimony (which includes the emphatic repetition of "mulier") that he thought this man was indeed a woman.

> Qui quidem Johannes Britby inde allocutus fatebatur quod ipse per vicum regium de Chepe die dominica inter horas supradictas transiens,

dictum Johannem Rykener vestitu muliebri ornatum, ipsumque mulierem fore suspicantem fuerat assecutus, petens ab eo, tanquam a muliere, si cum *ea* libidinose agere possit. (461, my emphasis)

John Britby confessed that he was passing through the high road of Cheap on Sunday between the above-mentioned hours and accosted John Rykener, dressed up as a woman, thinking he was a woman, asking him as he would a woman if he could commit a libidinous act with *her*. (463, my emphasis)

Rykener in turn solicits John Britby's desire on a heterosexual model, and apparently acts on one, too, since s/he mentions sex as a woman only with men, and mentions sex as a man only with women. Masculine/feminine in this model is correlated with active/passive: this is apparent in Thomas Aquinas's motto, repeated through the late Middle Ages, about the necessary evil of prostitution: he suggests that active penetration of a passive partner is what matters, in heterosexual prostitution as well as in its debased alternative, male-male sodomy: "Tolle cloacam, et replebis foetore palatium; et similiter de sentina. Tolle meretrices de mundo, et replebis ipsum sodomia" ("Remove the sewer and you will fill the palace with ordure; similarly with bilge from a ship; remove whores from the world and you will fill it with sodomy").[28] We have seen such associations of sodomy with purging in the last chapter, and have seen such universalizing of sodomitical proclivity, too, when the Lollards suggest that if there are no women around, men will engage in sodomy. But while the Lollard Third Conclusion did not deploy the language of feminization of the male passive partner (thus leaving open the possibility of masculine-masculine sex), modeling the act of penetration in the discourse of Rykener's case are the gender binaries of heterosexual relations—masculine and feminine—correlated implicitly with active and passive.

But those stark binaries do not preclude more complex—queerer—desires. The document, despite its normalizing moves, invites us to try to read otherwise, to try to explore bits that won't be assimilated into the hetero frame; the unspoken yet somehow already mentioned concept of sodomy, for starters, opens a moment—one of Bhabha's "new times," perhaps—in this narrative where queer desires emerge. Why did John/Eleanor choose this labor over other kinds of labor available even to very poor men? S/he learned how to have sex *modo muliebri* from the whore Anna; why did Anna teach him/her, or why did s/he ask for instruction? By the time s/he met up with Elizabeth Brouderer s/he had learned that lesson, and Elizabeth dressed him/her in women's clothing. Whose idea was that, and how did it arise? Perhaps his/her appearance was "feminoid," as Donald Howard said of the Pardoner, and it suggested this occupation.[29] Or perhaps s/he liked male-male sex, or liked dressing up—or embroidery—and either was impelled to exploit these desires for money, or learned through taking on this occupation that s/he liked aspects of it. Though the cross-dressing initially may have been merely a business opportunity, as Karras and Boyd note, it's also possible that passing had its pleasures: Rykener was apparently not only turning tricks but living and doing embroidery as a woman in Oxford.[30]

It is impossible to discern with any certainty what Rykener's various customers wanted, but it is no doubt too limited to assume simply that those desires can be understood in the binary gender terms of heterosexuality. John Britby insists that he had wanted a woman on that December night—but did he insist this mainly to save his own skin? The dogged repetition of "mulier" in the record can be read as an inflection of anger or humiliation—but it can also convey fear. The unfortunate rector of Theydon Garnon earlier seems clearly enough to have wanted a woman, and just as clearly never to have been disabused about what he got: after having sex, he was caught in a scam based on the idea that Rykener could have a husband.

> Item dixit quod quidam Philippus, Rector de Theydon Gernon, concubuit cum eodem Johanne Rykener ut cum muliere in domo cuiusdam Elizabeth Brouderer extra Bisshoppesgate, quo tempore dictus Johannes Rykener asportavit duas togas ipsius Philippi. Et quando idem Philippus illas petiit a prefato Johanne Rykener, ipse dixit quod fuit uxor cuiusdam hominis, et si ipse illas repetere vellet faceret maritum suum versus ipsum prosequi. (462)

> [He] further said that a certain Phillip, rector of Theydon Garnon, had sex with him as with a woman in Elizabeth Brouderer's house outside Bishopsgate, at which time Rykener took away two gowns of Phillip's, and when Phillip requested them from Rykener he said that [he] was

the wife of a certain man and that if Phillip wished to ask for them back [he] would make [his] husband bring suit against him. (463)

Further testimony notes that three friars had sex with Rykener numerous times—whether "ignotos" ([*sic*] "unsuspecting") only at first or during the entire time of their acquaintance in Oxford, where s/he was working and passing as a woman, it is not clear:

> Item dictus Johannes Rykener fatebatur quod per quinque septimanas ante festum santi Michaelis ultimo elapsum morabatur apud Oxonium et operatus est ibidem in veste muliebri in arte de brouderer nominans ipsum Alianoram. Et ibidem in marisco tres scolares ignotos, quorum unus nominatur dominus Willielmus Foxlee, alius dominus Johannes, et tertius dominus Walterus, usi fuerunt sepius cum ipso abominabile vitium supradictum. (462)
>
> Rykener further confessed that for five weeks before the feast of St. Michael's last [he] was staying at Oxford, and there, in women's clothing and calling himself Eleanor, worked as an embroideress; and there in the marh three unsuspecting scholars—of whom one was named Sir William Foxlee, another Sir John, and the third Sir Walter—practiced the abominable vice with him often. (463)

Not only is a "priuy asay" incapable of discerning very reliably which men commit sodomy with other men, as I have suggested in the previous chapter; it may be that these clerics *themselves* were always convinced that they were having sex with a woman.[31] Or further, it may be that in the male in feminine clothes they got exactly what they wanted.

We may find in fact that the binary gender terms of heterosexuality are used—by the accused, as well as in the common cultural discourse of sodomy and transvestism here—to express desires that nonetheless blur or exceed those very categories. As the instance of the three "scolares ignotos" can suggest, the desires that circulate around and through Rykener might be much more heterogeneous indeed: are those clerks *really* unsuspecting, or might they want a feminized man, or a phallic woman? Might they want something that's not a woman but not a man either, something that seems to them neither fully masculine nor fully feminine? Is that what makes them "ignotos"—not only unsuspecting, but profoundly unknown themselves, because what they want is unheard of? If and when they were disabused of the belief in this creature's femaleness, did they, anticipating Joe E. Brown in *Some Like It Hot*, chirp, "Nobody's perfect," and get on with it?

The male transvestite prostitute can in this way reveal not only the potential queerness of desires but also a certain malleability of gender. Rykener acts like a woman on certain occasions, like a man on others, and the prostitution context certainly highlights the performativity of gender here.[32] Women, particularly harshly regulated by gender in this culture (as we have seen in the previous chapter), are the ones who know best how to exploit the fact that gender can be performed. Women, subjected by gender so obviously in the Lollard Eleventh Conclusion, are the ones in Rykener's narrative who exploit the dominance of gender expectations. They capitalize on gender expectations, make gender work for them. They teach Rykener to mimic them, and femininity clearly takes practice: at first Rykener plays only the daylight role and Elizabeth's daughter does the heavy lifting at night.

> [Elizabeth] etiam conduxit quandam Aliciam filliam [*sic*] suam diversis hominibus luxuriae causa, ipsam cum eisdem hominibus in lectis eorum noctanter absque lumine reponens et eandem summo mane ab eisdem recedere fecit, monstrando eis dictum Johannem Rykener veste muliebri ornatum ipsum Alianoram nominantem, asserens ipsos cum ipsa sinistre egisse. (462)

> [Elizabeth] also brought her daughter Alice to diverse men for the sake of lust, placing her with those men in their beds at night without light, making her leave early in the morning and showing them the said John Rykener dressed up in women's clothing, calling him Eleanor and saying that they had misbehaved with her. (463)

But fairly soon, it seems, John/Eleanor can sustain whatever scrutiny is applied during sex; s/he goes on to testify to the authorities about that unlucky rector of Theydon Garnon. And in Oxford later still John/Eleanor seems to be passing successfully as a woman.

The interrogation of this cross-dressed male caught in a sodomitical act suggests that laws based on clear and apparent sex difference (that is, heterosexually based laws)—laws regulating prostitution, for example, that presume that only women act like women—are irrelevant or inadequate in the face of queer desires or queer truths about the inessentiality of gender, the inadequacy of binary gender categories of heterosexuality, and the resistance of bodies to their official gender constitution and categorization. Finally, John/Eleanor's feminine gender performance demonstrates that at least fundamentally—in regard to the fundament, that is—masculine and feminine are indistinguishable, and this is at least part of what would make him/her a nightmare for not only civil but also ecclesiastical authorities, as well as for dissenters such as the Lollards. The Wife of Bath, as we shall see, in her *Prologue* addresses the agendas behind the clerical regulation of gender behavior and constitution of normative anatomies; but the inconclusiveness of John/Eleanor's court proceedings may be a sign of a momentary failure of such laws and agendas, the result of his/her queer and queering presence.[33]

There seems to have been no pursuit of a formal legal case beyond this interrogation. But we can be certain (from the kinds of language we have seen in the previous chapter) that Rykener's queerness was not celebrated on those Guildhall premises. S/he embodies such indeterminacy as is unleashed by reverse accusations we have seen in the Lollard context—and indeed, s/he collapses crucial social distinctions: from his/her perspective, secular authorities who apprehended him/her look much like the heretics whose final punishment they will administer, as both groups seek to eradicate sodomy. S/he might be imagined standing on the street while insults and accusations fly around him/her, but that image must neither be idealized nor taken to represent a stable or safe situation of happy indeterminacy. The official inconclusiveness of the case, the apparent inapplicability of the law, of course do not preclude danger to him/her; the silence of the records regarding this case might be the final silence of a violent death, or the muteness of a maimed life. "I wolde I hadde thy coillons [balls] in myn hond / In stide of relikes or of seintuarie. / Lat kutte hem of [off], I wol thee helpe hem carie" (6.952–54), Harry Bailley bursts out after having been solicited by that figure of sexual and gender indeterminacy, the Pardoner. The Pardoner is, in his turn, silent; who knows what happened to John/Eleanor?

The sex and gender issues arising from the confrontation of John/Eleanor Rykener and the London authorities that December night in 1394—and the anxieties in public circulation that s/he seems proleptically to reify—can focus for us some issues that arise in the confrontational interactions between the Pardoner and other pilgrims in the literary representations Chaucer created at more or less this time just outside London.[34] When the Pardoner interrupts the Wife of Bath on the road to Canterbury in the *Tales*, he not only speaks but first "starts up" ("Up stirte the Pardoner" [3.163]), disturbing the air around him, sending shock waves into the body of pilgrims with whom he travels.[35] Chaucer had used the phrase "up stirte" before—in *Troilus and Criseyde*, when the "noyse of peple" bursts out in insistence on exchanging Criseyde for Antenor, revealing homosocial traffic in women as a structuring principle of the Trojan society that Hector and Troilus want to believe operates ethically, respectfully of women, and according to romantic rules of heterosexual relations.[36] On the Canterbury pilgrimage, where normative sexual parameters will be contested in many a narrative turn, the upstart Pardoner sends into a queer skid what has theretofore been confidently represented, and represented as perfectly natural—the robust heterosexuality of the Wife—and exposes it as a pose, something learned and exploited. If the John/Eleanor Rykener text has allowed us to specify how heterosexually based categories are confused by, inadequate to, and contaminated by the queer, the Chaucerian text allows us to see how a "felaweshipe" formed on such categories encounters and both deals with and is incapable of dealing with the queer.[37] That queer effect, in its contagious qualities, exceeds, persists, plagues the intended management and control. And if the force of the queer is relatively contained in the fourteenth-century context—detained by city authorities, interrogated in ecclesiastical courts, hounded by statutes and regulations, or burned—our latter-day bodies can not only fully feel the shock, I shall finally argue, but also appropriate that force for queer use.

Lately—after Donald Howard's brilliant 1976 reading in *The Idea of the* Canterbury Tales cleared the way—there has been growing critical interest in the Pardoner as queer and in claiming him as some kind of hermeneutic key to the *Tales*, or as a player in a "gay history," a complicated sort of gay "ancestor."[38] There is a growing literary tradition of gay invocations of the Pardoner, as Steven F. Kruger has noted—"the first angry homosexual," as Allen Barnett's character Preston called him—and of his *Tale* as, for example, part of the literature of "a community of doubt" that also includes Bob, the narrator of Robert Glück's *Margery Kempe*. These late-twentieth-century gay American writers, as we shall see, in very different ways are sensing something—a "vibration," as Foucault would put it, a "touch," according to Barthes—about his presence and place among the pilgrims, something, some shared marginality or uncategorizability, prepared in fact by the Pardoner's first audience itself.

When he begins to speak his own tale, for example, other pilgrims on the road to Canterbury seem to back away from the Pardoner. Recall the scene with its barbed jocularity: the Host invites him to tell a tale, in language that intentionally highlights the Pardoner's apparent sexual anomalousness: "Thou beel amy, thou Pardoner" (318), he taunts: "Hey, lover boy." The Host wants "som myrthe or japes [jokes]," and right away, to soothe his aching heart after the *Physician's Tale* of Virginia; the Pardoner responds by picking up and mimicking the Host's garbled oath to "Seint Ronyan" (320; cf. 310). This acid repetition of the Host's diction hints not just at a psychology, not just some sort of defensiveness or sensitivity, but at the Pardoner's denaturalizing power, denaturalization working here by means of parody.[39] Taking time to really make an impact, the Pardoner then draws the pilgrimage to a halt in order that he might have a snack. The Host has asked for mirth or jokes, but the "gentils"—Chaucer's joke on the mixed and rowdy nature of the pilgrimage, as Derek Pearsall suggests—seem to fear that some wasteful immorality is what this deliberate, willful creature will come out with; "japes" is, after all, what the narrator of the General Prologue has called the Pardoner's scams (1.705–06). Even before the Pardoner says another word they cry out: "Nay, lat hym telle us of no ribaudye [ribaldry]!" (324).[40]

This protest that the Pardoner should "Telle us som moral thyng" and the Pardoner's dry retort—"I moot [must] thynke / Upon som honest thyng while that I drynke" (6.325, 327–28)—introduces in a dramatically heightened way a major theme of the Pardoner's *Prologue,* the assertion that though he is a "ful vicious man / A moral tale yet I yow telle kan" (6.459–60). The representation of the Pardoner's hypocrisy plays on vibrant contemporary Wycliffite polemics against religious hypocrisy, as Alan J. Fletcher argues, and this statement in particular picks up a lively issue current among Chaucer's audience, which likely included some Lollard sympathizers: the fierce Lollard debate about whether a corrupt priest can nonetheless validly celebrate the sacraments.[41] The religious climate of the 1390s was drastically "unsettled," as Paul Strohm has described it, and we have seen in the preceding chapter the discursive instability that was operant; on the one hand Lollards were posting their *Conclusions* and on the other "an uneven but steady consolidation of the anti-Lollard position had continued throughout Richard's reign."[42] The volatility of this climate is perceptible in Harry Bailley's words to the Parson in the endlink to the *Man of Law's Tale,* words that may be intended to tweak the sensibilities of Lollards in the audience: "O Jankin, be ye there? / I smelle a Lollere in the wynd" (2.1172–73). Lollardy is in the air, and such a heretic can be sniffed out.[43] The atmosphere of Lollard and anti-Lollard propaganda sustains and nourishes the Pardoner's self-presentation as a hypocrite.

Chaucer's characterization of the Pardoner in fact hits many polemical hot-button issues. Here I rely on Fletcher's excellent work, which details the ready contemporary associations—some of which we saw in the last chapter—between hypocrisy and heresy; between selling holy things—an extension of simony—and heresy; and between greedy preaching, even greed itself, and heresy.[44] Buzzwords in Lollard polemic—"substaunce" and "accident," "kaityf" (6.539, 728)—ring out in the Pardoner's *Tale,* further stressing this character's location in the debates.[45] Fully conversant with the debates (his association with the so-called "Lollard knights" as well as with the anti-Wycliffites Gower, Strode, and Arundel has often been remarked),[46] Chaucer polemically engages Lollard issues, Fletcher argues—Chaucer not only makes the Pardoner a false preacher but also has him comment on false preaching in a general way: "For certes, many a predicacioun / Comth ofte tyme of yvel entencioun" (6.407–8)—while his representation of the pilgrim refrains from falling on either side; it is neither clearly heterodox nor obviously orthodox.

The structure of reverse accusation, the likes of which I discussed in the last chapter, is invoked and operant here as the Pardoner is associated with heresy in the very terms of heretics. Fletcher notes that "[i]n the polemic which the debate [on religious hypocrisy] produced, the same weapons of disparagement were equally available for each side to wield against the other." The reversibility of the insults contributes to the "polemical yet not identifiably partisan" nature of Chaucer's representation here.[47] We've seen the workings of the dense network of accusations of hypocrisy, heresy, and sexual perversion, the ways in which these phenomena interact to undermine knowledge and discernment; I argue that the uncertainty about the Pardoner's sexual nature is intertwined with accusations of heresy in precisely the ways I mapped out in the last chapter. Religious and sexual indeterminacies intersect in both Lollard and anti-Lollard polemics, and these indeterminacies derail efforts to *know one;* perversion shadows and crosses the norms, sexual and religious. The Pardoner's indeterminacy is produced in exactly this nexus, and the kind of contagion he threatens becomes more menacing even as efforts to discern who is not orthodox became ever more threatening, their Ricardian consolidation eventuating in the burning, in Henry's reign, of William Sautre in 1401. Fletcher concludes his article by maintaining that the neither-heretical-nor-orthodox indeterminacy of Chaucer's representation is yet another mark of his deft and politic elusiveness as a writer; shifting the focus, I frame my analysis of the Pardoner with the historical moment of John/Eleanor Rykener and the Lollard polemics, and suggest that the fierce silencing of the Pardoner on the pilgrimage marks a larger cultural response to the intertwined phenomena of sexual indeterminacy and intimations of heresy.

The narrator of the *Canterbury Tales* was the first to register his uncertainty about this creature. In the General Prologue, the Pardoner is introduced last among the pilgrim company assembled at the Tabard, and after describing his person the narrator speculates: "I trowe he were a geldyng or a mare" ("I guess he was a castrated horse or a female horse" [1.691]). Following his usual usage, the narrator does not condemn this pilgrim outright: he employs metaphor to indicate what he guesses about the Pardoner's sexual proclivities.[48] Suggestions of eunuchry emerge from the "geldyng" image, as do suggestions of effeminacy from "mare"; many critics have adduced various meanings and implications of these images.[49] Though I think it useful to explore the various sexual possibilities (both eunuchry and sodomy seem likely and have proved fruitful in modern-day analyses of this pilgrim), the first point to emphasize is that it is not quite clear to the narrator, just by looking at this pilgrim's physical person, *what* he is; maybe he is feminine in appearance, as Boyd and Karras suggest, and the "geldyng" or "mare" suggestions offer physical types that make sense of that femininity.[50] But it is apparent at the least that the Pardoner does not fit easily into the "felaweshipe" (1.32) of pilgrims gathered for the journey to Canterbury.

If we think back to the famous opening lines of the General Prologue, it will be clearer why this character seems illegible. These lines lay out the nexus of normative sexuality and religion for the *Canterbury Tales*, and, doing so, have become arguably the most famous in all of English poetry. In fact, I think they have come in the anglophone West to signify Literature itself—literature with a capital "L," the kind that is believed to underwrite the foundational values of Western Civilization. And if these lines signify Literature, it is perhaps because they may be indeed the first in English to articulate a normative heterosexuality with such clarity—normative heterosexuality, taken to be one of the founding markers and guardians of the Christian West:

> Whan that Aprill with his shoures soote [sweet]
> The droghte of March hath perced to the roote,
> And bathed every veyne in swich [such] licour
> Of which vertu [power] engendred is the flour;
> Whan Zephirus eek [also] with his sweete breeth
> Inspired hath in every holt [wood] and heeth
> The tendre croppes, and the yonge sonne
> Hath in the Ram his half cours yronne [run],
> And smale foweles maken melodye,
> That slepen al the nyght with open ye [eye]
> (So priketh hem nature in hir corages [hearts]),
> Thanne longen folk to goon on pilgrimages,
> And palmeres for to seken straunge strondes
> [seek foreign shores],

To ferne halwes, kowthe in sondry londes
    [faraway shrines, known in various lands];
And specially from every shires ende
Of Engelond to Caunterbury they wende,
The hooly blisful martir for to seke,
That hem hath holpen whan that they were seeke
    [who helped them when they were sick].

Chaucer's representation of the seasons combines various written traditions (the classical, the scientific, the natural-philosophical, the courtly French, as well as the paraliterary tradition of manuscript illustration) in a complex mixture, as Rosemond Tuve has demonstrated at length, and other critics have insisted that his representation here of seasonal change is verisimilar to boot.[51] This passage employs eloquent, highly poetic diction, making use of the conventional discourse of mythology; even as it thus places itself in a long classical and medieval literary tradition, and specifically locates itself among literary works (such as the *Roman de la rose* and Guido delle Colonne's *Historia destructionis Troiae*) that lavishly detail the coming of spring, it appeals to local experience of dry winters, wet springs, and farming chores.[52] This representation of general vernal awakening negotiates literary tradition with realism, linking humans on the one hand with the spiritual and, on the other, the material realms.

Given the density of its cultural reference, it is a remarkably structured passage, and not only syntactically: humans are located by a network of binary oppositions structuring the world that both produced and is produced by the *Tales:* April/March, summer/winter, masculine/feminine, active/passive, desire/inertia, fecundity/barrenness, generative/nongenerative, sky/earth, spiritual/physical, knowledge/the unknown, outside/inside, public/private, health/illness, local/national.[53] The mention of St. Thomas à Becket implies, as well, a contrast between tyranny/good governance (Henry II/holy subject Thomas).[54] And, of course, those who go on pilgrimages are implicitly contrasted with those who willfully do not, thus suggesting an opposition between orthodoxy and Lollardy. A large cultural paradigm, governing the cycle of the seasons, the energies of animal life and human labor, the dynamics of human community formation and of spiritual development, is specified in that firs stance in which masculine pierces feminine to the root.

Several recent commentators have remarked on the intense r culinization of spring fecundity in these lines.[55] And by the late-fourteenth century there was a long and varied tradition of sexualizing the coming of spring as a masculine/feminine event: not only does Lucretius draw on a concept of the generative union of father ether with mother earth, but a text in the pseudoscientific tradition closer to Chaucer's rendering in these lines, the *Secretum secretorum*, develops an elaborate allegorical image: in spring, "þe erthe holy takys his worschippe and fairhede, and bycomes as a fair damoysele, a spouse semly dighte of ryche ornements and dyuers colours, to be shewyd to men yn þe feste of weddynge" ("the earth wholly receives its honor and fairness, and becomes as a fair damsel, a spouse beautifully adorned with rich ornaments and various colors, to be shown to men in the wedding feast").[56] The *Riverside Chaucer* in fact reduces the multivalence of the Middle English when it glosses "his" in the first line only as Modern English "its." Of course, Middle English has no "its"; "his" is the third-person masculine as well as neuter possessive adjective, and it is clear that even in some definitely gendered contexts (such as the *Secretum* passage just quoted) the masculine gender value of the possessive adjective "his" may not be activated. But the whole context of personification here in the General Prologue ("Zephirus eek with *his* sweete *breeth*," "the *yonge* sonne / Hath in the Ram *his* half cours yronne") provides generous evidence for a reading of Middle English "his" not only as modern English "its" but "his" as well.[57]

A penetrative act that fosters generation is imaged in the inaugural moment of the *Canterbury Tales*. The liquor whose virtue rises and engenders the flower is, in the *Secretum secretorum*, the "moistures" that rise to make the greenery grow; here, the earthly moisture is from April's rain baths, whose force through the green fuse drives the flower.[58] This rain is generative (it is its "vertu" of which "engendred is the flour"), and April's piercing the earth with showers is an act which links humankind to the cycle of nature: not only is it the case that when this happens folks' longings arise; but further, April's piercing the earth with showers is the principle of all generation. This fecundating masculine act, performed on the feminine surface, is associated with the positive poles of those binary oppositions: desire, for example, and health, knowledge, public space, spiritual life. The act thus can be understood as the expression of a sexuality if we understand sexuality as the large cultural structure that locates the individual in relation to his or her desire. This act is, I argue, heterosexual, and normative heterosexuality in Chaucer's *Tales* is built up of this complex web of cultural relations that structures and locates individual subjectivity—as, conversely, these binary relations are "ineffaceably marked," to use Eve Kosofsky Sedgwick's elegant phrase, by normative heterosexuality in this work.[59]

The traditional figure of generation is of course Natura, well known to Chaucer most immediately through both Alain de Lille and Jean de Meun. In works of both authors Natura is garrulous, and in both *De planctu Naturae* and the *Roman de la rose* her ultimate message of proper human reproduction is somewhat tempered, if not ironically undercut, by her language and the whole literary project in which she is embedded. In the *De planctu* she both decries figurative language as sodomitical and uses it to make her case against sodomy; in the *Rose* she is part of a narrative which plays out a pleasurable conflict between a literal (masculine-masculine) erotic plot and an allegorical (masculine-feminine) plot, and thus, as Simon Gaunt writes, "challenges the repressive binary structure that subordinates nonheteronormative sexualities to a heterosexual matrix."[60] Chaucer's masculinizing the coming of spring here draws in the main on traditional materials that diverge from this tradition of figuring Natura, as I suggested above, but Chaucer's literary representation cannot entirely obviate the pervasive traditional associations of the femininity of Natura—and of the same-sex relations she in turn has not been able to extirpate.[61]

The celebrated General Prologue lines are voiceless, and the magisterial diction of that sweeping single sentence, without any "he said" or "I said," creates a silent authority of and for the text. This grand passage naturalizes a normative heterosexuality that is dialectical and wide-ranging, whose operations seem both cosmic and inevitable. It is no surprise, then, that these are the most famous of Chaucer's lines—Chaucer, who is himself revered for his generative powers, critically constructed as the father of English poesy.[62] These lines contribute to the scholarly establishment of a tradition of English literature consonant with larger heterosexualized literary structures: literary production itself has been construed as a heterosexual act, a masculine act of signifying performed on a feminine surface, and I have argued elsewhere that Chaucer makes extensive and creative use of that paradigm.[63] Literary history, too, has been written—by Harold Bloom, notably—as a heterosexual family romance, the poet seeking to couple with the Muse his mother, his place to be in turn usurped by his poet-son.[64] Less ostensibly oedipally but with notable similarities, literary history has been seen as a struggle of virility, only the strong surviving: the critical construction of Chaucer over the years has occurred at Gower's expense; while the two were seen early on as poetic equals, Gower later was feminized as Chaucer's poetic manliness grew.[65]

And yet a sodomitical shadow—in the figure of the feminized man—haunts even that bright heterosexualized tradition. The silent authority of normative heterosexual relations in the first eighteen lines is interrupted not only by the voice of the pilgrim narrator in the heterogeneous tavern world of the lines that follow, but also by the murmurs and echoes of the very oppositions that structure those normative relations—especially all that is *unkynde*.

The Most Abandoned

But given the text's ostensible emphasis, it is no surprise, either, that critics have rather routinely interpreted the *Canterbury Tales* as being structured in a major way by marriage. Early in this century, in a vastly influential argument whose effects are still widely (and especially pedagogically) felt, the august Chaucerian George Lyman Kittredge, apparently following Eleanor Prescott Hammond, analyzed the *Wife of Bath's Prologue* and *Tale* and tales following the Wife's as the Marriage Group, and various critics after him have extended this group to include just about all of the *Tales*.[66] Let me pause to consider in some detail Kittredge's reading, because I want to demonstrate how heterosexuality has configured this formative critical approach and what it might as a consequence have left out. Heterosexuality as a powerful norm introduced by the opening lines provides the critic a means of interpreting the *Tales* that follow; it is a hermeneutic whose surface accidents might be historicizable but whose substantial core is assumed by the critic to be transhistorical, according to which events and characters are rendered intelligible or unintelligible. Thus the language of normativity organizes Kittredge's reading: the Wife of Bath's tone, for example, is "frankly sensual,—unmoral, if you like,—but too hearty and too profoundly normal to be unwholesome." [67] Kittredge understands the Wife's desires and therefore knows how to put her in her place. She even can be associated with heresy (her two heretical doctrines, he comments, without further elaboration, are that "Human nature [rather than celibacy] is good enough for her," and that "the wife is the head of the house"), and she scandalizes, "of course," both Parson and Clerk with these beliefs.[68] Yet her recognizable zest and joviality overwhelm any grave threat or confusion that she might pose; her particular vigor is understood and deemed normal. "The Wife is an heresiarch after her own boisterous fashion," Kittredge writes. "She is not to be taken too seriously, but she deserves a rebuke." [69]

If the Wife of Bath's profound normality is worthy of Kittredge's note, there must be a contrasting figure of profound abnormality applying some pressure somewhere. Kittredge never describes the Pardoner's person—a notable omission, since he refers to the physicality of many of the other pilgrims—but he does make the Pardoner's exceptional status clear: "The most abandoned character among the Canterbury Pilgrims is the Pardoner"; he is their "one lost soul." [70] "Abandoned" by whom? Not Kittredge himself, who valiantly and at length tries to make sense of the Pardoner's performance. He famously describes that puzzling moment at the end of the Pardoner's performance—in which the Pardoner finally recommends *Christ's* real, not his own fake, pardons after he has gloated proudly over his own pardons, and then just as suddenly offers to the pilgrims his own pardons again—as a "paroxysm of agonized sincerity" that comes out of nowhere, "suddenly, unexpectedly, without an instant's warning." [71] The Pardoner's lines about Christ's pardon are part of an outburst that remains unclearly motivated for Kittredge. It is, I argue, a strange—queer—moment in which the character (crucial to Kittredge's dramatic reading) in fact breaks the formal boundaries established by the fiction.[72] This is a break hard to account for when the formalism of the *Canterbury Tales* (with its tales within tales within tales) requires identifiable and coherent entities as tellers—requires discrete bodies, not weird parasites and fragments; this break can make little sense when the *Canterbury Tales* is understood uncritically to have featured heterosexuality as its major organizational category. In this latter view, formalism and heterosexuality are mutually necessary and supportive.

Kittredge tries hard to make some sense of the Pardoner, but ends up performing interpretive contortions to account for his behavior. He describes first that "paroxysm," then, further, a "wild orgy of reckless jesting," then finally "another revulsion of feeling" in the last moments of the Pardoner's performance when "words stick in his throat."[73] The critic's phrases ring with sexual undertones as they trace an arc of spasm ("paroxysm") and "orgy," then "revulsion" as something sticks in the throat. Even given that some of his language has dated—so that "Dykes" on the next page of *Chaucer and His Poetry*, or "ejaculation" in the *Atlantic Monthly* version of this argument, do not have ready sexual connotations—the cumulative force of Kittredge's analysis of the Pardoner suggests a forbidden yet fascinating sexual experience rendered homophobically. And like the discourse of normalcy, the discourse of sincerity—"agonized sincerity"—cannot fail to be hetero-logical here: the Pardoner's only *normal* moment is that agonized one; all else is false. It seems that according to Kittredge the Pardoner's dedication to performance (his "histrionic temperament") is an index of the lostness of his soul.[74]

One might argue at this point that Kittredge could have known no better, and that analyses of the presumptive heterosexuality and even homophobia structuring his interpretive models are uninteresting blanket condemnations, routine activist gestures that miss the point of his century-old critical innovations. It is important, however, to insist on this heterosexist presumption because, as I stated above, Kittredge's criticism is still the basis of much teaching of Chaucer.[75] Further, the hints of homophobia in his reading (published in 1893 in the *Atlantic Monthly*, and carried into the 1914 lectures published in *Chaucer and His Poetry*) resonate with stereotypes and conceptions of sexual "queerness" circulating at the time he developed it. Thus a brief suggestion toward historicization of Kittredge's criticism can demonstrate some particularities of this heterosexism and homophobia, and show that other literary models of reading were available in his own day.

Kittredge's suggestion of something forbidden yet fascinating in the Pardoner's performance (in the 1893 *Atlantic Monthly* article, a reading adapted in the later lectures) may in fact echo something of his own early writing. As an undergraduate, Kittredge penned much journalism for the *Harvard Advocate*, which he edited in his senior year; it is useful to look at these light pieces for the kinds of cultural impresses that might have shaped Kittredge's later critical readings.[76] More likely than a direct or precise correspondence is a shared discourse of gendered and sexual peculiarity in Kittredge's discussion of Chaucer's Pardoner and in his creative reportage eleven years earlier, while a Harvard undergraduate, of the notoriously disastrous visit to Boston of Oscar Wilde.

In this short article for the *Harvard Advocate* (3 February 1882), Kittredge assumed the point of view of "an imaginary 'giddy girl,' " as his biographer calls it, remarking to an unheard interlocutor on the scene at the Music Hall. She has a naive, heterosexual eye: "Oh! Here the Harvard boys come! What a lot of them! Some of them are real handsome, too. Don't think so? Well, *I* do." There is plenty of Yale comparison, through the girl's reporting on her cousin Tommy ("[H]e's at Yale, you know"), though she herself comprehends none of it. She's equally out of it concerning the audience around her: "Oh! But see that pretty girl with the big hat in the midst of those Harvard boys! I should think she would be ashamed of herself, so there! Hear the people applaud her. What a brazen thing she must be! What? *She* a boy? One of the boys from Cambridge dressed up like a girl? Dear me, I did n't [*sic*] think of that." But—after some confusion with pronouns ("But what a pretty girl she makes. See the airs he puts on")—she does catch the affinity between the boy in flamboyant drag and Wilde himself: "Oh! Now he's chaffing the Harvard boys. See how they blush! All but that girl,—she's taking notes." Wilde that night was dressed in formal evening wear; he had been touring the United States appearing in knee breeches, which had caused a hostile stir; according to Kittredge's biographer, in Boston that night Wilde "outwitted the Harvard students who marched into the hall wearing knee breeches and languidly gazing at sunflowers. Wilde shifted from knee breeches to conventional evening dress and noticed with amused condescension those in the attempted travesty, who after the lecture had to travel back to Cambridge, in their knee breeches, through the snow." Wilde's knee breeches had been savaged in public and in the press on this American tour, and the giddy girl shares that negative public opinion on his aestheticism.[77] "Oh! Here's Oscar at last. What a funny-looking man. But where are his knee-breeches? Frightened out of wearing them by the Harvard boys, I do believe. Why, if they kept on, they might frighten him into common sense." The British man, affectedly dressed, without common sense—like the Pardoner, whom Kittredge described later as "so lacking in common sense"? [78] The Pardoner, dressed "al of the newe jet" (1.682), with that "voys . . . smal" (1.688), whose self-described "handes" and "tonge goon so yerne [eagerly]" (6.398)—like Oscar Wilde? "What a poor little voice Oscar has. He can't begin to fill the hall with it. And how unhappy he looks, too. And how funny he talks, and how queerly he makes his mouth go." The naive, satirized girlish voice seems to comprehend nevertheless the real importance (or, rather, lack of it) of the scene, and in the end dismisses Oscar:

> Oh dear! I'm tired. Have n't you heard enough? He does n't say anything new. He is n't half so bright in his lecture as he is in "Patience." Let's go home.
>
> And they went.

"Abandoned"? The silly, clueless feminine voice is of course one of the brunts of the satire, ordinary enough Harvard undergraduate fare; but the voice is, as well, positively invested with a certain naive truth-telling capacity that has as its major target the effeminacy and queer sensuality of Oscar Wilde. Finally, "And they went" breaks with that voice and moves into reportage; in fact the London *Daily News* received a "scurrilous" cable, hostile to Wilde, that reported that many of the audience indeed left after fifteen minutes.[79]

I have paused over this piece of Kittredgean juvenilia because it gives a vibrant sense of the atmosphere in which the critic's readings were developing. Kittredge's first teaching job, after undergraduate school, was at Phillips Exeter, whose nature as a school for "manly boys" he lauded.[80] In this overall context of masculine tutelage it might be expected, even if it is not inevitable, that Kittredge when reading the *Canterbury Tales* would be oriented by the ideology of those first eighteen lines of the General Prologue to use a normative concept of "man" in reading the *Tales,* and indeed he does. But the Pardoner's appearance itself on the pilgrimage, I argue, demonstrates the impurity of the norm, and within the confines of that norm Kittredge has a hard time interpreting the aberrant.

In dilating on the assumptions behind Kittredge's demarcation of a "Marriage Group," I am not arguing against the idea that marriage provides a powerful hermeneutic tool in the *Canterbury Tales.* It is clearly a pervasive theme and trope. Marriage, and the heterosexual relations around it, are salient, according to Pearsall, "both as a social reality and as a way of talking about the distribution of power in social relationships."[81] I don't question the importance of speaking about marriage in this text. But I do point to what such a critical focus might thereby leave out: phenomena in which Chaucer was clearly interested enough to imagine deeply and subtly.

The Pardoner Takes On a Wife

The Pardoner is on the negative or less valued side of those General Prologue binary oppositions: barrenness, for example, and nongenerativity, the physical, the unknown, illness, heresy. Perversion inheres in the normative sexuality mapped in those lines: as we saw in the last chapter, those opposites are not external to but inhere in the supposedly pure, positive concept.[82] I have demonstrated the way in which the General Prologue sets up a norm whose function is to configure the intelligible and unintelligible; but now I want to see what happens when the queer makes visible the workings of that norm, shows the unnaturalness in the bosom of the "natural," reveals the perversion at the heart of the orthodox. John Ganim has remarked on the ways in which what comes later in the *Canterbury Tales*—even in the General Prologue—provokes us to reread and reevaluate what has come first;[83] the shift from voicelessness to voiced narrative, from atopia to Southwark, lets us hear the sound of the norm working, as it were; similarly, the Pardoner's uncategorizable appearance at the end of the pilgrims' portraits makes us particularly aware of the categories that have been used up until that point in drawing them.

The Pardoner's first words on the pilgrimage (after the General Prologue description and before his own *Tale,* in the Ellesmere order) interrupt the Wife of Bath, the flamboyant and much-married *wife,* as she recounts her own "tale / Of tribulacion in mariage" (3.172–73). And those words swearingly associate her with Lollardy: " 'Now, dame,' quod he, 'by God and by Seint John! / Ye been a noble prechour [preacher] in this cas [situation]' " (3.164–65). Margery Kempe, as we'll see, is accused of preaching, an accusation that is linked with suspicions of heresy and of disruptive sexual behavior. Here in the *Tales* the discursive matrix is similar, even the same: the Wife's gender and sexual practices come to the fore as her heretical leanings are highlighted. The Pardoner protests her disruptive vision of marriage, specifically the rough use of her husband's body. She has just demonstrated familiarity with Scripture written apparently in the vernacular ("Right thus the Apostel tolde it unto me," she puts it [160]) and such ease puts her in the arena of Lollardy—as does her "preaching": Alcuin Blamires notes that "[t]he standard orthodox view of preaching held that 'no lay person or Religious, unless permitted by a Bishop or the Pope, and no woman, no matter how learned or saintly, ought to preach.' Lollards, on the other hand, challenged the licensing restriction, gave preaching a special priority, and argued that any lay Christian had the power to preach. Walter Brut . . . specifically championed also a woman's right to do so. In 1393 his submission that 'women have power and authority to preach and make the body of Christ' provoked elaborate refutation." [84] The archness of her interchange with the Pardoner is explicable in this context: put in relief by the queer, himself subject and object of heresy, the constructed and contested nature of the Wife's own heterosexuality starts to become visible. The two pose as bachelor and wife: "I was aboute to wedde a wyf," he asserts; "[W]han that I have toold thee forth my tale / Of tribulacion in mariage / Of which I am expert in al myn age," she replies, "Than maystow chese wheither thou wolt sippe / Of thilke tonne that I shal abroche" ("then you may choose whether you want to sip from the cask that I shall tap"). "[T]eche us yonge men of youre praktike" is his response (166–87).

The Pardoner's retort to the Wife leads us in a lateral contextual move to John/Eleanor Rykener's tutelage by Elizabeth Brouderer, another (probably) married woman who worked with cloth and taught that (presumably) young man about the practice of love, even as it leads us back into the Wife's explicit literary ancestry by recalling La Vieille, the old bawd in the *Roman de la rose* (whom the Wife virtually quotes later on, in recalling her own youth).[85] The structural connections are fascinating, and perhaps suggest the existence of a cultural constellation that merits further research—for the *Rose,* too, depicts a young masculine figure who is instructed by an experienced, feminine bawd on how to have sex like a woman. (Such a constellation may bear some discursive relation to Saint Paul's taking up, in his letter to the Romans, first women who turn from natural to unnatural sexual usage, and then men who do likewise; and it may relate as well to the early-sixteenth-century tradition of legal theorists who "contended that sodomy had begun historically with the practices of the women of Sodom and Gomorrah.")[86] Recall that La Vieille addresses her many lines to Bel Acueil, the personified aspect of receptivity—gendered masculine—of the feminine beloved: the old woman is advising *him* on how to get men and their money—how to act, dress, make love like a woman. She advises false hair, cosmetics, deceptive dressing as well as proper feminine hygiene, to "hide any defect she knows of"; she instructs in how to laugh and cry, how to disport oneself at table (which manners the Prioress in the General Prologue, that other woman who acts like a woman, gets from the old dame); she recommends faking orgasm when necessary.[87] "[T]eche us yonge men of youre praktike" insists that gender and sex are performances, not only in explicit prostitution but also in more apparently normative settings: La Vieille indeed suggests that all sexual behavior is a performance, since there is nothing but treachery and trickery on all sides. And the context of male-male sex provides a particularly pointed occasion in all three of these instances further to denaturalize—to queer—gender and sex.

Like Elizabeth Brouderer, like La Vieille as well, the Wife of Bath knows how to exploit gender, to make it work for her. The observation that the Wife's heterosexual subjectivity is an act suggests that it is produced in and by discourse—and this is something she seems to have some awareness of and some limited ability to manipulate.[88] Her *Prologue* is a veritable analysis of the constitution of the female heterosexual subject in and by late-fourteenth-century culture in England. Normative female sexual behavior is a contested territory in the Wife's *Prologue,* inculcated on the one, negatively restrictive hand, by orthodox biblical exegesis (since Christ went to only one wedding, at Cana, so the proper Christian only marries once [9–13]), traditional clerkly antifeminism (women's love is like fire: the more it burns, the more it desires to consume everything [373–75]), and age-old antimatrimonialism (a wife destroys her husband from the inside, as a worm does a tree [376–77]), and by the discourses of daily life, on the other, positively reinforcing, hand, including astrology (609–18), economics ("Wynne whoso may, for al is for to selle" [414]), and "dames loore" (old wives' tales [e.g., 575–76]). Discourse that blurs these negative and positive poles is found here as well: while Lollards exhort widows to remarry and (by implication) engage in lawful sexual relations, they do so (as I suggested in the last chapter) because they believe that self-restraint is impossible—especially when delicious drink is involved; thus the Wife's assertion, "For al so siker as cold engendreth hayl, / A likerous mouth moste han a likerous tayl" ("For as surely as cold engenders hail, / A lecherous mouth must have a lecherous tail" [465–66]). The Wife appropriates exegetical discourse (e.g., 158–60), rejects clerkly misogyny (e.g., 346–47), craftily deploys heretical concepts (e.g., 26–29),[89] masters customs in her community (e.g., 1.449–52), features her own sartorial style (e.g., 559), and structures the story of her life as a contemporary romance narrative. Such contestatory discursive fields constitute the Wife's subjectivity, and, as I have argued before, she mimics and turns them to her own ends, to achieve erotic and domestic satisfaction.[90]

But those ends, as I have contended, turn out to be much less subversive of gender and sexual norms than might be expected from the sheer vehemence of her autobiographical *Prologue.* And since those norms remain the same for Lollardy and orthodoxy, as I have demonstrated in the last chapter, her associations with heresy do not place her in the margins of the pilgrimage or serve to render her illegible in the ways they do the Pardoner. The Wife's associations with Lollardy are finally very difficult to pin down: she is on a pilgrimage, after all; she swears, too; she seems to have been characterized initially as protesting against Lollards, in the Man of Law's endlink. But I maintain that she remains legible not because her associations with Lollardy are not strong but because they *are,* and because those attitudes toward femininity are the same as orthodoxy's. Thus here, as in the Eleventh of the Lollard *Twelve Conclusions,* in regard to women, the divide between orthodox and Lollard is observably less fundamental than the one between masculine and feminine.

And these conventional gender values inform sexual relations in the Wife of Bath's performance. Indeed, romance narrative at the very end of her *Prologue* provides her with the final ideological resolution of the competing discourses I listed above: she ends with the assertion that she was "as kynde [to her husband] / As any wyf from Denmark unto Ynde, / And also trewe, and so was he to me" (823–25), this mutual affection and the vast geographical span of that assertion invoking romance. In her use of it, romance provides the literary form of and for finally resolved heterosubjectivity; it is one major narrative form whose ostensible task is to promote some version of heterosexuality against all odds: not only the sword-bridges and perilous beds, but also the homosexual potential of bonds between men and plots between women imperil heterosexual fulfillment. It is not inconsiderable that the Wife uses romance in her tale, too—as I shall detail in a minute—to elaborate her explication of the "natural" relations between men and women (she is "kynde" to her husband), and thus to facilitate the emergence of a unified, resolved feminine subject.

Not only are feminine gender and desire discursively produced—and revealed as such—in the Wife's *Prologue;* the body is discursively produced, too, *as* "the body." One of the profoundest insights into the constructed nature of the normative heterosexual subject comes from the Wife's comments on the creation and function of "membres . . . of generacion" (116) in her *Prologue.* She sees clearly that "clerkes" construe body parts according to their own dried-up clerkly desires; and since clerks were the ones producing the official anatomies and learned descriptions, their allegation that genitals are merely for purging and discriminating male from female seeks indeed to establish "the body" as pleasureless, nonreproductive, and altogether asexual. The Wife, in opposition to this outlook, is eager to propound that genitals must be for generation—for, as she puts it, "*ese* / Of engendrure" ("*ease* of generation" [127–28, my emphasis]), for the ready yoking of male and female together. What the Wife reveals here is that "the body" itself is a contested interpretive collation—articulated by either clerks or wives, each with differing agendas—of various and disparate corporeal parts. Thomas Laqueur has demonstrated vividly the early anatomists' masculinizing vision of the female body; but Chaucer's analysis of the production of the medieval body goes even further: he has the Wife naturalize "the body" as specifically *heterosexual*, arguing as she does in the voice of common sense, of "experience."[91] The force of this naturalization is felt when the Pardoner, with his apparently deviant body and desire confounding the fundamental categories of the natural, breaks in not long after.

"Abyde!" (169) is what the Wife says to the effeminate, perhaps castrated Pardoner—and she goes on, apparently unfazed, to tell her story.[92] But it is crucial that the "naturalness" of the heterosexual body be restored after the infectious influence of the queer, and thus the production of a normative, married feminine body becomes the ultimate achievement of the Wife of Bath's *Tale:* "Cast up the curtyn, looke how that it is" (1249), says the hag-turned-lovely-bride triumphantly at the denouement of the romance. "It" is a body transformed from foul to fair, possible now to look upon and touch because of the husband's duly granting "maistrie" to the wife (a "maistrie" that seems mainly to allow her to be true to him): that is, only in the space of heterosexual relations, the binary of masculine and feminine, can this body become speakable, tolerable, something to behold and embrace: "For joye he hente [took] hire in his armes two" (1252).

Comparison with other Middle English analogues of the Loathly Lady tale reveals the notable concentration in Chaucer's version on the masculine/feminine binary of marriage. Three other Middle English versions (Gower's tale of Florent, *The Weddynge of Syr Gawen and Dame Ragnell*, and *The Marriage of Sir Gawaine*) elaborate the basic plot in ways that emphasize familial, rather than marital, contexts.[93] In all these versions the blame for the lady's enchantment is placed on her stepmother; this is a traditional feminine antipathy, which tradition works to keep women away from one another (especially when they seem almost to be amorous rivals, as apparently in *The Marriage of Sir Gawaine*). Sibling relations enter into the narrative in both *The Weddynge* and *The Marriage*, as the knight challenging King Arthur to find out what women want most is revealed to be the loathly lady's sister; parental relations figure further in Gower's tale, wherein the parents and especially the grandparent of the slain Branchus set the challenge to the offending Florent. Chaucer's Wife's version, in contrast, focuses exclusively on the sexual and marital relations between men and women, stripping away the familial contexts and even bringing out the sexual politics of Arthur's own marriage.

In rendering an image of the loathly lady herself, Chaucer's Wife simply relies on the force of the adjective "foul" to convey a sense of her repulsiveness, whereas all three other versions, as has been often noted, are gruesomely visual (and viciously misogynistic) in their descriptions. They thus make the ordering power of properly gendered heterosexual relations more acutely visible than in the Wife's more philosophical version. Gower's hag has body parts in the wrong proportions and where they shouldn't be:

> Hire Nase bass [nose low], hire browes hyhe,
> Hire yhen [eyes] smale and depe set,
> Hire chekes ben with teres wet,
> And rivelen [wrinkled] as an emty skyn
> Hangende doun unto the chin,
> Hire Lippes schrunken ben for age, . . .
> Hir front [forehead] was nargh [narrow], hir lockes hore [gray], . . .
> Hire Necke is schort, hir schuldres courbe [stooped], . . .
> Hire body gret and nothing smal,
> And schortly to descrive hire al,
> Sche hath no lith [limb] withoute a lak. (1.1678–91)

It takes the "love and sovereinete" (1847) of the knight to undo the wicked stepmother's curse—that is, to organize and fix this sagging, pinched, and in-turned corpus as a normal, recognizable (read *marriageable*) body. In the space of marriage the woman is composed.[94]

Meanwhile, back on the pilgrimage, similar forces of ordering and naturalization are at work. If his effect is shaken off by the Wife and her gender and sexuality confirmed, the Pardoner is finally silenced after his own *Prologue* and *Tale*. Consider this performance again for a moment: as Donald Howard puts it, "he role-plays himself" in his own tale.[95] He openly and with great relish demonstrates how he bilks his gullible provincial audiences with fake relics, pardons, and tricks:

> By this gaude [trick] have I wonne, yeer by yeer,
> An hundred mark sith [since] I was pardoner.
> I stonde lyk a clerk in my pulpet,
> And whan the lewed peple is doun yset,

I preche so as ye han herd bifoore
And telle an hundred false japes [jokes] moore.
Thanne peyne I me to strecche forth the nekke,
And est and west upon the peple I bekke [nod],
As dooth a dowve sittynge on a berne.
Myne handes and my tonge goon so yerne [eagerly]
That it is joye to se my bisynesse. (6.389–99)

If his masculine histrionics were evident in his interchange with the Wife of Bath, the performance he is giving of his own performances is even more perceptible here. He then delivers a sample sermon, complete with exemplum set in a Flanders that seems very much the London world of John/Eleanor Rykener, in a tavern swirling with young women and bawds; he first decries lechery, gluttony (including wine to be found in Cheap), swearing, and gambling, then moves on to a moralizing narrative about three "riotoures," sworn brothers who set out in search of Death and end up dead of avarice, having not recognized Death in the form of bushels of money. The exemplum, as Steven Kruger puts it, "deploys a common medieval constellation of ideas about male homosexuality," some of which we have seen before: "an exclusion of the female, with heterosexual behavior replaced by a homosocial parody of procreative sexuality; a failure of reading; an involvement in and debasement of body."[96] In lines that betray his fascination with the body, the Pardoner stresses digestive processes associated with overeating, recalling the deliciously fed clerics of the Lollard Third Conclusion who had to release built-up sexual energy with one another:

O wombe [belly]! O bely! O stynkyng cod [bag],
Fulfilled of dong and of corrupcioun!
At either ende of thee foul is the soun [sound]. (6.534–36)

Note the virtual equation of "bely" with "cod" (a word used at this time to denote the scrotum as well), and the consequent association of overeating and purging with sex. He continues by characterizing the ministrations of cooks in language that directly recalls the intense eucharistic debates I discussed in the last chapter, speaking of "substaunce" and "accident";[97] he thus links overeating with not only sexual activity but with the Eucharist:

How greet labour and cost is thee to fynde!
Thise cookes, how they stampe, and streyne, and grynde,
And turnen substaunce into accident
To fulfille al thy likerous talent! (6.537–40)

In the narrative context here the eucharistic references work the same kind of queasy associations with sodomy that I suggested earlier in Lollard discourse about handling the body of Christ. For the three dissolute men celebrate an inverted Eucharist of "breed and wyn" (6.797) that brings a final bodily struggle to the death, not redemption. Not merely felicitous from our point of view but perhaps an indication of the close cultural interweaving of Eucharist anxiety and sodomy anxiety is the term used when the Pardoner turns his relic-selling scam on the pilgrims: he first baits "oure Hoost" (941).

He is singled out by the Pardoner to offer tribute to his fake relics first; the Host, of whom the narrator has said, "of manhod hym lakkede right naught" (1.756), is enjoined to "offre first anon [right away], / And thou shalt kisse the relikes everychon [each one], / Ye, for a grote! Unbokele anon thy purs" (6.943–45). In the context of the Pardoner's performance, this is sexualized language, even as sodomitical associations have already been exploited by this performance. And though the Pardoner may not be explicitly soliciting the Host, the latter nonetheless responds as if he is, in his anal fantasy of shit-stained breeches and of a relic made of the Pardoner's balls. He recoils, snarling "Thou woldest make me kisse thyn olde breech, / And swere it were a relyk of a seint, / Though it were with thy fundement depeint!" (948–50) and wishing to cut the Pardoner's "coillons" off to enshrine them in a hog's turd (952–55). The first threatened queer bashing in English literature? There is nothing like this outraged diction, the images so vividly imagined, on the rest of the pilgrimage; this "felaweshipe" does touch on some low-down things in its late moments, especially in the sloppy-drunk interaction of the Cook with the Manciple, but the unique severity of response to the Pardoner is an index of the depth of the threat he poses. A threat to the Host, who will soon complain of being cowed by his brawny wife Goodelief, who demands of him, "I wol have thy knyf" (Give me your knife [7.1906]); to the pilgrimage, which proceeds toward a saint's relics whose power derives from the unitary One, the Truth;

to the tale-telling game of stories that are supposed to represent "sentence"—some wisdom, some truth—as well as provide some "solaas"; to what constitutes the "felaweshipe" as, precisely, a *body*.

The Pardoner's performance is deeply disturbing to the "felaweshipe" of pilgrims, not least because the tale he tells depicts the self-destruction of what Clanvowe would call a "curside felashipe."[98] It is not only that sworn bonds of brotherhood are broken, either, though that is frightening enough; the whole heterosexual matrix, which constitutes and locates the pilgrim fellowship as a body, itself is threatened. After the "paroxysm" that Kittredge makes much of, when the Pardoner asserts that Christ's, not his own, pardons are best, he then turns to the pilgrim audience itself and apparently tries to bilk them. When can he be believed—when he tells everyone present that he is a fraud? When he expects them to purchase his fraudulent pardon? Is he sincere when he states that Christ's pardon is best? Is that, rather, his trump card in the game he's playing? Critics have hashed out these questions time and again: he's faking there, he's being sincere here. But the queer, *always* playing a role (and thereby revealing that others do), eliminating any idea of essence, obviates all question of originality, sincerity, even truth. The creature who is uncategorizable in the binary gender terms of heterosexuality confounds these criteria of originality, sincerity, and truth because those categories are of a piece with—they draw on and entail—notions of origin, wholeness, unity, sameness, the natural, the spiritual, the true. The queer empties out the natural, the essential (those conventional foundations of representation and identity), shakes the heterocultural edifice.

The Pardoner has been viewed initially with uncertainty; when he first opens his mouth, he is repellent to the group; and at the end of his *Tale* he is enraged into silence, shunted back into the margins, having been introduced last in the General Prologue, as Donald Howard remarks, like a bad memory.[99] He is the recipient of the Host's ostensibly reparative and apologetic kiss, elaborately staged by the Knight, a kiss whose subversive sexual potential (following on what has just happened) is refused by the pilgrim community. They want now to continue on their way, laughing and playing, and wishing this, I argue, they attempt to rid themselves of such uncomfortable uncertainties as Lollard polemics and sodomitical accusations unleash.

The Pardoner continues on the pilgrimage with them, with the immediate threat of his queerness diffused by that careful kiss of peace. But if that queerness is silenced in a reimposition of heterosexual order, it is nonetheless still around and, moreover, contagious: just as John/Eleanor Rykener's interrogation has suggested the indeterminacy of male and female, at least in certain acts, and has rendered dissenters, orthodox, and London authorities interchangeable when it comes to specific anticlerical social agendas, so has the Pardoner involved the Host in vividly engaging on the level of the body—"exactly what the Pardoner stands accused of."[100] The Pardoner still walks by the side of the other pilgrims, still goes where they go; the "dilemma of reading that the Pardoner poses for the other pilgrims is never solved," as Kruger argues,[101] and the Pardoner's very person remains an unwelcome but insistent reminder of normative heterosexual unnaturalness.

(You Make Me Feel) Mighty Real

Written at about the same time in about the same milieu, each of these texts demonstrates the unnerving effects of a queer presence on structures and lives around them. What difference does it make to queer historians' projects that the deposition of John/Eleanor Rykener is a document of practice, an instrument of the legal apparatus, while the Pardoner is a fiction? What kinds of evidence does each of these texts provide for queer history? To what ends can such evidence be used? To approach these questions, I want finally to turn to Foucault's short essay, "The Life of Infamous Men." It tells us a great deal about a practice of what I call queer history.

One day in the Bibliothèque Nationale Michel Foucault came across an account in an internment register, one of two that moved him to compile what he would later call "an anthology of existences": "Jean Antoine Tousard, sent to the chateau of Bicêtre 21 April 1701: 'Apostate, friar, seditious, capable of the greatest crimes, sodomite, atheist if it were possible; this is a veritable monster of abomination that there would be less inconvenience in suppressing than in letting go free.'"[102] This, and a similar fragment, made a "physical" impression on him—as if, Foucault drily observes, it were possible to have any other kind (77 [238]). He says he has assembled these and other extremely brief fragments into a collection—"Brief lives, chanced upon in books and documents," the experience of whose narrative rapidity and factual reality is so intense one doesn't know whether it is "the vividness of the words" or "the violence of the facts" that causes such a physical stir (76 [237]). It is not that the narratives provide "lessons to contemplate," he insists, but quite the opposite, "brief effects whose force fades almost at once" (76 [237]). In fact, it is not clear to Foucault that the "intensity" he feels from these materials can be "restore[d]" (*restituer*) "in an analysis," which is why he decides on presenting the collection—"This is in no way a history book," he maintains—with a minimum of editorial intervention (77, 76 [238, 237]). These, then, are "Lives which are as though they hadn't existed, lives which only survive from the clash [*du heurt*] with a power whose only wish was to annihilate or at least to efface them, lives which only return to us through the effect of multiple chances" (81 [243]).

What is it about these "singular lives" that causes "that vibration which I feel even today" (77 [238])? That causes him to "broo[d]," "gras[p]," seek? The repeated word "intensity" provides a key. In the Deleuzian scheme operating here, "intensity . . . is in itself pure difference" (as Foucault explained it in his 1970 review of Deleuze, "Theatrum Philosophicum"); intensity does not suggest a phenomenological relation between a "unified subject" and an "originary experience," and it does not suggest a relation of resemblance or similarity between two things. Intensity is difference "that displaces and repeats itself"; it propels thought which is itself "disintegration of the subject."[103] Intensity is affect, too, and sensation, "ardor of a different kind," as Brian Massumi puts it.[104] So Foucault's sensation of intensity as he reads these documents indicates postmodern *différance* ("the multiple . . . the nomadic and dispersed multiplicity that is not limited or confined by the constraints of similarity")[105] and at the same time it indicates a connectedness, a very desubjectified connectedness, between his life and those infamous ones, all considered fragmentary. As he put it on the cover of the French edition of *Herculine Barbin*, whose 1978 publication inaugurated the series "Parallel Lives," "The ancients loved to put in parallel the lives of illustrious men; one could hear the exemplary shadows speak across the ages." Parallel lines rejoin in infinity; but the lives of such infamous men are the inverse, "lives so parallel that no one could join them."[106] They diverge off the path of infinity or eternity into obscurity. But Foucault senses his own relatedness to them: Judith Butler remarks in *Gender Trouble* on his relation to Herculine: both of them contest "the literal as such, especially as it applies to the categories of sex."[107] And as he puts it in "The Life of Infamous Men," he is "shock[ed]" by "these words and these lives"; constrained and pained as he is by various vectors of power, he feels "a certain effect mixed with beauty and fright" (78 [239]). This is the beauty and terror, perhaps, of queer community, constituted by nothing more than the connectedness (even across time) of singular lives that unveil and contest normativity. As I mentioned in my introduction, one shift of emphasis in Foucault's final works—from the end of the 1970s to his death in 1984—is precisely toward collective self-fashioning, postidentitarian self-creation such as he found in the context of gay communities in the United States.[108] So though Foucault insists that "this book will not satisfy historians" (78 [239]), it might satisfy the *queer* historian who sees that a queer history can be made of just such affective relations across time.

John/Eleanor Rykener could perhaps have been in such a collection of infamous people, and mine would be the anthologizing body feeling the vibration from the document, crossing time, religion, nation, sexuality, in making a relation to that incommensurable creature who haunts the normative fourteenth-century London household, even as I haunt the (very different) normative household in current United States culture. Rykener's interrogation would definitely qualify: among the principles of selection for his anthology, Foucault insisted "that it should be a question of personages having really existed"; and "that these narratives not simply constitute strange or pathetic anecdotes, but that in one way or another (because these were complaints, denunciations, orders or reports) they should have really taken part in the miniscule history of these existences, of their misfortune, of their rage or of their uncertain madness" (78 [239]). The Plea and Memoranda Rolls in which Rykener's deposition is recorded are records of proceedings in London city court; they not only claim evidentiary status but they also performed an aspect of the legal process itself. Rykener's collision with the London law not only produced him for later gazes, such as my own, but had an effect on the court: it resulted in this document, however inconclusive, which may have been recorded in order to mark some sort of precedent.[109] This document performed in the real of which it speaks, as Foucault put it (78 [239]).

Foucault insists, in fact, that such documents of "real existences" caught by power strike him much more intensely than any products of literature or the imagination.[110] "Therefore I banished all that which could be imagination or literature: none of the dark heroes which the latter have been able to invent has appeared to me as intense as these cobblers, these deserting soldiers, these hawkers, these scriveners, these vagabond monks, all enraged, scandalous or pitiable; and this doubtless comes from the simple fact [*seul fait*] that one knows that they existed" (78 [239]). One of Foucault's major points in this essay concerns the rise of "literature" after the seventeenth century as "part of that great system of constraint by which the West compelled the everyday to bring itself into discourse"; even though it claims to be "outside the law," saying "the most unsayable [*le plus indicible*]," "we must not forget that this singular position of literature is only an effect of a certain apparatus of power [*un certain dispositif de pouvoir*] which traverses in the West the economy of discourse and the strategies of the true" (91 [253]). Obscure lives such as those that caused that stir in Foucault's own bodily system could not, presumably, be found in such modern literature; if they could, they would not be really beyond the law, but would be only the law's ruse. His brief comments in this essay about premodern Western literature intimate that its representations gain power (exemplary force) inasfar as they depart from the commonplace — the lowly — or even the verisimilar, and thus do not engage any problematic of truth or facticity.

I imagine that Foucault would have revised his account of premodern literature in a way similar to the one in which he revised his account of premodern subjectification when he came to study it after volume 1 of the *History of Sexuality.* Even as the whole process of subjectification had to be reproblematized, so would his hypotheses, I would guess, about premodern literature vis-à-vis truth, the exemplary, and the everyday. But I think, further, with Michael Lucey, that any clear divide between even modern literature and documents is blurred in this very essay.[111] Foucault speaks of a mixture of beauty and fright born of encounters with "these words and these lives" (78 [239]; there is a similar discourse of beauty and terror in the introduction to the text of Pierre Rivière's memoir, another fragment presented without interpretation or commentary).[112] This effect of contact sounds like the experience of the literary sublime. Further, he writes that these lives themselves become "strange poems" "through I know not what accidents"—of language, of events. This is no *ordinary* modern literature, these "poems," but Foucault finds the literary term useful and somehow descriptive. Finally, at the very end of the essay, Foucault remarks that "*Manon Lescaut* recounts one of the following histories" (91 [253]). In this very cryptic final statement, Foucault might be suggesting that *Manon Lescaut* disciplined his fragmentary narrative, or he might be suggesting that the literary work somehow managed to convey the excesses and the unassimilable, the kind of vibration that the document conveyed to him in the first place. Literature, I would maintain, like the lived lives he celebrates, seems to hold out a promise of intensity even in this essay.[113]

I want finally to suggest that the materials of queer histories can be the *Cook's Tale* as well as John/Eleanor Rykener's deposition, the *Twelve Conclusions of the Lollards* as well as the texts of the Pardoner and the Wife of Bath. Rykener's document has a different status and performs a different function from the texts of the Pardoner and the Wife: s/he provoked, and altered by that very provocation, the London legal apparatus. But beyond that time and place, there is, as Foucault acknowledges and as I quoted above, "a certain equivocation of the fictitious and the real."[114] As queer historical projects aim to promote a queer future, the possibility of queernesses in the past—of lived lives or fictional texts—becomes crucial. Rykener doesn't have to function as a role model for latter-day queers, but the mere idea that such an obscure life suggests queernesses in the past makes it seem less likely that queers could ever be completely exterminated in the future—not because there is a clear continuity of deviant identities or behaviors across time, but because queernesses seem always to haunt dominant structures. Fictions as well as documents of practice can end up promoting a queer future: "The most intense point of lives, the one where their energy is concentrated, is precisely there where they clash with power, struggle with it, endeavour to utilise its forces or to escape its traps," as Foucault put it.[115] Since that power can be deployed through, or as, literature, as Foucault rightly saw, then literature can be important in the defining life struggles he describes:

the fictions of the Pardoner, the Wife of Bath, even the wife of the friend of Perkyn Revelour are valuable to queer histories in that they can be, and have been, appropriated for queer use, struggled with, performed in order to fashion queer existences now—these texts, too, end up in this way performing in the real, which they help thus recreate.

The testament of such gay writers as Allen Barnett and Robert Glück suggests that the Pardoner forms part of queer history by offering a sensible (i.e., sensation-al), appropriable discourse. He is a fictional character that can be grasped and taken beyond an immediately homophobic textual and cultural environment and put to enabling queer use as a sort of reverse discourse in a different cultural context. But each writer approaches the construction of such queer history quite differently. In Barnett's 1990 short story, "Philostorgy, Now Obscure," Preston, a gay man just diagnosed with AIDS, obsessively and therapeutically cleans out his apartment but saves his college paper on the Pardoner, whom he therein called " 'the first angry homosexual' " with " 'the first camp sensibility in English literature.' " This emphasis on the "first," plus the accompanying college paper on Walt Whitman, in addition to Preston's fervent memory of the power of eternal love in Augustine's *Confessions* and his abiding interest in etymology—securing meaning through finding roots—all suggest a kind of history that seeks in the past forebears or models for gay people today.[116] In contrast, identifying with the historical can be a way of "disorganizing" a solid self, as Robert Glück has put it. In *Margery Kempe*, his novel of queer identification with the medieval woman who appears really to have lived, Glück writes: "Margery held a mistaken belief in the value of her experience. A tradition I *can* claim as my own links me to her—of farce and uncertainty, the broad comedy of terror, the fable a community of doubt tells itself: 'The Pardoner's Tale,' the *Talmud*, *The Ship of Fools*, Kafka's slapstick, Freud's case histories, the sarcasm of Marx, Brecht, Fassbinder—"[117] Here (as I shall discuss more fully in the next chapter) Glück claims not a tradition of sexual precursors but rather a community (such as Foucault's essay suggests) of abject others—marginal, ironic, self-parodying. But in both Barnett and Glück, diverse discourses such as autobiography, fiction, sacred writings, psychoanalytic case history, and political theory, all constitute traditions that underwrite these gay American male writers. What was, and what could be thought, contribute to an expanded future of what can be thought and what can be.

What interests me most as a medievalist is that such a concept of queer histories—affective relations across time—recognizes the historical past as a vibrant and heterogeneous source of self-fashioning as well as community building. Foucault in the archive plays out a sensible relation to the past that I am intrigued by as the form and matter of queer histories, as I touch on John/Eleanor Rykener, tracking him/her as s/he was caught in the gaze of municipal power and as s/he returned that gaze; as I sense a vibration when I read of Foucault in the archive; as I am caught by the norms of my time and place and as I seek to contest that normativity by tracing other kinds of relations—not reproductive, not mimetic, but rather affective and metonymic.

Finally, then, toting his relics of lives past and flashing them before a desiring public, the Pardoner can offer an image now of the queer historian, a subject even as he is also taken as an object of queer history. I have argued elsewhere that the Pardoner is a fetishist; lacking either male genitals or masculine gender identification, fragmentary in and of himself, he plays on his audiences' desires for wholeness and unity. He offers them bits and pieces of saints, insisting on their fakeness while nonetheless believing that they can make him, and them, whole again.[118] The queer historian, as I have described him/her in my introduction, is decidedly *not* a fetishist in this way, decidedly *not* nostalgic for wholeness and unity; but s/he nonetheless desires an affective, even tactile relation to the past such as a relic provides. *Queer* relics—*queer* fetishes—do not stand for the whole, do not promise integrity of the body; they defy the distinction between truth and falsehood, as do ordinary fetishes, but they offer the possibility of a relation to (not a mirroring or completing of) something or someone that was, or that was thought, or that was specifically *prevented* from being or even being thought. Wrenched out of its context of hypocrisy and of stagnant, nostalgic longing for wholeness, the queer Pardoner's preoccupation with the matter of past lives can reinforce the queer sense of the need for and prompt the creation *not* of the kinds of books that would please "historians," as Foucault sneered, but rather of another kind of "felaweshipe" across time.

Chapter Three

Margery Kempe Answers Back

Touch is something I could never take for granted.

Leslie Feinberg, *Stone Butch Blues*

White Clothes

In a tense moment during her confrontation with the abbot, the dean, and the mayor of Leicester, an abrupt question is put to Margery Kempe. In front of a crowd so eager to gawk at her that they are standing up on stools, she has successfully confuted an accusation of Lollardy by demonstrating to the abbot and his men her knowledge of the articles of the faith and by rehearsing her orthodox belief in the Eucharist. Unconvinced and alleging hypocrisy, the mayor then takes over. His accusations that she is "a fals strumpet, a fals loller, & a fals deceyuer of þe pepyl" have provoked this trial to begin with, and at last he gets down to what seems to be the bottom line of his discomfort with her in his town: "I wil wetyn why þow gost in white clothys, for I trowe þow art comyn hedyr to han a-wey owr wyuys fro us & ledyn hem wyth þe" ("I want to know why you go about in white clothes, for I believe you have come here to lure away our wives from us, and lead them off with you").[1] How are all of these accusations—of hypocrisy, sexual deviance, heresy, sociopolitical disruption—focused by the act of wearing white clothes? And why might Margery's sartorial practice evoke the suspicion that she intends to lead wives away from their husbands and homes? I want to begin this final meditation on queerness, community, and history with a consideration of Margery Kempe's clothing, that constant issue in the *Book* that records a life at odds with most every everyday thing in late-medieval East Anglia.[2]

Margery goes dressed in this white garb—is clothed in a color that stands out from the clothes of the other bourgeois matrons and chaste women of her community and causes a continual stir—because Christ asks her to do so. White clothes are a token of the merry life above: "[Y]f ȝe clothyn me in erth, owyr Lord Ihesu Cryst xal clothyn ȝow in Heuyn" (34; "[I]f you clothe me on earth, our Lord Jesus Christ shall clothe you in heaven" [69]), she tells the bishop of Lincoln, Philip Repyngdon. These clothes mark her as Christ's own: "þu xal ben arayd aftyr my wyl" (32; "You shall dress according to my will" [67]), he commands her. Saint Bridget, one of Margery's most important holy role models, was ordered to wear clothes that she herself interprets spiritually; in Bridget's *Liber Celestis* the Virgin Mary tells Bridget, "Mi son lufes [loves] [þ]e of all his herte, and þarefore lufe þou him. Þou buse [you should] be araied with clothes of grete honeste, and I sall shewe þe what þai sall be. Þe bose [You should] haue a shirt, a cote, a mantill, a nowche [jewel] in þi breste, a crown, and shone [shoes] on þi fete."[3] But Margery understands her orders very materially. Both she and her Christ, in their more or less daily conversations, use them as a sort of bargaining chip: Christ promises to bring her safely on her pilgrimage journey to Rome and then back to England *if* she wears white clothes; and she agrees, calculating that the protection he offers will be worth suffering the discomfort of being made a spectacle. Anomalously dressed, she is visually designated "as unique," Mary Erler writes, "a woman vowed to chastity, but wearing the garments of symbolic virginity."[4] Her worries that she will therefore be called "an ypocryt"—that people will slander her because she goes "arayd on oþer maner þan oþer chast women don" (32; "dressed differently from how other chaste women dress" [67–68])—are indeed confirmed, as when an English priest sneers when she is on her pilgrimage to Rome that she "weryd white clothyng mor þan oþer dedyn whech wer holyar & bettyr þan euyr was sche" (84; "wore white clothing more than did others who were holier and better than she ever was" [120]). Her priestly supporter,

Wenslawe, then orders her to leave off the white clothes, and she obeys. Later in her narrative, however, when she again understands that the Lord wants her dressed in white, she is less confident: she requires some further indication from him (thunder, lightning, and rain) that wearing them is indeed his will; when the Lord grants her this meteorological token, "þan sche purposyd hir fullych to weryn white cloþis" (104; "then she fully resolved to wear white clothes" [141]). With increasing, recurrent hesitancy, in fact, Margery obeys his behest, for the clothing is disruptive: it is "synguler," as Philip Repyngdon remarked in refusing her request for it (35 [70]); it comes between her and a spiritual advisor (103 [140]); it costs money she does not have (104 [141]); it provokes others again and again to rebuke and shame her (e.g., 105 [142]).

And it seems to confirm suspicions of heresy. After she has been released from Leicester, she gets into hot water in York, where the archbishop sharply demands of her, " 'Why gost þu in white? Art þu a mayden?' Sche, knelyng on hir knes be-for hym, seyd, 'Nay, ser, I am no mayden; I am a wife.' He comawndyd hys mene to fettyn a peyr of feterys & seyd sche xulde ben feteryd, for sche was a fals heretyke" (124; " 'Why do you go about in white clothes? Are you a virgin?' She, kneeling before him, said, 'No, sir, I am no virgin; I am a married woman.' He ordered his household to fetch a pair of fetters and said she should be fettered, for she was a false heretic" [162]).

Hope Emily Allen's notes on Margery's white garb refer to a new sect in Europe pretending great sanctity and wearing white that had been banned from England by the king in 1399, when a great influx of adherents had arrived in Italy from France. Perhaps Margery's white clothes were considered not only sanctimonious but also something of a foreign "contagion," something she might have brought back with her from her continental travels. The spread to England of continental heresies associated with free love and promiscuity "was constantly feared by the Church and the civil authorities," as Joyce Bazire and Eric Colledge write, and such deviant sexual practices seem to have been linked to Lollardy—in Roger Dymmok's refutation of the 1395 *Twelve Conclusions* as well as in William Ramsbury's 1389 heresy trial and in *The Chastising of God's Children*.[5] Indeed, fear of the English heresy, perhaps touched as well by fear of continental outlandishness, relentlessly follows Margery.

The world's wonder at her white outfits is thus not provoked only by what they see as hypocrisy or pride, though those are constant accusations. "Her style was Lollard," as Nancy F. Partner puts it, and Lollardy, as we have observed, was associated not only with hypocrisy and pride but with disruptiveness both social and sexual.[6] Despite her ostentatious orthodoxy on theological issues and in her devotional practices—her predilection for confession alone should attest that she is not a Lollard, as should her pilgrimages and her devotion to images (e.g., 77–78 [113–14])—her other habits draw on distinctly Lollard preoccupations: her opposition to swearing, her negative view of temporal interests among religious, her familiarity with the Bible in the vernacular, her teaching (if it is not in fact preaching). The specter of the latter, a woman teaching, brings forward orthodoxy's associations of Lollardy with feminine social upheaval, as Ruth Nissé Shklar has deftly outlined them.[7] And even as Lollards were associated with deviant sexuality, so do Lollards accuse others of deviant sexual practices, as we have seen: Margery's white clothes glisten in the polemical climate of the Lollard Eleventh Conclusion, on the one hand, which accuses supposedly chaste women of having sex, and Dymmok's countercharge regarding commonness among Lollard women, on the other. Enacting her unnameable combination of orthodoxy and heterodoxy, Margery steps right into this unstable environment, and she goes some distance in exploiting that instability. I shall detail this process in a moment; first I want to consider the particular challenges to sexual categories this heretical orthodox woman poses.

The people in Lynn, her home, rebuke her not only "for weryng of hir white clothys" (105; "for wearing her white clothes" [142]), as they say, but also, in the same breath, "for sche cryed so lowde whan owr Lord ȝaf hyr mende of hys Passyon" (105; "because she cried so loud when our Lord put her in mind of his Passion" [142]). They are responding to the whole weird, disruptive phenomenon, this mother of fourteen children wearing white and reenacting with lacrimose contortions the birth and Passion of Christ.[8] Her garb signals a disjunction between her multiparous body and her virgin desire, her desire, that is, to remake her body so that she is not merely *like* a virgin. As Hope Phyllis Weissman has written, Margery's agonized weeping and writhing, first experienced in Jerusalem, constitute a spiritual labor of childbirth that seeks to undo the effects of original sin and Eve's curse; "by reexperiencing her labor pains at the scene of the Virgin's Compassion," Weissman writes, "Margery demonstrates her passage beyond Eve's biological maternity to achieve a maternity suprasexual and faultlessly pure." [9] As I shall explain in a moment, I wonder about whether she achieves such a "passage beyond." But at the least, Margery's white clothes focus the disjunct nature of her bourgeois life in Lynn: she is expected to have children while she desires to be chaste, indeed virginal, for Christ. This is a disjunction that points up paradoxes that we have seen before within Christianity, both orthodox and heretical, on the issue of sexuality.

That the normative heterosexual expectations of her community in Lynn clash with the imperatives of her own call to spirituality is the burden of her anguished interchange with Christ:

> "Lord, I am not worthy to heryn þe spekyn & þus to comown wyth myn husbond. . . . Lord Ihesu, þis maner of leuyng longyth to thy holy maydens." "Ʒa, dowtyr, trow þow rygth wel þat I lofe wyfes also, and specyal þo wyfys whech woldyn levyn chast, ȝyf þei mygtyn haue her wyl . . . for, þow þe state of maydenhode be mor parfyte & mor holy þan þe state of wedewhode, & þe state of wedewhode mor parfyte þan þe state [of] wedlake, ȝet dowtyr I lofe þe as wel as any mayden in þe world." (48–49)

> "Lord, I am not worthy to hear you speak, and still to make love with my husband. . . . Lord Jesus, this manner of life belongs to your holy maidens."
>
> "Yes, daughter, but rest assured that I love wives also, and specially those wives who would live chaste if they might have their will. . . . For though the state of maidenhood be more perfect and more holy than the state of widowhood, and the state of widowhood more perfect than the state of wedlock, yet I love you, daughter, as much as any maiden in the world." (84–85)

Christ's response here—contradicting the powerful Hieronymian tradition that tends to imply that Christ loves virgins *better* than widows or wives, a tradition that Saint Bridget's Christ follows—points directly to the difficulty of living according to the logic of degrees of perfection. How does it feel to be "less perfect," to be the wooden vessel instead of the gold or silver? [10] Bridget's teachings on marriage convey the letdown: "Virginity merits the crown, widowhood draws near to God, matrimony does not exclude from heaven" ("Virginitas meretur coronam, viduitas appropinquat Deo, conjugium non excludit a caelo").[11] Human sexuality, even the fruitful kind ("I wyl þat þow bryng me forth mor frwte" [48; "I wish you to bring me forth more fruit" (84)], says Christ to the wearily pregnant Margery), is not only a distraction (Margery would prefer to spend her time differently), but is, more problematically, a deflection of desire from its ultimate, properly heavenly goal toward earthly objects.[12]

The deeply problematic nature of desire is evident in the works of Jean Gerson, whom we have already seen (in chapter 1) facing head on the problem of involuntary nocturnal pollutions and their gender-destabilizing effects on priests. In the section "De luxuria" in his *Regulae mandatorum*, Gerson writes of the inadequacy of the sacrament of marriage in addressing desire: "Facilior est saepe ab opere carnali totalis abstinentia, sicut in virginibus viduis et aliis multis continentibus, quam modeste maritalem, copulam exercere; sicut enim febris potu, ignis flatu et pruritus attactu magis succenduntur" ("Complete abstinence from carnal acts—as in virgins and widows—is often easier than exercising conjugal rights, just as a fever by drinking, a fire by blowing, and an itch by scratching, ultimately become more inflamed"). We hear similar imagery in Gerson's protest against false visions prompted by the canonization of Bridget (perhaps Margery's closest role model), with its misogynistic linking of women's speaking and women's body: among such fantasizing women there is "the insatiable itch to see and to speak, not to mention . . . the itch to touch" ("Habet insatiabilem videndi loquendique, ut interim de tactu silentium sit, pruriginem").[13] As we have seen in relation to Lollard polemics, the particular burden imposed on women by the inadequate orthodox Christian theology of sexuality is great.

Margery's clothes function as a signal of this unlivable difficulty of contradictory imperatives and the resulting disjunctiveness between her body and her desire. As a kind of transvestism, they mark a "category crisis" of the sort Marjorie Garber analyzes in *Vested Interests*, just as John/Eleanor Rykener's clothes did a little earlier in London.[14] When we look *at*, not *through*, the mother wearing the clothes of a virgin, and when we listen to her own words about her experience as well, we perceive a creature that itself is not clearly categorizable in her community's bourgeois heteronormative terms, terms that would ease the contradictions of Christian dogma by leaving perfection to others and adjusting desires accordingly. We perceive a creature whose body does not fit her desires. We perceive, that is, a queer. And the queer allows us to recognize not only the unlivable logic of that scale of perfection, and (as John/Eleanor Rykener suggests as well) not only a fundamental similarity between orthodoxy and Lollardy concerning gender and sexuality, but even more generally the perversion within the normative: Margery's white clothes point to the disjunction in an orthodox Christianity which establishes marriage as a sacrament yet always maintains its taint, maintains that it is a perversion from the ultimately perfect perfection.[15]

"Lawful" heteronormative relations are not only a perversion, their disjunctiveness signaled by the cross-dressing virgin mother Margery. They are limited, rigid, and Margery's queerness shows this up as well: how adequate, they challenge her community to ask, are the categories we use? Who can be a virgin, who is really chaste, who is most perfect, and how can you tell? Only a woman who has never been married? never had children? whose spouse is also chaste? Can a married couple live together chastely? What manner of living is appropriate to a person who is chaste? Margery and John finally live separately because everyone suspects that a husband and wife who live together will be having sex. Community categories in Lynn, especially concerning the domicile, are narrowly defined, as Lynn Staley argues.[16] But in the spiritual realm Margery can be "a very dowtyr to me & a modyr also, a syster, a wyfe, and a spowse" to Christ; he tells his daughter that he will be as meek as a child is to its father (31; cf. also 157 [66; cf. also 196]). Margery can marry the Godhead and also be wife to the Manhood, Christ who insists that they sleep together. The Virgin Mary calls Margery her "dowtyr," and says that she is Margery's mother, lady, and mistress who will teach her (50 [85–86]). And daughter/spouse/pupil Margery is received as the mother of several priests (e.g., 96 [133]).

This is, in fact, one big queer family. As Margery maps the relationships of earthly families onto her relationships in a spiritual family, she shows up the earthly family (as she knows it) for its limitations, especially for its lack of intimacy. As David Aers puts it, "Margery's religious identity involved a *rupture* with the earthly family, an energetic struggle *against* the nuclear family, its bonds, its defences in the lay community, and its legitimating ideologies."[17] Normative family relations are apparently routinely arduous and thankless (as is her relationship with her son at the beginning of book 2), or relatively inconsequential and irrelevant to what really matters in her life (as with the other thirteen of her offspring), or distant (as in her sexual relations with her husband); when such relations of son, daughter, mother, father, brother, sister, wife are mapped by Margery onto spiritual relations, they are given a new context and their significance changes. "To a much greater degree than any other pious woman," Susan Dickman observes, "Margery was inclined to interpret her spiritual experience in social terms."[18] The normative, earthly family itself, its structure manipulating and restricting the relations of bodies, needs, and desires, appears vacant, lonely, pinched, strange, in Margery's queer mapping—just as the assumption of an accord between an individual's anatomy, desire, and community standards of behavior is foregrounded—queered—when shattered by Margery in her white clothes.

Sarah Beckwith has made a similar point about what she calls Margery's "critiqu[e]" of "the medieval family household" in the "fluid, interchangeable relationships" between Margery and Christ.[19] Christ as perfect lover wants to know Margery inside out, wants to be "homly"; "I am in þe, and þow in me" (23), he says; "I knowe þe bettyr þan þow dost þi-self, what-[þat-euyr men] seyn of þe"(48; "I know you better than you do yourself, whatever people say about you" [83]). As Sheila Delany notes, the intimacy of Margery's mundane world was so limited that she could wear a hair shirt without her husband's knowing it, and bear him numerous children, and David Aers points out that the devastating contradictions of Christian sexuality show up in this practice of self-punishment in the course of licit sexual relations.[20] But in Christ's spiritual embrace Margery's interior fire keeps revealing itself, showing itself outwardly (185 [225]).

Margery feels Christ's touch, first in sickness (she was "towched be þe hand of owyr Lord with grett bodyly sekenesse" [2; "touched by the hand of our Lord with great bodily sickness" (33)]), then, as she is restored, in her "rauysched . . . spyryt" (16; "ravished . . . spirit" [51]). Using an image that stresses the physicality of Margery's connection with Christ, an anchoress reassures the wondering Margery that she indeed sucks on Christ's breast (18 [52]). Christ himself assures her that his very hands and feet—those parts made for tactile contact—are "wretyn" (30; "written" [65]) with her (a reference to Isaiah 49.16).[21] Christ's presence in her life, his spiritual ("gostly") touch, has a physical impact on Margery, and at times becomes hard to distinguish from actual physical contact. But more on this crossing of spiritual and bodily in a minute; what I want to develop now is the effect of that touch of Christ on Margery and, as she passes it on, on her community. It takes Margery out of her everyday patterns, habits, routines into a new "manner of living."

I am going to leave aside the thorny question of whether Christ's touch can meaningfully be called "queer"—though I have already opened the issue in my discussion of the Eucharist in chapter 1—because I want to focus on human queernesses and their effects on earthly communities. I focus on Margery's as the touch of the queer, a touch showing something disjunctive within unities that are presumed unproblematic, even natural. I speak of the tactile, "touch," because I feel queerness work by contiguity and displacement; like metonymy as distinct from metaphor, queerness knocks signifiers loose, ungrounding bodies, making them strange, working in this way to provoke perceptual shifts and subsequent corporeal response in those touched.[22] Margery's effect on her community is nothing if not corporeal: her bodily presence, loud and moist with tears, constantly weighs on the narrative. Her touch, salvific at times like Christ's, is welcomed by some people around her. She kisses and embraces two leprous women, at least one of whom is entirely changed by the encounters (177 [217]); she ministers to a woman newly delivered of a child who has, like Margery years earlier, gone out of her mind—and who will not allow other people to touch her (177–79 [217–19]). Margery reports many incidents in which her whole copious manner of bodily living is praised.

But to others, whom the narrative is at pains to record again and again, as if their discomfitting is the main subject of the book, Margery is *too* bodily, *too* loud.[23] She interrupts a calm Mass, she ruins a nice meal, and her companions want to be rid of her. Appearing on her peregrinations through England and Europe in her white clothes, Margery not only refuses normative relations between body, desire, and gender, but she also suggests that others can and should as well: her Jesus claims, in fact, that many wives would like to "be as frely fro her husbondys as þu art fro thyn" (212). Thus the mayor of Leicester links white clothes to leading wives away from their husbands, away from their enforced pair bonds and only fictitiously unified lives; he might also, as Ruth Nissé Shklar has suggested, be alluding to an all-female version of Oldcastle's Lollard rebellion.[24] "Social discomfort," as Lynn Staley puts it,[25] that is, the breaking up of the comfortable unities of gender, desire, and body on which her community, its sexual norms, and its family structure are founded, is indeed the point, and Margery's the queer touch that makes it.

It Takes One to Know One, Again

Calling this life of hers *queer* allows us to focus not only on individual acts of sex/gender manipulation, but on the relationship between such acts and other kinds of social disorder in Margery's narrative. It allows us, as we return our attention to that confrontation in Leicester, to understand links between the various behaviors that are cited and acted out in Margery's interview with the abbot and mayor: she wears white clothes, she allegedly intends to lead wives away, and—one of her key rhetorical strategies—she answers back. *Answering back* functions in this context of bodily disjunctions in a particularly queer way. To observe this, let's look further at the scene in Leicester.

The atmosphere of accusations slung back and forth is the general cultural atmosphere in which Margery Kempe moves. It is the propagandistic environment I analyzed in chapter 1 in which insults fly and authority and certainty are unhinged. It is the atmosphere of the Church of All Hallows, stuffed with onlookers, when she is brought to be examined there. There is no one, after all, who can answer back quite like Margery; and answering back in the faces of her accusers is a ploy very characteristic of her style: she seizes an accusation and works it to her own advantage. Margery not only tells people off (she castigates clerks at Lambeth, for example, for swearing [36 (71)]), but she also accuses people in kind who have accused her: the archbishop of York, for example, whom we have already seen badgering her about her white clothes, continues his examination:

"I am euyl enformyd of þe; I her seyn þu art a ryth wikked woman." And sche seyd a-geyn, "Ser, so I her seyn þat ȝe arn a wikkyd man. And, ȝyf ȝe ben as wikkyd as men seyn, ȝe xal neuyr come in Heuyn les þan ȝe amende ȝow whil ȝe ben her." Than seyd he ful boistowsly, "Why, þow, what sey men of me." Sche answeryd, "Oþer men, syr, can telle ȝow wel a-now." (125)

"I am told very bad things about you. I hear it said that you are a very wicked woman."

And she replied, "Sir, I also hear it said that you are a wicked man. And if you are as wicked as people say, you will never get to heaven, unless you amend while you are here."

Then he said very roughly, "Why you! . . . What do people say about me?"

She answered, "Other people, sir, can tell you well enough." (163)

It is true that at times accusations silence her, or leave her shaken; she quakes a lot—just before this particular interchange, for example. But the general outline of this interchange with the archbishop (the accusation, the reverse accusation, and the shifting and deferral of authority) links it up with other practices Margery undertakes, practices that produce social discomfort by undoing proper Christian identity and destabilizing generally recognized authority—practices like wearing those white clothes.

Margery has been jailed by the mayor of Leicester, who, as we have seen, accuses her of being "a fals strumpet, a fals loller, & a fals deceyuer of þe pepyl" (112). She is not actually *in* jail in Leicester, as it happens; she is in custody of the jailer, in his own house, and this is for a reason that is a constant refrain in the *Book*. If she is incarcerated among men, she fears, her chastity will be at risk. The jailer, heeding her tears, takes her safekeeping upon himself. I shall take up the issue of Margery's fears of rape further on in this discussion, but I do not want to leave it here without noting that the very next chapter of Margery's *Book* (chapter 47) records in detail an attempted rape by the steward of Leicester.

The following chapter (chapter 48) records Margery's examination at All Hallows Church: the abbot of Leicester, with some of his canons, and the worthy dean of Leicester, along with friars, priests, the mayor, and many laypeople, are there to hear Margery's profession of faith. She passes orthodox muster. The mayor, "hir dedly enmy," then accuses her of dissembling, and makes further accusations too scandalous to repeat (accusations "þe whiche is mor expedient to be concelyd þan expressyd" [115; "which it is more fitting to conceal than express" (153)]). It seems likely that in these unrecorded accusations he has dilated on his previous charge that she is a "strumpet," since Margery's orthodox recitation of "þe Sacrament of þe Awter" disproves his explicit charge that she is a "loller," and since Margery responds to these unrecorded reproofs by insisting on her fidelity to her husband and to her spiritual spouse.

But it is in what comes next that things really heat up, as Ruth Nissé Shklar has observed: Margery answers back to the mayor with a complex accusation of her own.[26]

> Sir, ȝe arn not worthy to ben a meyr, & þat xal I preuyn be Holy Writte, for owr Lord God seyde hym-self er he wolde takyn veniawnce on þe cyteys, "I xal comyn down & seen," & ȝet he knew al thyng. & þat was not ellys, sir, but for to schewe men as ȝe ben þat ȝe schulde don non execucyon in ponischyng but ȝyf ȝe had knowyng be-forn þat it wer worthy for to be don. &, syr, ȝe han do al þe contrary to me þis day, for, syr, ȝe han cawsyd me myche despite for thyng þat I am not gilty in. I pray God for-ȝeue ȝow it. (116)

> Sir, you are not worthy to be a mayor, and that shall I prove by Holy Writ, for our Lord God said himself before he would take vengeance on the cities, "I shall come down and see," and yet he knew all things. And that was for nothing else, sir, but to show men such as you are that you should not carry out punishments unless you have prior knowledge that they are appropriate. And, sir, you have done quite the contrary to me today, for, sir, you have caused me much shame for something I am not guilty of. I pray God forgive you it. (153)

Margery attacks his authority as mayor as he has wielded it in her case: not even a mayor, she implies, should punish an infraction that has not been investigated and proven. Even God did not do this, and he knows everything; God did not hastily destroy the cities, Sodom and Gomorrah, without coming down to check things out: he did this to set a precedent for investigation and appropriate punishment. As we have seen above in relation to the Lollards, this is indeed the reasoning behind procedures of "general inquisition" newly instituted in 1215 which took God's approach to rumors of unnatural sex in Sodom and Gomorrah as a model.[27]

What, exactly, did the mayor accuse Margery of? Did the priestly amanuensis or Margery herself, following a long tradition we have seen in operation throughout the present book, dare not speak this sin's name? Margery's counteraccusation, with its reference to the cities, may in fact be turning an accusation of sodomy back on the accuser. But if the mayor did not insinuate anything about homosexual activities initially, his response to her countercharge might well do so now: "I wil wetyn why þow gost in white clothys, for I trowe þow art comyn hedyr to han a-wey owr wyuys fro us & ledyn hem wyth þe" (116; "I want to know why you go about in white clothes, for I believe you have come here to lure away our wives from us, and lead them off with you" [153]). The mayor might be voicing fears about what a professedly chaste woman will do—with other women, suspicions that are articulated in the Lollard Eleventh Conclusion castigating female homosexual acts as well as contraception, abortion, bestiality, and the use of sex toys among women who have taken vows of chastity.[28] Vows of chastity are no guarantee, the Lollards maintain, that sexual relations are not taking place, either among the women themselves, or with animals, or with things; the mayor might be insinuating something similar about Margery's practices in return for her allusive remark about him.

In response to this, Margery defers her answer to his question about her clothes, apparently abandoning the strategy of answering back. She prefers, she replies, to convey it to several worthy clerks, who can themselves pass on her answer to the (unworthy) mayor. But her tactic actually extends the effects of answering back, for, as she points out to these clerks, the answer to the mayor will be neither lies nor falsehood: "[3]e may seye, 3yf 3ow likyth, þat my gostly faderys byddyn me gon so [i.e., in white clothes], & þan xal 3e make no lesynggys ne he xal not knowe þe trewth" (116; "[Y]ou may say, if you please, that my confessors order me to [wear white clothes]; and then you will tell no lies, yet he will not know the truth" [154]). As we have seen, answering back with a reverse accusation raises questions of authority, even of epistemology: if I call you a sodomite, and you call me one, who has the authority to make this accusation in the first place? Who really is guilty, and how can you tell? Here, a scene of accusations, with sodomy in the air, ends in an unhinging of the opposition between truth and falsehood and a further deferral of authority that is ironically undercut by its own past: the mayor finally insists that he is not responsible for Margery's case at all, but that she must go see the bishop of Lincoln, Philip Repyngdon—the former Lollard.

Sodomy is a queer act that only hovers as an implication in this narrative, but in this polemical atmosphere of accusations that remove the very ground on which they are made, the implication will not go away (just as we saw in chapter 1): Margery knows the articles of the faith, attest the archbishop of York's clerks, "but we wil not suffyr hir to dwellyn a-mong vs, for þe pepil hath gret feyth in hir dalyawnce, and perauentur sche myth peruertyn summe of hem" (125; "but we will not allow her to dwell among us, because the people have great faith in her talk, and perhaps she might lead some of them astray" [163]) "Dalyawnce," as Wendy Harding also observes, has a sexual denotation as well as its primary meaning of spiritual conversation, and the accusation of perversion strengthens this reference here.[29] Facing the archbishop yet again, Margery is accused by his suffragan:

> "[Þ]u cownseledyst my Lady Greystokke to forsakyn hir husbonde, þat is a barownys wyfe & dowtyr to my Lady of Westmorlonde, & now hast seyd j-now to be brent for." And so he multiplyed many schrewyd wordys before þe Erchebischop,—it is not expedient to rehersyn hem. (133)

> "[Y]ou advised my Lady Greystoke to leave her husband, and she is a baron's wife, and daughter to my Lady of Westmorland. And now you have said enough to be burned for." And so he multiplied many sharp words in front of the Archbishop—it is not fitting to repeat them. (172)

In this atmosphere of ringing implication—once again, "it is not expedient to rehersyn" allegations—Margery's answering back is a brash rhetorical touch of the queer: it is repetition with a difference, an appropriation that puts the ground of the original claim into question. We saw this process in operation in the pair of Latin poems and in other paired accusations in chapter 1, and the atmosphere is very similar here. We saw, too, that John/Eleanor Rykener's deposition in chapter 2 might be using the traditional language of sodomy and of heterosexuality in order to express queer desires. Answering back here—like parody, like drag—opens the possibility of a different kind of authority and different behaviors—like wearing white clothes—that shake up the ground of traditional categories and actions. Margery wants to use her body completely differently from the (reproductive) ways expected by her community: that desire is signaled by her white clothing. Her body is for expressing a relationship with Christ: it turns the color of lead (69, 140 [105; 179]); it gets hot with the fire of love (88–89 [124–25]); it writhes and screams; it seems like it is going to tear apart from the soul (138 [177]). The author of the *Cloud of Unknowing* writes that when people mistakenly interpret the bodily as spiritual, they "reuerse hem aȝens þe cours of kynde" ("they reverse the order of nature") and the devil produces in them false sounds, smells, tastes, "& many queynte hetes & brennynges in þeire bodily brestes or in þeire bowelles, in þeire backes & in þeire reynes, & in þeire pryue membres" ("and many other strange ardours and burnings in their bodily breasts or in their entrails, in their backs and their kidneys, and in their private parts"); such people, particularly hypocrites and heretics, end up with disordered and unseemly—queer—bodily bearings, using body parts in all the wrong ways.[30] As we shall see in more detail in the next section, Margery's melding of corporeal and spiritual is enabling—her convulsions are a somatic recasting of reproduction into a labor that has spiritual force; her white clothes suggest that she can remake a relationship between body and desire; and she can answer back to those who insinuate otherwise—and yet finally limited.

Stop Your Sobbing

As scholars have demonstrated, an intricate structure of saintly repetition—*imitatio*—forms an important context for Margery's corporeal enactments. Though her spiritual imperative comes directly from God and renders her part of a larger movement in medieval spirituality that emphasizes the inner self, she nonetheless engages outer models to imitate as well.[31] Her intensely visual, even bodily meditations suggest a role-playing that, through repetition, powerfully revalues her whole bourgeois life. In that role-playing, she replays

Christ's life in hers; she replays the Virgin Mary's, too, and Mary Magdalene's, and Saint Bridget's; and she hears Christ say he has given her to others as just such an example.[32] She spreads her arms wide in her participatory drama of the Passion, imitating Christ's crucifixion. Her somatic manipulations and manifestations put her in the company of the female saints Caroline Walker Bynum has studied.[33] Margery's amanuensis becomes convinced of her genuineness once he has read the Blessed Marie de Oignies (153 [191]), and thus the recording of Margery's life might indeed be modeled somewhat by this example. So why call this life of hers *queer*?

To put it another way, when we call it saintly *imitatio*, what do we leave out? What is left out, that residue, is the leavings of categories, the queer; and queerness is just that relation of unfittingness, disjunctiveness—that uncategorizability, that being-left-out.[34] Queerness denotes a relation that can be specified in a given time and place (Margery is queer in relation to her neighbors) and can be traced across time, as I have been demonstrating in this book (Margery and I are both queer—in different ways, in relation to our very different surroundings—and are thus queerly related to one another). The rubric *queer* names disjunctiveness, both *within* her individual person (as I have argued above) and *between* her person and established social forms.[35] Among the things elided here by the rubric of saintly *imitatio* for Margery Kempe's life is the disjunctiveness of that life in relation to saintly and divine lives that she admires and emulates.[36] The rubric *queer* links various disjunct bodies and practices and allows us to analyze their relationships, as queer, to one another; it allows us, as I've said, to understand links between these various queer sex/gender manipulations, on the one hand, and social disorder, on the other.

One might point out that female saints caused plenty of disruption in their families and communities as well. Dyan Elliott remarks that "one of the functions of saints' lives is to dramatize how frequently social and celestial expectations are at variance."[37] But I want to argue that Margery doesn't—ultimately, and to her great pain—fit the saintly molds, either. They are thus useful in analyzing a horizon of her world, and they may be usefully analyzed as queer in their own worlds; but because they operate in Margery's narrative as role models, we must reckon with the lack of fit between those pious models and the untranscendent particulars of Margery's own story.

And that lack of fit is crucial. Margery may be reenacting saintly exempla, but in an oft-cited moment of competitiveness, she notes that Christ says to her that Saint Bridget never saw him as Margery herself has: the narrative focus shifts immediately from the eucharistic miracle Margery has just witnessed toward her one-upping the Swedish mystic, the language of the following passage clearly appropriating Bridget's own style.[38] Margery weeps and agonizes *more* than the apostles, *more* than the Blessed Virgin Mary, and Christ finally tells her himself to chill out. People in Lynn snarl that she hasn't been to Heaven any more than they have (11 [46]); this may be merely ungenerous backbiting from a jealous and uncharitable neighborhood, as indeed Margery sees it. So, too, may be the comments by people at a vicar's grave: "We knew hym as wel as þu," they sneer, as Margery screams uncontrollably at his death (147 [186]); mean and small-minded as well is, perhaps, a priest's refusal of the whole style of saintly *imitatio:* "Damsel, Ihesu is ded long sithyn" (148; "Woman, Jesus is long since dead" [187]), he remarks drily upon seeing her convulsed with sorrow at a pietà. Maybe they just don't get it—as when, too, they complain that "þer was neuyr seynt in Heuyn þat cryed so as sche dede" (105; "there was never saint in heaven that cried as she did" [142]) and that the Blessed Virgin didn't cry like this (164 [203]). But the Blessed Virgin may have had enough herself, when she refuses Margery's lovingly prepared "good cawdel" (195; a "good hot drink" [236]) after Christ's burial. The apostles think she is overdoing it at the Blessed Virgin's death (175 [215]). Christ tells her "Be stille" (189 [229]) at his own death.

The priest recording Margery's story worries about her practice of weeping and crying. He elaborates on this specifically, in chapter 62, where he tells of his being swayed from his belief in her by a friar's preaching against her, only to read various devotional and hagiographical tracts and understand that Margery's sobbing is not unique in Christian devotion. Lynn Staley has argued that Margery Kempe, as author, deploys in her narrative the priestly scribe as a trope to authorize her own *Book*.[39] This is an appealing and productive hypothesis, but it cannot explain little gaps in the text that suggest the priest never stopped worrying about what he suspected to be Margery's excessive devotional manner. The impact of his doubt, perhaps shaping the whole progress of Margery's narrative as he records it, is difficult to assess, but specific moments in the narrative are notably nervous. At the close of the first book, for example, the text begins to sum up her life, and it registers her uncertainty about her own experiences:

> Sum-tyme sche was in gret heuynes for hir felyngys, whan sche knew not how þei schulde ben vndirstondyn many days to-gedyr, for drede þat sche had of deceytys & illusyons, þat hir thowt sche wolde þat hir hed had be smet from þe body tyl God of hys goodnesse declaryd hem to hir mende. (220)

> Sometimes she was greatly depressed about her feelings [revelations]—when she did not know how they should be understood for many days together, because of the dread that she had of deceptions and delusions—so that she thought she wished her head had been struck from her body until God, of his goodness, explained them to her mind. (261)

But then it hesitates: "*For sumtyme þat sche vndirstod bodily it was to ben vndirstondyn gostly,* & þe drede þat sche had of hir felyngys was þe grettest scorge þat sche had in erde" (220, my emphasis; "*For sometimes, what she understood physically was to be understood spiritually,* and the fear that she had of her feelings [revelations] was the greatest scourge that she had on earth [261, my emphasis]).[40] At this final moment of book 1, the text (echoing Margery's voice? or registering the priestly amanuensis's abiding concerns?) puts in question the "bodiliness" of her understanding throughout the whole of the narrative, hesitates as to whether Margery really should have interpreted and performed her spiritual impulses so corporeally. If this is the priest himself registering his uneasiness, he would seem to be confirming that sometimes Margery's touch is too heavy, queer rather than saintly.[41]

If the voice of that final summary passage is hard to identify, Margery's own narrated voice, late in the book, makes clear the discrepancy between her practice of devotion and that of the saints: "A, der Lady," she says to the Blessed Virgin as they experience the Passion together, "how may ȝowr hert lestyn & se ȝowr blisful Sone se al þis wo? Lady, I may not dur it, & ȝyt am I not hys Modyr" (189; "Ah, dear lady, how can your heart last, and see your blissful son see all this woe? Lady, I may not endure it, and yet I am not his mother" [229]). She is not, indeed. Neither is she an apostle. Neither is she Mary

Magdalene, although both of them are described as being inflamed with love. When Christ appears on the third day after his death in Margery's Passion vision, the Magdalene takes him for the gardener:

> Mary, not knowyng what he was, al inflawmyd wyth þe fyre of lofe, seyd to hym a-geyn, "Sir, ȝyf þu hast a-wey my Lord, telle me, & I xal takyn hym aȝen." Þan owr merciful Lord, hauyng pite & compassyon of hir, seyd, "Mary." And wyth þat word sche, knowyng owr Lord, fel down at hys feet & wolde a kyssyd hys feet, seying, "Maistyr." Owr Lord seyd to hir, "Towche me not." Þan þe creatur [Margery] thowt þat Mary Mawdelyn seyd to owr Lord, "A, Lord, I se wel ȝe wil not þat I be so homly wyth ȝow as I haue ben a-forn," & mad heuy cher. "Ȝys, Mary," seyd owr Lord, "I xal neuyr forsake þe, but I xal euyr be wyth þe wyth-owtyn ende." . . . And þan þe creatur thowt þat Mary went forth wyth gret joye, & þat was gret merueyl to hir þat Mary enioyid, for, ȝyf owr Lord had seyd to hir as he dede to Mary, hir thowt sche cowde neuyr a ben mery. (197)

> Mary, not knowing who he was, all enflamed with the fire of love, replied to him, "Sir, if you have taken away my Lord, tell me, and I shall take him back again."
>
> Then our merciful Lord, having pity and compassion on her, said, "Mary."
>
> And with that word she—knowing our Lord—fell down at his feet, and would have kissed his feet, saying, "Master."
>
> Our Lord said to her, "Touch me not."
>
> Then this creature [Margery] thought that Mary Magdalene said to our Lord, "Ah, Lord, I see you don't want me to be as homely with you as I have been before," and looked very miserable.
>
> "Yes, Mary," said our Lord, "I will never forsake you, but I shall always be with you, without end." . . .
>
> And then this creature thought that Mary went with great joy, and it was a great marvel to her that Mary rejoiced for, if our Lord had spoken to her as he did to Mary, she thought she could never have been happy. (238)

Margery can't figure out how Mary Magdalene can be happy after Christ says, "Touch me not." Her Christ, unlike the Christ of the Gospel of John, doesn't go on to explain, "for I am not yet ascended to my

Father." Sheer physical withdrawal and distance obtrude in Margery's vision. Christ's aloofness in this biblical episode of his resurrection in fact posed a problem for meditators: even as Christ's assertion ("Touch me not") was interpreted by some exegetes to refer to his unity with the Father,[42] or to the limits of carnal ways of knowing and the deceptions of human experience,[43] or to his own transience, crossing between humanity and divinity,[44] other writers seem to have felt its potential harshness: following the Pseudo-Bonaventuran *Meditationes vitae Christi* (whose devotional style was deeply influential for Margery), Nicholas Love has to contradict the Scripture in order to agree with orthodox exegesis at last. Love translates the Pseudo-Bonaventure's comments on this scene:

> [Þ]ouh oure lorde so straungely as it semeþ answerede hir at þe bygin-nyng biddyng hir þat she sulde not touch him.' neuereles I may not trowe, bot þat afterwarde he suffrede hir to touch him, & to kysse boþe handes & feete, or þei departeden. For we mowe suppose & godely trowe þat siþen he wolde so affectuously & specialy after his owne modere first before alle oþere visete & apere to.' þat he wolde not þereby in any maner disturble hir or heuye hir, bot raþer in alle poyntes confort hir. And þerfore þe goode lorde þat is so benynge & ful of swetnes, namely to alle þoo, þat trewly louene him spake not to hir þe forseide wordes in straunge manere & bostesly.' bot in misterye, shewyng hir in perfite affeccion as it is seide, & willing lift vp hir herte holly to god & to heuenly þinges, as seiþ seynt Bernerde.

> [T]hough our Lord spoke to her so aloofly, as it seems, at the beginning, asking that she not touch him, nevertheless I cannot believe but that afterward he suffered her to touch him before he departed, kissing his feet and his hands. For we may suppose and goodly believe that, since he would so earnestly and particularly visit and appear to her, after his own mother, first, he would not thereby in any manner disturb or weigh her down but rather comfort her in all ways. And therefore the good Lord who is so benign and full of sweetness, and namely to all those who truly love him, did not speak the aforementioned words to her in an aloof or rude manner, but, rather, mysteriously, revealing himself in perfect affection, as it is said, and wanting to lift up her heart entirely to God and to heavenly things, as Saint Bernard said.[45]

Margery, ever after Christ's words, is marked by this visionary experience of corporeal rejection. Her text goes on:

> Þat was whan sche wolde a kissyd hys feet, & he seyd, "Towche me not." The creatur had so gret swem & heuynes in þat worde þat euyr whan sche herd it in any sermown, as sche dede many tymys, sche wept, sorwyd, & cryid as sche xulde a deyd for lofe & desir þat sche had to ben wyth owr Lord. (197)

> That was when she would have kissed his feet, and he said, "Touch me not." This creature had such great grief and sorrow at those words that, whenever she heard them in any sermon, as she did many times, she wept, sorrowed and cried as though she would have died, for the love and desire that she had to be with our Lord. (238)

"[T]ouch sets as it were a limit to knowledge" ("Tactus enim tamquam finem facit notionis"), Saint Augustine writes on this Gospel passage in the *De trinitate*.[46] But "Touch me *not*" marks the unhappy limit for Margery Kempe. It signals the limit of her saintly, mystical experience: it marks her difference from Mary Magdalene; it marks her distance from the apostles, the Blessed Virgin, Christ. "Why does the hand endeavor to examine that which is beyond its range?" ("Et manus quid explorare conatur, quod supra ipsam est?") asks Bernard of Clairvaux as he dilates on Christ's words.[47] That is not a question that would occur to Margery, because her whole style of living is based on her belief in the redemptive power of a spiritual relation with Christ which is expressed in corporeal terms. Yet there is clearly in her *Book* an unresolved tension between the spiritual and the corporeal—the greater pull (as we see in this Passion vision) going toward the bodily.[48] "Touch me not": no wonder Margery is devastated by this admonition. She is not and cannot be satisfied without touching Christ, but that *is* after all something that is beyond her range. In Jerusalem she stood on the very spot where Mary Magdalene stood when Christ asked her, "Mary, why wepyst þu?" (75 [111]). The final writing of her *Book* was begun on the day after Mary Magdalene's Day (6 [38]). But Margery's whole story is a record of her inability to will that tactile contact or accept its inaccessibility—she is unable finally to write herself out of her earthly community and into a spiritual one, just (and for the same reasons) as she is unable to remake her body as virginal again.

This "Touch me not" is the line between divine and human, registering her subjection to the material. It is the distance between the corporeal refashioning she attempts in her *imitatio* and her body as it exists in the world. She can put white clothes on and look like all the "oþer holy maydens & virgynes" dancing in Heaven (52 [88]). She can twist and turn in an enactment of spiritual childbirth. She can call upon a spiritual family in contrast to an unsatisfyingly intimate earthly one. But that body of hers remains intractably part of the earthly world and all its designs.

My point is not that the body is in itself intractable materiality; that would not take seriously the context of female saintly discourse in which Margery lived and fashioned herself. But she does experience her body as a "drag" on her spiritual possibilities (to adapt Biddy Martin's phrase to my purposes here),[49] and, moreover, the world's interpretation of her body constantly keeps its grip tight in this text. The number of times Margery fears rape, for example, is really notable, and her fears seem justified; the steward of Leicester episode (chapter 47) makes this clear. She cannot get out of the reproductive cycle without a monetary bargain with her husband, and without divine aid; and still, having gotten that divine aid, her life is constrained by her society's construction of femininity as penetrability: on her travels in book 2, when she is over sixty years old and well past her reproductive years, she does not sleep all night for fear (236–37, 241 [281, 285]).

Her body is an ill-fitting robe for her desiring soul. And cross-dress as she may, invent her own manner of living as she does, in very basic ways she still is subject to her community's standards. The female body in her world is still configured as passive material to be penetrated. Earthly kinship relations still apply pressure and exact their dues.[50] Christ's "Touch me not" is not in the first instance intended to enforce a normative heterosexuality, but it does set a limit that focuses and enforces a difference between Margery's body and what she aspires to, between Margery's body and her desires. Virginal cross-dressing, answering back, both are queer acts in the *Book*, and neither has much material effect, finally, on the expectations of her community.[51] There's always someone, in other words, who is going to say no—"don't touch me"—to the touch of the queer.

Don't Leave Me This Way

But that incommensurability between body, gender, and desire is exactly what allows Bob, the present-day narrator, to identify with Margery in Robert Glück's 1994 novel, *Margery Kempe*.[52] Bob is a San Francisco fag, and he loves too much (*MK*, 137), and the mismatch between Margery and her world is what allows him to make *her* story *his* as well. What Glück sees in Margery is excessiveness born of that disjunction—"a greed for more life" (*MK*, 6)—and he finds a culture of excess to which her story is suited: late-twentieth-century gay male America. In Bob/Margery, there is a powerful urge for sex and more sex; there is the romance of identification with a lover; there is the high camp drama of an intense love affair. Glück gets, too, what I have called the queerness of the Holy Family: not only does his Jesus act maternal ("Jesus lowered his eyes and said, 'Like a mother I give you my breast to suck'" [*MK*, 22]), as Jesus does in Margery's book, but Glück's Virgin Mary "blather[s]" on in incomprehensible fragments, leading Margery to wonder, "Is the whole family simple-minded?" (*MK*, 24).

In *Margery Kempe* an engulfing, shattering affair between Margery and Jesus is assimilated to Bob's ill-fated affair with his rich boyfriend L. The novel blends characters and voices in a postmodern narrative strategy that is, according to Earl Jackson Jr., a distinctly gay one: "[T]o the Glückian narrator, literary praxis itself is founded on a willingness for penetration, abandonment, kaleidoscopic invasion of voices, bodies, memories, fantasies, dreams, and media messages."[53] The penetration into and invasion by history here are, as well, distinctly what I call queer (thus linking gay male sexual practices to other nonnormative practices and lives), for reasons that will I hope become clear through the course of this section.

The text is woven of various narrative threads. Long passages are adapted closely from B. A. Windeatt's modern English translation of the *Book of Margery Kempe*, sometimes in more or less straightforward paraphrase, sometimes with fictionalized additions that do not appeal to any historical veracity, sometimes with specific changes that, while fictional, nonetheless resonate with historical conditions. Fictional additions run the gamut from husband John's impression of "stiff as a board" Master Allyn after dinner with him: " 'Master Allyn, Master Allyn, first you *squeeeeze* your *asshole,*' and he jerked upright" (*MK*, 30); to an elaboration of the birth of Christ to include details not in Margery's book but in other Middle English works and in received scholarly tradition, details such as two midwives who "took the liberty of confirming Mary's virginity" (*MK*, 24); to some additions that tell of sexuality in medieval England in ways close to what I have been outlining in this book. The scenes in a monastery in chapter 12 of the *Book of Margery Kempe* (where Margery accuses a monk of lechery [with wives], despair, and keeping worldly goods) and at Canterbury in chapter 13 (where she is for the first time in the narrative charged with being a Lollard) are reworked in Glück's rendition to meld heresy and sodomy in ways we have seen before: the novel adds a scene of a sodomitical encounter (plus a suggestion of heresy), makes Margery's accusation imply sodomy, and then moves to the monk's accusation of her in turn as a Lollard:

> She challenged a monk in high office in Canterbury. "Sir, I accuse you of lechery, despair, and keeping worldly goods." . . .
>
> (Three decades earlier, some men the monk met in a latrine invited him to a party. One of them had eaten a very hot meal with a lot of pepper. He asked, "Is that okay?" The monk didn't understand until he kissed the man, licked him, fucked him, found that every orifice was peppery, a prickly sensation, wildly stimulating. The man could twist into any position yet keep the monk's cock in his ass, heretic in a fire. . . .)
>
> The monk asked, "Say, with wives or single women?" He would not look at her directly.
>
> "Neither, Sir."
>
> The monk was fearful and assertive by turns. He followed Margery out. "We'll burn you, false Lollard. Here's a cartful of thorns ready for you, and a barrel to burn you with!" (*MK*, 31–32)

Another passage slyly revises the *Book's* scene of competitive mystical vision, picking up (as does the whole novel, in fact) on the sexual undertones of the Eucharist I've been suggesting: while Margery in her *Book* sees the Host fluttering in ways Jesus claims even Bridget wasn't privileged to see, in *Margery Kempe* the fluttering is the body of Christ in orgasmic spasm:

> Jesus was the world and Margery rode panting on top. . . . "I spasmed eleven times," he mused. He'd been counting absentmindedly. . . .
>
> "Be thankful, St. Bridget never saw me fluttering like a dove." (*MK*, 15; cf. 13)

Yet another passage demonstrates changes that register some big differences between the medieval and the postmodern works, differences whose problematic nature I shall suggest in a moment: the passage reworks Margery's attempted rape by the steward of Leicester ("& þan had sche meche drede & meche sorwe, crying hym mercy," etc. [*The Book*, 113]) into a scene of seduction by the mayor: "He rubbed himself and wet his lips. Margery felt giddy, that her body betrayed her by blushing" (*MK*, 111).[54]

Another thread in the narrative describes Bob's relationship with L. in the present day. But the main interest of the novel lies in the melding of the narratives, characters, and voices, most passages in Bob's voice, one in Margery's (chapter 9), others in a hybrid of those two voices: "I'm Margery following a god through a rainy city. The rapture is mine, mine the attempt to talk herself into existence" (*MK*, 13). And once the narrative assumes L.'s voice, which is assimilated to Jesus's, an exasperated, fragmented paragraph perhaps approximating "a hollow space inside meaning" that Bob reconstructs as the memory of access to Jesus's body (*MK*, 161). The articulation and collapse of characters are intricate: "Jesus's new lover brushes against me as he climbs. Now he's as young as Jesus, with soft brown curls and Jewish features as aquiline as an arrowhead. He's serious, rich, more troubled by my pain than Jesus is. He arouses me; I can't breathe thinking of them together" (*MK*, 88). Here Jesus's new lover, young and rich, is identified with L., but as he is Jewish he is identified with Bob, who, aroused by this young thing, is identified with Jesus too, having sex with the new one; Bob is also in the position of Margery, jealous of Jesus's new love.

Historical difference is, similarly, alternately registered and collapsed, and history is both incommensurate with and mimetic of our own era. "I wanted to mingle the near and distant," Glück writes, "present a jumpy, heterogeneous physical life, and assert the present, which projects in every direction" (*MK*, n.p.). Glück's Middle Ages functions in reference to the present, in ways in fact similar to those we'll see (in the coda) in Foucault's works: the era is both alterity and origin, a time different from our own and the beginning of our modernity: "Margery lived during the Hundred Years War, the collapse of feudal systems, and the plague. Towns had walls; at night the gates shut. At the beginning of modernity the world and otherworld lay in shambles. Margery was an individual in a recognizable nightmare: the twentieth century will also be called a hundred years war" (*MK*, 31). History is a teleological narrative; the passage continues: "A simpler individual, she went by her first name except once before a high court. The same individual who now disintegrates." And the development of the individual is a capitalist story: "Inner life is a kind of greed, desire a form of personal profit." The meeting of Margery and Bob consists of simultaneous movements forward and backward: "She pushes out of the flat pictorial plane into personality and suspense, illusion of escape, while I go back to the ruins of overall pattern and to the somber murmur of the already known" (*MK*, 31).

And as in Foucault's volume 1 of *The History of Sexuality* and other works, the Middle Ages seems in this novel a time in which bodies made a display of themselves and sex was not disciplined by modern power. "Mary and Joseph squatted naked, combing each other for nits, cracking lice between fingernails. Physical life was new to the gods; deity had no shame. The tips of Mary's nipples were long and Joseph's cock was a length of rotten rope below a pad of gray curls. Being human was a costume party—dressing up in flesh and blood" (*MK*, 24). Polymorphous perversity is not unique to the gods, either: "[A] peasant drove a pig from market with a goad, the peasant's alcoholic face so bright with need that Margery responded with unwilling arousal; a blind man begged on the grass; a young woman stared shyly at the retreating back of a lady with coiled yellow hair—she wanted to press that lady's low-slung breasts together and suck both nipples at once" (*MK*, 18). At this moment as they walk toward Norwich a dog is tagging alongside Jesus (who has "the forward stiff-legged gait of an athletic woman" and the clothes of a dandy) and Margery (with whom the dog senses "a gleeful camaraderie"): "When they last saw

Poochkins she was at attention, transfixed by a rib roast on a plank, eyes misty and tail rotating behind. Jesus said, 'Her hunger seems ageless' " (*MK*, 17–18). Jesus's comment here links canine appetite to a previous moment in the novel, in which Bob, fucking L., observes of his boyfriend's ass that "[i]ts hunger seems ageless" (*MK*, 9). Through a relation with the medieval, postmodern sex can move beyond the oppressive organization of modern sexuality: "The motion of his ass makes me simple" (*MK*, 9), like that "simpler individual," Margery.

Identifying with the historical story, even as its main character bursts out of her own medieval context, becomes a way not of organizing a self—as, say, John Boswell's use of history as something of a mirror would suggest—but of "disorganizing" one, as Foucault's use of the medieval suggests too.[55] Bob's identification with Margery's tale—"I push myself under the surface of Margery's story" (*MK*, 49)—recalls Foucault's writing practice, explicated in his introduction to *The Archaeology of Knowledge* ("opening up underground passages . . . in which I can lose myself"),[56] even as Bob questions the ethics of such writing: "I perform my story by lip-synching Margery's loud longing but I wonder if that visible self-erasure is just a failure to face L." (*MK*, 49).

Though I think the ethical question remains unresolved in the novel, the disorganizing function of historical identification is facilitated by the premise shared in both pre- and postmodernity that the self is textual, is a fictive creation, not an original or even an individual being. Margery's self and experience *are* her *Book* and, further, are themselves imitations of written saints' lives. (This textuality may be behind the observation that "Margery identified with fabrics" (*MK*, 8)—Latin *textus.*) Similarly, *The Book of Margery Kempe*, the medieval text, structures Bob's self and his experience of his world.[57] If you're a text, a fiction, already written, it is important nonetheless, according to Glück, not to conclude that there is thus no experience of self. He has stated in an interview with Earl Jackson Jr. that

> People often say that Margery knew [various hagiographies], and that she had organized some of her book around other books. So maybe Margery was creating a fiction in her book. That is, how much was appropriated ideas? How much did Margery live through? If she did live through them, does that mean they weren't appropriated?

EJ: Right. Because she could have lived through them because she read them, you mean.

RG: Exactly. That quandary over what experience means and how the authority, or whatever authenticates experience, runs back and forth between yourself and the world.

Glück then concurs with Jackson's formulation that "the self is . . . a collaborative effort." [58] Pre- and postmodern subjects are in this view disaggregate, indiscrete, without origin; identities are built up of crossings "back and forth between yourself and the world"—built up, that is, of relations between aspects of individual existences and other, ineluctably textual, phenomena (what Glück calls the "already-known"):[59] creatures, books, people, religions, eras. Intensities, as Deleuze and Foucault put it. Bob's queer subjectivity is built up through such cross-identifications in the realm of sexuality and gender, as they, in turn, relate to other realms: he is a man who identifies with a woman who is herself likened to a dog; a gay man who identifies with a straight woman whose experience crosses the line between spiritual and material, divine and human; a twentieth-century man who finds a relation to a medieval woman; a Jew who touches Christian myth; a writer who takes " 'The Pardoner's Tale,' the *Talmud*, *The Ship of Fools*, Kafka's slapstick, Freud's case histories, the sarcasm of Marx, Brecht, Fassbinder— " (*MK*, 82) as his own tradition. Bob's and Margery's may be "lives so parallel," just as Foucault writes on the cover of the French edition of *Herculine Barbin*, "that no one could join them"—that is, Margery's and Bob's are lives queerly related, just as are the lives of Herculine and infamous men and Foucault, so that, unlike parallel lines in infinity, and unlike the parallel lives of Plutarch, they will never meet.[60] But through such a sensation of "vibration" as Foucault discusses in "The Life of Infamous Men," a sensation of relatedness in their very isolation, their very abjection, Bob crosses lines of identification. A queer tracing a history—as Bob is tracing a history—is engaged in a process of building a self through just such crossings; and seen in this way doing queer history becomes a profound act (and future source) of subject formation.

It is at the same time a profound act of (and resource for) community building. Glück has written about his use of "real" (mostly contemporaneous) people in his narratives, stressing that he does so not only in order "to evoke the already-known, to make writing co-extend with the world and history, and also to examine the fiction of personality"; but further, in naming names, "The story floats—as gossip does—between the lives of the people who are its characters, and the lives of its readers (in that thorny field of reader/writer dynamics)."[61] The work is thus an "open form," opening the possibility of relations between characters and readers, not all of which are controlled by the writer. Connections and disjunctions are reordered. In *Margery Kempe* the Middle Ages as well as Robert Glück's present-day circle are opened up in order that the reader may establish some kind of relation to them. The social space that results is a community—of indiscrete, temporally extended, collaborative selves; such a community is contingent and finite ("A community is founded on finitude; there can be no community of immortal beings" [*MK*, 46]), and riven: "The tension between masculine-feminine and inside-outside pervades all levels of my community" (*MK*, 48). Such is "a community of doubt," constituted by a shared condition of fragmentation, nourished by "farce and uncertainty, the broad comedy of terror," and the historical-textual tradition of irony, sarcasm, and slapstick (*MK*, 82). Doubt, in fact, as Earl Jackson Jr. explains, is the wished-for "dissipation" of which belief is only "a prelude," and any lack—in the subject, in a community of such subjects—is but "a capacity for tangible ecstacy to be realized."[62]

In comments about crossing lines of identification, Eve Kosofsky Sedgwick writes in her essay "Across Gender, Across Sexuality," "For a particular gay or lesbian subject, then, to choose a figure in a different position with whom to identify even partially always has the potential of being revelatory in *some* way about *some* aspect of the positioning of the subject her- or himself: not through a vague invocation of the commonality of all people of all genders and sexualities, though that may also be at work, but through the complex and conflictual specificities of what different positionings may have in common under the contradictory definitional aegises of our century."[63] We must expand Sedgwick's important early formulation to include many different sites of identification, and when we include identification across time, we can learn "what different positionings may have in common under . . . definitional aegises" of *different* centuries, too. We learn a lot about the positioning of the postmodern novelist by his relation to a woman so queer in her own time: his queerness—his feminine maleness and his desire for transcendent being—seeks out another who crossed lines of identification. But we learn, further, about crucial differences between these two whose historical contexts, "definitional aegises," and drags on their respective significatory possibilities were so drastically different; we thus must continue to respect the queerness of queerness. The medieval of Glück's *Margery Kempe* is a time in which disaggregation, disjunctiveness, lack of unity can offer the postmodern subject an ideal, can offer a creative potential for community: "We are a village common producing images" (90), says Bob of his friends who supply him with textual bodies in which to clothe the characters who assimilate and blend into one another, whose stories, in turn, lead him into productive instability, and whose realness invites the reader into a new social space. But the disjunctiveness in and of Margery Kempe's life in her own time elicited, finally, the arresting barrier of her own Christ's "Don't touch me."

That arrest and suspension focus queer Margery's unassimilable nature. Bob, who has several times worried about the ethics of appropriation but cooled those anxieties in a sort of Barthesian bath of the writerly (*MK*, 80–81), leaves her at last "in a suspended moment," shifting into an impossible postmodern aporetic knowledge of her own textual abandonment and eventual dry-as-dust death, "comfortable for the moment—the moment that lives and dies" (*MK*, 161). But at a final point in the novel that seems to take away this delicate queer suspension and use the medieval character in a broad, essentializing way, Bob—having pushed himself under the surface of Margery's story—emerges into happy postmodern instability. While earlier he has been in anguish, complaining, "I have no position—what can *I* reject?" (*MK*, 108), finally he is triumphant: "I leave Margery in a suspended moment as the inevitability of L. subsides along with my fear of dying. I dreamt that Margery wants to see me. Who would know to pass himself off as her? Only L., I surmise, because I asked him not to contact me. Now *I* am the god of nonrelation. If he takes my place as Margery, do I take his place as Jesus? At last my position is not so fixed. I feel the anguish of rejecting him, but I'm not sure I do—a quandary of wanting and not wanting" (*MK*, 161–62). Bob's postmodern ideal, for all its brilliant queerness throughout the book, becomes at this late moment similar to the other postmodern ideals in the works of Bhabha and Foucault that totalize something, somewhere; even though Margery's unassimilable queerness is recognized, and even though her story is through the narrative allowed to go its own way while being reworked as well, Bob's final emotional settlement appears to be achieved over Margery's dead body, as it were. This abjection—not necessary to a postmodern use of history, however inevitable it might seem by this point in my inquiry—having taken place, Bob can at the last focus on the language of his story: "I want to contain my rambling story in a few words. *exult, exasperate, abandon, amaze*" (MK, 161). If "the fragment of language evokes the melancholy pleasure of a ruin," as Glück has written elsewhere, its "eternal" and "shared" qualities here are nonetheless limited at last.[64]

Absurd Projects

There's always someone who is going to say no to the queer, "don't touch me." Don't touch me, because you're sick and you'll contaminate me—such were the anxieties of the U.S. postman, for example, who refused to deliver mail to a couple with AIDS.[65] Or you'll contaminate Western civilization—such was the anxiety expressed by those cultural warriors on the national scene who wanted to eliminate queer art and queer history by, for starters, trying to defund the National Endowments for the Arts and for the Humanities.[66] I first presented these ideas about Margery Kempe's—and Robert Glück's—queer touch in an NEH summer institute at Notre Dame in 1995 entitled "Sex and Gender in the Middle Ages," just as congressional debate over the next year's budget for the Endowments was heating up—more precisely, just a week after U.S. congressman Steven J. Chabot, Republican from Ohio, ridiculed that very NEH Institute on the floor of Congress.[67] One year later, in budget negotiations for fiscal 1997, Representative John N. Hostettler (R-Indiana) took up the burden of mocking this institute, and a year after that, the institute was yet again being scorned on Capitol Hill (" 'Sex and Gender in the Middle Ages.' Boy, a burning issue in my district," sneered Representative Jack Kingston [R-Georgia]).[68] In both Chabot's and Hostettler's remarks, on which Kingston's were later based, explicit reference to contamination (used by others in the arts and humanities debates) had given way to a discourse of derision; but the underlying force of abjection — get away, don't touch me — still operated.

As I write, the debate over the Endowments has cooled, after a particularly heated period in which some members of the 105th Congress tried to reverse the course of the 104th and others stepped up the attack. (Arguments about both Endowments tended to blend together, even when just the NEH was being debated.) In 1997 alone, the Endowments were subjected to much volatile public discourse. In January 1997 President Clinton expressed support for the arts and humanities in his State of the Union speech; the President's Committee on the Arts and Humanities February 1997 report, *Creative America*, argued on the basis of public policy that federal support of the "cultural sector" is crucial; Representative John Conyers Jr. (D-Michigan) stated in March 1997, "I believe those who pursued a strategy of defunding and dismantling the NEA in the 104th Congress made a mistake"; dozens of college presidents wrote to influential congresspeople in support of federal funding for the NEH in May 1997; scores of lawmakers wrote in favor to Representative Ralph Regula, chair of the House subcommittee in charge of NEH appropriations.[69] But House Majority Leader Dick Armey pledged to end the NEA in a letter to its chair in March 1997; and Representative John T. Doolittle (R-California), brought a new twist to the debates in his April 1997 remarks, delivering the testimony of Patrick Trueman of the far-right American Family Association.[70] The following July the House indeed voted to defund the NEA; a Senate committee two days later voted to increase its 1998 budget slightly over 1997. Both Endowments managed to survive fiscal 1998 appropriations deliberations; new chairs were sworn in at both agencies, with sheer survival in Congress and recovery of some losses on the agenda.[71] With increased congressional oversight and regulation of the NEA and explicit efforts on the part of both endowments to "exten[d] the reach" of their programs (which, in this context, may be just another way of steering away from marginal subjects and viewpoints), "Congressional death squads," as Michael Bérubé called them, seem to have been at least temporarily satisfied: the Endowments' federal budgets having already been slashed drastically, moderate Republicans saved the NEA from yet another conservative Republican attack in 1998, and that same year was the first in several that saw no attempt to defund the NEH.[72]

In this section I want to consider the remarks by Representatives Chabot and Hostettler about the Notre Dame seminar, proffered in the 104th Congress, in some detail. The language, arguments, and lists marshaled in 1995 proved to be templates for congressional discussion in the following years. It is not all that common that the study of the Middle Ages is made the matter of public debate, after all, and these very public references demonstrate with unusual clarity the cultural politics of doing history at this moment in the United States. After I analyze these remarks, I shall look at the broader contexts of these attacks. And I shall ask, finally, how these ideas about queer history that I have been developing in this book can help us craft an approach to these marauding culture warriors.

As he did subsequently for the 1998 budget, Representative Chabot proposed an amendment to the 1996 House appropriations bill that would have eliminated the NEH entirely.[73] Chabot, in making his case for immediately zeroing out the NEH rather than following a proposed three-year phaseout, read a list of five projects sponsored by the Endowment as examples of its squandering ways. He began by mentioning the Conversation Kit (part of the National Conversation Project, one of the NEH's large grants) whose goal, as he put it, is "to educate the American public so we can all talk to each other." (He mentioned this project again in his 1997 statements even as he maintained that he would not waste time enumerating the "silly projects" funded by the Endowment.) This is an "absurd" way to spend tax dollars, he argued, and went on to mention other "wastes" of taxpayers' money: "[The NEH] spent $114,000 to [*sic*] Catholic University to support the preparation of a database for indexes for Gregorian chants. They spent $135,000 for 24 college teachers to travel to a summer institute to chat about sex and gender in the Middle Ages. They spent $201,000 for Laurie Conlevit of Filmmakers Collaborative for a feature length documentary of the life and world of the 18th century midwife, Martha Ballard. They gave $400,000 to Doran H. Ross at UCLA for something called the 'Art of Being Cuna,' which is an expressive culture of some islands in Panama."[74]

I take for granted the anti-intellectualism of this attack on the NEH, though the representative from Ohio made his resentment absolutely clear: "[T]he problem is not just that the NEH wastes tax dollars," he stated; "it also breeds arrogance in the culture bureaucrats who sneer at the citizens who pay the freight." From his language it is apparent that Chabot views these projects as trivial entertainments at best, ridiculous scams at worst.[75] His opening statement frames the proposal in financial terms: "Mr. Chairman, we face a lot of hard budget choices"; but the point is not ultimately a budgetary one. Chabot's rhetoric delivers the message that the NEH is a waste of money in any fiscal climate. "Now, many of these projects I am sure," he argues, "are nice to do if we have got the money to do it." "Nice," but not *important*. College teachers don't "study" or "research" the Middle Ages—in his words, they "*chat* about sex and gender," topics that thus appear not worthy of or amenable to serious study. "The Art of Being Cuna" is apparently without connection to life in the United States: it's "*something called* the 'Art of Being Cuna,'" its unfamiliarity—its foreignness—marking it as minor and irrelevant; the culture is found in "*some islands* in Panama," no matter exactly where. Preparing a database of research materials on Gregorian chants or making a film about a woman who practiced midwifery several centuries ago are activities so arcane or so marginal that Mr. Chabot considers their mere mention enough to demonstrate their absurdity. And the idea that the American public needs to spend money to learn how to talk to each other is as well, he implies, patently nonsensical.

When Representative John Shadegg (R-Arizona) proposed an amendment aimed at increasing cuts to the 1997 NEH budget in June 1996, Representative Hostettler argued in favor, returning the House discussion to the subject of the Notre Dame NEH summer institute. His tone was less measured than Chabot's, though his pseudo-budgetary rhetoric and anti-intellectualism were shared: "Mr. Chairman, how, when faced with a $5 trillion national debt that continues to grow, can we continue to spend money on projects like these: Sex and gender in the middle ages, 1150–1450. This course received $135,000. Let me give a free lesson here and save the money—there were men—and there were women. The fact that we are here today lets us assume some of them had conjugal relations." And he continues with his own waste list: "Representation of gender and sexuality in opera. This course received $34,000. There's another hint: The sopranos are usually women. The bass voices are men—no charge."[76] The next speaker in this House debate over the 1997 budget was Representative Chabot, highlighting his own list from a year earlier: the National Conversation Kit, and the "Art of Being Cuna," "And how about the $135,000 handout to a couple of dozen college professors so that they could take a summer trip to Chicago to talk about sex and gender in the middle ages?"[77] When Representative Kingston took up the topic again for the 1998 budget, his list included the same projects.[78]

What is it about "Sex and Gender in the Middle Ages" that proved so compelling to the Republican imagination? On the most practical level, the project was mentioned repeatedly because the same lists tend to be repeated year after year in these congressional debates. So let's look at that first list, Representative Chabot's 1995 waste list, to see what his five demonized projects have in common. It's easy to recognize resistance to multiculturalism, of course, and to a diversified, "PC" history. Lynne V. Cheney, former head of the NEH (to whom Chabot referred approvingly), said that the Endowment should be supporting "traditional" scholarship; what, then, could be more traditional than indexing Gregorian chants?[79] I argue that motivating this list is a thorough resistance to such ideas as those that Robert Glück bases *Margery Kempe* on—resistance to the very concepts of engagement and relation across time as well as across other divides (of gender, sexuality, religion, race, class, nationality). Because the very basic idea that history lives, that even distant and relatively unexplored times and places are relevant to twentieth-century American lives, suggests sites of cultural relation that are unpredictable, uncontrollable.[80] In the mention here of at least half of these funded projects, the possibility that we can forge dynamic relations to the past, even the distant or unfamiliar past, even if at present we cannot know where such relations will lead, is closed off; thus the deployment of very current technologies (films, databases, analyses of sex and gender) on such dead historical materials is intended to sound preposterous. This ridicule is used to reinforce an American modernity whose history is short and already known, a modernity that just doesn't inquire.[81] This American present abjects the medieval—in such manifestations as Gregorian chants—as irrelevant, by definition lifeless and inaccessible.

It is no mere coincidence that the 1995 legislative attempt on the

NEH's life occurred in the wake of two national controversies over how to teach and, indeed, how to *do* history. In his June 1996 remarks Representative Hostettler moved from deriding the NEH project on gender and sexuality in opera to objecting to the National History Standards, and in his statement in July 1997 Chabot links Hackney's Conversation Kit to the National History Standards as well. In January 1995, the newly elected Republican-controlled Senate passed a resolution (99 to 1) condemning the National History Standards, a project to create standards for teaching high school U.S. and world history that was sponsored by the NEH. Former chairs of the NEH Lynne Cheney and William Bennett appeared before a congressional subcommittee to press for the Endowment's elimination because of its role in sponsoring these history standards. Cheney had actually called the standards her "favorite grant" when she was chair of the Endowment; but after the draft volumes of U.S. and world standards were released in 1994, she stated in an op-ed piece in the *Wall Street Journal* that though "[t]he professors in charge of the project had presented the NEH with a balanced and reasonable model of what they intended to do," the resultant volumes "could not be described that way." She found them, instead, distorted and unbalanced, taken over by academic revisionism: "Imagine a version of American history in which race, ethnicity and gender provide the overriding theme. Such a telling of the American story would distort one of our country's most important contributions to the world: the unique insistence on the individual that has characterized us from the beginning."[82] Cheney as head of the NEH "pushed the history standards with the expectation that they would promote her view of history," as John K. Wilson analyzes the situation. "When the standards were finished, she was shocked to find that the process of consensus and debate had produced a document far more neutral and even-handed than she ever expected."[83]

The Senate would have none of them either, and the discourse of contamination spewed forth in condemnation in early 1995: the standards "must be recalled," urged Senator Slade Gorton (R-Washington), "like a shipload of badly contaminated food." Fears of what might be fomented by an improper view of history emerge as he characterizes as "perverted" the very idea that the standards should be a guide for teaching.[84] Cheney argued that there is not enough treatment of "things that have happened in this country that are good"; later, in the July 1995 House debate of Chabot's amendment to defund the NEH, Representative Martini pointed out that some members of Congress seem in fact to prefer to forget painful history.[85] The controversy over the standards continued: John Fonte in the *National Review* lambasted their use of the plural "peoples," and President Clinton, riding the wave, called the standards a failure. They were duly revised and rereleased in the spring of 1996; defending them, UCLA historian Joyce Appleby identified the "politics of nostalgia" behind the debate. (Lynne Cheney thought them improved, but still problematic.)[86] With the perceived "infect[ion]" of American education at stake (the image is Senator Spencer Abraham's) no federally funded Endowments, no such history standards—and soon *no history*, I argue—will prove the better option to those who prefer "a kind of Fourth-of-July historiography" to a more inclusive historical investigation. "Fourth-of-July historiography" is a phrase used by M.I.T. historian John W. Dower in another virtually concurrent national controversy over doing history—the one that erupted over 1995's Enola Gay exhibit at the federally authorized and funded Smithsonian Institution.[87] This exhibit, scheduled to appear in May of 1995, by January had provoked a congressional movement to have the museum's director fired.

The threat to the concept of an analyzable past—a living, unknown, unpredictable source—posed by such attacks functions in a general "undermin[ing]" of higher education, as John Wilson writes, and as a powerful tool in the "current corporate redistribution of wealth and organization of life" in the United States.[88] Since the NEH "is the single largest source of support for the humanities" in the United States, a point that is repeated year after year,[89] the move to eliminate it, a move that used projects such as mine to demonstrate its own necessity, must be seen as part of an effort to produce a country in which there is no troublesome humanities research. And if that effort has so far failed, the future is nonetheless curtailed. The current effort to raise private-sector funds for the NEH (by the Office of Enterprise at the NEH, created in 1996, and the new National Trust for the Humanities) links humanities research to foundations and corporations with their own agendas; "The corporations," according to one observer, "will be much more bottom-line oriented." Though "[t]he fund-raising climate is unquestionably better than it was a couple of years ago [i.e., in 1996]," as another put it,[90] the question of which humanities projects will be funded by such private-sector money or government partnerships with private institutions is still very much an open one. And when we consider, too, the chilling effect of the Supreme Court's 1998 decision to allow "general standards of decency" as criteria for federal arts funding—the effect not only on the arts, of course, but potentially on the humanities as well—there is plenty of reason to fear that queer projects in the humanities as well as the arts may not make the cut.[91]

Representative Chabot argued again and again that the federal government should not fund humanities projects and humanities research, and such an argument seems partly to have succeeded, since "[t]he push in Congress to cut the budgets of the NEH and the National Endowment for the Arts was driven partly by lawmakers' views that the government should not subsidize the arts."[92] But as I have been suggesting, Chabot's rhetoric went further: he denied the credibility or exigency of these projects altogether in his presentation as he called such expenditures "absurd." To which we might reply that *he* is absurd, a grown man who does not know the value of studying Gregorian chants. We would then set in motion the dynamics of answering back—except that there really is not any destabilization such as we have seen before. That is, *we* may have the intellectual authority to make the accusation, but he is bigger than we are—he has another kind of authority as a Republican in a Republican Congress. We can see the necessity of embedding our formal analysis of the dynamic—answering back, parody—in a context of institutional power relations. Even if Margery Kempe did have a momentary or local victory over the authority of the mayor of Leicester, for example, he remained mayor, got her out of his town, and she continued in her search for authority—one which never ceased in her lifetime. Representative Chabot's amendment was in fact defeated in July of 1995, Representative Shadegg's amendment to increase projected cuts went down in June 1996, and Chabot's amendment lost in July 1997, but the Endowments' futures remain limited.[93]

What can be done to counter the massively organized forces behind attacks on open and analyzable history, on humanities research, on higher education in general? What can we scholars, notoriously isolated, do? One intrepid medievalist, longtime SUNY history professor Bill Cook, outraged by these attacks on the NEH, ran for Congress himself in the 1998 election season. It is indeed clear that purely formal analyses will get us nowhere. But we can attempt to take up, occupy, and *use* the central—centrally abjected—position that has already been so fully appointed for us in these congressional culture wars. Even if we do not mount our own congressional campaigns, we can start to construct and draw on a queer history of answering back, of even momentary destabilizations (such as we identify in the life of Margery Kempe) to provide models of possible actions. We can make alliances across conventional boundaries. And as we try to recontextualize the debates, to empower different players and audiences, I see the necessity of doing what I am doing here: preaching to the converted.

As Tim Miller (one of the notorious "NEA Four") and David Román have written, preaching to the converted is crucial for community building.[94] Everyone reading this, I would hazard, already believes in academic freedom. But not everyone reading this, I imagine, is queer or queer-friendly. Neither is everyone, I suppose, NEH-positive, supportive of the Endowment despite all of its faults. We are all already converts to and partisans of various causes; "the converted" is never a single, monolithic category. The risks of proceeding as if it is are clearly stated by one Modern Language Association member, who complained in a letter to the *MLA Newsletter* that then-MLA President, Sandra Gilbert, was using her column therein "as a bully pulpit to castigate conservatives, or what she calls the right wing. Please be aware that there are many conservatives among the MLA membership, though such comments as [Gilbert's] may increasingly lead them to wonder why they would belong to an organization that routinely anathematizes them."[95] What my discussion here can do is point out links between *causes*—between the politics that undergird queer history, the politics that support academic freedom at all educational levels, and the politics that would preserve the NEH. We can then form a coalition of interests—taking our crossed, disjunctive, and open identities and articulating them with one another, forming a movement in which queers associate with humanities scholars, advocates of higher education ally with schoolteachers and education officials not because we recognize in these allies who we are—this is not a politics of essentialized identities—but rather, as Heather Findlay puts it, because we recognize in these others who we are *not;* Ernesto Laclau and Chantal Mouffe maintain that in any "overdetermined" social field "the presence of some in the others hinders the suturing of the identity of any of them," and, as Findlay continues, "this hindrance is the condition, not the failure, of politics."[96] Queer history, queer medieval studies, queer-friendly scholarship, the fight for preservation of funding for the humanities, the defense of open inquiry in education at all levels—each will be altered once such an articulation has taken place. Even as activism for the humanities and for higher education gains an energized contingent in queers and the queer-friendly, so queers can demonstrate the value of destabilization, disjunction, queerness in the projects that most deserve preservation and funding. And (in the spirit of Margery Kempe) all of us—not just the elect—can preach: each of us can embrace the project of building coalitions (those postmodern communities), and we can each participate in building coalitions in which such abjected figures as queers and scholars of early periods are armed and empowered in the fray of the culture wars, not merely tolerated as a liberal free-speech cause or resolutely sunk in some distant, dank past. And in defense of our united (but not necessarily unified) interests as queers, as medievalists, as proponents of queer scholarship, as humanities researchers, as advocates of higher education, and as supporters of academic freedom, we say to those who would eliminate us: *Don't touch me.*

Coda

Getting Medieval: *Pulp Fiction*, Foucault, and the Use of the Past

I'm proud of my country's past, but I don't want to live in it.
Tony Blair, in comments on a recent effort
to update Britain's image

Quentin Tarantino's Middle Ages

My title derives from some lines in a dark scene deep within *Pulp Fiction*. They are spoken by Ving Rhames acting the part of Marsellus Wallace, the big black boss presiding over the underworld of the movie—that world's heretofore unmoved mover. To this point virtually all we have seen of him is the back of the neck. Due to circumstances definitely beyond his control, Marsellus has been raped by a sadistic white southerner in an S/M dungeon; and after he has been rescued by the very man he has been chasing, Butch Coolidge (Bruce Willis), he snarls back to "Mr. Rapist," now shot in the crotch and writhing on the floor:

> I'm gonna call a coupla pipe-hittin' niggers, who'll go to work on homes here with a pair of pliers and a blow torch.
>
> (to Zed)

Hear me talkin' hillbilly boy?! I ain't through with you by a damn sight. I'm gonna git Medieval on your ass.[1]

Get Medieval. The phrase caught on like wildfire: street-smart teenage boys (the "young male viewers" whom *Variety* pegged as an obvious primary audience for this movie) could be heard in San Francisco slinging the phrase around the neighborhood; Courtney Love, speaking of her dead husband, Kurt Cobain (reluctant idol of such teenage boys), picked it up to describe how she wanted to treat his remains;[2] magazine headlines used it; *Saturday Night Live* created a skit around it; *Film Threat* magazine in early 1995 voted Ving Rhames "Bastard of the Year" for pronouncing the phrase, and noted approvingly, "Ving gets bonus points for combining the words *ass* and *medieval* in the same sentence."[3] Even after this first flush of publicity, the phrase stuck: Altoids in the spring of 1997 launched an ad campaign featuring mint-green billboards reading menacingly, "Get Medieval on Your Breath."[4] The phrase has entered American public culture. Why has it proved so popular?[5] What exactly makes it so useful? To get a clue, I want to look first at what it means in this film: why this word here? Does it perform any function other than to inflict a slight sting on the medievalist, buried in the past but finally getting out to see a movie?

The phrase is not repeated in the fast-talking film; the Middle Ages are not mentioned again. But medievalists, especially queer medievalists, instead of sinking even lower beneath the pop-culture surface, might instead conceive of ourselves as specially equipped to view this movie. With a whole armature of narratives, discourses, and images that look in fact much like *Pulp Fiction*—sodomitical insults (such as we saw in chapter 1), Arthurian romances and the discourse of normative heterosexuality (in chapter 2), Christian expressions of a desire for transcendence (in chapter 3)—we can suggest ways in which what was seen to be Hollywood's latest, from the hot-hot-hot Quentin Tarantino, turned out indeed to be an old, old story—even as the temperature around Tarantino subsequently cooled.[6] We can train our long, queer gazes on *Pulp Fiction*'s use of the medieval to understand the film's concomitant construction of the postmodern present, and to open up other options for thinking not only the past but the future. In this final chapter I play the movie's idea of the medieval off another use of the medieval—that of Foucault, whose thematic preoccupations are very similar but whose political intentions mark his radicality.

Back, then, to the dungeon. There's a lot of violence in *Pulp Fiction,* lots of gore splattered: on my count, five bodies blown away altogether onscreen, an additional three wounded, plus two others busted offscreen or in the prehistory of the narrative—not counting the casualties in this scene. Violence happens routinely; it causes practical problems ("Now you got a corpse in a car, minus a head, in a garage. Take me to it," says Harvey Keitel as Mr. Wolf, who fixes messes [128]). One hit man's qualms (in the film's last scene) cannot alter the whole moral economy: killing, maiming, and terrorizing are what happens, and they continue to happen in the in-folded narrative events that diegetically occur *after* the film's last scene.

But in the dark scene with which I began, in the dungeon-basement of the "Mason-Dixon Pawnshop," with its sadomasochism and its southern proprietors, there is what *Time* magazine, picking up on the film's priorities, called "a fate worse than death": not only rape, but, crucially, sodomitical rape.[7] Butch, having freed himself from the sadists' bonds and fleeing the perverts' pawnshop, suddenly hesitates; he decides he cannot leave Marsellus, his mortal enemy, "in a situation like that" (scr. 105), and selects the largest weapon the pawnshop has to offer in order to free his enemy from being sodomized: not the hammer, not the chainsaw, not the Louisville slugger, but a "magnificent" Samurai sword (scr. 106). After Butch stealthily returns to the basement and "THRUSTS" it into one of the brothers (scr. 107), Marsellus is freed from the other startled brother, shoots him in the crotch, and makes his medieval plans: as was the provision of a secular law in France in 1270 (discussed above, in chapter 1), the punishment for sodomy was castration for the first offense, death by fire for repeat offenders—rather like pliers and a blow torch.[8]

The sodomitical violence in this scene is different from any other violence in the film, and it calls for a different remedy: it is ritualized sexual torture, it is dark and perverse, and it must be met by a personal vengeance that is itself ritualized, torturous, dark, and perverse. This is the realm of the medieval in *Pulp Fiction:* it isn't exactly another *time,* in this movie in which time is peculiarly flattened out both by the manipulations of narrative and by the drenching of everything in postwar cinematic and pop culture references; Marsellus's line about "a pair of pliers and a blow torch" is in fact a direct quotation from the 1973 cult gangster movie *Charley Varrick*.[9] The medieval, rather, is the space of the rejects—really, the abjects—of this world. Despite the *New York Times*'s liberal claim that the film is "completely and amicably integrated," we can see what must be eliminated: sodomy, sadomasochism, southerners.[10] Even the status of black men is degraded by this scene, despite the fact that it is a black man who speaks these lines and who clearly participates in the process of abjecting those country perverts. At the end of this sequence we're left with the vision of the triumphant Butch, roaring away on the Harley owned by the homo whose medieval torture is being planned—white hypermasculine Butch, drawing on the sexually powerful look of a macho gay man but whose ass, we know for sure now, is straight, male, modern.

We might well have wondered about Butch's butthole. The film plants the doubt itself. In a scene at least one critic found gratuitous, the dream that chronologically begins his story, Butch recalls that as a young boy he was visited by a Vietnam War buddy of his father's.[11] Captain Koons, played by Christopher Walken, tells the young Butch the story of the gold watch that he is now delivering from Butch's dead father, who didn't make it out of "that Hanoi pit of hell" (67). I am always interested in what seems gratuitous in a narrative, since these are the things that, for some reason, the author simply cannot leave out. What we get here is not just a "gross-out . . . anecdote" (Janet Maslin) or a lousy "joke" (Anthony Lane); the anatomy, as it were, of male bonding—the relationship of homosocial and homosexual male relations in this movie about gangsters—is opened to view.

In a deadpan monologue, Captain Koons tells the little Butch that the watch he is being given was his "great granddaddy's war watch" from the First World War, handed down to his "granddad for good luck" in World War Two, in turn handed down to his infant father, who grew up to be "shot down over Hanoi" with the watch on his wrist: "Now he knew if the gooks ever saw the watch it'd be confiscated. The way your Daddy looked at it, that watch was your birthright. And he'd be damned if any slopeheads were gonna put their greasy yella hands on his boy's birthright. So he hid it in the one place he knew he could hide somethin'. His ass. Five long years, he wore this watch up his ass. Then when he died of dysentery, he gave me the watch. I hid this uncomfortable hunk of metal up my ass for two years. Then, after seven years, I was sent home to my family. And now, little man, I give the watch to you." (68) The captain puts a "hunk" up his ass, the same "hunk" that has been up his buddy's ass; the suggestions of sodomy are obvious. They are only suggestions, of course: the hunk is "uncomfortable," not pleasurable; there is no necessary anal contact between the giver and the receiver of the watch; and the detail about death from dysentery works hard to make the whole monologue laughably disgusting. Sodomy is only hinted at here, both suggested and at the same time deflected into a sophomoric bathroom joke.[12]

But what is explicitly confirmed in this initial scene is the centrality of the anus in male bonding, or, more precisely, in the maintenance of patriarchy: the interanal storage and bequeathal of the watch by father to son ("little man") is the monologue's focus. What is not clear is the *limit* of the uses of the anus between and among men. This is an issue obsessively raised in Tarantino's films (including the *True Romance* screenplay, *Reservoir Dogs,* and his bit part in *Sleep with Me*) but never patiently worked out.[13] In ways more superficial and conservative than in the deeper and more pointed—yet still unresolved—*Reservoir Dogs,* the whole Butch episode undertakes to limit the uses of the anus.[14] We might call this episode's project "anus-surveillance," following John J. Winkler's studies of classical Athens: sodomy, implicitly suggested and denied in the opening monologue as a possibility in male bonding, is then explicitly represented, in the pawnshop basement, as nonconsensual and violent—rape—so that it cannot be seen as in any way acceptable.[15] In this racist straight white male imaginary, sodomy puts one in the passive and feminine, which is equal to the black, position here. Sodomy is combined with sadomasochism, which figures sexual torture as an unmistakable perversion and thus safely distances the everyday torture hit men perform from any perverse desire.[16] Butch can ride off on that chopper with his French girlfriend (who insists that he give her "oral pleasure" before she does him [81])—he can even "hum[p] a hot hog," as the script puts it (109, probably referring particularly to *Deliverance*), he can look like a Castro fag, and because of these representational strategies the audience can *still* rest assured that his straight masculinity is unthreatened.[17] Earlier in the movie, the marriage of queer "love birds"—the Three Stooges—is broadcast on a TV that Lance the drug dealer is watching ("Hold hands, you love birds," we hear); but that queer parody is comfortingly replaced by the real thing now: as the final stage directions for this episode read, "the two lovebirds [Butch and Fabian [*sic*] PEEL AWAY" (scr. 111) on the chopper.

This anal surveillance project makes sense, too, of the fact that John Travolta, as Vincent Vega, spends so much time on the toilet in this movie. He misses out on crucial action twice when he goes to "take a shit" (and once when he "take[s] a piss"). This is part of the film's anal project: it is trying to reassure the (putatively straight) audience by this reminder that anuses *are* used for shitting. But that fact might not turn out to be so reassuring, after all.[18] Vince's time in the toilet has been not only useful but pleasurable—he dallies in a leisurely read of an action novel at Butch's apartment—and thus its distinction from another pleasurable use of the anus has become blurred. Shitting is problematic in this movie, as Sharon Willis has shown; just as little Butch's father is said to have died of it, Vince himself must be eliminated. He is blown apart by Butch, the film's representation of the triumph of homo/hetero distinction.

Homosexual sex *is* a constant possibility between men, Tarantino's movies affirm. In major and minor moments throughout *Pulp Fiction* the possibility of homosex is raised in an attempt to manage it—to distance and foreclose it. The attempt to construct straight white maleness and armor its body is thorough: men's bodies, black and white, must remain on guard against the possibilities of pleasurable opening.[19] But by the end of the film, one black man has been "fuck[ed] . . . like a bitch" (as Jules puts it, referring to another situation [24]); the "armour" of Vince's and Jules's black suits, as Tarantino said in an interview, has been completely stripped off and turned into "the exact antithesis—volleyball wear";[20] and Vince is a lost cause in the project of constructing masculinity. As it turns out, neither Vince nor Jules can finally survive in this world in which any play with open and shut, clear-cut, and stable distinctions proceeds according to an all-too-predictable straight white male agenda.

The medieval signals all the abjected Others of this world of *Pulp Fiction*. But as with all such abjection, the medieval inheres in the (post)modern, perversion inheres in the straight, hicks in the urban, black in white. The very postmodern *Pulp Fiction*'s concern to police the borders of male homosociality is continuous with various medieval attempts (as we've seen throughout this book) at drawing the line. Marsellus's "pipe-hittin' " city "niggers" will end up acting like the white hillbilly sadist they torture; similarly, Butch "THRUSTS" (scr. 107) his giant, uh, sword into the other homo. And shortly after he has rescued Marsellus, Butch's question sounds like a proposition: "[W]hat now, between me and you?" (108). If the medieval represents things that cannot be eradicated, despite efforts to construct something free of them—represents, that is, the impurity of these apparently pure concepts (straightness, whiteness, identity)—then "getting medieval" redoubles that impurity by making the medieval (the abject) itself a role or game. *Getting* medieval—playing in an abjected space, adopting an abjected role—doubly gets at the impossibility of absolute straightness, whiteness, modernity, of the purely dominant, of essentially *being* anything. And this condition of inessentiality, the basic condition of the impossibility of essential being, becomes an explicit fear at the film's end. It is an impossibility so thorough in this postmodern cinematic world of simulation and citation that it takes a putative miracle from God to suggest—to Jules, the hit man with qualms—any chance of being (as he puts it) "just . . . Jules . . . no more, no less" (147). *Being*, not just acting.

Jules worries, at last, about his own rituals of performance as he struggles to extract himself from a world in which he and Vince "get into character" (17) in order to stage a killing: he has been accustomed to quote a biblical text just before he blows his victims away, but what role is it, exactly, he wonders, that he has been playing in the Ezekiel verses he quotes? (157–58). That he could worry about the potential interchangeability of roles in themselves means that he must already be through with this acting and this whole world. As the character—black—in whom authenticity has been located in the film, he prefers, as he states at the end, to wander the earth "Until God puts me where he wants me to *be*" (147, emphasis added). Jules is the only one trying to opt out at this point, and the figure of Jimmie (formerly in the life and still plagued by his hit-man pal) suggests that any break Jules tries to make isn't going to be clean. Furthermore, in the racist "new world order" of this film, as bell hooks notes, the "resident black male preacher/philosopher death-dealing mammified intellectual," thus enlightened, doesn't have anywhere to go: Vince makes it clear that Jules will be a bum if he quits.[21]

Jules's is not the only response to the impossibility of true identity, of course, to simulation and roles, in this movie whose deepest (and most expensive) visual delight is the simulation of a simulated fifties diner in nineties L.A. The film revels in role-playing so deeply that its own actors refer to their earlier roles: John Travolta's dancing the twist and Christopher Walken's POW monologue are the most obvious examples. But it is crucial to remember that shaping all this reveling is the film's desire to limit what, exactly, can be performed and by whom—which roles or positions can be taken up as empowering and which ones cannot be. This is an agenda that has used Jules to articulate its own desire for authenticity, for the solid ground of being. Dennis Cooper has remarked on Tarantino's "fascination with the amoral," a fascination that is itself "moralistic." [22]

But couldn't *Pulp Fiction*, then, for all the obviousness of its asshole narrative, for all its joy in cross-race male homosociality, be pointing out and critiquing homophobia? Couldn't it be critiquing the way homophobia dissolves even racial boundaries in its corrosive patriarchal politics? Butch cannot leave the black man "in a situation like that"; sodomy is the worst thing, bar no explosive violence, in the world of this movie. Isn't Tarantino showing how absurd an attitude this is? Maybe, at times; there is certainly a send-up of *Deliverance* in this scene.[23] But with bell hooks, who has posed these questions as well, I contend that it doesn't finally *matter* if you read it that way or not, if you catch the parody or if you don't: "Yeah, like it's really funny when Butch the hypermasculine phallic white boy—who has no name that means anything, who has no culture to be proud of, who comes straight out of childhood clinging to the anal-retentive timepiece of patriarchal imperialism—is exposed. Yet exposure does nothing to intervene on this evil, it merely graphically highlights it." [24] Jules, she points out further, is not shown "grieving or seeking revenge" for Vince when he is killed: so much for enduring male bonding. And if it is a twist on the usual scenario that this black man is not eliminated, no place to which he tries to exit will have changed: as Sharon Willis remarks more mildly, "we need to entertain the possibility that *Pulp Fiction* might resecure racialized representations for a racist imaginary, even as it tries to work them loose from it."[25]

"[S]ubversive possibility" may "titillate" in a narrative sequence such as "The Gold Watch," but then "everything," as hooks observes, "kinda comes right back to normal."[26] Band-Aids will still be made in the color "flesh," like the one that sticks, gleaming, to Marsellus's black neck; and the black woman will still be a just-barely-visible phantasm.[27] White Butch and Fabian have a place to go (Bora Bora, Tahiti, Mexico? [83]) and a big bike, courtesy of a dead homosexual, to take them there. And Jules, not mourning for Vince, will wander, will have adventures, and thus will continue to represent authenticity for a sped-up dominant culture—the culture in and of this film, including the hordes of its appreciative viewers—that revels in but ultimately fears really getting medieval.

Michel Foucault's Middle Ages

The medieval; sodomy and sadomasochism in male-male relations; the desire for transcendent, essential identity: the dense cluster of themes I have been tracing is not itself unique, however startling and showy Quentin Tarantino's saturated-color, no-grain handling of it. These preoccupations are deeply intertwined in Western culture, in popular fantasy outlets as well as in more analytical and political spheres—such as in Foucault's landmark *History of Sexuality*, volume 1. The coincidence of movie and book, I contend, is not haphazard; I want to get at not only the similarities but also the very significant differences between them. In the rest of this coda I shall look closely at volume 1 of Foucault's *History* and support that look with glances at various others of Foucault's works. Generalizations about Foucault's practice of the history of sexuality in volume 1 have to be tempered by consideration of volumes 2 and 3, but I focus on volume 1 here because it has had the most impact on lesbian and gay studies to date.[28] Foucault's claims about the medieval shifted across the years of reformulating his *History of Sexuality;* and yet, as I shall argue, the pervasive political and ethical dispositions that inform these claims in volume 1 persist through his late thought. His use of the medieval—contradictory, nostalgic, and above all tactical—finds possibilities for creativity where *Pulp Fiction* has found shit.

I am walking something of a tightrope through the course of my analysis here, as I both celebrate Foucault's usefulness and critique aspects of his work. Foucault is not unassailable, a high-culture club with which I shall beat pop-culture fictions to a pulp; recalling to us the racial agenda linked to sexuality in *Pulp Fiction*, for example, Foucault in volume 1 uses various, mostly eastern civilizations—"China, Japan, India, Rome, the Arabo-Moslem societies" (57 [76])—as uniform, idealized, and unproblematically eroticized societies of the *ars erotica* in order to develop and analyze the concept of the Western *scientia sexualis*—a use so troublingly imperialist that he disavowed it later.[29] What I do want to suggest, though, is that *Pulp Fiction* takes an easy way out of the labyrinth of cultural problems it maps; it is easy at least in part because of its long history—a history that includes such essentializing and abjecting strategies as we have seen in this book but which is not inevitable, as Foucault helps us recognize. My aim is to understand how the all-too-familiar dynamics of a work like *Pulp Fiction* can be exploded and how—instead of the abjection of the past and the inessential, and the longing for pure truth—a postidentitarian and postmedieval ethos and history can be forged.

I shall begin my discussion of Foucault's use of the medieval with one of his famous claims in volume 1 of *The History of Sexuality*, the notorious historical distinction between the sodomite and the homosexual. "As defined by the ancient civil or canonical codes," he writes, "sodomy was a category of forbidden acts; their perpetrator was nothing more than the juridical subject of them." But in the late nineteenth century, Foucault maintains, there occurred "an *incorporation of perversions* and a new *specification of individuals*" (42–43 [58–59], emphasis original); and therefore follows the distinction that Foucault, as David M. Halperin has recently explained, posited in the service of his larger claims about modernity: "The sodomite had been a temporary aberration [*un relaps*]; the homosexual was now a species" (43 [59]).[30] Thus the paradoxical but thoroughly Foucauldian proclamation in Halperin's earlier, influential essay, "One Hundred Years of Homosexuality": "[A]lthough there have been, in many different times and places . . . persons who sought sexual contact with other persons of the same sex as themselves, it is only within the last hundred years or so that such persons . . . have been homosexuals."[31] (We might note that this shift finds its counterpart in a shift, at around the same time, that Foucault hypothesizes in *Discipline and Punish*, from the offender to the delinquent: "The delinquent [*le délinquant*] is to be distinguished from the offender [*l'infracteur*] by the fact that it is not so much his act as his life that is relevant in characterizing him.")[32] The historical argument about the sodomite in particular has been pursued by Alan Bray and, following him, Jonathan Goldberg, as I have mentioned in chapter 1, who contend that European Renaissance society, intensely homosocially bonded, is built not only on male social bonds but also on sexual acts unrecognized or unacknowledged as sodomy. Goldberg, in his intricate investigation of the opposition of "acts" to "identities," comments that:

> [A]lthough sodomy is, as a sexual act, anything that threatens alliance—any sexual act, that is, that does not promote the aim of married procreative sex . . . and while sodomy involves therefore acts that men might perform with men, women with women (a possibility rarely envisioned), men and women with each other, and anyone with a goat, a pig, or a horse, these acts—or accusations of their performance—emerge into visibility only when those who are said to have done them also can be called traitors, heretics, or the like, at the very least, disturbers of the social order that alliance—marriage arrangements—maintained.[33]

Thus, according to this strand of Foucauldian argumentation, men could engage in sexual relations with one another and not only did they not identify themselves as homosexuals, but the acts themselves, part of and continuous with the male-dominated structure of culture, were not even visible as sodomy unless performed in "particularly stigmatizing contexts."[34] My argument in this book has demonstrated the pervasive relation of the discourses of Lollardy and sodomy, thus confirming Goldberg's viewpoint.[35] The homosexual, in contrast, is a sexual identity deployed in the process of the subjectivation of modern individuals (the making of subjects, and their domination); in a crucial argument about the nature and operations of modern power, Foucault opposes what he calls the "repressive hypothesis" to his contention that modern power works not merely to repress—to block or negate—but to produce sex, to multiply and implant all forms of it. Modern power constitutes "sex" as the truth—

which we tell ourselves is taboo—of each individual. Thus sexual, and in particular homosexual, *identity* (though Foucault does not use this word here).

We can see the applicability of Foucault's analysis of modern homosexual identity as we consider *Pulp Fiction* once again. Though the film shows a world of male bonding (in this respect picking up from *Reservoir Dogs,* in which there are no major female characters, as well as from *True Romance* and *Natural Born Killers,* in which the female characters are not terribly nuanced),[36] sexual relations between men cannot be acknowledged as an inevitable part of the structure of that society. Thus Mr. Wolf, having detailed and begun to implement a plan to clean up a particularly bloody mess, warns everybody not to congratulate each other too soon: "[L]et's not start suckin' each other's dicks quite yet" (134), he sneers, the scorn in his statement making it clear that only homos would stop to enjoy this point, taking pleasure when it should not be taken. Homosexual relations are on the horizon of male bonding, but must be kept there. A divide must be erected and anxiously maintained; on the one side are homosexuals, those whose same-sex desires are at the center of their identities; on the other are straight men, whose absence of homosexual desire and aggressive gender style define their identities. The fact that Marsellus has participated in even forced homosexual sex acts must be hidden forever: "[D]on't tell nobody about this" (108), he orders Butch, lest he be thought a fairy.

Foucault's contrast between the sodomite and the homosexual has had a big impact on scholarly work on sexuality. It has been taken as a dictum, and scholars of early and late periods have taken up and run with it, analyzing what, exactly, sexual identity is, how it is constituted and manifested, whether or not one can indeed talk about sexuality as a constructed core of identity in premodern times. When the assertion about the sodomite has been taken to imply something about the entire premodern Western sexual landscape, the dictum has been used to authorize reductive and ignorant views of sex in the Middle Ages. In fact, as we have seen in this book, any stark historical opposition between the categories of premodern subjects of sodomitical acts, on the one hand, and modern people who are identified on the basis of sexual preference, on the other, is wrong: that is, it is clear from a number of different kinds of premodern sources (some of which we have seen in chapter 1, for example) that men who engaged in acts of male-male sex were thought to be visibly marked, known at least to others if not to themselves, grouped with others of the same kind, and defined by sexual desire. In the same chapter we have also seen that female-female sex is codified by "ancient civil and canonical codes" as sodomy, but females who have sex with other females are not (at least in the *Twelve Conclusions*) identified visibly in themselves, as a group, or by a specific desire; in other words, we see that a description of "the sodomite" that works for men does not work for women.

More on that gender dissymmetry, invisible to Foucault's analysis, in a moment. For now, we must allow that it may be, indeed, a distortion of the kinds of claims Foucault makes in this introductory volume 1 to try to fasten onto an absolute and precise historical opposition between sexual acts and sexual identities. He specifically refers in this passage to the juridical subject of ancient civil or canonical codes, thus implying that one particular discursive formation is what he is talking about at this moment; as Halperin has pointed out, Foucault is talking about a particular premodern "discursive style" of "disqualifying" male-male sex, against which he plays the modern "discursive style" of doing so (via the construction of a modern homosexual identity). Foucault does not state here that premodern people could *not* have made "connections" between "specific sexual acts and the particular ethos, or sexual style, or sexual subjectivity, of those who performed them," Halperin explains; he more simply, heuristically, suggests here that premodern ways of "regulating and delegitimating" male-male sex differ from modern ways.[37] In a later piece, a 1982 interview in *Salmagundi* in which homosexuality is discussed and references to the Middle Ages are pursued, Foucault blurs any starkly drawn opposition between sexual acts and sexual identities.[38] Certainly by that time, as Halperin contends, and witnessed most fully in the later volumes of the *History of Sexuality*, Foucault had shifted away from contrasting sodomy and homosexuality, sexual practices and categories of individuals, and toward what Halperin has summarized as "defining different historical forms of sexual experience—different ways of being, different sets of relations to others and to oneself, different articulations of pleasure and meaning, different forms of consciousness."[39]

But a sharp contrast between acts and identities is drawn, and that opposition, however heuristic, is deployed for certain *effects* in the particular paragraph in volume 1, in the whole volume, and in the later work.[40] However Foucault might have changed his mind about the history of sexuality, a contrast between acts and identities provides something of a structuring principle for Foucault's thinking about history—and about the future. Foucault in volume 1 evinces a particular desire for a premodern realm of (as he sees it) clearly apprehensible sexual acts as opposed to the hypocritical and surreptitious world of modern sexual identities. I want to look more closely at volume 1 to see, first, what kind of history this is. We can then discern carefully what the medieval is for Foucault, and understand the kind of liberatory potential that is offered by a realm of acts without essential identities—in contrast to the fear of such a realm and the desire for true being in *Pulp Fiction*.

In looking at Foucault's deployment of the Middle Ages, we must keep in mind—if it has been forgotten over the course of this book—that he refuses to write "history" as it has been traditionally formulated. In brief discussions of Foucault's treatment of the Middle Ages, what Pierre Payer has not acknowledged, and what Anne Clark Bartlett has, is Foucault's crucial and thorough assertions of his projects' difference from "history." From *Madness and Civilization* (1961) through *The Order of Things* (1966), *The Archaeology of Knowledge* (1969), and "Nietzsche, Genealogy, History" (1971), to *The History of Sexuality* (1976–84), he resists the search for determinative origins and "the discourse of the continuous."[41] Yet what makes this antihistorical perspective difficult to keep in mind is the fact that Foucault has also chosen to retain some markers placed by very conventional history, such as "medieval," "modern," and "the rise of the bourgeoisie" (not to mention eras defined by centuries); he retains as well some concepts that derive from totalizing historical analyses ("capital," for one), and some dates that are often taken by conventional historians as watersheds or as moments of origin (1215, for example, the date of the Fourth Lateran Council). That he employs these conventionally accepted historical concepts in his discussion of the repressive hypothesis—that is, that he critiques, via conventional historical markers, a conventional historical story that we moderns tell ourselves, a story that he says is not the whole truth (11)—makes his investment in "history" difficult to ascertain. But, as he put it in an interview about volume 1: "I am well aware that I have never written anything but fictions. . . . One 'fictions' history on the basis of a political reality that makes it true, one 'fictions' a politics not yet in existence on the basis of a historical truth."[42]

The History of Sexuality, volume 1, offers a vision of a future politics based on a politically "fictioned" "true" past. And as opposed to the final desire in *Pulp Fiction*, at the base of Foucault's "fictioned" politics is the *inessential* identity of its author. Foucault suggests in another introduction—this one to *The Archaeology of Knowledge*—that his writing is a kind of performance, whose gaps and lapses seek the dissolution of his own identity. This introduction clarifies Foucault's relation to historical markers: he uses them strategically to clear a space ("this blank space from which I speak") for his own project.[43] How, exactly, he uses the conventionally delineated Middle Ages in his project of disaggregating identity is the issue to which I now turn.

In volume 1 Foucault posits (by using conventional markers) two major historical "ruptures," shifts in the history of sexuality mapped, as he puts it, as the history of "mechanisms of repression": one in the seventeenth century, one in the twentieth: "The first . . . was characterized by the advent of the great prohibitions, the exclusive promotion of adult marital sexuality, the imperatives of decency, the obligatory concealment of the body, the reduction to silence and mandatory reticences [*pudeurs impératives*] of language. The second . . . was really less a rupture than an inflexion of the curve: this was the moment when the mechanisms of repression were seen as beginning to loosen their grip [*se desserrer*]" (115 [152]). "The chronology of the techniques [of repression] themselves," he notes with a characteristically broad stroke," "goes back a long way [*remonte loin*]." Making this dating more precise, he goes on: "Their point of formation must be sought in the penitential practices of medieval Christianity, or rather in the dual series" of changes imposed by the Fourth Lateran Council of 1215 and then by devotional practices of the sixteenth century (115–16 [153]). We might ask, for starters, what gain Foucault makes in adhering to a paradigm of ruptures and periods, particularly since the points of rupture seem so constantly revised, so labyrinthine (note the "or rather" in this passage, and such revisions throughout the book). This is the whole (ruptured) style of his Nietzschean model of effective history.[44] But it might also be read as itself having a specific rhetorical effect: perhaps it affords him what early in volume 1 he calls "the speaker's benefit [*le bénéfice du locuteur*]" (6 [13]): the verbal act of speaking of a time before "the great prohibitions" puts the speaker prophetically outside of or beyond them, and thus "anticipates the coming freedom [*la liberté future*]" (6 [13]). Foucault's analysis of the discourse of liberation (the ruse of the repressive hypothesis) can be applied to his own use of the Middle Ages in "a discourse that combines the fervor of knowledge, the determination to change the laws, and the longing for the garden of earthly delights [*le jardin espéré des délices*]" (7 [14]). I shall pick up on such longed-for past delights in a moment.

But notice first what role the medieval period plays in this passage about the two major historical ruptures: it is the time period in which techniques of modern subjectivation took form. Specifically, the medieval is the time in which, after 1215, the obligation of annual confession began the process of putting of sex into discourse (a process completed by the seventeenth century [20 (29)]). The Middle Ages here are the time of the seeds of modern "men's subjection [*l'assujettissement des hommes*]: their constitution as subjects in both senses of the word" (60 [81]); "Since the Middle Ages at least," Foucault contends (58 [78]), confession has been a mainstay of such subjection; the Christian pastoral made sex an "enigma," creating "modern societies" who speak and exploit sex as "*the* secret" (35 [48–49]). Further, Foucault claims that modern power's suppression of its own actual multiplicity originated in the Middle Ages (86 [114–15]). Even if these "beginnings" of modern sexual subjectivity were "surreptitious," they were "long ago . . . already making" themselves "felt at the time of the Christian pastoral of the flesh" (156 [206])—already long in evidence before the sixteenth century.

Thus there is a powerful and continuous use of the Middle Ages in volume 1 as the site of the beginnings of modern sexual subject formation. We have seen in relation to John/Eleanor Rykener in chapter 2 at least one potential context in which this analysis of putting sex into discourse is right on target. I am not going to evaluate further Foucault's particular claims about the institution of confession here; my intent is only to present his general claims about periodization.[45] And what I find in general counterpoint to this pervasive use of the Middle Ages is another use, wherein the Middle Ages form the firm border between us moderns and a very different age with its own systems of codes governing sexual practices: codes that center sexual practices on matrimonial relations, that still determine "nature" as "a kind of law," and that do not differentiate the concept of the "unnatural" into a specific field of sexuality (37–39 [51–54]). It was a time, this theme goes, of a "markedly unitary" discourse ("*un discours assez fortement unitaire*") around "the theme of the flesh and the practice of penance," a uniformity that was "broken apart" ("*décomposée*") more recently (33 [46]). At this point I hear something like a note of nostalgia tuning Foucault's historical song.

Such nostalgia is even more audible in the claim that "[l]ittle by little, the nakedness of the questions formulated by the confession manuals of the Middle Ages, and a good number of those still in use in the seventeenth century, was veiled" (18 [27]). Foucault argues that increasing discretion of early modern confessors was advised so that less detail would be articulated: no longer was there, as he puts it, a complete "description of the respective positions of the partners, the postures assumed, gestures, places touched, caresses, the precise moment of pleasure—an entire painstaking review of the sexual act in its very unfolding" (19 [27]). In his style that mimes the rhythms of the medieval confession itself, Foucault seems here to assert that medieval language was able to record so precisely as itself to mime "the sexual act in its very unfolding [*dans son opération même*]" (27). It is difficult to pin down the historical value or even the place in his own argument of Foucault's idealizing assertion here.[46] This description in volume 1, which Foucault offers as an accurate account of modern power (the beginning of the proliferative modern process of putting sex into discourse) sounds much like the mocking description of the repressive hypothesis that opens the volume: "it would seem [*dit on*]," he writes in the opening, that the beginning of the seventeenth century was still "a time of direct gestures, shameless discourse, and open transgressions, when anatomies were shown and intermingled at will, and knowing children hung about amid the laughter of adults: it was a period when bodies 'made a display of themselves.' "[47] Is this time of direct gestures, easy contact between body parts, and naked descriptions of nakedness a rhetorical effect or genealogical-historical fact? (More generally, and hearkening back to my earlier observation about the repressive hypothesis: is this repressive hypothesis a story Foucault must tell to produce a certain modernity, or one he believes we moderns really believe?) Following his comments on politics, fictioning, and history, I think both propositions are true: the Middle Ages plays a role in the history of sexuality formulated around the mechanisms of repression—the period works for his effective history, he deploys it for certain effects—and he believes, or at least desires, that it really was like that.

Now it may well be that these two perspectives on the Middle Ages—seen as a period that produces our modernity, and as a period quite separate and different from our own—are conceptually coherent, part of a whole genealogical approach to the modern subject. The demonstration of modern contingency traces the forces that produce us and at the same time suggests that we can be different in the future because we were not always like this. But I do not want to harmonize these two strains completely and thus elide not only the obviously tactical use of the Middle Ages in volume 1 but also—crucially—the desire that emerges from this contradictory history. Central to discerning the value of this double position is in fact that nostalgic tone; various critics have noted an idealization and have assigned varying importance to it. Medievalists have always taken exception to a Middle Ages that functions "as a lost and golden age," as Bartlett puts it; yet I don't want to discard utopianism altogether.[48] The utopian, the elegiac, what I have been calling the nostalgic, functions as part of a serious ethical and aesthetic vision of the present and the future: a view of political reality informs Foucault's historical pronouncement about the sodomite and the homosexual, and, in turn, the historical pronouncement allows Foucault to fiction a future politics.

Foucault has insisted that he does not study historically distant periods in order to find an alternative to the present: "I am not looking for an alternative; you can't find the solution of a problem in the solution of another problem raised at another moment by other people." Indeed, he maintains, "[T]here is no exemplary value in a period which is not our period . . . it is not anything to get back to";[49] and yet genealogical analysis, he suggests, can be useful in showing us that, and perhaps how, such a "fictitious unity" as modern sexuality (vol. 1, 154 [204]) can be broken apart and reconfigured. Foucault uses the opposition of acts to identity, surface to depth, premodernity to modernity, in order to show that future sexuality does not have to be dominated by current notions of identity. The potential for acts (not entailed with identity) to shatter the modern liberal subject is great; insofar as such a category of acts is associated with the premodern in his historiography, Foucault expresses a desire for the premodern.

What I find in Foucault's work, carried through the late interviews, is not only an analytical focus on the body as imprintable surface[50] but a desire—which is mistakenly reduced to *mere* nostalgia—for a realm of clearly apprehensible acts and legible surfaces. In *Discipline and Punish* the premodern offender's acts were clearly motivated by "a free, conscious will," Foucault writes, while the delinquent's internal "instincts, drives, tendencies, character" muddy the surface.[51] In the Middle Ages invoked in the 1980 Introduction to *Herculine Barbin,* the hermaphroditic body is clearly legible, not clouded over by the necessity of interpretation.[52] At the beginning of *The History of Sexuality,* vol. 1, the scene opens on "this bright day [*ce plein jour*]" (3 [9]) of bodies displayed and accessible, on the surface and without mediation. And at the end of volume 1, Foucault calls for a resistance to coercive modern "sexuality" and its "fictitious unity" in order "to counter the grips of power with the claims of bodies, pleasures, and knowledges" (157 [208])—calls, as Leo Bersani puts it, for a "reinventing of the body as a surface of multiple sources of pleasure."[53] There is an emphasis on the visible and apparent, on the apprehensible in its immediacy; it even sounds "prediscursive," as Judith Butler points out, despite Foucault's "official" line that (as she puts it) "there is no 'sex' in itself"—and certainly no body—"which is not produced by complex interactions of discourse and power."[54] This pre- or extradiscursive reinvention project has as its basis "desexualization," as Foucault put it in an interview at about the time of volume 1's publication: a reinvention "with the body, with its elements, its surfaces, its volumes, its depths, [of] a nondisciplinary eroticism: that of a body in a volatile and diffuse state given to chance encounters and incalculable pleasures" not centered on genitalia.[55] Foucault suggests in a 1978 interview, "Le Gai savoir," that in anonymous sexual encounters there is "an exceptional possibility of desubjectivization, of desubjection, perhaps not the most radical but in any case sufficiently intense to be worth taking note of. . . .

It's not the affirmation of identity that's important, it's the affirmation of non-identity": the act, the surface, and the loss of identity are linked.[56] The body is turned inside out; its depths become surfaces; this body is "diffuse," "exploding," and without the old hierarchical conceptualizations of internal drives and impulses.[57]

In the later volumes of *The History of Sexuality* as well as in late discussions in the gay press, Foucault's emphasis on *becoming* rather than on *being*, performance rather than ontology, is marked; in studying the "arts of existence" in volume 2, for example, Foucault clarifies that he means "those intentional and voluntary actions by which men not only set themselves rules of conduct, but also seek to transform themselves, to change themselves in their singular being, and to make their life into an *oeuvre*" (2: 10–11 [16]). And in a 1981 interview, he insists, "[W]e have to work at becoming homosexuals and not be obstinate in recognizing that we are." [58] Finally, recalling to us the very different treatments we have seen in the other visions of the medieval, Foucault happily links such an acts-centered disposition against depth to sadomasochism in a 1982 interview: "I think that S/M . . . [is] the real creation of new possibilities of pleasure. . . . The idea that S/M is related to a deep violence, that S/M practice is a way of liberating this violence, this aggression, is stupid." And in the same interview, he links S/M to the "strategic game" of medieval " 'courtly love.' " [59]

But the valorization of surfaces and thus clearly apprehensible acts needs to be considered carefully. "Acts" of course cannot be imagined to be immediately self-apparent. Foucault, genealogist, certainly is not suggesting that they are. Earlier, in *Discipline and Punish,* he suggests that the modern penal state itself problematizes the notion of a proven and punishable act (19 [27]). At specific moments in volume 1, too (elaborated in volume 2 [e.g., 92 (106–7)]), Foucault makes perfectly clear the complexities of judging acts, especially in the Christian tradition. In his discussion of the expansion of the scope of confession in volume 1, for example, he notes that an "evolution tended to make the flesh into the root of all evil, shifting the most important moment of transgression from the act itself to the stirrings—so difficult to perceive and formulate—of desire" (19–20 [28]). I assume that the biblical precedent for this shift is Matthew 5.28, Christ's warning in his Sermon on the Mount: "But I say unto you, That whosoever looketh on a woman to lust after her hath committed adultery with her already in his heart" (King James Version); the act, that is, has already taken place even before the act has occurred. This is a deconstruction of the act pursued with moral vigor by patristic writers such as Saint Augustine and Saint Jerome.[60] What we see in the act, in its "concrete realization" (2: 63 [74]), on the surface, does not necessarily indicate—and certainly does not exhaust—its meaning or function in social context. We only have to recall the intense anti-Lollard polemics on the Eucharist to appreciate that in the Middle Ages (as in any other time) what you see is not necessarily what you get: remember Roger Dymmok's argument that inner change is not always accompanied by outer change. And Foucault, ever suspicious of the ways modern power can infuse and saturate the body from the interior, would not presume that a visible surface at any time is a reliable indicator of meaning or function; indeed, who would?

To be historiographical tools, then, and not mere heuristic devices, the "category of forbidden acts" and the concomitant "juridical subject of them" must be supplemented in order to accommodate (among other things) differences in social context and empowerment among such subjects. The mechanisms of the premodern codes' prohibitive functioning—exactly *how* these civil and canon laws worked to regulate specific communities—need further analysis; such mechanisms matter because (for one reason) these codes clearly had different relations to male and to female perpetrators of sodomy. In the case of the 1270 legislation of Orléans that I cited above, for example, female sodomites were mentioned but not really envisioned at all (their punishment makes little practical sense, as I pointed out in chapter 1), whereas males definitely were; the law therefore has a different evidentiary status in relation to male sodomites from the one it has to female sodomites. More generally, any historical observation that depends on an understanding of legal codes or even more broadly, some category of "acts," must register the fact that historically women's acts are not recorded and not codified as fully as men's because women don't act in public spheres as do men, and thus women tend to be regulated differently. The *Twelve Conclusions of the Lollards* makes this point, as we have seen. I argued in chapter 1 that the Eleventh Conclusion makes a very different kind of accusation about women than the Third Conclusion makes about men; a concept of gender, the secondariness and perversion of femininity itself, informs the indictments of female sexual behaviors in the Eleventh Conclusion. Acts are not separable from gender categories; acts have values and effects that differ as they are practiced by different people and in different contexts. As feminist scholars have continually insisted we ask, "*Who* can act, when, and under what circumstances?"

But as a mere heuristic device, the Foucauldian distinction between identity and act proved immensely fruitful in queer political organizing in the United States. The importance of volume 1 for queer activist practice in the late 1980s and early 1990s was immense: Halperin observes in *Saint Foucault*, on the basis of an "unsystematic" 1990 survey of people active in ACT UP/New York in the late eighties, that "the single most important intellectual source of political inspiration for contemporary AIDS activists—at least for the more theoretically-minded or better-outfitted among them" was volume 1 of the *History of Sexuality*.[61] Just as an analytical model of sex acts challenges models of identity, so does a model of political acts: current queer resistance to identity politics is informed by an acts-centered model of coalition politics (such as I outlined in chapter 3) that picks up on Foucault's preference for acts. Such an acts-centered model is politically efficacious in particular circumstances, countering the persecution of already marginalized identity-based groups—efficacious when, for example, the concept of "high-risk acts" in AIDS activist discourse counters the phobic, racist, and misogynist concept of "high-risk groups." But queer politics can constantly benefit from feminist tutelage, as the connotations of the term "queer" themselves suggest (still young, white, and male): who gets to act—and who gets to act up?[62]

The very concept of self-identical and thus self-apparent acts apprehensible via the surface, then, needs to be nuanced in scholarly and in activist practice. Identities may be constituted by acts—the theory of nonessentialized, performative identity so fully enunciated in *Gender Trouble* has conceptual roots in Foucault's genealogy of modern sexual identity in volume 1, and volume 1 in turn continues to perform the dissolution of essential identity that we saw in the preface to *The Archaeology of Knowledge*—but acts are not themselves fully self-identical or self-apparent. From a conventional historicist point of view, Foucault's locating self-apparent acts in the Middle Ages in volume 1 of *The History of Sexuality* seems both essentializing and nostalgic. Essentializing it is not, as I have suggested. Furthermore, nostalgia isn't what it used to be. Foucault, tactical, forward-looking and resistant, is fictioning history on the basis of a political reality that makes it true, in order that he can fiction a politics not yet in existence. Sexual identity now is constructed as truth, so that only in resistance to modern sexual subjectivation is there any possibility of reinvention or "explosion" of the body into surface.

In contrast to the medieval in *Pulp Fiction*, then, that space of abjection and otherness—the space where sodomy, sadomasochism, southernness, and blackness get dumped in the creation of a unified straight white masculinity—the Middle Ages Foucault most deeply desires is a time whose lack of unified sexuality is *preferable* to the present with its "fictitious unity" of normative heterosexuality, a time whose sexual disaggregation is not to be feared but can for the future offer a creative, even liberatory, potential. "There is a creation of anarchy within the body," Foucault comments in a 1975 interview suggesting such disaggregation, "where its hierarchies, its localizations and designations, its organicity, if you will, are in the process of disintegrating. . . . This is something 'unnameable,' 'useless,' outside of all the programs of desire. It is the body made totally plastic by pleasure: something that opens itself, that tightens, that throbs, that beats, that gapes."[63] Here is that prediscursive body gaping wide open.

So when Hayden White analyzes, and goes on to condemn, Foucault's historiography as "all surface," I can agree with the terms of the analysis but value them entirely differently.[64] "Of course," states Ed Cohen on this late material, "Foucault does not characterize these new possibilities of pleasure as inherently 'political' or 'resistant' "; thus his qualification, for example, of the radicality of anonymous sexual encounters (quoted above).[65] But he does place them at the center of any future deliberations of a "homosexual movement" about the organization of a given society.

The ethos of this disaggregative project underwrites a coalition politics such as I delineated in relation to queer medieval studies, funding for the humanities, and academic freedom in chapter 3. This view of the fragmented self enables contingent relations with the past, such as we have seen Foucault making in the archive in chapter 2—and, in my introduction, as we have seen Michael Camille and Roland Barthes make, too—and those relations, I have been arguing throughout this book, can be the material not only of selves but of communities. And we can insist that such a project of disaggregation be specifically informed and guided by feminist analyses and goals of transforming the "social relations within which sexuality is organized and articulated."[66]

Getting medieval: not undertaking brutal private vengeance in a triumphal and unregulated bloodbath, as Marsellus Wallace threatens in *Pulp Fiction;* and not turning from an impure identity to some solidity guaranteed by God, as Jules is made hopefully to do; but using ideas of the past, creating relations with the past, touching in this way the past in our efforts to build selves and communities now and into the future. What could be better, after all, as the Altoids advertising executives obviously knew, than getting medieval on—or with—your very breath?

Notes

Introduction: Touching on the Past

1. A brief and provisional description, to be elaborated and documented in the course of this book: "Lollards"—initially a term of disapprobation that seems to have been picked up and used by the disapproved themselves—refers to followers of John Wyclif (c. 1330–84), philosopher and theologian at Oxford. Wyclif was concerned with—among other things—what he saw as the illegitimacy of the established church hierarchy and clerical privilege, including the church's material holdings, clerical claims to perform a miracle in the sacrament of the Eucharist, and deviations from the will of God as it was expressed in the Bible. Certain of Wyclif's doctrines were condemned as heretical in 1382. From the 1380s through the 1390s Lollards were found in a relatively wide range of English society, high and low; opposition consolidated against Lollardy during Richard II's reign (1377–99) and the first Lollard was burned in 1401. The social level of Lollardy in the fifteenth century became more decidedly nonaristocratic. Note, too, that the term refers to dissenters whose ideas, though "born" of Wyclif (as Anne Hudson puts it), were not necessarily entirely uniform across the movement. For a capsule description, see *The Concise Oxford Dictionary of the Christian Church*, ed. E. A. Livingstone (Oxford: Oxford Univ. Press, 1977); for the standard scholarly work, see Anne Hudson, *The Premature Reformation: Wycliffite Texts and Lollard History* (Oxford: Clarendon, 1988), to whose rich scholarship I am deeply indebted.

Modern English translations are my own unless otherwise indicated.

2. *John Mirk's Instructions for Parish Priests*, ed. Gillis Kristensson (Lund: Gleerup, 1974). This edition updates the 1868 EETS edition by Edward Peacock, revised by F. J. Furnivall in 1902 (EETS o.s. 31 [London: Kegan Paul, Trench, Trübner, 1902]). My modern English translations are informed by Kristensson's glosses. On the genre of religious instruction manuals in the thirteenth through fifteenth centuries, see H. G. Pfander, "Some Medieval Manuals of Religious Instruction in England and Observations on Chaucer's Parson's Tale," *Journal of English and Germanic Philology* 35 (1936): 243–58;

see also W. A. Pantin, *The English Church in the Fourteenth Century* (Cambridge: Cambridge Univ. Press, 1955), 189–219.

3. On the relationship of Mirk's *Instructions* to the *Oculus sacerdotis* of William of Pagula (canonist, theologian, and parish priest of Berkshire), see L. E. Boyle, "The *Oculus sacerdotis* and Some Other Works of William of Pagula," *Transactions of the Royal Historical Society*, 5th ser., no. 5 (1955): 81–110, esp. 86, 89; and Pantin, *The English Church*, 214.

4. For references to this traditional belief, see below, note 22. In the *Book of Vices and Virtues*, ed. W. Nelson Francis, EETS 217 (London: Oxford Univ. Press, 1942), a fourteenth-century translation of the *Somme le roi*, the air itself is said to be befouled by mention of this sin: see 46, and compare Dan Michel's earlier fourteenth-century translation, *Ayenbite of Inwit*, ed. Richard Morris, EETS o.s. 23 (London: Kegan Paul, Trench, Trübner, 1866), 49–50. Mirk may indeed have represented a "conservative" viewpoint about speaking of this sin, as James Brundage opines, but it is one nonetheless represented as a current possibility for a priest in a late-fourteenth-century English context (we shall see this in the Parson's Canterbury tale). For a brief discussion of the "terse[ness]" of late medieval English sources about this sin, see Allen J. Frantzen, "The Disclosure of Sodomy in *Cleanness*," PMLA 111 (1996): 451–64, esp. 455, where he mentions some of the sources I discuss here. In the very different, Italian context, Saint Bernardino of Siena "devoted three consecutive sermons in his 1424 [Lenten] cycle and one more in 1425 exclusively to sodomy," as Michael Rocke writes in his *Forbidden Friendships: Homosexuality and Male Culture in Renaissance Florence* (New York: Oxford Univ. Press, 1996), 36–44, at 36. See in particular *Sermo* 15, "De horrendo peccato contra natura," in *Opera omnia*, 9 vols. (Florence: Ad Claras Aquas, 1950–65), 3: 267–84. On Bernardino see also James Brundage, *Law, Sex, and Christian Society in Medieval Europe* (Chicago: Univ. of Chicago Press, 1987), 534, and Vern L. Bullough, "The Sin against Nature and Homosexuality," in *Sexual Practices and the Medieval Church*, ed. Vern L. Bullough and James Brundage (Buffalo, N.Y.: Prometheus, 1982), 55–71, at 66.

5. P. P. A. Biller, "Birth-Control in the West in the Thirteenth and Early Fourteenth Centuries," *Past and Present* 94 (February 1982): 3–26, at 22 n. 82, cites a passage that is the likely source here: it occurs both in William of Pagula's *Oculus sacerdotis* and in his *Speculum prelatorum*. Biller comments: "A lengthy section about modes of emission of seed and the sin against nature commences with a warning against contraceptive action during intercourse between man and wife or man and woman." See, further, 24 n. 89, acknowledging that the term "sin against nature" is very general, while arguing that "the context here suggests that contraceptive *coitus interruptus* was uppermost in William's mind."

6. Clearly, then, "unspeakable" does not mean "unspoken"; it indicates

not ineffability, either, but a moral judgment: the sin can, but should not be, spoken of. In the *Parson's Tale* the speaker declares that "though that hooly writ speke of horrible synne, certes hooly writ may nat been defouled, namoore than the sonne that shyneth on the mixne [dunghill]" (10.910 in *The Riverside Chaucer*, 3rd ed., gen. ed. Larry D. Benson [Boston: Houghton Mifflin, 1987], 320). All reference to Chaucer's works refer to this edition, by fragment and line number; translations are my own, informed by *A Chaucer Glossary*, Norman Davis et al. (Oxford: Clarendon, 1979). On the context, see below. On the interlinking of the unspeakable with the sin against nature, see Jacques Chiffoleau, who points out (among other things) the relationship between unspeakability and being outside the norm: "Dire l'indicible: Remarques sur la catégorie du *nefandum* du XIIe au XVe siècle," *Annales ESC* 45 (1990): 289–324, esp. 295. The problem of speaking the unspeakable, as Chiffoleau fully sees, is linked to the required practice, especially after 1215, of confession; see below in this introductory chapter. For the pleasure of speaking the unspeakable, see Catherine Brown, who cites Chiffoleau: "Queer Representation in the *Arcipreste de Talavera*, or, The *Maldezir de Mugeres* Is a Drag," in *Queer Iberia*, ed. Josiah Blackmore and Gregory S. Hutcheson (Durham, N.C.: Duke Univ. Press, 1999).

7. *The Book of Vices and Virtues*, 46. See also the parallel translation of *Somme le roi* in Michel's *Ayenbite of Inwyt*, 49–50.

8. Foucault comments specifically about the term "sodomy," which he calls "that utterly confused category [*cette catégorie si confuse*]" (*The History of Sexuality*, vol. 1: *An Introduction*, trans. Robert Hurley [New York: Vintage, 1978], 101; *Histoire de la sexualité* 1: *La Volonté de savoir* [Paris: Gallimard, 1976], 134). Jonathan Goldberg takes up this concept in his "Introduction: 'That Utterly Confused Category,' " in *Sodometries: Renaissance Texts, Modern Sexualities* (Stanford: Stanford Univ. Press, 1992), 1–26; and Mark D. Jordan extends this idea into an argument about Christian theology: *The Invention of Sodomy in Christian Theology* (Chicago: Univ. of Chicago Press, 1997), 9 and passim.

9. For full definition, see the *Middle English Dictionary*, *kinde;* for the Old English *cynd*, see *An Anglo-Saxon Dictionary*, ed. Joseph Bosworth and T. Northcote Toller (Oxford: Oxford Univ. Press, 1882–98), supplement, 140, and cf. *ġecynd*.

10. Interrelations among sex/gender deviance and heresy, leprosy, witchcraft, Judaism, Islam, and treachery are widely noted in European continental high- and late-medieval contexts: see, for a sampling of the scholarship over the last twenty-five years on these topics, Arno Karlen, "The Homosexual Heresy," *Chaucer Review* 6 (1971): 44–63; Michael Goodich, *The Unmentionable Vice: Homosexuality in the Later Medieval Period* (Santa Barbara, Calif.: ABC-Clio, 1979), esp. "Appendix: The Trial of Arnold of Verniolle for Heresy and Sodomy," 89–123; John Boswell, *Christianity, Social*

Tolerance, and Homosexuality: Gay People in Western Europe from the Beginning of the Christian Era to the Fourteenth Century (Chicago: Univ. of Chicago Press, 1980); Vern L. Bullough, "Postscript: Heresy, Witchcraft, and Sexuality," in *Sexual Practices and the Medieval Church*, ed. Bullough and Brundage, 206–17; Guido Ruggiero, *The Boundaries of Eros: Sex Crime and Sexuality in Renaissance Venice* (New York: Oxford Univ. Press, 1985), 109–45; R. I. Moore, *The Formation of a Persecuting Society: Power and Deviance in Western Europe, 950–1250* (New York: Basil Blackwell, 1987); Daniel Boyarin, "Are There Any Jews in 'The History of Sexuality'?" *Journal of the History of Sexuality* 5 (1995): 333–55; David Nirenberg, *Communities of Violence: Persecution of Minorities in the Middle Ages* (Princeton: Princeton Univ. Press, 1996); José Piedra, "In Search of the Black Stud," in *Premodern Sexualities*, ed. Louise Fradenburg and Carla Freccero (New York: Routledge, 1996), 23–43; Steven Kruger, "Conversion and Medieval Sexual, Religious, and Racial Categories," *Constructing Medieval Sexualities*, ed. Karma Lochrie, Peggy McCracken, and James A. Schultz (Minneapolis: Univ. of Minnesota Press, 1997), 158–79; *Queer Iberia*, ed. Blackmore and Hutcheson; Kathleen Biddick, *The Shock of Medievalism* (Durham, N.C.: Duke Univ. Press, 1998).

11. For Mirk and Lollardy, see *Mirk's Festial*, ed. Theodor Erbe, EETS e.s. 96 (London: Kegan Paul, Trench, Trübner, 1905), 171: in a sermon for Corpus Christi Mirk argues against Lollards on roods and images. See Alan J. Fletcher, "John Mirk and the Lollards," *Medium Ævum* 55 (1987): 217–24, for a discussion of this passage and of another passage in the sermon for Trinity Sunday that precedes it, and for a suggestion that Mirk's intention may well have been to counter in the *Festial* the heretical activities of the Lollards.

12. Well-documented secondary works on the concept of the sin against nature include Boswell, *Christianity, Social Tolerance, and Homosexuality*, esp. 303–32; John T. Noonan Jr., *Contraception: A History of Its Treatment by the Catholic Theologians and Canonists* (Cambridge, Mass.: Harvard Univ. Press, 1966), esp. 238–46; Vern L. Bullough, "The Sin against Nature and Homosexuality," in Bullough and Brundage, *Sexual Practices and the Medieval Church*, 55–71.

13. *Book of Vices and Virtues*, 45; cf. *Ayenbite of Inwit*, 48.

14. Noonan, *Contraception*, 243, describing sex in Thomas Aquinas; there are some exceptions to the judgment of unnaturalness of nonprocreative married sex (see Noonan, 243–44). But in general, the act of generative coitus was taken as the norm. Thus Saint Thomas Aquinas, *Summa theologica*, 2-2.154.1. Resp. (Parma ed., 1852–73; rpt. New York: Musurgia, 1949, 3: 511–12): "peccatum luxuriae consistit in hoc quod aliquis non secundum rectam rationem delectatione venerea utitur. . . . Quae quidem [matter in

which pleasure is sought] potest non convenire rationi rectae dupliciter. Uno modo, quia habet repugnantiam ad finem venerei actus: et sic in quantum impeditur generatio prolis, est *vitium contra naturam,* quod est in omni actu venereo ex quo generatio sequi non potest." Trans. Fathers of the English Dominican Province, 3 vols. (London: Burns Oates and Washbourne; New York: Benziger Bros., 1921), 2: 131–32: "[T]he sin of lust consists in seeking venereal pleasure not in accordance with right reason. . . . Now this same matter [wherein this pleasure is sought] may be discordant with right reason in two ways. First, because it is inconsistent with the end of the venereal act. In this way, as hindering the begetting of children, there is the *vice against nature,* which attaches to every venereal act from which generation cannot follow" (Emphasis in original). In this section of the *Summa* Thomas discusses unnatural vice as including masturbation, heterosexual intercourse that does not observe the right manner of copulation, male-male and female-female homosexual relations (i.e., *vitium sodomiticum*), and bestiality, in order of ascending gravity (2-2.154.12); unnatural vice is the worst species of *luxuria*. But the value of "nature" in the *Summa* shifts in sometimes conflicting ways, and here, as Boswell points out, there is no definition of the "nature" against which these sins militate; senses range here from "the 'nature' of the venereal act to the 'order of nature,' " which proceeds from God himself, with "human nature" most common (*Christianity,* 323). Boswell analyzes the contradictions in Thomas's use of "natural" and "unnatural" in reference to homosexual acts; while his conclusions are arguable, the analysis of contradictions seems sound. For a critique of Boswell's analyses of the "natural" in Aristotle and Aquinas, see Glenn W. Olsen, "The Gay Middle Ages: A Response to Professor Boswell," *Communio: International Catholic Review* 8 (1981): 119–38; Mark Jordan argues against Boswell as well but on different grounds, maintaining that the instability in Thomas's discussions is in fact endemic to the category of sodomy (*The Invention of Sodomy,* 136–58).

15. *Fasciculus morum: A Fourteenth-Century Preacher's Handbook,* ed. and trans. Siegfried Wenzel (University Park: Pennsylvania State Univ. Press, 1989), 686–89. Cf. the mention of the devil in Venetian sex-crime discourse, combined with the discourse of the unnatural to indicate sodomy: Ruggiero, *Boundaries of Eros,* 111.

16. *Purity* [*Cleanness*], ed. Robert J. Menner, Yale Studies in English 61 (1920; rpt. Hamden, Conn.: Archon, 1970), ll. 693–710. On the precision of this poem's denotation of sodomy as anal intercourse, see Frantzen, "The Disclosure of Sodomy in *Cleanness,*" esp. 455–64. On gender violation as the primary concern in medieval discourses of sodomy and unnatural sexual relations, see Karma Lochrie, *Covert Operations: The Medieval Uses of Secrecy* (Philadelphia: Univ. of Pennsylvania Press, 1999), chap. 5,

"Sodomy and Other Female Perversions." Lochrie's excellent, far-reaching chapter takes up several texts that I discuss here, and her well-focused argument helped me sharpen my own.

17. *The Parson's Tale* 10.864–65, in *The Riverside Chaucer*, 318. This proper end of coitus includes the proper upbringing and advancement of a child, as Thomas Aquinas maintains. See Thomas Aquinas, *Summa theologica* 2-2. 154. 1 (Parma ed., 3: 511–12; Blackfriars ed., 2: 132).

18. Lochrie, *Covert Operations*, 185.

19. *The Holy Bible . . . Made from the Latin Vulgate by John Wycliffe and His Followers*, ed. Josiah Forshall and Frederic Madden, 4 vols. (Oxford: Oxford Univ. Press, 1850), 4: 305–6.

20. Jean Gerson, *De confessione mollitiei*, in *Oeuvres complètes*, ed. P. Glorieux (Paris: Desclée, 1971), 8: 71–75, esp. 72; Antoninus of Florence, *Summula confessionis* (Flach: Strasbourg, 1499), 5, both cited and discussed by Thomas Tentler, *Sin and Confession on the Eve of the Reformation* (Princeton: Princeton Univ. Press, 1977), 92, 89. See Ruggiero, *Boundaries*, for still differing denotations and prosecutions of sodomy in fourteenth- and fifteenth-century Venice. James Brundage maintains that in this late period "[w]riters on moral questions lumped together as sodomy any and all sexual practices that they considered unnatural, including masturbation, mutual masturbation, oral sex, and anal sex, either homosexual or heterosexual" (*Law, Sex and Christian Society*, 533). For a historical narrative of sodomy that follows Foucault in arguing that the category of sodomy becomes both more inclusive and less spoken about as the Middle Ages in England progress, see Frantzen, "The Disclosure of Sodomy." For a contrasting view, see Anne Gilmour-Bryson, "Sodomy and the Knights Templar," *Journal of the History of Sexuality* 7 (1996): 151–83, esp. 164: while earlier theologians differed in their usages, referring to any illicit sexual coupling, she is "convinced that by the fourteenth century, the term 'sodomy' was used by theologians and inquisitors almost entirely in reference to male intercourse, anal intercourse in particular."

21. The variant "*by* oþer way" (my emphasis) might tend to support this reading. See Mirk, *Instructions*, 80.

22. Worries about providing the occasion for sin are traditional in the penitential literature: see, for two examples among many, Robert of Flamborough's early-thirteenth-century *Liber poenitentialis*, sec. 223, ed. J. J. Francis Firth (Toronto: Pontifical Institute of Mediaeval Studies, 1971), 196: "Postea potest quaeri si umquam plus contra naturam peccavit, si extraordinarie habuit aliquem. Si quaerat quomodo extraordinarie, non respondebo ei; ipse viderit. Numquam ei mentionem de aliquo faciam de quo peccandi occasionem accipere possit, sed tantum de generalibus quae omnes sciunt esse peccata." Trans. in Goodich, *Unmentionable Vice*, 57: "Afterward the penitent may be asked if he had sinned against nature at any other time and

if he had sex with anyone in any particular way. If he should ask what is meant by a 'particular way,' I would not answer him, for he would know. I never make mention of anything that might become an occasion for sinning, but rather speak of generalities that everyone knows are sins." And William Peraldus's mid- to late-thirteenth-century *Summa de virtutibus et vitiis* (Venice, 1497), 8 (where pagination numbers refer to two pages, and pagination starts anew for the vices). See Tentler, *Sin and Confession*, on this commonplace; see also Frantzen, "The Disclosure of Sodomy," and *The Literature of Penance in Anglo-Saxon England* (New Brunswick: Rutgers Univ. Press, 1983), esp. 7–8, 14, 117–18, on the discretion of confessors in the early English period.

23. Thanks to Nicolas Watson for suggesting this to me.

24. Compare Goodich, *The Unmentionable Vice*, 111–12, for a fourteenth-century realization in southern France of the same-sex sexual potentials of the shared bed (the 1323 testimony of Arnold of Verniolle, accused of sodomy and heresy in Bishop Jacques Fournier's campaign against heresy). See also 18, on monastic reformers' anxieties about adolescent experimentation in the close physical proximity of all-male communities. And see V. A. Kolve on early monastic strictures on and pleasures of same-sex desire: "Ganymede/*Son of Getron:* Medieval Monasticism and the Drama of Same-Sex Desire," *Speculum* 73 (1998): 1014–1067.

25. For the anti-Lollardy of the *Confessio*, see, e.g., ll. 346–51 of the Prologue (*The English Works of John Gower*, ed. G. C. Macaulay, 2 vols. EETS 81–82 [London: Oxford Univ. Press, 1900]), 1: 14.

26. *Confessio amantis* 4.494–95 (ed. Macaulay, 1: 314). Note in the textual apparatus that two manuscript groups change the same-sex reference to an opposite-sex one here: "he and sche" or "sche and he": such is the normalizing power of the binary gender relations of heterosexuality.

27. Kurt Olsson, "Natural Law and John Gower's *Confessio Amantis*," *Medievalia et Humanistica* n.s. 11 (1982): 229–61, carefully distinguishes "five separate meanings of the *jus naturae*" that occur in the poem, thus necessarily discussing varying meanings of *natura* along the way. The argument about a gradual development across the poem of Gower's teachings about natural law (and "kinde" love), though, does not help elucidate contradictory uses of the term *natura* that occur—as in this passage—in the space of a few lines. For a sharp analysis of this episode, see Lochrie, *Covert Operations*, 213–16.

28. For methodological ruminations about queer history and particularly its relation to lesbian/gay history, see *The Queer Issue: New Visions of America's Lesbian and Gay Past*, ed. Jeffrey Escoffier, Regina Kunzel, and Molly McGarry, spec. issue of *Radical History Review* 62 (Spring 1995), esp. "Editors' Introduction" and articles by Martha M. Umphrey, Donna Penn, and Henry Abelove. For an important statement that attempts to work

against an undue polarization of queer theory (with its emphasis on systems of representation) and lesbian/gay history (with its emphasis on empirical methods), see Lisa Duggan, "The Discipline Problem: Queer Theory Meets Lesbian and Gay History," *GLQ: A Journal of Lesbian and Gay Studies* 2 (1995): 179–91. Duggan's own work exemplifies well a kind of historical analysis that treats sexual subjectivity as a story of representation: see "The Trials of Alice Mitchell: Sensationalism, Sexology, and the Lesbian Subject in Turn-of-the-Century America," *Signs* 18 (1993): 791–814.

29. See the introduction and essays in Teresa de Lauretis, ed., *Feminist Studies/Critical Studies* (Bloomington: Indiana Univ. Press, 1986); Barbara Johnson, *A World of Difference* (Baltimore: Johns Hopkins Univ. Press, 1987); Carole S. Vance, ed., *Pleasure and Danger: Exploring Female Sexuality* (Boston: Routledge and Kegan Paul, 1984), particularly Hortense Spillers, "Interstices: A Small Drama of Words," 73–100; Audre Lorde, *Sister Outsider* (Freedom, Calif.: Crossing Press, 1984). Feminist theorists and historians are not the only ones who have understood sex's indeterminacy, of course; see Carole S. Vance for discussion of the evolution of this perspective among early lesbian/gay historians such as Jonathan Ned Katz: "Social Construction Theory: Problems in the History of Sexuality," in *Homosexuality, Which Homosexuality? International Conference on Gay and Lesbian Studies,* by Dennis Altman, Carole Vance, Martha Vicinus, Jeffrey Weeks, et al. (Amsterdam: Uitgeverij An Dekker/Schorer, 1989; London: GMP, 1989), 13–34. For medievalists developing queer theoretical insights, see below.

30. *De civitate Dei,* 14.18, ed. Bernard Dombart and Alphonse Kalb, 2 vols., Corpus christianorum, 47–48 (Turnhout: Brepols, 1955), 2: 441; *The City of God,* 14.18, trans. Henry Bettenson (1972; Harmondsworth, U.K.: Penguin, 1984), 580. For discussion of Augustine that traces his notion of the perversion even within God, see Jonathan Dollimore, *Sexual Dissidence: Augustine to Wilde, Freud to Foucault* (Oxford: Clarendon Press, 1991). I have discussed elsewhere a particular instance of the inessentiality of heterosexuality: in the late-fourteenth-century English romance *Sir Gawain and the Green Knight,* an intricate narrative logic specifically produces the possibility of homosexual relations (between the exemplary knight Gawain and his robust host, Bertilak) only in order that that potential be foreclosed as impossible and the heterosexual be reinscribed as the only legitimacy. For my discussion of heterosexuality's contingency in *Sir Gawain and the Green Knight,* see "A Kiss Is Just a Kiss: Heterosexuality and Its Consolations in *Sir Gawain and the Green Knight,*" *diacritics* 24.2–3 (1994): 205–26.

31. See Karma Lochrie, "Sodomy and Other Female Perversions," chap. 5 of *Covert Operations,* for the connection of the exegesis of femininity to a notion of inessential heterosexuality.

32. This view is such a basic one in the field of queer studies and is so widely held that specific documentation seems at once futile and unnecessary. For theoretical starters, see Judith Butler, "Critically Queer," *GLQ: A Journal of Lesbian and Gay Studies* 1 (1993): 17–32; for a full-length discussion of modern heterosexuality, see Jonathan Ned Katz, *The Invention of Heterosexuality* (New York: Dutton, 1995); for emphasis on social and political theory, see the essays in Diane Richardson, ed. *Theorizing Heterosexuality: Telling It Straight* (Buckingham, U.K.: Open Univ. Press, 1996).

33. For a statement of the perils of making methodological distinctions, particularly between gender and sexuality, see Judith Butler, "Against Proper Objects," *differences* 6.2–3 (Summer–Fall 1994): 1–26. Analysis of interrelations between sexuality and other cultural phenomena is indeed often not pursued: Geeta Patel remarks, for example, that most of the essays in *Radical History Review*'s "Queer Issue" "speak through whiteness as though it were given and transparent" ("Homo, Homo, Hybrid: Translating Gender," *College Literature* 24 [1997]: 133–50, quotation at 147 n. 10). See Edward W. Said, "The Problem of Textuality: Two Exemplary Positions," *Critical Inquiry* 4 (1978): 673–714, esp. 710–11, on the absence of accounting for European hegemony in Foucault's work; see also Ann Laura Stoler's observation of the occlusion and centrality of race in Foucault's *History of Sexuality*, in her *Race and the Education of Desire: Foucault's* History of Sexuality *and the Colonial Order of Things* (Durham, N.C.: Duke Univ. Press, 1995).

34. For an extended debate on the "linguistic turn" conducted in the pages of the *American Historical Review,* see John E. Toews, "Intellectual History after the Linguistic Turn: The Autonomy of Meaning and the Irreducibility of Experience," *American Historical Review* 92 (1987): 879–907; David Harlan, "Intellectual History and the Return of Literature," *American Historical Review* 94 (1989): 581–609; David A. Hollinger, "The Return of the Prodigal: The Persistence of Historical Knowing," *American Historical Review* 94 (1989): 610–21; Joyce Appleby, "One Good Turn Deserves Another: Moving beyond the Linguistic; A Response to David Harlan," *American Historical Review* 94 (1989): 1326–32. And see Roger Chartier, *On the Edge of the Cliff: History, Language, and Practices,* trans. Lydia G. Cochrane (Baltimore: Johns Hopkins Univ. Press, 1997), 68–69, for these references and a discussion apropos of Foucault. For a discussion in a medieval context of the linguistic turn, see Gabrielle M. Spiegel, "History, Historicism, and the Social Logic of the Text," chap. 1 of her book whose entirety is relevant here: *The Past as Text: The Theory and Practice of Medieval Historiography* (Baltimore: Johns Hopkins Univ. Press, 1997).

35. Joan W. Scott, "The Evidence of Experience," *Critical Inquiry* 17 (1991): 773–97, at 793.

36. Spiegel, *The Past as Text,* xxi. See also Nancy F. Partner's review

essay of medieval historiography, "Making Up Lost Time: Writing on the Writing of History," *Speculum* 61 (1986): 90–117, which explores the linguistic status of history writing.

37. Donna J. Haraway, "Situated Knowledges: The Science Question in Feminism and the Privilege of Partial Perspective," in *Simians, Cyborgs, and Women: The Reinvention of Nature* (New York: Routledge, 1991), 183–201, quotation at 187 (first published in 1988; emphasis in original). See also "The Promises of Monsters: A Regenerative Politics for Inappropriate/d Others," in *Cultural Studies,* ed. Lawrence Grossberg, Cary Nelson, and Paula A. Treichler (New York: Routledge, 1992), 295–337.

38. Haraway, "Situated Knowledges," 193 (emphasis in original); Foucault, "La Vie des hommes infâmes" (1977), rpt. in *Dits et écrits, 1954–1988,* ed. Daniel Defert and François Ewald, 4 vols. (Paris: Gallimard, 1994), 3: 237–53, at 238; trans. as "The Life of Infamous Men" by Paul Foss and Meaghan Morris, *Michel Foucault: Power, Truth, Strategy,* ed. Meaghan Morris and Paul Patton (Sydney: Feral Publications, 1979), 76–91, at 77.

39. Joan Scott, "The Evidence of Experience"; Dominick LaCapra, *History and Criticism* (Ithaca: Cornell Univ. Press, 1985); Michel de Certeau, "History: Science and Fiction," in *Heterologies,* trans. Brian Massumi (Minneapolis: Univ. of Minnesota Press, 1986), 199–221, and *The Writing of History,* trans. Tom Conley (New York: Columbia Univ. Press, 1988), esp. 19–55; Roger Chartier, *On the Edge of the Cliff.* Medievalists in addition to Gabrielle Spiegel and Nancy Partner (notes 34, 36, above) include Kathleen Biddick, *The Shock of Medievalism* (note 10, above); Michael Camille, *Master of Death: The Lifeless Art of Pierre Remiet, Illuminator* (New Haven: Yale Univ. Press, 1996); Umberto Eco, "Dreaming of the Middle Ages" and "Living in the New Middle Ages," *Travels in Hyperreality,* trans. William Weaver (San Diego: Harcourt Brace Jovanovich, 1986), 61–72, 73–85; Louise O. Fradenburg's essays, " 'So That We May Speak of Them': Enjoying the Middle Ages," *New Literary History* 28 (1997): 205–30, " 'Voice Memorial': Loss and Reparation in Chaucer's Poetry," *Exemplaria* 2 (1990): 169–202, " 'Be Not Far from Me': Psychoanalysis, Medieval Studies, and the Subject of Religion," *Exemplaria* 7 (1995): 41–54, "Introduction: Caxton, Foucault, and the Pleasures of History" (with Carla Freccero), *Premodern Sexualities* (New York: Routledge, 1996), xiii–xxiv; Aaron I. Gurevich, "The Double Responsibility of the Historian," *Diogenes* 42.4, no. 168 (Winter 1994): 65–83; Brian Stock, *Listening for the Text: On the Uses of the Past* (Baltimore: Johns Hopkins Univ. Press, 1990); Nicholas Watson, "Desire for the Past," *Studies in the Age of Chaucer* 21 (forthcoming 1999); Paul Zumthor, *Speaking of the Middle Ages,* trans. Sarah White (Lincoln: Univ. of Nebraska Press, 1986). And see Helen Solterer, ed., *European Medieval Studies under Fire, 1919–1945,* spec. issue of *Journal of Medieval and Early Modern Studies* 27 (Fall 1997), for a range of explorations of personal schol-

arly engagement (Willem Otterspeer, "Huizinga before the Abyss: The von Leers Incident at the University of Leiden, April 1933," 385–444, at 388, trans. Lionel Gossman and Reinier Leushuis, led me to the epigraph from Nietzsche for the present book).

40. See Jacques Derrida, "Cogito and the History of Madness," *Writing and Difference,* trans. Alan Bass (Chicago: Univ. of Chicago Press, 1978), 31–63 (originally delivered as a lecture in 1963 and published in 1964); and Foucault's response in the appendix to the later edition of *Folie et déraison: Histoire de la folie à l'âge classique* (Paris: Gallimard, 1972), 583–603; rpt. *Dits et écrits,* 2: 245–68; trans. as "My Body, This Paper, This Fire," by Geoff Bennington, *Oxford Literary Review* 4.1 (1979): 9–28. For discussion, see Ann Wordsworth, "Derrida and Foucault: Writing the History of Historicity," in *Post-Structuralism and the Question of History,* ed. Derek Attridge, Geoff Bennington, and Robert Young (Cambridge: Cambridge Univ. Press, 1987), 116–25. Wordsworth's essay and the introduction to the volume polarize the issues and seem to side with Derrida, and the complexities of Foucault's position do not seem fully represented or appreciated. I take up the issue in Foucault's work of what might not be reconstitutable by discursive analysis in chapter 2. On "practices" that are not reducible to discourses in Foucault, see Chartier, "The Chimera of the Origin: Archaeology of Knowledge, Cultural History, and the French Revolution," in *On the Edge of the Cliff,* 51–71, esp. 68–69.

41. I want to demonstrate how the theoretical purchase of such postmodern work is weakened because of the binary historiographical narratives—they are modernist narratives, after all, of rupture and dissociation from a unified past—deployed in setting up their frameworks and strategies. As Caren Kaplan points out, "[T]he kind of history staged by the invocation of 'post'-ness will tend to be oversimplified, even mystified." Kaplan, *Questions of Travel: Postmodern Discourses of Displacement* (Durham, N.C.: Duke Univ. Press, 1996), 21. While she notes that " '[p]ost' will always privilege a temporal language and agenda over a spatial one," Kaplan does not find spatial terms particularly satisfactory, either, and discusses, further on, the contingent utility of the terms "postmodern" and "postcolonial" (21).

Such a complaint against binary readings of a medieval/modern-postmodern opposition has been forcefully articulated by Lee Patterson, who reproachfully documents instances in which scholars of the English Renaissance dismiss the Middle Ages as mere premodernity so that they can argue that individual selfhood and historical consciousness were invented in their own period. Patterson's argument opens with a discussion of the fate of history in postmodernism, and intimates that though postmodern theorists such as Lyotard seem to abolish the very possibility of historical understanding, "a genuine postmodernist return to history" is also possible; he suggests, further, that a rethought medieval studies can intervene in postmodernist debates about history, disciplinary practice, and social existence. Though in the space of this article he does not specify how, I concur with his general stance, and in this book I work to make just such an intervention. See Lee Patterson, "On the Margin: Postmodernism, Ironic History, and Medieval Studies," *Speculum* 65 (1990): 87–108, esp. 90–99. For further discussion of an "old/new binarism," see his "The Place of the Modern in the Late Middle Ages," in *The Challenge of Periodization: Old Paradigms and New Perspectives*, ed. Lawrence Besserman (New York: Garland, 1996), 51–66, presenting an argument about the risks but eventual necessity of "the master narrative of modernization" (54). David Aers observes acidly the conservative politics of so-called radical analyses of early modernity. See David Aers, "A Whisper in the Ear of Early Modernists; or, Reflections on Literary Critics Writing the 'History of the Subject,' " in *Culture and History, 1350–1600: Essays on English Communities, Identities and Writing*, ed. David Aers (Detroit: Wayne State Univ. Press, 1992), 177–202. See also Nancy F. Partner, "Did Mystics Have Sex?," in *Desire and Discipline: Sex and Sexuality in the Premodern West*, ed. Jacqueline Murray and Konrad Eisenbichler (Toronto: Univ. of Toronto Press, 1996), 296–311, esp. 296–301.

42. Homi K. Bhabha, "Postcolonial Criticism," in *Redrawing the Boundaries: The Transformation of English and American Literary Studies*, ed. Stephen Greenblatt and Giles Gunn (New York: MLA, 1992), 437–65, at 437.

43. Bhabha, "Signs Taken for Wonders: Questions of Ambivalence and Authority under a Tree outside Delhi, May 1817," in *The Location of Culture* (New York: Routledge, 1994), 102–22, at 113.

44. Bhabha, "Signs Taken for Wonders," 116.

45. "New times": Bhabha, "Postcolonial Criticism," esp. 441–45, and "Postcolonial Authority and Postmodern Guilt," in *Cultural Studies*, ed. Grossberg, Nelson, and Treichler, 56–68, esp. 59–60.

46. Bhabha, "Postcolonial Authority," 59, 60.

47. Walter Benjamin, "Theses on the Philosophy of History," in *Illuminations*, ed. Hannah Arendt, trans. Harry Zohn (New York: Schocken, 1969), 253–64, at 255: "To articulate the past historically does not mean to recognize it 'the way it really was' (Ranke). It means to seize hold of a memory as it flashes up at a moment of danger. Historical materialism wishes to retain that image of the past which unexpectedly appears to man singled out by history at a moment of danger. The danger affects both the content of the tradition and its receivers. The same threat hangs over both: that of becoming a tool of the ruling classes."

48. Bhabha, "Postcolonial Criticism," 443–44. Similarly, attending to "the place and time of the enunciative agency," he emphasizes "the *present* of utterance," the performative over the pedagogical. "Postcolonial Authority," 57 (emphasis in original).

49. Bhabha, "Postcolonial Criticism," 457. "Internal difference" is Derrida's term, qtd. in "Postcolonial Criticism," 448.

50. Bhabha, "Postcolonial Criticism," 445.

51. Benjamin, "Theses on the Philosophy of History," 263.

52. Carolyn Dinshaw, "A Kiss Is Just a Kiss" (see note 30, above).

53. Bhabha, "DissemiNation: Time, Narrative, and the Margins of the Modern Nation," *Nation and Narration*, ed. Homi K. Bhabha (London: Routledge, 1990), 291–322, at 308.

54. Bhabha seems to reduce Anderson's more nuanced view of the medieval linguistic environment here. See Benedict Anderson, *Imagined Communities: Reflections on the Origins and Spread of Nationalism* (London: Verso, 1983): although the analysis is at points reductive and condescending (e.g., pp. 28–29), see the subtler accounts of the nonarbitrariness of the medieval sign on 21, and on the fall of Latin and the use of the vernacular on 25.

55. Paul Strohm's sharp summary remarks at the "Cultural Frictions" conference at Georgetown University (October 1995) focused my thoughts here. Through this deadening of the Middle Ages Bhabha creates a very conventional history of his own imagined community: as Eric W. Hobsbawm notes in "The Historian between the Quest for the Universal and the Quest for Identity," *Diogenes* 168 (1994): 51–64, at 59: "Reading the desires of the present into the past, or, in technical terms, anachronism, is the most common and convenient technique of creating a history satisfying the needs of what Benedict Anderson has called 'imagined communities' or collectives, which are by no means only national ones." Qtd. in Chartier, *On the Edge*, 8.

56. Since Bhabha is challenging the foundations of Western nationalism and finding other locations of culture, that tired foundational idea of periodization should be challenged wherever it can be found—as feminist historians, among others, have stressed. Bhabha might extend his concept of betweenness: if we follow Donna Haraway (as she makes use of Bruno Latour), we might elevate the middleness of the so-called Middle Ages into a principle here: "[T]he world has always been in the middle of things, in unruly and practical conversation, full of action and structured by a startling array of actants and of networking and unequal collectives." Donna Haraway, "The Promises of Monsters," 304. See also Jeffrey Jerome Cohen and Bonnie Wheeler, "Becoming and Unbecoming," in *Becoming Male in the Middle Ages*, ed. J. J. Cohen and B. Wheeler (New York: Garland, 1997), vii–xx, esp. xviii. Feminist challenges to conventional historical periodization include Joan Kelly, "Did Women Have a Renaissance?" *Women, History and Theory* (Chicago: Univ. of Chicago Press, 1984), 19–50; Jo Ann McNamara and Suzanne Wemple, "The Power of Women through the Family in Medieval Europe: 500–1100," *Feminist Studies* 1 (1973): 126–41.

Since Bhabha has called for culturally productive processes of identification requiring "direction and contingent closure but not teleology and holism," narratives that refuse such "continuous history" would seem to be crucial. "Continuous history [*l'histoire continue*]" is from Foucault, *The Archaeology of Knowledge*, trans. A. M. Sheridan Smith (1972; New York: Barnes and Noble Books, 1993), 12; *L'Archéologie du savoir* (Paris: Gallimard, 1969), 21.

Also grappling with Bhabha's usefulness in analyzing cultural phenomena while observing his lack of engagement with medieval culture is Kathleen Davis, in a paper delivered at the 1996 New Chaucer Society Congress: "Post-Colonial Nationalism Theory and the Medieval English Text."

57. Paul Zumthor, *Speaking of the Middle Ages*, trans. Sarah White (Lincoln: University of Nebraska Press, 1986), 67. See Marina S. Brownlee, Kevin Brownlee, and Stephen G. Nichols, eds., *The New Medievalism* (Baltimore: Johns Hopkins Univ. Press, 1991), esp. "The New Medievalism: Tradition and Discontinuity in Medieval Culture," by Stephen G. Nichols, for demonstrations of medieval awarenesses of "the uncertainties, undecidability, mutability and finiteness of the world" (22).

58. Bhabha, "Postcolonial Authority," at 56, 57, emphases in original.

59. Bhabha, "Postcolonial Authority," 56. Barthes's text reads: "Un soir, à moitié endormi sur une banquette de bar, j'essayais par jeu de dénombrer tous les langages qui entraient dans mon écoute" (*Le Plaisir du texte* [Paris: Seuil, 1973], 79).

60. Quoted phrases from D. A. Miller in *Bringing Out Roland Barthes* (Berkeley: Univ. of California Press, 1992), 23; the negative force of the term "phobic" is mitigated by Miller's discussion of the warrants of such "quasi-paranoid mistrust." For Barthes's own explication of the problematics of gay self-naming, see his preface to Renaud Camus's *Tricks* (1979) in *The Rustle of Language*, trans. Richard Howard (New York: Hill and Wang, 1986), 291–95; *Le Bruissement de la langue* (Paris: Seuil, 1984), 327–31.

61. Bhabha, "Postcolonial Criticism," 441.

62. Roland Barthes, *Incidents* (Paris: Seuil, 1987); trans. as *Incidents* by Richard Howard (Berkeley: Univ. of California Press, 1992).

63. Bhabha, "DissemiNation," 292.

64. Geeta Patel writes that hybridity can be seen as related to queerness: "I want to put the seamless uniformity of heterosexuality to the test, not merely by pointing to its culturally contingent construction, but by asking what happens when you assume sexuality is neither fixed nor uniform, by asking how it would look if it were hybrid. Queerness then becomes a way to make the center ambivalent, hybridize it, so that hybridity and queerness no longer sit in for 'otherness,' but, in continuity with Homi Bhabha's injunctions, unsettle the self." Patel, "Home," 134. But she also observes that Bhabha's reliance on a psychoanalytic framework cannot help but limit the possibility of his engagement with homosexuality and gender; she

also notes Gayatri Spivak's limitations with regard to homosexuality in the South Asian context ("Home," 138–39).

65. Here I want to make clear that Bhabha is hardly the only postmodern theorist who totalizes the medieval past in order that an arbitrary modernity may emerge. Jean Baudrillard provides another fulsome example. Baudrillard's discussion of "The Orders of Simulacra" in *Simulations* (published in English in 1983 [New York: Semiotext(e)]) traces a temporal procession from the *counterfeit*, characteristic of the era spanning the Renaissance and the Industrial Revolution, to *production*, characteristic of the industrial era, to *simulation*, which reigns over the current phase wherein the real is "that which is always already reproduced." Such an analysis undertakes to explicate the emptying-out of the sign, of history, and of all cultural phenomena under capitalism: these processes, shattering any possibility of a humanistic subject, produce a sort of vertiginous postmodern exhilaration. Such a shattering can be seen to have its queer uses, as I suggest via Foucault in my coda. (Lest this very general characterization of a conceptual similarity between Baudrillard and Foucault mislead, however, let us not forget that Baudrillard wrote *Oublier Foucault* [Paris: Editions Galilée, 1977] in addition to later remarks in *Cool Memories, 1980–85* [Paris: Editions Galilée, 1987], 197–201, that homophobically reduce Foucault's AIDS to a loss of confidence, to letting oneself die. Baudrillard's relation to Foucault is taken up in David M. Halperin's "Forgetting Foucault: Acts, Identities, and the History of Sexuality" [*Representations* 63 (Summer 1998): 93–120]; Halperin's title inspired the title of my third section of this introduction.) But it is telling that a recent queer historical project, Michael Camille's look at medieval book collecting, deploys Baudrillard on the twentieth century, not on the premodern period; see Michael Camille, "The Book as Flesh and Fetish in Richard de Bury's *Philobiblon*," in *The Book and the Body*, ed. D. W. Frese and K. O'Brien O'Keeffe (Notre Dame: Univ. of Notre Dame Press, 1997), 34–77, esp. 61. Baudrillard's entirely conventional, humanist historiographical narrative renders his work less useful to the queer historian of premodernity than it might be to queer modernists. We will see in chapter 3, in the congressional discussions concerning the National Endowment for the Humanities, a dangerous relationship between a desire to have a safely lost, foundational past, a United States whose history is disappearing, and neoconservative politics in the United States; as with Bhabha's use of the past, Baudrillard's offers a troubling link to conservative politics. It is no mere coincidence that *Cool Memories* includes a homophobic characterization of AIDS.

66. See Bhabha, "Postcolonial Criticism," 450–51; Bhabha derives the concept of identification that eludes resemblance from Slavoj Žižek in *The Sublime Object of Ideology* (New York: Verso, 1989), 109. The "time lag" of signification opens up "a disjunctive space of temporality"—"new times"

in which emergent cultural identificatory strategies can be pursued: "Such a disjunctive space of temporality is the locus of symbolic identification that structures the intersubjective realm — the realm of otherness and the social — where 'we identify ourselves with the other precisely at a point at which he is inimitable, at the point which eludes resemblance' (Žižek 109). . . . [T]his liminal moment of identification — eluding resemblance — produces a subversive strategy of subaltern agency that negotiates its own authority through a process of iterative 'unpicking' and incommensurable, insurgent relinking" (Bhabha, "Postcolonial Criticism," 450–51). If we take the "other" here as the past, such identification (or as I prefer, removing the concept from its psychoanalytic frame here, relations or partial connections) does not require the past to provide a model to mime but rather offers the past as part of a range of possible relations.

67. Cf. Michel de Certeau, "History: Science and Fiction," *Heterologies: Discourse on the Other,* trans. Brian Massumi (Minneapolis: Univ. of Minnesota Press, 1986), 199–221, at 218: "Questioning the subject of knowledge demands that one rethink the concept of time, if it is true that the subject is constructed as a stratification of heterogeneous moments and that whether the scholar is a woman, black, or Basque, it is structured by relations to the other. Time is precisely the impossibility of an identity fixed by a place. Thus begins a reflection on time. The problem of history is inscribed in the place of this subject, which is in itself a play of difference, the historicity of a nonidentity with itself." See also Fradenburg and Freccero, "Introduction: Caxton, Foucault, and the Pleasures of History," in *Premodern Sexualities,* xix, and Fradenburg, " 'So That We May Speak of Them.' "

68. Scott Bravmann, in *Queer Fictions of the Past: History, Culture, and Difference* (Cambridge: Cambridge Univ. Press, 1997), has recently taken up this very issue, exemplifying his theoretical discussion with analyses of current uses of Greek antiquity and of Stonewall in constituting queer communities now.

69. There is a rich postmodern theoretical literature on "community," engaging the problems of being-in-common after metaphysics: for starters, see Jean-Luc Nancy, *The Inoperative Community,* ed. Peter Connor, trans. Peter Connor et al. (Minneapolis: Univ. of Minnesota Press, 1991); Giorgio Agamben, *The Coming Community,* trans. Michael Hardt (Minneapolis: Univ. of Minnesota Press, 1993). But my thinking about the term has derived mainly from discussions of identity politics in feminist and in lesbian/gay/queer contexts; the literature here is overwhelming, but for a succinct summary of some of the problems, see Joshua Gamson, "Must Identity Movements Self-Destruct? A Queer Dilemma," *Social Problems* 42 (1995): 390–407. For a sharp rejection of the term, see Cindy Patton, *Inventing AIDS* (New York: Routledge, 1990), 7–8. And see Stephen O.

Murray, *American Gay* (Chicago: Univ. of Chicago Press, 1996), chap. 8, "Gay Community," 182–214, for a defense.

70. Ralph Hexter, "John Boswell, 1945–1994," *Radical History Review* 62 (1995): 259–61, at 260. On Judeo-Christianity as the cause of "the anti-homosexuality taboo," see John Lauritsen, "Religious Roots of the Taboo on Homosexuality," in four parts, in *GALA [Gay Atheists League of America] Review* 1.2–5 (1978).

71. See the essays by Warren Johansson, Wayne Dynes, and Lauritsen that comprise *Homosexuality, Intolerance, and Christianity: A Critical Examination of John Boswell's Work* (New York: Scholarship Committee, Gay Academic Union, 1981), esp. Lauritsen's "*Culpa ecclesiae:* Boswell's Dilemma," at 20. See also Lauritsen's review of Boswell's book in *GALA Review* 3.12 (1980): 9–18. For Christianity as an important cause of homosexual oppression, see Arthur Evans, *Witchcraft and the Gay Counterculture: A Radical View of Western Civilization and Some of the People It Has Tried to Destroy* (Boston: Fag Rag Books, 1978). For Christian moral theology as cause of lethal oppression, see Louis Crompton, "The Myth of Lesbian Impunity: Capital Laws from 1270 to 1791," *Journal of Homosexuality* 6 (1980/81): 11–25. For analysis of the historical specificity of Christian intolerance, see David F. Greenberg and Marcia H. Bystryn, "Christian Intolerance of Homosexuality," *American Journal of Sociology* 88 (1982): 515–48.

72. Jean Strouse, "Homosexuality since Rome," *Newsweek*, 29 September 1980, 79–81; "Eros, Ethos, and Going to College: An Interview with John Boswell," *Yale Daily News Magazine*, December 1983, 6–9, at 9.

73. Richard Hall, interview with John Boswell, in "Historian John Boswell on Gay [*sic*], Tolerance and the Christian Tradition," *The Advocate*, 28 May 1981, 20–23, 26–27.

74. Letter, 15 September 1980. I cite Boswell's personal correspondence with permission, and use only dates to identify individual letters in order to protect the privacy of the correspondents.

75. Letter, 6 May 1983.

76. Letter, no date.

77. Letter, 3 July 1980.

78. Letter, 19 January 1984.

79. The two new translations are *The New International Version* and *The New Jerusalem Bible*. See Boswell's statement, 8 October 1993, for the plaintiffs.

80. Letter, 6 January 1981.

81. See letters, 16 August 1982; 3 June 1982; transcript, 19 August 1982.

82. Transcript, 19 August 1982, n.p.

83. Letter, no date ("Books like yours," the correspondent writes, "will help educate the public").

84. See, e.g., letter, 16 September 1981.

85. Letters, 28 September 1980; no date.

86. Letters, 24 September 1980; 28 September 1980; 15 November 1980.

87. Letter, 1 October 1980.

88. Letter, 9 June 1983.

89. Boswell, "Revolutions, Universals, and Sexual Categories," originally published in 1982. Rpt. with postscript in *Hidden from History: Reclaiming the Gay and Lesbian Past,* ed. Martin Duberman, Martha Vicinus, and George Chauncey Jr. (New York: Meridian, 1990), 17–36, at 20.

90. E.g., letters, 22 December 1978; 18 December 1980.

91. "No Such Word as Gay?" *Gay News,* 4–17 September 1980.

92. Letter from John Boswell to Louis Evrard, 10 July 1984: the French were balking at the non-Frenchness and apparent militance of the word "gay."

93. Site maintained by Paul Halsall, who wrote there, "Gay history and gay liberation have ever gone together": the utopian drift of this assertion is reinforced by the instantaneous utopia of global availability that many believe is promised by the Internet. Thanks to Halsall for extensive online bibliographies and strenuous MEDGAY Internet discussion of Boswell.

94. Boswell, "Revolutions," 35. In "Sexual Categories, Sexual Universals: A Conversation with John Boswell," Lawrence Mass presses Boswell about the positions expressed in "Revolutions, Universals, and Sexual Categories." Boswell explains repeatedly that he is using the term "gay" the way he thinks most Americans do now, to refer to people who prefer sex with their own gender; this rubric is broad and unspecific, he notes, while still meaningfully referring to something distinctive and real, and thus it can serve to group rather diverse people together. Interpreting the "gray areas"—"people in ambiguous categories"—does form part of the practice of gay history, Boswell implies (209). At the same time, his stance that "there were people with sensibilities much like those of modern gay people in almost every pre-modern society" (209) tends to limit the range (and, I think, the impact on the practice of history) of those ambiguities. See the interview in Lawrence Mass, *Homosexuality as Behavior and Identity: Dialogues of the Sexual Revolution,* 2 vols. (New York: Harrington Park, 1990), 2: 202–33.

95. Louise Fradenburg and Carla Freccero make such a point in their "Introduction: Caxton, Foucault, and the Pleasures of History," xix: "What has to be asked is whether the observation of similarities or even continuities between past and present inevitably produces an ahistoricist or universalizing effect."

96. See "Gay History," Boswell's review of David F. Greenberg's *The Construction of Homosexuality* in *Atlantic* (February 1989): 74–78, esp. 74–75.

97. On *Christianity, Social Tolerance, and Homosexuality,* see letter, 5 January 1981, and David M. Halperin's work in his *One Hundred Years of Homosexuality and Other Essays on Greek Love* (New York: Routledge, 1990); on Boswell, *Same-Sex Unions in Premodern Europe* (New York: Villard Books, 1994), see Mark D. Jordan's review of *Same-Sex Unions,* "A Romance of the Gay Couple," *GLQ: A Journal of Lesbian and Gay Studies* 3 (1996): 301–10; and Randolph Trumbach, review of *Same-Sex Unions* in *Journal of Homosexuality* 30.2 (1995): 111–17.

98. Boswell, *Same-Sex Unions,* 280–81. But neither this qualifier nor, as Joan Cadden notes, the choice of the term "same-sex union" can or should "mask Boswell's conviction that the institution reflected in the texts is, in some significant sense, 'gay marriage.' " Cadden, review of *Same-Sex Unions, Speculum* 71 (1996), 693–96, at 695.

99. Randolph Trumbach, review of *Same-Sex Unions;* Bernadette J. Brooten, *Love between Women: Early Christian Responses to Female Homoeroticism* (Chicago: Univ. of Chicago Press, 1996), 12; see her discussion of the gender problems in Boswell's work, 10–13. Brooten's own groundbreaking book may indeed be guilty of problems similar to the ones I am analyzing in Boswell: not of ignoring gender but of creating an image of lesbians (in this case) in history that is acceptable in the Western mainstream now, that even mirrors the mainstream lesbian image. As Natalie Boymel Kampen writes in The *GLQ* Forum on Brooten's book, "Lesbian Historiography before the Name?" *GLQ: A Journal of Lesbian and Gay Studies* 4 (1998): 595–601, at 600–601: "Placing love and nonexploitative same-sex relationships at the heart of her Roman and early Christian women's lives, [Brooten] presents these women to modern Christians as legitimate ancestors for lesbians who seek a legitimate place in today's church."

100. E. Ann Matter, review of *Christianity, Social Tolerance, and Homosexuality, Journal of Interdisciplinary History* 13 (1982): 115–17, at 117.

101. "Introduction," *Homosexuality, Intolerance, and Christianity,* n.p.

102. Noted by Trumbach in his review of *Same-Sex Unions,* at 112. One of Boswell's correspondents (25 September 1980) in the wake of the phenomenal success of *Christianity, Social Tolerance, and Homosexuality* predicted that the book would sell to gay markets for years, like Katz's *Gay American History* (1976).

103. Trumbach, review of *Same-Sex Unions,* at 112.

104. See Michael Warner, "Normal and Normaller: Beyond Gay Marriage," *GLQ: A Journal of Lesbian and Gay Studies* 5 (1999): 119–71.

105. "Revolutions, Universals, and Sexual Categories," 19–20.

106. Larry Kramer, "Report from the Holocaust," *Reports from the Holocaust: The Making of an AIDS Activist* (New York: St. Martin's, 1989), esp. 240–42, 273.

107. Letter to Douglas Mitchell, 19 November 1979.

108. Didier Eribon, *Michel Foucault,* trans. Betsy Wing (Cambridge, Mass.: Harvard Univ. Press, 1991), 317.

109. *The History of Sexuality,* vol. 2: *The Use of Pleasure,* trans. Robert Hurley (New York: Pantheon, 1985), 3–13; *Histoire de la sexualité,* 2: *L'Usage des plaisirs* (Paris: Gallimard, 1984), 9–19.

110. "Sexual Choice, Sexual Act," interview with James O'Higgins, trans. James O'Higgins, *Salmagundi* 58–59 (Fall–Winter 1982), rpt. in *Foucault Live,* 322–34, at 323.

111. *Christianity, Social Tolerance, and Homosexuality,* 44.

112. Michel Foucault, "Histoire et homosexualité," interview with J. P. Joecker, M. Ouerd, and A. Sanzio, *Masques* 13 (Spring 1982), 15–25, at 22; rpt. in *Dits et écrits, 1954–1988,* ed. Daniel Defert and François Ewald, 4 vols. (Paris: Gallimard, 1994), 4:286–95, at 292; trans. as "History and Homosexuality" by John Johnston in *Foucault Live: Collected Interviews, 1961–1984,* ed. Sylvère Lotringer (New York: Semiotext[e], 1996), 363–70, at 367–68. Note also Foucault's appreciation of Lillian Faderman's *Surpassing the Love of Men,* another 1980 book that has been seen as essentializing by some American readers; he sees that Faderman is tracing historical phenomena that might well demonstrate the kind of "diversification" of modes of life that could show us possibilities for the future: "De l'amitié comme mode de vie," *Le Gai pied* (April 1981): 38–39, at 39; rpt. *Dits et écrits,* 4: 163–67, at 166; trans. as "Friendship as a Way of Life" by John Johnston, *Foucault Live,* 308–12, esp. 311; see also "Histoire et homosexualité," *Dits et écrits,* 4: 289.

113. Postscript of 1988 to his 1982 article, "Revolutions, Universals, and Sexual Categories," 34–36.

114. "Sexual Choice, Sexual Act," 323, 322.

115. Didier Eribon, "S'acharner à être gay," *Ex Aequo,* no. 5 (1997).

116. Jordan, *Invention of Sodomy,* 158. See Ralph Hexter's generous review of *The Invention of Sodomy* (*Medieval Review,* http://www.hti.umich.edu/b/bmr/tmr.html) for observations of Jordan's occasional failure to eschew teleology and occasional reliance on what he ostensibly decries in historiography, "verisimilitude and sequence" (*Invention of Sodomy,* 1).

117. Louise Fradenburg, " 'So That We May Speak of Them,' " 220. See her series of articles developing an argument about mourning, loss, history, and pleasure: Fradenburg, " 'Voice Memorial,' " " 'Be Not Far from Me,' " and "Introduction" (with Carla Freccero) in *Premodern Sexualities.*

118. Fradenburg and Freccero, "Introduction," xix.

119. Ibid., xix.

120. Camille, *Master of Death,* 7.

121. Camille, *Master of Death,* 4, 7.

122. Ibid., 245. Camille quotes Foucault's essay, "La Vie des hommes in-

fâmes," and differentiates his project from such an approach that treats only the archive of the aberrant, recorded in verbal records: "But what of other kinds of archives, those that are retained in scraps not of words but of images, and those which represent not the unique but the ordinary, the repeatable" (3). Remiet's ordinariness is crucial for Camille's study "because he is rooted in a world he can never transcend" (3). Yet of course Foucault's infamous men do not transcend their worlds, either, but rather reveal something of the workings of those worlds. Camille's critique of the neglect of the image in such archival studies is important; but his approach here nonetheless bears some palpable similarities to Foucault's: both speak of something like "sensation" in trying to interpret or analyze their material (Camille, *Master of Death*, 9; Foucault, "La Vie," 238 [see note 38]).

123. Though I don't seek to oppose postcolonialism to postmodernism, I am nonetheless moved by what Kwame Anthony Appiah calls postcoloniality's humanism. He writes that the "post" in postcoloniality, like that in postmodernism, "is also a 'post' that challenges earlier legitimating narratives. And it challenges them in the name of the suffering victims of 'more than thirty [African] republics.' But it also challenges them in the name of the ethical universal; in the name of *humanism*. . . . For what I am calling humanism can be provisional, historically contingent, and antiessentialist (in other words, postmodern) and still be demanding. We can surely maintain a powerful engagement with the concern to avoid cruelty and pain while nevertheless recognizing the contingency of that concern." The ethical concerns about cruelty and pain that African postcolonial writers address have affinities with (but are not commensurate with) ethical concerns about cruelty and pain that queers address. Kwame Anthony Appiah, "Is the 'Post-' in 'Postcolonial' the 'Post-' in 'Postmodern'?" in *Dangerous Liaisons: Gender, Nation, and Postcolonial Perspectives*, ed. Anne McClintock, Aamir Mufti, and Ella Shohat (Minneapolis: Univ. of Minnesota Press, 1997), 420–44, quotation on 438. Cf. Jeffrey Weeks's focus on "radical humanism" in the context of social constructionist analysis of sexuality: *Invented Moralities: Sexual Values in an Age of Uncertainty* (New York: Columbia Univ. Press, 1995).

124. The past inheres in the present, as C. S. Lewis wrote in 1936; the present forms the past, as Marc Bloch, before he was killed by the Nazis, insisted. C. S. Lewis, *The Allegory of Love* (1936; rpt. New York: Oxford University Press, 1958), 1: "Humanity does not pass through phases as a train passes through stations: being alive, it has the privilege of always moving yet never leaving anything behind. Whatever we have been, in some sort we are still." Qtd. by Boswell, *Same-Sex Unions*, 282. Marc Bloch, *The Historian's Craft*, trans. Peter Putnam (New York: Knopf, 1953), 43–47, esp. 44; cited by David Nirenberg, *Communities of Violence*, 3; I found Nirenberg's introductory discussion useful in formulating my own project.

125. E. N. Johnson, "American Mediaevalists and Today," *Speculum* 28 (1953), 844–54, at 854; cited in Patterson, "On the Margin," 107–8. See Judith M. Bennett, "Our Colleagues, Ourselves," in *The Past and Future of Medieval Studies,* ed. John Van Engen (Notre Dame: Univ. of Notre Dame Press, 1994), 245–58, for an argument that "medieval studies boasts a long and distinguished alternative tradition" of engagement with the modern world (246).

126. Steven Justice, "Inquisition, Speech, and Writing: A Case from Late-Medieval Norwich," *Representations* 48 (Fall 1994): 1–29, at 27. Though our conclusions differ radically, I have benefited a great deal from Steven Justice's help in my approach to the Lollards—the encounter early on with his expertise and translations of Lollard material influenced my subsequent work deeply—and I thank him for his collegial generosity.

In "Inquisition," commenting on the place of historians in the story of "dissent and its antagonists," Justice likens historians to John of Exeter, a clerk of Lollard heresy trials in East Anglia at the end of the 1420s. John's "investment in the proceedings" is in the main in "keeping himself awake and aware, getting through days of work that, though well remunerated and hardly on the larger scale of things laborious, still have their *longueurs* and their provocations of restlessness and resentment, and in finding something there worth fixing the mind on" (26–27). These activities characterize the daily grind of scholars as well, Justice finds in the conclusion of his essay. Justice's rich and dense historical analysis seeks to recover the clerk's experience of labor, to humanize the scribe, to understand his "detached curiosity" and indeed celebrate that detachment for enabling him to record the voice of the heretics on trial "without judgment and without commitment" (25). Noting that historical situations such as heresy trials demand that we modern historians "take sides," Justice nonetheless maintains that our place is more like that of the detached, institutionally secure scribe and cautions that "[i]f as historians we cultivate sympathies, we should in all conscience admit that it is ourselves for whom we cultivate them" (26). While I may be able to agree in general with this admonition, I can't agree with the implication of dead-end narcissism or the sense of inconsequence that Justice seems to suggest is the inevitable result of this admission: "Even when we nourish motives more pointed than [the daily grind described in the above quotation], we ought not to pretend that our work is on our subjects' behalf, or that it is in any direct or unambiguous way political; it is perhaps at most a cultivation of the soul. We may claim other motives than John's, but I am not sure that as historians we can claim any other lineage; like him, we engage with these Lollards, if we engage with them at all, from the safety of privilege and inconsequence" (27). But not all historians are alike, of course, and surely Justice (revising the work of previous historians) knows this; that "we" covers over great multiplicity and diversity.

127. That vulnerability occurs in all arenas—in hiring, promotion, and teaching. For varied discussions of lesbian presences and vulnerabilities in academe, see Greta Gaard, "Anti-Lesbian Intellectual Harrassment in the Academy," in *Antifeminism in the Academy*, ed. VèVè Clark, Shirley Nelson Garner, Margaret Higonnet, and Ketu H. Katrak (New York: Routledge, 1996), 115–40; Linda Garber, ed., *Tilting the Tower: Lesbians, Teaching, Queer Subjects* (New York: Routledge, 1994); Bonnie Zimmerman and Toni A. H. McNaron, eds., *The New Lesbian Studies: Into the Twentieth Century* (New York: Feminist Press of CUNY, 1996); Susan Krieger, *The Family Silver: Essays on Relationships among Women* (Berkeley: Univ. of California Press, 1996); Beth Mintz and Esther D. Rothblum, eds., *Lesbians in Academia: Degrees of Freedom* (New York: Routledge, 1997). For teaching in particular, in addition to materials in the above books, see Sue-Ellen Case, "The Student and the Strap: Authority and Seduction in the Class(room)," in *Professions of Desire: Lesbian and Gay Studies in Literature*, ed. George E. Haggerty and Bonnie Zimmerman (New York: MLA, 1995), 38–46; and see the discussions of Jane Gallop's pedagogy and sexual harassment case in *Lingua Franca*, the *Chronicle of Higher Education*, and her own story, *Feminist Accused of Sexual Harassment* (Durham, N.C.: Duke Univ. Press, 1997). For rich testimonies and analysis of hundreds of faculty survey respondents, see Toni A. H. McNaron, *Poisoned Ivy: Lesbian and Gay Academics Confronting Homophobia* (Philadelphia: Temple Univ. Press, 1997). For a sociological study addressing "the implications of institutionalized heterosexuality for structuring the conditions of women's work" (2), see Gillian A. Dunne, *Lesbian Lifestyles: Women's Work and the Politics of Sexuality* (Toronto: Univ. of Toronto Press, 1997).

128. Stephen O. Murray, in *American Gay*, at 36–37, has recently lashed out against social constructionists: "Not since German(-speaking) Jewish professionals in the late nineteenth and early twentieth centuries tried to convince themselves that they were assimilated has there been a people with a set of intellectuals so bent on denying the existence of their own people, attacking any attempts to discover tradition, and deriding any affirmations of identity and pride in the identity." See Carole S. Vance's clear explication of the "considerable backlash" against social construction theory of sexuality in "Social Construction Theory: Problems in the History of Sexuality," esp. 27–30.

129. For one high-level claim about historical grounding of sodomy laws in the United States, see the 1986 Supreme Court decision in *Bowers v. Hardwick*. Writing for the majority, Justice White declared, "The issue presented is whether the Federal Constitution confers a fundamental right upon homosexuals to engage in sodomy and hence invalidates the laws of the many States that still make such conduct illegal and have done so for a very long time. . . . Proscriptions against that conduct [consensual sodomy]

have ancient roots." But the problems in determining exactly what is proscribed in any "ancient" sodomy statutes or canons should be clear from my first section, above; on the intensely equivocal legal-historical record and the confusion of sodomitical acts with homosexual persons, see Janet E. Halley's brilliant "*Bowers v. Hardwick* in the Renaissance," in *Queering the Renaissance*, ed. Jonathan Goldberg (Durham, N.C.: Duke University Press, 1994), 15–39; for an earlier, similar analysis of the case, see Jonathan Goldberg, "Introduction: 'That Utterly Confused Category,'" *Sodometries: Renaissance Texts, Modern Sexualities* (Stanford: Stanford Univ. Press, 1992), 1–26.

130. I focus on fragmentation and conflict in medieval communities even as I delineate the pressures of homogeneity. Thus I take into consideration both sides of the debate among late medieval historians that Katherine L. French describes in "Competing for Space: Medieval Religious Conflict in the Monastic-Parochial Church at Dunster," in *From Medieval Christianities to the Reformations*, 215–44, ed. David Aers, spec. issue of *Journal of Medieval and Early Modern Studies* 27 (1997).

131. See Ruth Mazo Karras and David Lorenzo Boyd, "'Ut cum muliere': A Male Transvestite Prostitute in Fourteenth-Century London," in Fradenburg and Freccero, *Premodern Sexualities*, 101–16, esp. 110; and see below, chapter 2.

132. Foucault, "De l'amitié comme mode de vie," 4: 167; trans. "Friendship as a Way of Life," at 312. Michael Lucey quotes this passage in his essay, "Balzac's Queer Cousins and Their Friends," which engages similar concerns about queer relations across time (in *Novel Gazing: Queer Readings in Fiction*, ed. Eve Kosofsky Sedgwick [Durham, N.C.: Duke Univ. Press]), 167–98, at 195 n. 10.

133. Bhabha, "Postcolonial Criticism," 452. "Metonymy" here does not indicate continuity; my use of the term in relation to historiography is thus different from Nancy F. Partner's, in her "Making Up Lost Time" (see note 36, above). She interprets metonymy as a relatively inflexible trope: "[I]t always produces more of the same" (106). But metonymy is not merely a part for the whole, as Partner's first example ("three head of cattle" [106]) would indicate; and it seems to me premature to dismiss "contiguity," "consubstantiality," and "coexistence" as inappropriate to discussions of historical relations—they are the kinds of phenomena I am exploring in this book.

134. Carlo Ginzburg, "Clues: Root of an Evidential Paradigm," in *Clues, Myths, and the Historical Method*, trans. John and Anne Tedeschi (Baltimore: Johns Hopkins University Press, 1989), 96–125. My queer history follows such clues as Carlo Ginzburg has isolated: discarded information, marginal data, anomalies, "details usually considered of little importance, even trivial or 'minor,'" "individual cases, situations, and documents, precisely *because they are individual*" (101, 106). My paradigm is "conjectural," to use

Ginzburg's term, not "Galilean," and it uses a "low" intuition of relations between "unique and indispensable" things: "This 'low intuition' is based on the senses (though it skirts them) and as such has nothing to do with the suprasensible intuition of the various nineteenth- and twentieth-century irrationalisms. It can be found throughout the entire world, with no limits of geography, history, ethnicity, sex, or class—and thus, it is far removed from higher forms of knowledge which are the privileged property of an elite few. . . . It binds the human animal closely to other animal species" (125).

135. Roland Barthes, *S/Z*, trans. Richard Miller (New York: Hill and Wang, 1974), 252; *S/Z* (Paris: Seuil, 1970), 256. Henceforth in my text I shall refer to page numbers first of the English translation, and then of the French edition; all emphases are original.

136. *S/Z*, 28 (translation modified); *S/Z*, 35: "[C]'est au niveau du corps que la barre de l'adversion doit sauter, que les deux *inconciliabilia* de l'Antithèse (le dehors et le dedans, le froid et le chaud, la mort et la vie) sont appelés à se rejoindre, à se toucher, à se mêler par la plus stupéfiante des figures dans une substance composite (sans *tenue*)."

137. Leslie Hill, "Barthes's Body," *Paragraph* 11 (1988): 107–26, at 122.

138. "[T]he castration is transposed onto Sarrasine's own body and we ourselves, second readers, receive the shock [*l'ébranlement*]" (165 [171]); the emptiness of the model contaminates the statue/copy (199); "The Author himself—that somewhat decrepit [*vétuste*] deity of the old criticism—can or could some day become a text like any other" (211 [217]).

139. *S/Z* 154–55; *S/Z* 160.

140. The "scene" is also used in *S/Z* in relation to "The Declaration of Love," when Barthes suggests that such a declaration is "a contestant discourse, like the 'scene' . . . : two languages with different vanishing points (metaphorical perspectives) are placed back to back; all they have in common is their participation in the same paradigm, that of *yes/no*, . . . so that the contestation (or the declaration) appears as a kind of obsessive game of meaning" (177 [183]). Declaration or disputation, the important thing is that each very different kind of linguistic situation is or can be ludic.

141. *Camera Lucida: Reflections on Photography*, trans. Richard Howard (New York: Hill and Wang, 1981), 96; *La Chambre claire* (Paris: Seuil, 1980), 150.

142. "Reflections on a Manual," trans. Sandy Petrey, PMLA 112 (1997): 69–75, at 74–75; "Réflexions sur un manuel," rpt. in *Le Bruissement de la langue* (Paris: Seuil, 1984), 49–56, at 55.

143. Hill, "Barthes's Body," 124; see Andreas Bjørnerud, "Outing Barthes: Barthes and the Quest(ion) of (a Gay) Identity Politics," *New Formations* 18 (Winter 1992): 122–41, esp. 139–41, for a smart discussion of the gender politics of the neuter; though I agree wholeheartedly with the analysis of feminist identity politics, and appreciate the analysis of the political poten-

tial in Barthes's late writings, at this date seven years later I sense the utopianism of Bjørnerud's argument and would continue to insist on feminist vigilance about misogyny and gender oppression. For feminist critiques of the neuter (which Bjørnerud takes up), see Naomi Schor, "Dreaming Dissymmetry: Barthes, Foucault, and Sexual Difference," in *Men in Feminism,* ed. Alice Jardine and Paul Smith (New York: Methuen, 1987), 98–110; and "Women in the Beehive: A Seminar with Jacques Derrida," *Men in Feminism,* 189–203, esp. 194.

144. "The absence of sexual relation" is Lacan's hypothesis in "God and the *Jouissance* of ~~The~~ Woman," in *Feminine Sexuality: Jacques Lacan and the* école freudienne, ed. Juliet Mitchell and Jacqueline Rose, trans. Jacqueline Rose (New York: W. W. Norton, 1985), 137–48, esp. 138–41. "That rancid solipsistic pit" is the notorious phrase of D. W. Robertson Jr., in his 1969 essay, "Some Observations on Method in Literary Studies," in *Essays in Medieval Culture* (Princeton: Princeton Univ. Press, 1980), 73–84, at 82. See Louise O. Fradenburg's analysis of the interrelations of the past with femininity, particularly in the genre of romance: "The Wife of Bath's Passing Fancy," *Studies in the Age of Chaucer* 8 (1986): 31–58.

145. Sometimes, as in the 1968 "The Death of the Author," a fairly traditional historiographical narrative is followed: the Middle Ages is the premodern age, different from but out of which our modern society emerged. "The *author* is a modern character, no doubt produced by our society as it emerged from the Middle Ages, inflected by English empiricism, French rationalism, and the personal faith of the Reformation, thereby discovering the prestige of the individual." Trans. Richard Howard, in *The Rustle of Language* (New York: Hill and Wang, 1986), 49–55, at 49; "La Mort de l'auteur" (1968), rpt. *Le Bruissement de la langue,* 61–67, at 61–62.

146. *The Pleasure of the Text,* trans. Richard Miller (New York: Farrar, Straus and Giroux, 1975), 14; *Le Plaisir du texte,* 26.

147. *Writer Sollers,* trans. Philip Thody (Minneapolis: Univ. of Minnesota Press, 1987), 37; passage qtd. in Annette Lavers, *Roland Barthes: Structuralism and After* (London: Methuen, 1982), 212. *Sollers écrivain* (Paris: Seuil, 1979), 8: "Nous acceptons (c'est là notre coup de maître) les particularismes, mais non les singularités; les types, mais non les individus. . . . Mais l'isolé absolu? Celui qui n'est ni breton, ni corse, ni femme, ni homosexuel, ni fou, ni arabe, etc.? Celui qui n'appartient *même pas* à une minorité? La littérature est sa voix."

148. Michael Holland, "Barthes, Orpheus . . . ," *Paragraph* 11 (1988): 143–74, at 145.

149. Patrizia Lombardo, *The Three Paradoxes of Roland Barthes* (Athens: Univ. of Georgia Press, 1989), 44.

150. *Roland Barthes by Roland Barthes,* trans. Richard Howard (New

York: Hill and Wang, 1977), 139; *Roland Barthes par Roland Barthes* (Paris: Seuil, 1975), 124.

151. "Michelet, Today," trans. Richard Howard, in *The Rustle of Language*, 195–207, at 201; "Aujourd'hui, Michelet," *Le Bruissement de la langue*, 225–36, at 231 (originally published in *L'Arc*, 1972).

152. Lombardo, *Paradoxes*, 138.

153. *Camera Lucida*, 94; *La Chambre clair*, 147: "Michelet conçut l'Histoire comme une Protestation d'amour."

154. *Michelet*, trans. Richard Howard (New York: Hill and Wang, 1987), 81; *Michelet par lui-même* (Paris: Seuil, 1954), 73.

155. *Le Peuple*, qtd. in Lombardo, *Paradoxes*, 138.

156. Roland Barthes, *Michelet*, 18–19 [18]. In a related somatic writing, as Barthes observes years later, "Having to describe the terrible storm of 1859 [in his natural history], by a bold stroke which relates him to the symbolist poets, Michelet describes it *from within*. . . . [T]he storm provokes him to make an experiment *on his own body*, like any taker of hashish or mescaline: 'I went on working, curious to see if this wild force would succeed in oppressing, fettering a free mind.' " "Michelet, Today," 200; "Aujourd'hui, Michelet," 230.

157. Hill, "Barthes's Body," 115. Compare Barthes twenty years after his *Michelet:* "We must be grateful to Michelet (among other gifts he has given us—gifts ignored or suppressed) for having represented to us, through the pathos of his period, the *real conditions* of historical discourse, and for inviting us to transcend the mythic opposition between 'subjectivity' and 'objectivity' (such a distinction is merely propaedeutic: necessary on the level of research), in order to replace it with the opposition between *statement* [*énoncé*] and speech-act [*énonciation*], between the product of investigation and production of the text" (198 [228]). In this 1972 essay, "Michelet, Today," Barthes analyzes Michelet's accomplishments in the structuralist terms of the early 1970s; here he understands that Michelet's somatic historical reenactments effectively critique traditional historical discourse.

158. "The Surrealists Overlooked the Body" (1975), *The Grain of the Voice: Interviews, 1962–1980*, trans. Linda Coverdale (New York: Hill and Wang, 1985), 243–45, at 245, apropos of the Surrealists; "Les Surréalistes ont manqué le corps," *Le Grain de la voix* (Paris: Seuil, 1981), 230–32, at 232. See "Performing Pasts: A Dialogue with Paul Zumthor," in which medievalist Helen Solterer interviews the eminent medievalist Zumthor, discussing theatricality in Zumthor's work and in such a context mentioning the shifts and changes in Barthes's oeuvre (*European Medieval Studies under Fire, 1919–1945*, 595–640, esp. 625).

159. *Sade, Fourier, Loyola*, trans. Richard Miller (New York: Hill and Wang, 1976), 7–8; *Sade, Fourier, Loyola* (Paris: Seuil, 1971), 12–13.

160. Barthes discusses the problematics of the analysis announced by the title of the series, *X par lui-même: "moi par moi?"* (in *Roland Barthes*, 135).

161. *Roland Barthes*, 109, translation modified [102]: it is a factitious anamnesis, "celle que je prête à l'auteur que j'aime."

162. Miller, *Bringing Out Roland Barthes*, 7, 18.

163. "The Grain of the Voice," trans. Stephen Heath, in *Image, Music, Text* (New York: Hill and Wang, 1977), 179–89, at 181; "Le Grain de la voix," *Musique en jeu* 9 (1972): 57–63, at 58.

164. "The Grain of the Voice," 188; "Le Grain de la voix," 62.

165. See Miller, *Bringing Out*, 32–33.

166. Compare Roger Chartier's introduction to *On the Edge of the Cliff*, in which he outlines the problems facing historians who know that knowledges are situated but who nonetheless seek refounding; he evokes Paul Ricoeur: "It is perhaps paradoxical to evoke Paul Ricoeur's hermeneutic and phenomenological approach at the end of the introduction to a book that accentuates historical thinking about rupture and difference. But perhaps it is only within that tension that we can think about and comprehend the past or the 'other' and can get beyond the discontinuities that separate historical configurations" (9).

167. Barthes, *Camera Lucida*, 30 [54].

168. Note, too, Benjamin on early photographs: "Immerse yourself in such a picture long enough and you will recognize how alive the contradictions are, here too: the most precise technology can give its products a magical value, such as a painted picture can never again have for us. No matter how artful the photographer, no matter how carefully posed his subject, the beholder feels an irresistible urge to search such a picture for the tiny spark of contingency, of the Here and Now, with which reality has so to speak seared the subject, to find the inconspicuous spot where in the immediacy of that long-forgotten moment the future subsists so eloquently that we, looking back, may rediscover it." "A Small History of Photography" (1931), in *One-Way Street and Other Writings*, trans. Edmund Jephcott and Kingsley Shorter (London: NLB, 1979), 243. Quoted in Christopher Cutrone, "Glenn Ligon: 'A Feast of Scraps' and *Photos and Notes*" (http://www.xsite.net/~ccutrone/ligon.html), whose brief discussion of Barthes I found illuminating.

169. *Camera Lucida* 96 [150]. Perhaps this Barthes as viewer can give us some inkling of a queer historian, working in a zone of instability wherein his/her desire for the past ("*this has been*") is caught up in dialectical relation with his/her enactment of a present agenda that is just taking shape ("*this will be*"). In this formulation I draw on Bhabha's discussion of Fanon and Kristeva in "DissemiNation."

170. *Sade, Fourier, Loyola*, 7 [12].

171. "Historical Discourse," trans. Peter Wexler, rpt. in *Structuralism: A Reader,* ed. Michael Lane (London: Jonathan Cape, 1970), 145–55, at 154–55; "Le Discours de l'histoire," *Le Bruissement de la langue* (Paris: Seuil, 1984), 153–66, at 164–66; originally published in *Information sur les sciences sociales* (1967).

172. Very early on, in a 1951 article on Michelet, Barthes had argued that the historian is like a photographer, not in relation to the reality effect but in his ability to reveal historical traces in the flesh of men: "Thus the flesh of men who follow each other preserves the obscure trace of the incidents of History, until the day when the historian, like a photographer, *reveals* through a chemical operation that which has previously been experienced." "Michelet, l'histoire et la mort," *Esprit* 178 (April 1951): 497–511, at 509. Trans. in Lombardo, *Paradoxes,* 139.

173. Lombardo, *Paradoxes,* 138.

174. See above, note 168, on Benjamin. As full of conventions, deploying effects in representing reality just as realist narrative—or historical discourse—does, photographs are neither sheer authentication in any simple sense nor the thing itself. Donna Haraway's analysis in "Situated Knowledges" of the functions of visual systems and partial perspectives in the construction of knowledges might point to one way of restoring the dynamism and objectivity Barthes seeks while at the same time coming to terms with partiality and loss.

175. For critical comments on Barthes's turn toward "autobiography and a celebration of the fragment," see Gayatri Chakravorty Spivak, "Subaltern Studies: Deconstructing Historiography," in *In Other Worlds: Essays in Cultural Politics* (New York: Routledge, 1988), 197–221, esp. 208–9.

176. Michael du Plessis accuses D. A. Miller's project of just such idiosyncracy in his review of *Bringing Out Roland Barthes* in *Discourse* 16.1 (Fall 1993): 174–79.

1 It Takes One to Know One: Lollards, Sodomites, and Their Accusers

1. Thomas Walsingham, *Annales Ricardi Secundi,* ed. Henry Thomas Riley, Rolls Series (London: Longmans, Green, Reader, and Dyer, 1866), 182–83. For consistency, I have capitalized "Sodomorum." Cf. John Foxe's translation in *Acts and Monuments* (London, 1853–70; rpt. New York: AMS Press, 1965) 3: 206, which refuses to name the crime at all:

> The English nation doth lament of these vile men their sin,
> Which Paul doth plainly signify by idols to begin.
> But Giezites full ingrate, from sinful Simon sprung,

This to defend, though priests in name, make bulwarks great and strong.
Ye princes, therefore, whom to rule the people God hath placed,
With justice' sword why see ye not this evil great defaced?

Compare the version in the *Fasciculi ʒiʒaniorum*, ed. Walter Waddington Shirley, Rolls Series (London: Longman, Brown, Green, Longmans, and Roberts, 1858), 369, with its variation in the final line (to be translated "How can you prohibit swordplay in response to such deeds?"):

Plangunt Anglorum gentes crimen sodomorum.
Paulus fert horum sunt idola causa malorum.
Surgunt ingrati Gyezitae Symone nati
Nomine praelati, hoc defensare parati.
Qui reges estis, populis quicunque praeestis,
Qualiter his gestis gladios prohibere potestis?

2. There seem to be two independent Latin versions, which in itself might argue for their belatedness with respect to the English; but the English version, in turn, seems at points a mere transliteration of one of the Latin versions, the latinate syntax retained and the meaning not quite understood, as I will demonstrate later. H. S. Cronin's introduction to Dymmok (*Liber contra duodecim errores et hereses Lollardorum* [London: Wyclif Society, 1922], xxxiii n. 6) and Anne Hudson support English primacy; see Anne Hudson, ed., *Selections from English Wycliffite Writings* (Cambridge: Cambridge Univ. Press, 1978), 150: "It seems likely . . . that the original version was in English; certainly an English version must have existed early enough for its inclusion in Dymmok's refutation which was presented to Richard II on his return from Ireland in 1396." H. G. Richardson, "Heresy and the Lay Power under Richard II," *English Historical Review* 51 (1936): 1–28, on 21 n. 5, suggests that the English version of the *Conclusions* was posted on the door of Westminster Hall, that one Latin version was perhaps "prepared for the door of St. Paul's on the occasion of the meeting of convocation" of Canterbury (5 February 1395, after the English posting which would therefore have taken place between 27 January and 5 February), and that Dymmok's Latin seems an independent translation of the English. (Richardson also suggests that a copy of the *Conclusions* was sent to Pope Boniface IX.) The *Fasciculi* and *Annales* redactions seem to be made from the same Latin, while Dymmok does seem to prepare his own translation of the English; the *Fasciculi/Annales* version, compared with the English, seems more semantically precise and lexically varied, and thus perhaps prior. In this chapter I quote from Anne Hudson's edition of the English version (*Selections from English Wycliffite Writings*, 24–29) and Walsingham's Latin, from the Rolls Series edition of the *Annales* (174–83).

The very existence of this little Latin poem might be taken to support a hypothesis about the original Latin language of the *Conclusions;* at the least (given the uncertainties of poem's provenance) it suggests that the Latin version of the *Conclusions* had a popular and perhaps wide dissemination.

3. According to Roger Dymmok and implied by the *Fasciculi zizaniorum,* the *Conclusions* were posted on the doors of Westminster Hall; Walsingham adds the doors of Saint Paul's as well. See Dymmok, *Liber contra duodecim errores et hereses Lollardorum,* 15; *Fasciculi zizaniorum,* 360; Thomas Walsingham, *Annales Ricardi Secundi,* 174; Walsingham, *Historia Anglicana,* 2 parts, ed. Henry Thomas Riley, Rolls Series (London, 1864; rpt. Kraus Reprint, 1965), 2: 216. Thomas Netter's *Doctrinale antiquitatum fidei catholicae ecclesiae,* 3 vols. (ed. B. Blanciotti [Venice, 1759; rpt. Farnborough, U.K.: Gregg Press, 1967]), like the *Fasciculi zizaniorum,* is vaguer but might be taken to imply posting (rather than formal presentation, which seems unlikely) at Parliament (3: 404).

4. The paragraph, unexampled in other sources, mentions Thomas Latimer and Richard Stury as among the supporters of the *Conclusions,* wherein, it goes on, the Lollards wrote under cover (or, in a variant, openly), as is revealed through the verses that follow (*sicut patet per versus sequentes*), that if a remedy for the aforementioned ills were not put forward, they themselves, not as rebels or destroyers of the peace but as correctors of enormous vices, would serve up a remedy in a strong hand (*Annales Ricardi Secundi,* 182). See Cronin's introduction to Dymmok for a discussion of this paragraph (xxxvii–xli); note that Cronin argues against Walsingham's authorship of the *Annales,* but V. H. Galbraith, "Thomas Walsingham and the Saint Albans Chronicle, 1272–1422," *English Historical Review* 47 (1932): 12–30, demonstrates conclusively otherwise. Thomas Wright, *Political Poems and Songs,* Rolls Series, 2 vols. (London: Longman, Green, Longman, and Roberts, 1861), 2: 128, prints the version in the *Fasciculi zizaniorum* and dates the poem in question here to the reign of Henry V (but see discussion below).

5. "And this is the great insurrection," Bale goes on, emphasizing the nonviolence of the incident, "that Walden, then the king's confessor, complaineth of to Pope Martin V., and afterwards Polydorus, the pope's collector, and other papists more, wherein never a one man was hurt." John Bale, conclusion, *A Brefe Chronycle concernynge the Examinacyon and death of the blessed martyr of Christ Syr Johan Oldecastell* ([Antwerp?] 1544), fols. 50–51 (qtd. in Foxe 3: 819 n.). Bale's Latin follows the *Fasciculi* version and his translation at least mentions the Sodomites:

> Bewayle maye Englande the synne of Sodomytes.
> For Idolles and they are grounde of all theyr wo.
> Of Symon Magus a secte of hypocrytes
> Surnamed prelates are up with them to go.
> And to upholde them in all that they maye do.

Yow that be rewlers peculyarlye selected
How can ye suffre soche myscheues uncorrected?

On sixteenth-century chroniclers' treatments of Lollardy, especially Bale's treatment of Anne Askewe's narrative, see Thomas Betteridge, "Anne Askewe, John Bale, and Protestant History," in *From Medieval Christianities to the Reformations*, spec. issue of *Journal of Medieval and Early Modern Studies* 27 (1997): 265–84.

6. Heretics, at least on the European continent, were the ones usually accused of sodomy; see discussion below. For terminology linking heresy and sodomy, see Michael Goodich, *The Unmentionable Vice: Homosexuality in the Later Medieval Period* (Santa Barbara, Calif.: ABC-Clio, 1979), 8–9: *bougre/bougeron*, for an Albigensian, by about 1170 synonymously denoted a sodomite, as did the Old French *erite*, 'heretic.' See the fourteenth-century Jacob Twinger von Königshofen, *Chronik*, in *Chroniken der deutschen Städte* (Leipzig: S. Hirzel, 1871), 9: 904; the fall of Sodom and Gomorrah was a punishment for heresy. Cited in Robert E. Lerner, *The Heresy of the Free Spirit in the Later Middle Ages* (Berkeley: Univ. of California Press, 1972), 4.

7. Henry Knighton comments in his account of 1382 that the sect was enjoying such prestige and was multiplying so rapidly that if you saw two people in the road, most likely one was a disciple of Wyclif: see *Knighton's Chronicle, 1337–1396*, ed. and trans. G. H. Martin (Oxford: Clarendon Press, 1995), 308–9. Paul Strohm notes this passage and argues in "Chaucer's Lollard Joke," *Studies in the Age of Chaucer* 17 (1995): 23–42, that "fourteenth-century Lollards seem from the beginning to crop up at all points on the social scale" (33), and that the 1380s and 1390s were "unsettled" with regard to Lollardy, witnessing both aggressive Lollard actions like the posting of the *Conclusions* and "an uneven but steady consolidation of the anti-Lollard position" (29, 31). Geoffrey Martin argues recently for the importance of Knighton's testimony in "Knighton's Lollards," *Lollardy and the Gentry in the Later Middle Ages*, ed. Margaret Aston and Colin Richmond (New York: St. Martin's; Stroud, U.K.: Sutton, 1997), 28–40.

8. See Anne Hudson, *The Premature Reformation: Wycliffite Texts and Lollard History* (Oxford: Clarendon Press, 1988), quotation at 389. For other scholarly opinions on the heterogeneity of Lollardy, see Hudson, *Premature Reformation*, 382 and notes; for a further viewpoint, see Strohm, "Chaucer's Lollard Joke," 32–34. Note Steven Justice's critique of Hudson for reducing the voices of Lollards to Wyclif's: see "Inquisition, Speech, and Writing: A Case from Late-Medieval Norwich," *Representations* 48 (Fall 1994): 1–29. It must be recalled that the *Twelve Conclusions*, even as they provide a guide to Lollard beliefs at this time, were only one of numerous lists of tenets; they achieved a sort of canonical status when Dymmok reinscribed and refuted them. For another guide to Lollard beliefs, see a late-fourteenth-

century list of Lollard answers to orthodox accusations: "Sixteen Points on Which the Bishops Accuse Lollards," in Hudson, *Selections from English Wycliffite Writings*, 19–24.

9. Hudson, *Selections*, 24. See Hudson, *Premature Reformation*, 387, on the characteristics of the sect, including "a concentration upon secular society, its evils and their remedies," with an allusion to the beginning of the *Twelve Conclusions*. A note on Lollard terms: Hudson remarks that *prelacye*, very derogatory in Lollard writings, indicates "not only the bishops but the whole system of ecclesiastical government based upon provincial and episcopal jurisdiction"; and *priuat religion* "is another Wycliffite term of condemnation, used to signify the religious life adopted by any who have taken formal vows involving separation from the life of the community, and thus covering the life of monks, nuns, hermits, anchorites, friars or secular canons" (*Selections*, 151 n.).

10. John Bale, *A Brefe Chronycle*, fol. 50v.

11. Thanks to Larry Scanlon for pointing out the royalist view of lay monarchy in these lines, in his response to my paper in the "Lollardy and Authority" session at the International Congress on Medieval Studies, Kalamazoo, Michigan, May 1997.

12. Ruth Nissé Shklar has recently demonstrated the nationalistic intentions of the Lollards, scrupulously finding them in Lollard exegetical practices that assert a distinctly British history for right reading: see "History at a Loss," chap. 2 of her Ph.D. dissertation, "Spectacles of Dissent: Heresy, Mysticism and Drama in Late Medieval England" (University of California at Berkeley, 1995). Anne Hudson, *Premature Reformation*, 456–83, shows the geographical reach of the later Lollard network: it connects various communities across the whole of England. See also Shannon McSheffrey, *Gender and Heresy: Women and Men in Lollard Communities, 1420–1530* (Philadelphia: Univ. of Pennsylvania Press, 1995), 77.

13. Steven F. Kruger, "Conversion and Medieval Sexual, Religious, and Racial Categories," in *Constructing Medieval Sexuality*, ed. Karma Lochrie, Peggy McCracken, and James A. Schultz (Minneapolis: Univ. of Minnesota Press, 1997), 158–79, at 160. On the geographical metaphor's functioning, see also Mark D. Jordan, *The Invention of Sodomy in Christian Theology* (Chicago: Univ. of Chicago Press, 1997), 6–8.

14. General Prologue, chap. 10, in *The Holy Bible . . . Made from the Latin Vulgate by John Wycliffe and His Followers*, 4 vols., ed. Josiah Forshall and Frederic Madden (Oxford: Oxford Univ. Press, 1850), 1: 29–34, esp. 30–31. On the date of the General Prologue—between January–February 1395 and January–February 1397—see Margaret Deanesly, *The Lollard Bible and Other Medieval Biblical Versions* (1920; rpt. Cambridge: Cambridge Univ. Press, 1966), 256–58.

15. On Lollard resistance to swearing, see Henry G. Russell, "Lollard

Opposition to Oaths by Creatures," *American Historical Review* 51 (1946): 668–84. For Chaucer's Parson, see *Canterbury Tales* 2.1163–77, *The Riverside Chaucer*, 3rd ed., gen. ed. Larry D. Benson (Boston: Houghton Mifflin, 1987). For cautions about the textual status of this Chaucerian passage, see my chapter 2, note 43.

16. *The Lanterne of Liȝt*, ed. Lilian M. Swinburn, EETS 151 (London: Kegan Paul, Trench, Trübner; Oxford: Oxford University Press, 1917), chap. 12, p. 90; cited in Russell, "Lollard Opposition," 676.

17. Romans 1.23–27, Later Version, *The Holy Bible*, ed. Forshall and Madden, 4: 305–6. In the Vulgate:

> Et mutaverunt gloriam incorruptibilis Dei in similitudinem imaginis corruptibilis hominis, et volucrum, et quadrupedum, et serpentium. Propter quod tradidit illos Deus in desideria cordis eorum, in immunditiam, ut contumeliis afficiant corpora sua in semetipsis: qui commutaverunt veritatem Dei in mendacium; et coluerunt, et servierunt creaturae potius quam Creatori, qui est benedictus in saecula. Amen. Propterea tradidit illos Deus in passiones ignominiae. Nam feminae eorum immutaverunt naturalem usum in eum usum qui est contra naturam. Similiter autem et masculi, relicto naturali usu feminae, exarserunt in desideriis suis in invicem, masculi in masculos turpitudinem operantes, et mercedem, quam oportuit, erroris sui in semetipsis recipientes.

His rhetoric against idolatry is aimed, according to Bernadette J. Brooten, at both gentiles and Jews in his audience (Bernadette J. Brooten, *Love between Women: Early Christian Responses to Female Homoeroticism* [Chicago: Univ. of Chicago Press, 1996], 232). Paul may have believed that heathen deities allowed all kinds of sexual expression among their worshipers, or he may have viewed homosexual activity as the "divine punishment for the primal sin of exchanging 'the truth about God for a lie,' " or he may have seen homosexual relations as a shameful threat to a culture based on honor (*Love between Women*, 205, 204); in some way idolatry yields homosexual relations between females and between males. The recompense for this indecent sexual behavior in turn might be venereal disease, or the effeminacy associated with the passive partner in sodomy, or the sexual behavior itself, viewed as diseased. See Brooten, *Love between Women*, 258.

18. The Wycliffite *Apology for Lollard Doctrines* (written sometime after 1378) may be deploying just this set of associations to implicate members of "private orders" in sodomitical activity: "þei are tokunid bi þe wif of Loth, þat, after þe going out of Sodom, loking aȝen, was turnid in to an image of salt. An image haþ þe similitud of a man, but not þe trowþ" ("They are represented by Lot's wife, who, after leaving Sodom, looking back, was turned into an image of salt. An image has the semblance of a man, but not the truth"). *Apology for Lollard Doctrines*, ed. James Henthorn

Todd (1842; rpt. London: Johnson Reprint Co., 1968), 105, citing "Lincoln," i.e., Grosseteste. Cited by Hudson, *Selections,* 152 n. Here the mention of Sodom resonates beyond its immediate rhetorical focus on Lot's wife and the spiritual evacuation she represents: opposition to sodomy is suggested not only by the reference to the city but more strongly by that reference coupled with the indictment of images. Peter Cantor had earlier made Lot's wife's fate an index of the horror of the sexual sin in *Verbum abbreviatum,* 138, *Patrologia latina,* ed. J.-P. Migne (Paris, 1855), 205: 335: "Etiam pro solo respectu ad Sodomam, uxor Loth conversa est in terram et statuam salis, quasi diceret Dominus: Nolo ut hujus criminis aliqua sit memoria, aliquis respectus, aliquod vestigium pro enormitate illius" ("For just one look back at Sodom, Lot's wife was changed into earth and a pillar of salt, as if the Lord were saying, 'I wish that no memory of this crime should remain, no reminder, no trace of its enormity.' ") Trans. John Boswell, *Christianity, Social Tolerance, and Homosexuality: Gay People in Western Europe from the Beginning of the Christian Era to the Fourteenth Century* (Chicago: Univ. of Chicago Press, 1980), 375–78; at 377.

19. Wyclif is following William Peraldus in the latter's vastly influential twelfth-century treatise on the vices, "De avaritia," *Summa aurea de virtutibus et vitiis* (Venice, 1497), 41b (pagination, for every two pages, beginning with the vices); Wyclif, *De simonia,* ed. Sigmund Herzberg-Fränkel and Michael Henry Dziewicki, Wyclif Society (London: Trübner, 1898), esp. 8–9; trans. *On Simony,* trans. Terrence A. McVeigh (New York: Fordham Univ. Press, 1992), esp. 36–37. On Wyclif's wide-ranging debt to Peraldus, the Dominican born at Pérault, see J. Loserth, *Johann von Wiclif und Guilelmus Peraldus: Studien zur Geschichte der Entstehung von Wiclifs Summa Theologiae* (Vienna: Alfred Hölder, 1916).

20. Penn R. Szittya comments on the antifraternal use of these figures by William of Saint-Amour (whose writings helped found the antifraternal tradition in which Lollard polemics take their place), who makes Gehazi "an exemplar of all simoniac friars who beg after preaching"; and by the Lollard *Jack Upland,* wherein friars are depicted as heirs of Simon Magus. Penn R. Szittya, *The Antifraternal Tradition in Medieval Literature* (Princeton: Princeton Univ. Press, 1986), 49 on William of Saint-Amour; 211 on *Jack Upland.* See 62–122 for a discussion of the circulation in England of the works of William of Saint-Amour. On *Jack Upland,* see below, notes 47 and 78.

21. Jan Hus, letter to Archbishop Zbyněk defending himself against complaints by anti-reformist clergy, in *M. Jana Husi Korespondence a dokumenty,* ed. Václav Novotný (Prague: Komise pro vydávání pramenu náboženského hnutí českého, 1920), no. 12, pp. 30–41, esp. pp. 33–34; trans. Matthew Spinka in *The Letters of John Hus* (Manchester: Manchester Univ. Press; Totowa, N.J.: Rowman and Littlefield, 1972), 24–35, esp. 27–28. See also

Hus's letter in 1404 to John Hübner in defense of Wyclif, quoting Wyclif's *De simonia* (Novotný, *Jana Husi,* no. 6, 11–15, esp. 1–14; Spinka, *Letters,* 3–7, esp. 5–6). On the relation between Wyclif and Hus as reformers, see Gordon Leff, "Wyclif and Hus: A Doctrinal Comparison," in *Wyclif in His Times,* ed. Anthony Kenny (Oxford: Clarendon Press, 1986), 105–25, and Leff, *Heresy in the Later Middle Ages: The Relation of Heterodoxy to Dissent c. 1250–c. 1450,* 2 vols. (Manchester: Manchester Univ. Press; New York: Barnes and Noble, 1967), esp. 2: 620–44; on Wycliffite-Hussite contacts, see also Hudson, *Premature Reformation,* 514–15.

The Lollard poem here may link these two even lexically: the verb "surgere," used to refer to Simon Magus's boasting that he could raise men from the dead in, for example, fairly contemporaneous sermon literature by Bishop Thomas Brinton, is used in the poem for the actions of the Giezites, to denote their rising up. See Sermon 101 on the Feast of Mary Magdalene, according to the editor the last sermon Brinton preached at Cobham (22 July 1382), on the theme *De nocte surrexit, Prouerbiorum 31;* the end of the sermon includes a refutation of the heresies of Wyclif, linking the verb "surgere" to him as well as to Simon Magus earlier: "*pseudoprophete surgent et seducent multos.*" *The Sermons of Thomas Brinton, Bishop of Rochester (1373–1389),* ed. Mary Aquinas Devlin, O.P., Camden Society 86, 2 vols. (London: Royal Historical Society, 1954), 2: 462–66, esp. 465–66. See G. R. Owst, *Preaching in Medieval England: An Introduction to Sermon Manuscripts of the Period c. 1350–1450* (New York: Russell and Russell, 1965), 19–20. Brinton, Bishop of Rochester, died in 1389, having lived near the "centre of stirring events in the general life of his times," including having taken his place at the Blackfriars Council of 1382 at which Wyclif's ideas were condemned; see Owst, *Preaching,* 17.

22. Williell R. Thomson, *The Latin Writings of John Wyclyf: An Annotated Catalog* (Toronto: Pontifical Institute of Mediaeval Studies, 1983), 64. The treatise was written in late 1379 or 1380. Note Terrence A. McVeigh's comments on the treatise's dissemination beyond Oxford in *On Simony,* 17.

23. Wyclif's theory of dominion provided a general foundation for his doctrine of simony. See McVeigh, introduction, *On Simony.*

24. *De simonia,* 8–9; *On Simony,* 36. Note that Jan Hus repeats this passage more or less verbatim in his 1404 letter to Hübner defending Wyclif's teachings (*Jana Husi,* ed. Novotný, 13–14; *Letters,* tr. Spinka, 6).

25. General Prologue, chap. 13, *The Holy Bible,* ed. Forshall and Madden, 1:51. The Peraldus analysis, repeated by Wyclif, recurs in various Lollard works: see also, e.g., "Of Prelates," in F. D. Matthew, ed. *The English Works of Wyclif,* EETS 74, 2nd rev. ed. (London: Trübner, 1902), esp. chap. 5, p. 68. Written in the 1380s, "Fifty Heresies and Errors of Friars," also rehearses this analysis in English. See *Select English Works of John Wyclif,* ed. Thomas Arnold, 3 vols. (Oxford: Clarendon, 1871), 3: 399–400. On "gostli sodom-

ite" as an exclusively Lollard formulation, deployed "as a tool by which to conceptualize what they saw as the contemporary clergy's insufficient attention to pastoral duties, particularly preaching," see Kevin Gustafson, " 'Gostli Sodomites': The Rhetoric of Deviance in Lollard Translation Polemic," paper delivered at the 1993 Columbia Medieval Guild, New York.

26. See Sir Lewis Clifford's apparent characterization of clerical nonmarriage as homicidal (in his so-called confession in 1402): *Historia anglicana*, 252. See discussion of Clifford's words below.

27. For examples of simony as selling God's body, see *Jack Upland*, in *Chaucerian and Other Pieces*, ed. Walter W. Skeat (Oxford: Clarendon, 1897), 191–203, at 195; *The Lanterne of Li3t*, 62.

28. "Namque symoniaci nedum vendunt iusticiam et graciam pro vili precio, ac si quis duceret ad forum pro vili precio iumentum et servum vendendum, sed Christum qui est persona iustissima, quantum in ipsis est, inhonestissime comedunt et consumunt" (*De simonia*, 11). ("For not only do simoniacs sell justice and grace cheaply in the same way as a beast and slave might be led to the marketplace for a cheap sale, but they also shamefully eat and consume the most just person of Christ as much as they can" [*On Simony*, 39].)

29. *De simonia*, 1–2; *On Simony*, 1.

30. *De simonia*, 10; *On Simony*, 38.

31. R. I. Moore has adduced an economic explanation for the development of such a process of abjection in the twelfth century in Europe: *The Formation of a Persecuting Society: Power and Deviance in Western Europe, 950–1250* (Oxford: Blackwell, 1987). See also Vern L. Bullough, "The Sin against Nature and Homosexuality," in *Sexual Practices and the Medieval Church*, ed. Vern L. Bullough and James Brundage (Buffalo, N.Y.: Prometheus Books, 1982), 55–71, quotation at 70: the sin against nature was a confused, catchall category, and "anyone who did not conform to the Church standards on sex could be regarded as a heretic. Inevitably, most medieval heretics were accused of committing sexual sins and invariably one of the charges mounted against anyone whom one did not like was that he was a sodomist or that he committed crimes against nature." See also Bullough, "Postscript: Heresy, Witchcraft, and Sexuality," in *Sexual Practices*, 206–17. Continental heretics were from at least the twelfth century associated with sodomy; John Boswell, *Christianity*, 283–84, notes that by the thirteenth century "[i]t became a commonplace of official terminology to mention 'traitors, heretics, and sodomites' as if they constituted a single association of some sort": "Numerous heretics of the twelfth and thirteenth centuries and some whole movements, like the Albigensians, were accused of practising 'sodomy,' often (though not always) in the specific sense of homosexual intercourse. Civil and ecclesiastical records of trials dealing with heresy mention 'sodomy' and crimes 'against nature' with some regu-

larity." Boswell traced the philosophical development of such intolerance in the concept of a normative Natura.

32. Jan Hus, letter (in Czech) from the Franciscan prison at Constance in 1415 to Wenceslas of Dubá and John of Chlum (*Letters*, tr. Spinka, 177–79, esp. 177–78; *Jana Husi*, ed. Novotný, no. 139, 290–92, esp. 291: "že jest mordéř, svatokupec, kacieř, sodomský hřéšník"). As far as I can tell, the charges against John XXIII did not in fact specify that he was a "sodomite": see Karl Joseph von Hefele, ed., rev. Henri Leclercq, *Histoire des conciles d'après les documents originaux*, 11 vols., 10 vols. (Paris: Letouzey et Ané, 1907–52), 7.1, 234–9, 245.

33. For another example in the Lollard context, vernacularizing Wyclif's discussions of simony, see "Of Prelates," esp. chap. 5, where simony is linked to treason, leprosy ("gostly lepre" [67]), hypocrisy, heresy, and sodomy.

34. Alan Bray, *Homosexuality in Renaissance England* (London: Gay Men's Press, 1982) and "Homosexuality and the Signs of Male Friendship in Elizabethan England," in *Queering the Renaissance*, ed. Jonathan Goldberg (Durham, N.C.: Duke Univ. Press, 1994), 40–61; Jonathan Goldberg, *Sodometries: Renaissance Texts, Modern Sexualities* (Stanford: Stanford Univ. Press, 1992).

35. *Upland's Rejoinder*, ll. 58–59, in *Jack Upland, Friar Daw's Reply*, and *Upland's Rejoinder*, ed. P. L. Heyworth (London: Oxford Univ. Press, 1968); see Heyworth's notes on these lines and on ll. 257–63 (see below). The immediate point is preemptive, in preparation for a counteraccusation: no Lollard in turn can be proved guilty of such a sin—even for a hundred pounds:

> Bot lat see Dawe if þou or any lyer of þin ordre
> Can preue þis on oon of hem þat clepist my secte,
> And sicurly shalt þou haue of me an hundriþ pounde. (60–62)

One fifteenth-century poem speaking specifically of friars' sex crimes contends: "Thei weyl assaylle boyth Jacke and Gylle," perhaps enhancing our understanding of the constant accusations that friars steal boys and take them away to live in their orders. Wright prints this macaronic fifteenth-century poem against friars, warning husbands and fathers to be watchful of wives, daughters, and sons (Wright, *Political Poems*, 2: 249–50). That the friars in Wright's macaronic poem pose a sexual danger to both females and males is relevant to the Third Conclusion's framing of the issue of sodomy, as we shall see below. On friars' improper relations with women, see also, for example, Richard FitzRalph, *Defensio curatorum*, trans. John Trevisa, ed. Aaron Jenkins Perry, EETS o.s. 167 (London: Oxford Univ. Press, 1925), 73; for stealing boys, see 55–56, 65. The Lollard *Upland's Rejoinder* indeed blames friars for making such abducted boys sodomites; see ll. 257–63:

> Bot þus to stele a childe is a gretter theft
> Þan to stele an oxe, for þe theft is more.

Dawe, for þou saist ȝe robbe hym fro þe worlde,
ȝe maken hym more worldly þan euer his fadir—
ȝee, þowȝ he were a plowman lyuyng trwe lyf,
ȝe robbe hym fro þe trwe reule & maken hym apostata,
A begger & 'a' sodomit, for suche þai ben many.

Ecclesiastics, especially monks and friars, and sodomy had long been stereotypically linked. For one famous example out of many in the eleventh and twelfth centuries: Walter Map recounts a story in *De nugis curialium* that he heard from a Cistercian abbot about Bernard of Clairvaux. This narrative, between several chapters that detail monastic abuses and bad habits, shows clearly that in the 1180s monastic sodomy was not only a commonplace but material for jokes: " 'There was a man living on the borders of Burgundy who asked him to come and heal his son. We went, and found the son dead. Dom Bernard ordered his body to be carried into a private room, turned everyone out, threw himself upon the boy, prayed, and got up again: but the boy did not get up; he lay there dead.' 'Then he was the most unlucky of monks,' said I; 'I have heard before now of a monk throwing himself upon a boy, but always, when the monk got up, the boy promptly got up too.' The abbot went very red, and a lot of people left the room to have a good laugh." *De nugis curialium: Courtier's Trifles*, ed. and trans. M. R. James, rev. C. N. L. Brooke and R. A. B. Mynors (Oxford: Clarendon, 1983), 81.

36. Sodomites, Ruth Nissé Shklar suggests, are represented by the Lollards as part of a whole cultural economy of bad transactions. See Ruth Nissé Shklar, paper read at the 1995 MLA conference, "Widows Deliciously Fed: Appetite and Economy in the 1395 *Conclusions* of the Lollards and the *Wife of Bath's Tale*."

37. Wright, *Political Poems and Songs*, 2: 128: the first stanza is headed "Versus Lollardorum contra praelatos ecclesiae ad excitandum dominos temporales contra eos" (Verses of the Lollards against the prelates of the church to arouse secular lords against them), and the following lines are headed "Versus quidam catholici contra eosdem Lollardos" (Certain catholic [i.e., orthodox] verses against the same Lollards).

38. Alan J. Fletcher, "The Topical Hypocrisy of Chaucer's Pardoner," *Chaucer Review* 25 (1990): 110–26, at 112. Among the items in the codex are another anti-Lollard poem, composed around 1381; a history of the Carthusian order; a record of an assembly of Benedictine abbots; a narrative of Clairvaux; and letters from the Council of Basel to heretics in Bohemia and in England; see *A Catalogue of the Manuscripts in the Cottonian Library Deposited in the British Museum* (London: L. Hansard, 1802). Fletcher's study of the manuscript, briefly reported in "The Topical Hypocrisy," has determined that there was "an earlier, discrete compilation which has now been broken up and dispersed throughout the present codex" (112); materials on fols. 44–49, including (on fol. 48r) the two Latin poems I am discussing,

formed part of this core, as did, perhaps, the anti-Lollard poem on fols. 163–66v which Wright prints on 1: 231–49. The hand of "W. Mede" wrote fols. 44–49 and fol. 167v. On Mede as a Carthusian of Sheen, Fletcher points to N. R. Ker, *The Medieval Libraries of Great Britain*, 2nd ed. (London: Offices of the Royal Historical Society, 1964), 305, 417. I am indebted to Professor Fletcher for his study of the manuscript and confirmation of the new foliation since Wright's time.

For Carthusian scribal activity, see Michael G. Sargent, "The Transmission by the English Carthusians of Some Late Medieval Spiritual Writings," *Journal of Ecclesiastical History* 27 (1976): 225–40. For a complication of clear-cut anti-Lollardy among Carthusians, see J. Anthony Tuck, "Carthusian Monks and Lollard Knights: Religious Attitude at the Court of Richard II," in "Reconstructing Chaucer," *Studies in the Age of Chaucer*, Proceedings, no. 1 (1984), ed. Paul Strohm and Thomas J. Heffernan (Knoxville, Tenn.: New Chaucer Society, 1985), 149–61. Tuck argues that interest in the Carthusians in Richard's court "is an important, if seldom discussed, aspect of the lay piety of the late fourteenth century and is consistent with hostility to many aspects of the monastic life as it was lived in the houses of the Benedictine rule" (160), just as it is consistent with some beliefs of the so-called Lollard Knights as well.

39. I am here picking up a suggestion made by Alan J. Fletcher about the translation of the last line, its reference to *De heretico comburendo*, and the dating of the poem (personal correspondence).

40. See David Aers, "Preface," in *From Medieval Christianities to the Reformations*, ed. David Aers, spec. issue of *Journal of Medieval and Early Modern Studies* 27 (1997): 139–43, at 141, commenting on the importance of relations of church and monarch in the historical analysis of the continuity between late-medieval Catholicism and the sixteenth-century English Reformation. A. K. McHardy, "*De heretico comburendo*, 1401," in *Lollardy and the Gentry in the Later Middle Ages*, ed. Margaret Aston and Colin Richmond (New York: St. Martin's; Stroud, U.K.: Sutton, 1997), 112–26, analyzes the timing and circumstances of the enactment of the statute and its other "odd features" in arguing that "crown and church cooperated, perhaps in some haste" (122–23).

41. As Richard M. Wunderli remarks in *London Church Courts and Society on the Eve of the Reformation* (Cambridge, Mass.: Medieval Academy of America, 1981), 83–84, "Only one person out of 21,000 defendants in ecclesiastical court between 1470 and 1516 were accused of sodomy. Wunderli surmises that the "sudden appearance" of the 1533 antibuggery law in England only codified what had become common, trying sodomy cases in secular court. But the punishment for sodomy is very unclear in secular law in medieval England: though various treatises suggest capital punishments, their provisions conflict. For late-thirteenth-century examples, see *Britton*

1.10, recommending burning alive (ed. and trans. Francis Morgan Nichols [1865; rpt. Holmes Beach, Fl.: W. W. Gaunt, 1983], 1: 41–42), and *Fleta* 1.35, prescribing burial alive (ed. and trans. H. G. Richardson and G. O. Sayles, Selden Society, 72 [London: Bernard Quaritch, 1955]), 2: 90. Indeed, according to David Greenberg, they seem to state what their authors thought should be the case, not what really was. Greenberg reports the opinion of Samuel Thorne that "there was no criminal statute prohibiting sodomy in medieval England"; for citations and discussion, see the MEDGAY Internet discussion, especially 6 December 1995 and 7 December 1995.

42. Note McSheffrey, *Gender and Heresy:* "Despite the views of Colyn, Ramsbury, and Becket, it is worth noting that although continental heretics were assumed to be sexual deviants . . . Lollards were rarely accused of this" (197 n. 8).

43. Written around 1449, *The Repressor of Over Much Blaming of the Clergy*, ed. Churchill Babington, Rolls Series (London: Longman, Green, Longman, and Roberts, 1860), states: "summe ben founde and knowun openli among hem silf [themselves] and of othere neiȝboris to be greet lecchouris, summe to be avoutreris in greet haunt and contynuance [practiced, persevering adulterers], summe to be theefis, euen aȝens [against] her owne leernyng and aȝens her owne holding and doctrine" (1: 103). See Hudson, *Premature Reformation*, 172. Note that Pecock makes much of knowing this by "experience," "the grettist certeinte which mai be had in oure knowing"; this is reminiscent of the Lollard Third Conclusion, wherein Lollards claim to know by "experience" which clergy are sodomites.

44. Parody—appropriation—is characteristic of Lollard discourse: Lollards themselves appropriated the pejorative term "loller" for their own use. (On the name "Lollard," see Wendy Scase, *Piers Plowman and the New Anticlericalism* [Cambridge: Cambridge Univ. Press, 1989], 120–60, esp. 149–60). For discussion of Lollard strategy of "furnish[ing] established theological and political concepts with new 'slanted' meanings," see Matti Peikola, " 'Whom cl̄epist þou trewe pilgrimes?': Lollard Discourse on Pilgrimages in *The Testimony of William Thorpe*," in *Essayes and Explorations: A 'Freundschrift' for Liisa Dahl*, ed. M. Gustafsson, Anglicana Turkuensia 15 (Turku, Finland: Univ. of Turku, 1996), 73–84, at 77.

45. See the Pardoner's *Prologue, The Canterbury Tales*, 6.427–28.

46. Dymmok observes Lollard hypocrisy throughout his response; see, for example, his notes on their clothes (307; qtd. in Hudson, *Premature Reformation*, 145).

47. *Jack Upland* is dated by its most recent editor, P. L. Heyworth, "not earlier than about 1390" (17); Daw's *Reply*, perhaps 1419–20; and the *Rejoinder*, about 1450—though it is noted that Wright and Skeat date "all three pieces to the year 1402" (Skeat, qtd. in *Jack Upland*, ed. Heyworth, 9). I am interested in the structure of rejoinder, and thus, though the *Rejoinder*

itself is later than the *Conclusions* and Dymmok's reply, the whole sequence seems to have begun at about the same time, the 1390s. This phenomenon of reverse accusation is different from the phenomenon noted by John Boswell (*Christianity*, 217), in which reformers were accused of sodomy because they oppose clerical marriage.

48. Margery Kempe, often perceived as a Lollard, was threatened (after she castigates clerks at Lambeth for swearing) by a woman who snarled, "I wold þu wer in Smythfeld, & I wold beryn a fagot to bren þe wyth" ("I wish you were in Smithfield, and I would bring a bundle of sticks to burn you with") (*The Book of Margery Kempe*, ed. Sanford Brown Meech and Hope Emily Allen, EETS 212 [Oxford; Oxford Univ. Press, 1940], 36; *The Book of Margery Kempe*, trans. B. A. Windeatt [Harmondsworth, U.K.: Penguin, 1985], 71–72). William Sautre was burned at Smithfield for heresy in 1401.

49. They thus follow Matthew 10.15 here, as Wyclif did before (see discussion above). See Hudson, *Premature Reformation*, 217, quoting BL Cotton Titus D.i and citing J. Forshall's edition, called *Remonstrance against Romish Corruptions in the Church* (London: Longman, Brown, Green, and Longmans, 1851), 156–57.

50. *On Simony*, 40; *De simonia* 12: "Hec [symonia] autem periculosior est sodomia."

51. "On the Seven Deadly Sins," in *Select English Works of John Wyclif*, ed. Thomas Arnold (Oxford: Clarendon, 1871), 3: 162.

52. General Prologue to the Wycliffite Bible, chap. 13, p. 51. For dating, see Deanesly, *Lollard Bible*, 257. The *Historia vitae et regni Ricardi Secundi* records another event at that parliament in 1395 that carried a sodomitical charge—though it seems that this event must have in fact occurred at an earlier date. It is interesting and perhaps telling that the author, the monk of Evesham, associates this sodomy accusation with the 1395 parliament at which accusations of sodomy in the Lollard Conclusions (and perhaps poem) were publicly circulated. And it also may shed some light on the General Prologue statement that immediately follows the statement about "the last parlement": "Dyuynys [theologians] . . . ben moost sclaundrid of this cursid synne aȝens kynde." According to the monk of Evesham, John Bloxham, warden of Merton College, Oxford, and doctor of theology, was accused by two fellows (*socii*) of Merton "de crimine pessimo, non nominando." The accusers were egged on and aided by several lords; Bloxham denied the charges, and because nothing could be proven, no judicial action was pursued. The monastic chronicler adds: "Rex autem, cum de ista nephanda materia audisset, in iram contra predictos dominos et accusantes ualde commotus est" ("The king, too, when he heard of this unspeakable matter, was powerfully moved in anger against these lords and accusers"). See *Historia vitae et regni Ricardi Secundi*, ed. George B. Stow Jr., Haney Foundation Publications 21 (Philadelphia: Univ. of Pennsylvania Press,

1977), 135. Note that H. S. Cronin, Dymmok's editor, apparently misreads the passage, symptomatically assuming the lords supported the doctor of theology against the accusations of sodomy [xlvi]. The *Vita Ricardi*, whose post-1390 records are "hopelessly confused," according to its editor (1), temporally misplaces this event: John Bloxham died by July 1387; see A. B. Emden, *Biographical Register of the University of Oxford to a.d. 1500*, 3 vols. (Oxford: Clarendon, 1957–59), 1: 204.

53. Hudson, *Selections*, 25; cf. Walsingham, *Annales*, 175–76:

> Tertia Conclusio, et dolorosa, est.—Quod lex continentiae injuncta sacerdotibus, quae in praejudicium mulierum fuit primo ordinata, inducit sodomiam in totam Sanctam Ecclesiam. Sed nos excusamus nos per Bibliam, quia suspectum decretum dicit quod non nominaremus illud. Ratio; et experientia probant istam Conclusionem. Ratio; quia delicata cibaria virorum ecclesiasticorum volunt habere necessarie purgationem, naturalem vel pejorem. Experientia; quia secreta probatio talium hominum est, quod non delectantur in mulieribus; et cum probaveris talem, nota eum bene, quia ipse est unus ex illis. Corollarium istius est;—privatae religiones, inceptores, seu origo, istius peccati, essent maxime dignae annullari. Sed Deus, de potentia sua, super peccatum occultum talium in Sanctam Ecclesiam immittat vindictam aptam.

54. Wyclif, *Opus evangelicum*, 3.12, ed. J. Loserth (London: Trübner for the Wyclif Society, 1896), 2: 42. Anne Hudson mentions this reference and maintains that this criticism of the private religions was never his main theme or complaint (*Selections*, 152 n.).

55. *Knighton's Chronicle*, 306–7; this incident is mentioned by Strohm, "Chaucer's Lollard Joke," 33. That Lollardy was associated with both pro- and antifeminist positions is a prospect I shall pick up later in this chapter.

56. Joan Cadden, "Sciences/Silences: The Natures and Languages of 'Sodomy' in Peter of Abano's *Problemata* Commentary," in *Constructing Medieval Sexuality*, ed. Lochrie, McCracken, and Schultz, 40–57, at 44.

57. As one witness, consider the *Breviarium Practice*, written in a late-thirteenth-century monastery troubled by satyriasis: "In different monasteries and religious places one comes across numerous men who, sworn to chastity, are often tempted by the Devil; the principle cause is that every day they eat food that leads to flatulence. This increases their desire for coitus and stiffens their member; that is why this passion is called satyriasis." The author goes on: "As I am writing this book in the Cistercian monastery of Casanova, for the love of the abbot, the prior, and the monks, I will say what may be of use *ad removendum coitum*." Quoted by Danielle Jacquart and Claude Thomasset, *Sexuality and Medicine in the Middle Ages*, trans. Matthew Adamson (Cambridge: Polity Press, 1988), 147, from the edition in *Opera Arnaldi de Villanova* (Lyon: F. Fradin, 1504), fol. 176v;

their note states that "ascription of this work to Arnald of Villanova is no longer generally accepted."

58. John Gower, *Vox clamantis*, in *The Complete Works of John Gower*, ed. G. C. Macaulay, 4 vols. (Oxford: Oxford Univ. Press, 1899–1902), 4: 166–200; *The Major Latin Works of John Gower*, trans. Eric W. Stockton (Seattle: Univ. of Washington Press, 1962), 165–95.

59. That tradition is expressed by Peter Cantor, for example: *Verbum abbreviatum*, 138, in *Patrologia latina*, ed. J.-P. Migne, 205: cols. 21–554, at 333–35. Note that Peter links sodomy with murder, and distinguishes sodomites from *androgynos*, hermaphrodites; see Boswell, *Christianity*, 375–78.

60. *Fasciculus morum: A Fourteenth-Century Preacher's Handbook*, 6.2, ed. and trans. Siegfried Wenzel (University Park: Pennsylvania State Univ. Press, 1989), 628, 629.

61. Note the variations between *Fasciculi zizaniorum* and Walsingham's *Annales* at this point: while Walsingham has "volunt habere necessarie purgationem, naturalem vel pejorem," *Fasciculi* has a version closer to the English: "volunt habere naturalem purgationem, vel pejorem."

62. Cadden, "Sciences/Silences," 46–47.

63. B 14.75–77, ed. George Kane and E. Talbot Donaldson, rev. ed. (London: Athlone, 1988), 517. Pearsall places the related passage in C 15.231–32 in the exegetical tradition represented by Peter Cantor: *Piers Plowman by William Langland: An Edition of the C-Text*, ed. Derek Pearsall, York Medieval Texts, 2nd ser. (1978; Berkeley: Univ. of California Press, 1982), 257 and note.

64. See Mark Jordan's argument about Thomas Aquinas's reticence ("Homosexuality, *Luxuria*, and Textual Abuse," in *Constructing Medieval Sexuality*, 24–39, esp. 30–32), for this kind of point about the Pauline passage; the quotation is on 31. In the *Pardoner's Tale* (6.538–40) Chaucer may in fact be parodying such a Lollard tendency toward biologistic explanation in the Pardoner's ugly joke on Lollard eucharistic theology, linking Lollard theology itself with what comes out of either end in the digestive process. See Paul Strohm, "Chaucer's Lollard Joke," 36–37.

65. I am not arguing that such a treatment of sodomy is unexampled; see the earlier *Liber Gomorrhianus*, for example (according to Kruger, "Conversion," 164), where the vice is represented metaphorically in terms of biological sickness—a spreading cancer—even as it is assumed to be amenable to eradication via punishment (see the preface addressed to Pope Leo IX in *Liber Gomorrhianus* [ed. C. Gaetani, in *Patrologia latina*, ed. J.-P. Migne (Paris, 1853), 145: 161]). I argue, rather, that this treatment, if not unique, is nonetheless part and parcel of a Lollard reformist belief system.

66. Note that Foxe, refusing to follow the Lollard passage in his translation, garbles the logic: the secret test, he suggests, reveals that "such men . . . do delight in women." The antipathy of some sodomitical men toward

women is traditional: see, for example, the *Seven Sages of Rome,* wherein a king is described thus: "Wimmen he louede swiþe (*very*) lite, / And usede sinne sodomiȝte" (Southern Version, ed. Karl Brunner, EETS 191 [London: Oxford Univ. Press, 1933], ll. 1553–54, p. 66). Cited in Gustafson, " 'Gostli Sodomites,' " 2. And sometimes that antipathy is mutual: Laȝamon's *Brut* describes the mass exodus of women shamed by the repugnance that man-loving men in King Malgus's reign felt for them (*Brut,* 2 vols., ed. C. L. Brooke and R. F. Leslie, EETS 250, 277 [London: Oxford Univ. Press, 1973, 1978], 2: 756). Thanks to Jim Hinch for pointing out this passage to me.

67. Peter of Abano earlier deploys "naturalistic explanations at the anatomical, physiological, and psychological levels," Joan Cadden says ("Sciences/Silences," 43).

68. Hudson notes of later Lollards that "it is credible . . . that continued persecution by civil as well as ecclesiastical authorities should have removed from Lollard consciousness even the possibility of lay reformation" (*Premature Reformation,* 470). Here, I suggest that perhaps a certain view of human nature, expressed here, had already removed any very keen sense of possibility.

69. Naturalistic explanations, of course, do not always suggest that the activity might be performed by any man: anatomical explanations, for example, may indicate that certain men are anatomically predisposed toward sodomy, especially the "passive" role (as in Peter of Abano, according to Cadden ["Sciences/Silences," 46–47]).

70. Jordan, "Homosexuality," 28.

71. *Vox clamantis,* 4.3.187–90, 4: 171 in Macaulay ed.; *The Major Latin Works,* trans. Stockton, 169.

72. Alanus de Insulis, *De planctu Naturae,* ed. Nikolaus Häring, *Studi medievali,* 3rd ser., no. 19 (1978), 797–879, esp. 845–46.

73. Peter Brown, "Augustine and Sexuality," Protocol of the Forty-Sixth Colloquy, Center for Hermeneutical Studies, Berkeley, 22 May 1983, p. 12.

74. An offer of a male would be needed to confirm this diagnosis, one would suppose.

75. *Knighton's Chronicle,* 292–93; see Paul Strohm's treatment of this incident in "Chaucer's Lollard Joke," 33.

76. Hudson, *Selections,* 27. On Lollard scepticism regarding postbiblical saints, see Hudson, *Premature Reformation,* 197, 302–3. Note several threads of possible intersection between Lollard communities or discourses and Bridget: Cardinal Adam Easton, former Benedictine monk of Norwich (the town whose Lollard community apparently thrived from 1418 or so), had in 1386 promised to work for Bridget's canonization if he were saved from execution for a conspiracy against the pope. See *Saint Bride and Her Book: Birgitta of Sweden's Revelations,* ed. and trans. Julia Bolton Holloway, Focus Library of Medieval Women (Newburyport, Mass.: Focus, 1992), xiv.

Two hundred and twenty-eight books bequeathed by Easton were shipped from Rome to Norwich in 1407; see Norman P. Tanner, *The Church in Late Medieval Norwich, 1370–1532* (Toronto: Pontifical Institute of Mediaeval Studies, 1984), 35. And we'll see later (in chapter 3) that Margery Kempe, frequently accused of Lollardy, was in Rome in 1413 as the Council of Constance considered (and eventually confirmed) Bridget's canonization; Margery took special interest in the saint and in the truth of the revelations.

77. H. Ansgar Kelly, "The Right to Remain Silent: Before and after Joan of Arc," *Speculum* 68 (1993): 992–1026, esp. 995. See also James A. Brundage, "Playing by the Rules: Sexual Behavior and Legal Norms in Medieval Europe," in *Desire and Discipline: Sex and Sexuality in the Premodern West*, ed. Jacqueline Murray and Konrad Eisenbichler (Toronto: Univ. of Toronto Press, 1996), 23–41, at 27–28.

78. *Jack Upland*, in *Chaucerian and Other Pieces*, ed. Skeat, 191–203, at 192; William Woodford, *Responsiones contra Wiclevum et Lollardos*, ed. Eric Doyle, *Franciscan Studies* 43 (1983): 17–187, at 128–29; cited by Hudson, *Premature Reformation*, 146. Doyle, *Franciscan Studies*, p. 71, writes that a Latin version of *Jack Upland* was "the original version from which the English version came"; Skeat edited the 1536 printed version, which Doyle shows to be closer to "what the first English version must have been" (76) than are Heyworth's MSS. H and C.

79. *Purity* [*Cleanness*], l. 696, ed. Robert J. Menner, Yale Studies in English 61 (192; rpt. Hamden, Conn.: Archon, 1970).

80. Even though gender inversion is a prominent, even primary, issue in male-male sexual relations—as Augustine sees them, for example, speaking specifically about monastic settings, and as does Alain de Lille, following in the same tradition—as important a theologian as Thomas Aquinas does not comment on sodomites as effeminate, nor does Peter of Abano describe sodomites in this way. On Augustine, see Brooten, *Love between Women*, 352–53; on Thomas Aquinas, see Jordan, "Homosexuality," 33; on Peter of Abano, see Cadden, "Sciences/Silences," 52.

81. For William Smith, see *Knighton's Chronicle*, 292–93; for the Pardoner, see my discussion in the next chapter.

82. Fiona Somerset, in " 'Mark him wel for he is on of þo': Training the Lay Gaze in the Conclusions, Dymmok's Reply, and Chaucer," a paper delivered at the 1996 International Congress on Medieval Studies at Kalamazoo, cites Robert Mannyng's *Handlyng Synne*, 10233–36 on the blackness of the faces of lechers; see Robert Mannyng of Brunne, *Handlyng Synne*, ed. Idelle Sullens (Binghamton, N.Y.: MRTS, 1983), 255. Somerset's careful argument, using physiognomic treatises, emphasizes that both Lollards and their opponents promise to train the lay gaze to discern hypocrites but they do not make good on such promises because "no polemic . . . can afford to leave [its readers] space to decide for themselves" (9).

83. Hudson, *Selections*, 26; cf. Walsingham, *Annales*, 177: "[T]emporale et spirituale sunt duae partes activae, et ideo ille qui posuit se ad unum, non intromitteret se de alio; quia—'Nemo potest duobus dominis servire, etc.' Videtur nobis quod hermaphrodita vel ambidexter essent bona nomina pro talibus hominibus duplicis status." For a discussion of the urgency of the problem in the eyes of the Lollards, see Anne Hudson, "*Hermofodrita or Ambidexter:* Wycliffite Views on Clerks in Secular Office," in *Lollardy and the Gentry*, ed. Aston and Richmond, 41–51. And note an earlier incident, in 1379–80, wherein hermaphroditism was deployed in an argument against clerical privilege: W. A. Pantin, *The English Church in the Fourteenth Century* (Cambridge: Cambridge Univ. Press, 1955), 164–65, describes one Richard Helmslay, a Dominican of Newcastle on Tyne, and his "ingenious interpretation of the decree of the Lateran Council obliging everyone to confess to his parish priest; strictly speaking, he argued, this decree, *Omnis utriusque sexus*, only applied to those who were literally *utriusque sexus*, that is to say, hermaphrodites! The indignant clergy of the diocese of Durham cited him to Rome, and a contemporary correspondent tells us that Helmslay was known throughout the Roman Curia as *Frater Ricardus utriusque sexus*. In the end, he was ordered to make a public recantation of his teaching, at Durham and at Newcastle." The Dominican Dymmok perhaps knew of Frater Ricardus, whose reputation may have spread to the Lollards and maybe to Chaucer. Thanks to Robert Hanning for pointing this incident out to me.

84. See *Medieval Latin Word List from British and Irish Sources*, J. H. Baxter and Charles Johnson (Oxford: Oxford Univ. Press; London: Humphrey Milford, 1934), *ambidexter* and *ambisinister;* and the *Middle English Dictionary, ambidexter*. See Trevisa's translation of Bartholomaeus Anglicus, *De proprietatibus rerum*, 18. 51, "De fetu," on hermaphrodites among humans and animals: "þilke in þe whiche kynde goþ out of [þe weye]. . . . For in suche oon is yfounde boþe *sexus*, male and femele, but alway vnparfyte (those in which nature goes off the track . . . for in such a one is found both sexes, male and female, but always imperfect)" (*On the Properties of Things*, gen. ed. M. C. Seymour, 3 vols. [Oxford: Clarendon, 1975–88], 2: 1202). See, further, the fifteenth-century Middle English translation of a fourteenth-century French treatise, *The Cyrurgie of Guy de Chauliac*, bk. 7, chap. 7: "Hermofrodicia is þe nature of double kynde" (ed. Margaret S. Ogden, EETS 265 [London: Oxford Univ. Press, 1971), 529. Note that Guy de Chauliac lumps together "passiouns of þe ȝerde [penis], as þe priapasme and schettynge [shutting] of þe ȝerdes ende, circumscicioun, geldynge, hernyofrosis [hermaphroditism]" (bk. 7, chap. 7, p. 501).

85. For anxieties about sodomitical acts expressed in medieval treatments of hermaphroditism, see Joan Cadden, *Meanings of Sex Difference in the Middle Ages: Medicine, Science, and Culture* (Cambridge: Cambridge Univ.

Press, 1993), 223–27. On Dante's linking of sodomites and hermaphrodites, see Bruce W. Holsinger, "Sodomy and Resurrection: The Homoerotic Subject of the *Divine Comedy*," in *Premodern Sexualities*, ed. Louise O. Fradenburg and Carla Freccero (New York: Routledge, 1996), 243–74, esp. 261.

86. Hudson, *Selections*, 25; cf. Walsingham, *Annales*, 176: "Quarta Conclusio.—Quae maxime damnificat innocentem populum est, quod fictum miraculum Sacramenti panis inducit omnes homines, nisi sint pauci, in idolatriam; quia ipsi putant quod corpus Dei, quod nunquam erit extra coelum, virtute verborum sacerdotis includeretur essentialiter in parvo pane, quem ipsi ostendunt populo."

87. John Burrell in Norman P. Tanner, ed., *Heresy Trials in the Diocese of Norwich, 1428–31*, Camden Fourth Series 20 (London: Royal Historical Society, 1977): Richard Belward, William White, and Thomas Burrell taught

> quod nullus sacerdos habet potestatem conficiendi corpus Christi in sacramento altaris; et quod Deus creavit omnes sacerdotes, et in quolibet sacerdote capud et oculos ad videndum, aures ad audiendum, linguam ad loquendum et omnia membra cuiuslibet hominis; et illud sacramentum quod tales sacerdotes asserunt esse verum corpus Christi nec habet oculos ad videndum, aures ad audiendum, os ad loquendum, manus ad palpandum nec pedes ad ambulandum sed est torta panis facta de farina frumenti. (73)
>
> that no priest has the power of making the body of Christ in the sacrament of the altar; and that God created all priests, and in each priest, a head and eyes to see, ears to hear, tongue to speak, and all the parts of any man; and that sacrament which such priests claim to be the true body of Christ has neither eyes to see, ears to hear, mouth to speak, hand to shake nor feet to walk on, but is a cake of bread made from wheat flour.

88. For Burrell, see note 87. For a discussion of the varieties of belief even among the Norwich heretics, see Margaret Aston, "William White's Lollard Followers," in *Lollards and Reformers: Images and Literacy in Late Medieval Religion* (London: Hambledon Press, 1984), 71–100. Thanks to Steven Justice for his explanation of transubstantiation.

89. Dymmok, *Liber contra duodecim errores*, ed. Cronin, 130, trans. Strohm in "Chaucer's Lollard Joke," 40.

90. *De blasphemia, contra fratres*, in *Select English Works of John Wyclif*, ed. Arnold, 3.402–29, at 404.

91. Hudson, *Premature Reformation*, 285, quoting the Salisbury register of Bishop Audley of 1517.

92. "[I]f mony oostis, sacrid and unsacrid, were mengid togedir, a blaspheme þat knewe not þo medelynge of hom, kouthe not knowe accident fro bred, ne telle what is þis more þen a beeste" ("If many hosts, sacred and unsacred, were mixed together, a blasphemer who did not know that they

were mixed could not tell accident from bread, neither could he discern this better than an animal"): *De blasphemia*, in *Select English Works of John Wyclif*, ed. Arnold, 3.405, cited in Hudson, *Premature Reformation*, 285. Note that most of the works in the nineteenth-century editions by Arnold and by Matthew were incorrectly attributed to Wyclif.

93. *De blasphemia*, in *Select English Works of John Wyclif*, ed. Arnold, 3.405.

94. *Nicholas Love's* Mirror of the Blessed Life of Jesus Christ, ed. Michael G. Sargent (New York: Garland, 1992), 154; reference in Elizabeth B. Keiser, *Courtly Desire and Medieval Homophobia: The Legitimization of Sexual Pleasure in* Cleanness *and Its Contexts* (New Haven: Yale Univ. Press, 1997), 193.

95. "Women Mystics and Eucharistic Devotion in the Thirteenth Century," in *Fragmentation and Redemption: Essays on Gender and the Human Body in Medieval Religion* (New York: Zone Books, 1991), 119–50, at 133–34: "Although scholars have, of course, suggested that such reactions are sublimated sexual desire, it seems inappropriate to speak of 'sublimation.' In the eucharist and in ecstacy, a male Christ was handled and loved; sexual feelings were, as certain contemporary commentators (like David of Augsburg) clearly realized, not so much translated into another medium as simply set free." The David of Augsburg text referred to here strongly condemns sensuous response to seductive, false visions of Christ (and of his Mother) as blasphemy: see David of Augsburg, quoted in Peter Browe, *Die eucharistischen Wunder des Mittelalters*, Breslauer Studien zur historischen Theologie (Breslau: Verlag Müller und Seiffert, 1938), 110–11.

96. Bynum, "Women Mystics," 131, 129.

97. Dyan Elliott, "Pollution, Illusion, and Masculine Disarray: Nocturnal Emissions and the Sexuality of the Clergy," in *Constructing Medieval Sexuality*, ed. Lochrie, McCracken, and Schultz, 1–23, esp. 10–11; Jean Gerson, *De praeparatione ad missam*, in *Oeuvres complètes*, ed. P. Glorieux (Paris: Desclée, 1973), 9: 35–50, at 35.

98. Elliott, "Pollution," 11.

99. Elliott, "Pollution," 16.

100. Miri Rubin, *Corpus Christi: The Eucharist in Late Medieval Culture* (Cambridge: Cambridge Univ. Press, 1991), 11. See also her article, "The Eucharist and the Construction of Medieval Identities," in *Culture and History, 1350–1600: Essays on English Communities, Identities and Writing*, ed. David Aers (Detroit: Wayne State Univ. Press, 1992), 43–64; Kathleen Biddick's discussion of the body of Christ and "[t]he fantasy of exclusion and the boundary it creates," in "Genders, Bodies, Borders: Technologies of the Visible," in *The Shock of Medievalism* (Durham, N.C.: Duke Univ. Press, 1998), 135–62, at 152; and Sarah Beckwith, "Ritual, Church and Theater: Medieval Dramas of the Sacramental Body," in *Culture and History, 1350–1600*, ed. Aers, 65–90.

101. See *Cleanness,* ll. 1–48, esp. 11, concerning priests celebrating the Eucharist: "Þay hondel þer his aune body and usen hit boþe" ("They both handle his own body and use it [in the sacrament]").

102. *Mirk's Festial,* ed. Theodor Erbe, EETS e.s. 96 (London: Kegan Paul, Trench, Trübner, 1905), 21–26, at 23. See also the version in Jacobus de Voragine's *Legenda aurea,* ed. T. Graesse, 3rd ed. (Bratislava: William Koebner, 1890), 45–46, and the *Fasciculus morum,* ed. Wenzel, 688–89. For a mention in a fourteenth-century Cistercian sermon, see Hervé Martin, *Le Métier de prédicateur en France septentrionale à la fin du Moyen Age (1350–1520)* (Paris: Cerf, 1988), 381–82; and for discussion in the context of subversion of nature, see Jacques Chiffoleau, "Dire l'indicible: Remarques sur la catégorie du *nefandum* du XIIe au XVe siècle," *Annales ESC* 45 (1990): 289–324.

Other scholarly discussions forming a context for my suggestions about sodomy and the Eucharist include Stephen D. Moore, *God's Gym: Divine Male Bodies of the Bible* (New York: Routledge, 1996)—which led me also to the epigraph for my chapter 2—and Howard Eilberg-Schwartz, *God's Phallus and Other Problems for Men and Monotheism* (Boston: Beacon, 1994), esp. chap. 9.

103. Note that there is a considerable modern literature on the topic of the homoerotics of the Eucharist. See, e.g., psychiatrist Margaretta K. Bowers, *Conflicts of the Clergy: A Psychodynamic Study with Case Histories* (New York: Thomas Nelson, 1963), especially chap. 5, "Psychodynamic Implications Underlying Holy Communion," sec. D, "Sexual Deviations Expressed in Holy Communion." Bowers observes that in cases of "perversions of love" there can be a "sodomistic" experience of Holy Communion (63). As James C. Waller puts it in " 'A Man in a Cassock Is Wearing a Skirt': Margaretta Bowers and the Psychoanalytic Treatment of Gay Clergy," Bowers also "notes that celebration of the Mass has served as the occasion for psychological breakdown among a sizable portion of her Anglican and Roman Catholic priestly clientele, and Bowers appears to have used performance of the Eucharist as a kind of practical ritual or psychodrama—a medium for working through Oedipal conflict—in her group-therapy sessions." And, Waller continues:

> Bowers herself seems conflicted over whether the homoerotic dimension of the celebrant's experience during the Eucharist is an entirely regrettable thing. For example, Bowers reacts in an uncharacteristic way to the case of a celibate priest who, to his distress, always gets an erection during Mass. Rather than trying to help him get rid of what is, for him, a dreadfully embarrassing symptom, she responds with approbation. He is, after all, a man (that is, a desiring, sexual being); he has given his manhood entirely over to God; God deserves to be worshiped with every part of ourselves, including our sexuality; therefore, it is completely understandable and ap-

propriate that this priest should get an erection at the "sacrificial moment" of the Eucharist!

Bowers's discussion of this "devout and magnificent celibate priest" is in *Conflicts of the Clergy,* 67–68. See Waller, " 'A Man in a Cassock Is Wearing a Skirt': Margaretta Bowers and the Psychoanalytic Treatment of Gay Clergy," *GLQ: A Journal of Lesbian and Gay Studies* 4 (1998): 1–15, at 10.

104. Tanner, *Heresy Trials,* 91.

105. Tanner, *Heresy Trials,* 44–45; trans. by Steven Justice, "Inquisition, Speech, and Writing," 24.

106. Rubin, *Corpus Christi,* 320. See also Strohm, "Chaucer's Lollard Joke."

107. Hudson, *Premature Reformation,* 23.

108. How would one Lollard recognize another? Reginald Pecock in the *Repressor* reports: "whanne oon of hem talkith with an other of hem of sum other iije. man. the heerer wole aske thus: "Is he a knowen man?" and if it [be] answerid to him thus: 'Ȝhe, he is a knowen man,' al is saaf, perel is not forto dele with him; and if it be answerid to him thus: 'He is no knowen man,' thanne perel is castid forto miche homeli dele [too intimately deal] with him." *The Repressor of Over Much Blaming of the Clergy,* ed. Babington, 1: 53. Quoted by Hudson, *Premature Reformation,* 142–43. Hudson notes that russet clothes were associated with Lollards from early on, around the 1380s, but also notes that "evidently, not all Lollards wore the colour, nor was that colour peculiar to heretics," maintaining that there was diversity in many practices in the communities (147).

109. Hudson, *Selections,* 28; cf. Walsingham, *Annales,* 181:

> Undecima Conclusio.—Est miserabile ac verecunda loqui, quod votum continentiae factum in Ecclesia nostra per mulieres, quae sunt fragiles et imperfectae in natura, est causa inductionis maximorum peccatorum possibilium humanae naturae; quia licet interfectio puerorum antequam baptizentur abortivorum, et destructio naturae per medicinam, sint turpia peccata, adhuc communicatio cum seipsis, vel irrationabilibus bestiis, vel creatura non habente vitam, transcendit indignitate, ut puniatur poenis inferni. Corollarium est;–quod viduae et tales quae acceperunt mantellum et annulum, delicate pastae, vellemus quod essent desponsatae; quia nos nescimus excusare eas a privatis peccatis.

110. See the Lollard version, which lists various sins attributed to sloth, "þat is þe fierþe Moder of þe seuen synnes þat fordoþe childe wiþ drynche. oiþer fordoþe þat no childe may on hir ben ystrened" ("that is the fourth mother of the seven sins that destroys a child with a potion or spoils herself so that no child may be conceived in her"). *The English Text of the Ancrene Riwle edited from Magdalene College, Cambridge, MS Pepys 2498,*

ed. A. Zettersten, EETS 274 (London: Oxford Univ. Press, 1976), 96. For discussion, see B. D. H. Miller, " 'She Who Hath Drunk Any Potion' . . . ," *Medium Ævum 31* (1962): 188–93, esp. 188. For homosexual relations in this text (discussed below), see Bullough, "The Sin against Nature," 68.

111. Saint Augustine, Letter 211, *Epistvlae*, ed. A. Goldbacher (Vienna: F. Tempsky; Leipzig: G. Freytag, 1911), 4: 356–71, at 369. *The Confessions and Letters of St. Augustin*, trans. Philip Schaff, Nicene and Post-Nicene Fathers 1 (rpt. Grand Rapids, Mich.: Eerdmans, 1956), 563–68, at 568. Cited by Brooten, *Love between Women*, 351.

112. *The English Text of the Ancrene Riwle*, ed. Zettersten, 94.

113. Thomas Aquinas, *Summa theologica*, 2a.2ae.154.11–12 (Parma ed. [New York: Musurgia, 1948], 3: 520–21; Blackfriars trans. [London: Burns Oates and Washbourne, 1921], 2:157–61). See the discussion of unnatural vice in Thomas in my introduction. Thomas does not refer specifically in question 154 to sex with inanimate objects. As Monica Green notes, abortion and infanticide are "mechanisms of fertility control" ("Female Sexuality in the Medieval West," *Trends in History* 4 (1990): 127–58, esp. 148–50. See P. P. A. Biller, "Birth-Control in the West in the Thirteenth and Early Fourteenth Centuries," *Past and Present* 94 (February 1982): 3–26, esp. 24 n. 89 and 22 n. 82, for the suggestion that "the sin against nature" in certain contexts (in William of Pagula's *Oculus sacerdotis* and *Speculum prelatorum*) refers to *coitus interruptus* as a contraceptive strategy. B. D. H. Miller notes that "use of contraceptives was . . . rather a stock reproach against heretics" ("She Who Hath Drunk," 191 n. 45), a stock reproach that these heretics turned against the orthodox.

114. If not artificially "sewed on," as Seneca put it, then the women were suspected of anatomical abnormality; William of Saliceto (in the late thirteenth century) remarks on such phenomena, as does Simon of Genoa in the fourteenth century. See Seneca the Elder, *Controversiae* 1.2.23, ed. and trans. M. Winterbottom, Loeb Classical Library 463 (Cambridge, Mass.: Harvard Univ. Press, 1974), 87, quoted by Brooten, *Love between Women*, 43, 307, who translates the Greek term in the Latin text as "sewed on." The eminent Bolognese doctor William of Saliceto's *Summa conservationis et curationis* (completed 1285) mentions *ragadiae*, fleshy growths that are "caused by difficult childbirth, or by an abscess in the womb, and sometimes grow out of the vagina in the form of a penis. . . . Women who have these penis-like growths sometimes use them to have sexual intercourse with other women" (cited by Helen Rodnite Lemay, "William of Saliceto on Human Sexuality," *Viator* 12 [1981]: 165–81, at 179). In his *Synonyma*, Simon of Genoa explains: "*Batharum* in Arabic is a fleshy protuberance in the vulva of certain women which is sometimes so large that it is comparable to the penis" (Jacquart and Thomasset, *Sexuality and Medicine*, 45).

115. Thus gender roles and behaviors are paramount in this discussion

of females who take vows of chastity. And gender violation, the violation of active-passive roles, underwrites the condemnation of female sex acts without men as the worst problem among humankind. The hierarchical importance of gender over sexuality found here in the Lollard castigation of female perversion is consonant with representations of female-female homoeroticism found in the long tradition from Artemidorus to Ptolemy to Caelius Aurelianus to Cino da Pistoia to Shakespeare: only sexual acts between women that violate gender hierarchy emerge into visibility; they are consistently represented in relation to masculinization, facts suggesting that gender rules are regarded as much more serious than rules for sexual behavior insofar as they can be separated. See Karma Lochrie, *Covert Operations: The Medieval Uses of Secrecy* (Philadelphia: Univ. of Pennsylvania Press, 1998), esp. ch. 5; Brooten, *Love between Women*, passim; Louis Crompton, "The Myth of Lesbian Impunity: Capital Laws from 1270 to 1791," *Historical Perspectives on Homosexuality*, spec. issue of *Journal of Homosexuality* 6.1–2 (1980–81): 11–25, esp. 15; E. Ann Matter, "My Sister, My Spouse: Woman-Identified Women in Medieval Christianity," *Journal of Feminist Studies in Religion* 2 (1986): 81–93; Valerie Traub, "The (In)Significance of 'Lesbian' Desire in Early Modern England," in *Queering the Renaissance*, ed. Jonathan Goldberg (Durham, N.C.: Duke Univ. Press, 1994): 62–83; Thomas Laqueur, *Making Sex: Body and Gender from the Greeks to Freud* (Cambridge, Mass.: Harvard Univ. Press, 1990), 53 and note. Since there is no such gender violation mentioned in the Third Conclusion, its hint of masculine-masculine attraction leads me to suspect that gender violation in the case of male same-sex relations is not as important as it is in the case of women's, *even though* the stereotypical representation of the sodomitical activity refers to men's acting like women.

116. Bernadette Brooten remarks that "[w]hile ancient female homoerotic behavior probably included a full range of sexual expression, the ancient (and often modern) male imagination seems limited to postulating a physical substitute for the penis on the apparent assumption that sex occurs when a male organ penetrates a human orifice. Thus, ancient male representations of female homoeroticism show an obsessive preoccupation with trying to imagine what women could ever possibly do with each other" (*Love between Women*, 154). "What did she do? How? That's what I'm most interested to hear," are questions that needle a woman in Lucian of Samosata's *Dialogues of the Courtesans* 5 (*Lucian*, ed. and trans. M. D. Macleod, Loeb Classical Library [Cambridge, Mass.: Harvard Univ. Press, 1961], 7: 378–85, at 385); qtd. by Brooten, *Love between Women*, 154. As Brooten demonstrates throughout her book, there is an overwhelming continuity of opinion about female homosexual practice in the early Christian era, and this continuity is sustained, we see, in this Lollard conclusion. The mention of sex acts between women here continues this tradition of rep-

resentational indifference, to adapt Teresa de Lauretis's term. See her 1988 article, "Sexual Indifference and Lesbian Representation," rpt. in *The Lesbian and Gay Studies Reader*, ed. Henry Abelove, Michèle Aina Barale, and David M. Halperin (New York: Routledge, 1993), 141–58.

117. Natalie Boymel Kampen, review of Brooten in The *GLQ* Forum: "Lesbian Historiography before the Name?" *GLQ: A Journal of Lesbian and Gay Studies* 4 (1998): 595–601, at 596. *Li Livres de jostice et de plet* 18.24.22, ed. Pierre Rapetti (Paris: Didot Frères, 1850), 279–80. Quoted and translated in Crompton, "The Myth of Lesbian Impunity," 13.

118. For discussions of anatomical knowledge in the high and late Middle Ages, see Jacquart and Thomasset, *Sexuality and Medicine*, 7–47, esp. 22–47; for "member" as a standard, indiscriminate anatomical term, see 30. For an emphasis on the inversion model of female anatomy, see Laqueur, *Making Sex*, esp. 63–113; and for a critique of Laqueur's focus and his exclusion of other possibilities, see Valerie Traub, "The Psychomorphology of the Clitoris," *GLQ: A Journal of Lesbian and Gay Studies* 2 (1995): 81–113, esp. 84–85.

119. See the medieval lexicon, the Suda: "*Olisbos:* Leathern genitals that the Milesian women, as *tribades* and obscene women [or: masturbating women], used. Widows also used them" (Brooten, *Love between Women*, 153 n. 30).

120. The Penitential of Theodore, although much earlier, is useful for comparison and contrast with the Eleventh Conclusion because it distinguishes the two possibilities: "Mulier cum muliere fornicando . . . Si sola cum se ipsa coitum habet . . ." ("If a woman commits fornication with a woman . . . If she has sex with herself alone . . ."). Even so, the same penance is imposed for both these female sins, as if the acts are comparable, perhaps even not really quite distinct. See *Poenitentiale Theodori*, ed. Arthur West Haddan and William Stubbs, in *Councils and Ecclesiastical Documents Relating to Great Britain and Ireland* (Oxford: Clarendon, 1871), 3:173–213, at 178; trans. altered from *Medieval Handbooks of Penance*, trans. John T. McNeill and Helena M. Gamer (1938; rpt. New York: Columbia Univ. Press, 1990), 179–217, at 185. On Theodore's innovative treatment of women, see Allen J. Frantzen, *The Literature of Penance in Anglo-Saxon England* (New Brunswick: Rutgers Univ. Press, 1983), 66–67.

121. Chrysostom thought women who seek sodomy worse than men who do so, since they should have more modesty—but his priorities here are unusual. English translation of the Greek "Commentary on Romans, Homily 4," in Boswell, *Christianity*, 359–62: "And it is even more shameful that the women should seek this type of intercourse, since they ought to have more modesty than men" (360).

122. I explore the problem of representing female-female desire in *Sir Gawain and the Green Knight* in "Getting Medieval: *Pulp Fiction*, Gawain,

Foucault," in *The Book and the Body,* ed. Dolores W. Frese and Katherine O'Brien O'Keeffe (Notre Dame: Univ. of Notre Dame Press, 1997), 116–63, at 149–53. In various other Lollard denunciations of vows of celibacy for priests (in addition to the Conclusions, see, e.g., William White in *Fasciculi ȝiȝaniorum,* 425–26, and John Burrell in Tanner, *Heresy Trials,* 73) there is indeed no mention of women religious.

123. See Albertus Magnus, *Quaestiones super De animalibus* 15.2 ("Utrum generatio feminae intendatur a natura"), in vol. 12 of *Opera Omnia,* ed. members of the Institutum Alberti Magni Coloniense (Münster: Monasterii Westfalorum in Aedibus Aschendorff, 1955); and Thomas Aquinas, *Summa theologica* 1a.75.4 (on the distinction between universal nature and individual nature); and 1a.92.1 (on the creation of the female). For discussion, see my *Chaucer's Sexual Poetics* (Madison: Univ. of Wisconsin Press, 1989), 19–20.

124. Anne Hudson, ed., *English Wycliffite Sermons* (Oxford: Clarendon, 1990), 3: 199. See McSheffrey, *Gender and Heresy,* who refers to this and several other sermons and claims that Lollards "sometimes specifically targeted the credulity of the female sex" when ridiculing the worshippers of images, citing several other sermons and Wyclif's writings themselves (146). See also McSheffrey, *Gender and Heresy,* 85–87, on wives' subjection to husbands in the Lollard context: from the beginning, claims *The Lanterne of Liȝt,* "God ordeyned man. to [as] heed & lord ouir þe womman / & aȝenward [in turn] þe womman to be vndirloute & suget [submissive and subject]. vnto þis man" (*Lanterne of Liȝt,* ed. Swinburn, 31).

125. Hudson, *English Wycliffite Sermons,* 1:355, cited by McSheffrey, *Gender and Heresy,* 55.

126. McSheffrey, *Gender and Heresy,* 61.

127. Tanner, *Heresy Trials,* 142; McSheffrey, *Gender and Heresy,* 56.

128. For the argument that women Lollards were powerfully enabled, see Claire Cross, "'Great Reasoners in Scripture': The Activities of Women Lollards, 1380–1530," in *Medieval Women,* ed. Derek Baker (Oxford: Blackwell, 1978), 359–80; McSheffrey, *Gender and Heresy,* 138.

129. For a recent example of idealization of Lollard social resistance along gender lines, see David Aers's "Figuring Forth the Body of Christ: Devotion and Politics," in *Figures of Speech: The Body in Medieval Art, History, and Literature,* ed. Allen J. Frantzen and David A. Robertson, spec. issue of *Essays in Medieval Studies: Proceedings of the Illinois Medieval Association* 11 (1994): 1–14. Aers attempts to understand the body of Christ and its various imitations as "effects of power, of an identifiable historical power," and argues for a "thoroughly radical dissolution of the sacralized hierarchy of gender, and of the fundamental, hierarchical division between priesthood and laity" advocated by the Lollards. But with McSheffrey, I would argue that any claims about the political value of a particular phenomenon

of gender dissolution must be considered in context of Lollard conservatism in regard to gender. See Kathleen Biddick's response to Aers's essay, in *Figures of Speech*, 15–20: she analyzes the ways Aers idealizes the Lollards "as the sign of active resistance to the control of the medieval church" (15).

In addition to this deepened understanding of the specific contexts of Lollard sexual and gender politics, there is a methodological consequence of my discussion of Lollardy and sodomy. If, as I've argued, the Eleventh Conclusion makes a very different kind of accusation about women from the psychological accusation about men that adduces an antipathy to women as motive for acts of sodomy; and if a concept of gender, the secondariness and perversion of femininity itself, informs the indictments of female sexual behaviors here; then we have a specific basis for nuancing the Foucauldian discussion of the premodern sodomite as the juridical subject of a "category of forbidden acts" as opposed to the homosexual as an individual with a sexual identity. See Michel Foucault, *The History of Sexuality*, vol. 1: *An Introduction*, trans. Robert Hurley (1978; New York: Vintage, 1990), at 43, and my discussion below, in the coda. Acts are not separable from gender categories; acts have values and effects that differ as they are practiced by different people and in different contexts. Women's acts, as we see here, are forbidden by codes different from those that forbid men's: in the discussion of women, theological, moral, and social discourses of gender underwrite the physiological treatment of female perversion; in the discussion of men, laws of physiology, psychology, and sociality, unmarked and thus only implicitly gendered, combine to form something like a secret code of sexuality.

130. They do, but Dymmok did not know—or did not acknowledge—this. On the problem of using exempla from animal nature, see Boswell, *Christianity*, 319–21, regarding Thomas Aquinas.

131. Dymmok, *Liber contra duodecim errores*, ed. Cronin, 80; trans. Terrence G. Kardong, in *Cassian on Chastity: Institute 6, Conference 12, Conference 22* (Richardton, N.D.: Assumption Abbey Press, 1993), 40.

132. *Liber*, ed. Cronin, 81, 87.

133. *Liber*, ed. Cronin, 273; see also 279, for example.

134. Dymmok rehearses in particular the story of Jason, brother of Onias, elaborating on the received narrative in 2 Maccabees 4 by insisting that the Greek high priest Jason—wickedly imposing his own Hellenic customs—set up a whorehouse of women and a "locum prostitucionis pulcherimorum iuuenum masculorum" ("a place of prostitution of the most beautiful male youths"). *Liber*, ed. Cronin, 87–88.

135. See K. B. McFarlane, *The Origins of Religious Dissent in England* (1952; New York: Collier Books, 1966), 149 (translation adapted); he doubts Walsingham's assertion that Lollardy is involved here. But Patteshull's association with the chamber knights makes an association with Lollardy likely.

136. Walsingham, *Historia anglicana,* ed. Henry Thomas Riley, Rolls Series (1864; rpt. New York: Kraus Reprint, 1965), 2: 158.

137. Walsingham, *Historia anglicana,* 2: 252–53; speculations about the list and its sources are from Steven Justice, personal communication.

138. God's command to increase and multiply had always provided the mandate for sexual relations in orthodox Christian marriage, and Clifford's notion (shared by other Lollards, especially the East Anglians in Bishop Alnwick's heresy trials, e.g., Margery Baxter) that no ritual solemnization of marriage is necessary is not in itself unprecedented in orthodox belief: since the sex act itself had always constituted the sacramental act, according to standard theological argument, the canon law of this period did not hold ritual solemnization of marriage necessary. See McSheffrey, *Gender and Heresy,* 84 and note. McSheffrey outlines the varieties of emphasis in Lollard opinions on marriage: Lollards emphasize anticlericalism and privacy, even to the point of silence in the ceremony of marriage. When Clifford speaks of a single will to marry that in itself is sufficient to unite a man and a woman, the suspect, slightly frightening nature of this will, this desire ("ipsa voluntas"), and the Lollards' engagement of it, is heard in his statement "et sic conjuncti plures quam nos cognoscamus" ("and thus are married more than we would know"; Walsingham, *Historia anglicana,* 2: 253). Margery Baxter in her 1428 trial alludes outright to a "consensus mutui amoris" (Tanner, *Heresy Trials,* 46) itself linking two individuals in marriage.

139. Walsingham, *Historia anglicana,* 2: 252. For examples of this homicidal discourse, see the General Prologue to the Wycliffite Bible (mentioned above), and, earlier, the twelfth- or thirteenth-century poem printed and translated in Boswell, *Christianity,* app. 2, 400, 399:

> Turpiter et dire peccas, cogisque perire,
> Quod recte fusum uite prodiret inusum,
> Materiam proli generande tollere noli.
> Semiuir et mollis scorto sua gaudia tollis,
> Certa dico fide tibi inest homicide.
>
> Vilely and dangerously you sin and plot to destroy
> In vain what, rightly expended, would produce life.
> Do not waste the material for creating offspring.
> A half man, a debauchee, you steal the prostitute's joys:
> Truly, I say, you have the makings of a murderer. (ll. 27–31)

140. For a similar belief later, see Margery Baxter (Tanner, *Heresy Trials*). See Anne Hudson, *Premature Reformation,* 291–92, on the range of opinions about infant baptism: some denied that the administration of such a sacrament was necessary to a child born of married Christian parents, since the faith was passed on in the womb; others (such as Swinderby) held that

baptism was not effective if the priest was in mortal sin; others favored the retention of the form of baptism exemplified in the New Testament.

141. Walsingham, *Historia anglicana,* 2: 253.

142. See Miri Rubin, *Corpus Christi,* 9, on the "dialectical inscription of opposition within assertions"; note also Jonathan Dollimore, *Sexual Dissidence; Augustine to Wilde, Freud to Foucault* (Oxford: Clarendon Press, 1991), 138 n. 7, contending that "heresy becomes the attack on the Christian community *from within*" (emphasis in original) and citing Jeffrey Burton Russell on Tertullian as a precursor of such a tradition of thinking about heresy (*Satan: The Early Christian Tradition* [Ithaca: Cornell Univ. Press, 1981], 94–96, 98–99, 106).

2 Good Vibrations: John/Eleanor, Dame Alys, the Pardoner, and Foucault

1. On the commercial structures in Soper's Lane, seemingly well-suited for this kind of transaction, see John Schofield, *Medieval London Houses* (New Haven: Yale Univ. Press, 1994), 71–73.

2. The interrogation was uncovered by Sheila Lindenbaum and edited by David Lorenzo Boyd and Ruth Mazo Karras, in "The Interrogation of a Male Transvestite Prostitute in Fourteenth-Century London," *GLQ: A Journal of Lesbian and Gay Studies* 1 (1995): 459–65. See also the expanded version by Karras and Boyd, " 'Ut cum muliere': A Male Transvestite Prostitute in Fourteenth-Century London," in Louise O. Fradenburg and Carla Freccero, eds., *Premodern Sexualities* (New York: Routledge, 1996), 101–14. Both the edited Latin text and English translation appear in *GLQ,* 461–65; brackets in their translation indicate that gender is not marked in the Latin. I am much indebted to Boyd and Karras's excellent work.

3. All quotations of Chaucer are from *The Riverside Chaucer,* gen. ed. Larry D. Benson, 3rd ed. (Boston: Houghton Mifflin, 1987).

4. See Muriel Bowden, *A Commentary on the General Prologue to the* Canterbury Tales (1967; rpt. London: Souvenir Press, 1975), 187–88, on speculations about the "flesh-and-blood Roger of Ware." Edith Rickert, in a letter to the *Times Literary Supplement,* 20 October 1932, 761, lists documents that seem to identify the Cook. See Earl D. Lyon, "Roger de Ware, Cook," *Modern Language Notes* 52 (1937): 491–94, on the ward presentment; it is preserved in A. H. Thomas and Philip E. Jones, ed., *Calendar of Plea and Memoranda Rolls. . . .* 6 vols. (Cambridge: Cambridge Univ. Press, 1926–61), 2: 156. And see V. A. Kolve, *Chaucer and the Imagery of Narrative* (Stanford: Stanford Univ. Press, 1984), 257–79, esp. 259, for discussion of Chaucer's representation of the Cook.

5. See Ruth Mazo Karras, *Common Women: Prostitution and Sexuality in*

Medieval England (New York: Oxford Univ. Press, 1996), passim for prostitution in the trades, and 57–60 for prostitution of apprentices in particular; for Elizabeth Moryng, who was perhaps the same as Elizabeth Brouderer, see Henry Thomas Riley, *Memorials of London and London Life* (London: Longmans, Green, 1868), 484, translating Letter-Book H, fol. 194; for discussion of Moryng, see Karras, *Common Women,* 59–60 and note; 70 and note.

6. See Derek Pearsall, *The Life of Geoffrey Chaucer: A Critical Biography* (Oxford: Blackwell, 1992), 252–53, on the gaps in Chaucer's representations of the London of his day and on the unrepresentative nature of the five guildsmen of the General Prologue; see Kolve, *Chaucer and the Imagery of Narrative,* 266, on the ambitious nature of the guildsmen.

7. See Kolve's finely tuned analysis of this tonal variation in *Chaucer and the Imagery of Narrative,* 257–85.

8. For Elizabeth's name, see Boyd and Karras, "Interrogation," 460, and above, note 5; for this observation about Rykener's adopted name "Eleanor"—"se Elianoram nominans," "nominans ipsum Alianoram"—I thank Jim Cain, who notes such play on Eleanor of Aquitaine's name earlier.

9. Thanks to Steven Kruger for this observation about the *Shipman's Tale.*

10. "The Life of Infamous Men," trans. Paul Foss and Meaghan Morris, in *Michel Foucault: Power, Truth, Strategy,* ed. Meaghan Morris and Paul Patton (Sydney: Feral Publications, 1979), 76–91, at 80–81; Michel Foucault, "La Vie des hommes infâmes" (1977), rpt. in *Dits et écrits, 1954–1988,* ed. Daniel Defert and François Ewald, 4 vols. (Paris: Gallimard, 1994), 3: 237–53, at 241–42.

11. Karras and Boyd, "'Ut cum muliere,'" 105; at 113 n. 9, they cite the fourteenth-century Venetian case of Rolandino Ronchaia, who "was a male transvestite, working as a prostitute, but he was accused of sodomy, not prostitution." For this case, see Guido Ruggiero, *The Boundaries of Eros: Sex, Crime and Sexuality in Renaissance Venice* (New York: Oxford Univ. Press, 1985), 136; details therein help open interpretive possibilities for John/Eleanor Rykener: Rolandino became known as Rolandina, living and working as a female prostitute because of his feminine appearance.

12. See V. J. Scattergood, "Perkyn Revelour and the *Cook's Tale,*" *Reading the Past: Essays on Medieval and Renaissance Literature* (Portland, Or.: Four Courts Press, 1996), 183–91, esp. 191: "[I]t may be worth considering the possibility that [Chaucer] abandoned the *Cook's Tale* because it may have approximated too closely to what he had written or intended to write for the Pardoner." Scattergood notes that the Pardoner's three riotors are the characters in Chaucer closest in type to Perkyn Revelour. For analyses of gender and sexual dynamics in the first fragment, especially the *Miller's Tale,* see Elaine Tuttle Hansen, *Chaucer and the Fictions of Gender* (Berke-

ley: Univ. of California Press, 1992), 208–44; Karma Lochrie, "Women's 'Pryvetees' and Fabliau Politics in the Miller's Tale," *Exemplaria* 6 (1994): 287–304; and Glenn Burger, "Erotic Discipline . . . Or 'Tee Hee, I Like My Boys to Be Girls': Inventing with the Body in Chaucer's *Miller's Tale*," in *Becoming Male in the Middle Ages*, ed. Jeffrey Jerome Cohen and Bonnie Wheeler (New York: Garland, 1997), 245–60.

13. I use masculine pronouns for the Pardoner because the narrator of the *Canterbury Tales* does so and the Pardoner's self-presentation does not clearly contradict this (though the Pardoner plays with exaggerated masculinity); in contrast, I have chosen the hybrid forms "s/he," "him/her," "his/her," and "John/Eleanor" for several reasons: because the Latin document varies in its reference to this creature (using the feminine pronoun twice, in indirect discourse); and because John's self-reference, even apparently to the court officials, is "Eleanor." On the narrator's use of "he" to denote the Pardoner and the complex performance and deconstruction of masculinity in the *Pardoner's Prologue* and *Tale*, see Robert S. Sturges, "The Pardoner, Veiled and Unveiled," in *Becoming Male in the Middle Ages*, ed. Cohen and Wheeler, 261–78, esp. 263.

14. Didier Eribon, *Michel Foucault et ses contemporains* (Paris: Fayard, 1994), 266–69, at 266.

15. "The Life of Infamous Men," 78; "La Vie des hommes infâmes," 239.

16. Karras, *Common Women*, 16, quoting Corporation of London Records Office, Letter-Book L, fol. 189v (Reginald R. Sharpe, *Calendar of Letter-Books, L* [London: John Edward Francis, 1899] 11: 216).

17. According to Richard Wunderli's study of London church courts, "Venereal offenses dominate court records" (*London Church Courts and Society on the Eve of the Reformation* [Cambridge, Mass.: Medieval Academy of America, 1981], 81).

18. Karras and Boyd, " 'Ut cum muliere,' " 105.

19. For a discussion of the language of the rolls, see Thomas and Jones, ed., *Calendar of Plea and Memoranda Rolls* 4: vii–xix, esp. xii on the verbatim confession of John Russell; see Riley, *Memorials*, 630–34, for Russell's confession itself.

20. See Thomas and Jones, *Calendar of Plea and Memoranda Rolls*, for the character of the rolls: "Actions which seemed noteworthy to the clerks as illustrating City custom or recording City privileges were set out fully" (2: vii).

21. Thomas picks up on this emphasis: in his very brief summary of the document, he notes, "Examination of two men charged with immorality, of whom one implicated several persons, male and female, in religious orders" (*Calendar of Plea and Memoranda Rolls*, 3: 228). See Boyd and Karras, "The Interrogation," 459–60 on Thomas's obscurantist treatment of this examination.

22. Boyd and Karras, "The Interrogation," 464 n. 4. See chapter 1, esp. n. 41, on the status of sodomy laws and punishments in England at this time.

23. Marjorie Garber, *Vested Interests: Cross-Dressing and Cultural Anxiety* (New York: Routledge, 1992), 16.

24. For this point about Garber's effacement of transgender subjectivity, see Susan Stryker, "Introduction," *The Transgender Issue, GLQ: A Journal of Lesbian and Gay Studies* 4 (1998): 145–58, at 148.

25. Michel Foucault, *The History of Sexuality,* vol. 1: *An Introduction,* trans. Robert Hurley (New York: Vintage, 1978), 101.

26. See Karma Lochrie, *Covert Operations: The Medieval Uses of Secrecy* (Philadelphia: Univ. of Pennsylvania Press, 1998), chap. 5, on gender roles. It seems, as I shall discuss in a moment, that the heterosexual lens cannot clarify exactly what the crime or crimes were: as Karras and Boyd put it, "He was feminine, if not literally a woman; but this was not a crime. He was not a prostitute as medieval people understood that concept, and it was unclear whether he was a sodomite. . . . If, in fact, they did not prosecute him, but took his statement and released him, this may have been because they did not know quite what to make of him" (110).

27. *Purity* [*Cleanness*], ed. Robert J. Menner, Yale Studies in English 61 (1920; rpt. Hamden, Conn.: Archon, 1970), ll. 695–96. Karras and Boyd also bring this text to bear on the interrogation.

28. Thomas Aquinas, "De regimine principum ad regem Cypri," 4.14, *Opera omnia* (Parma: Pietro Fiaccadori, 1864; rpt. New York: Musurgia, 1950), 16: 225–91, at 281. According to Karras, who translates the passage in *Common Women,* 185 n. 7, the authorship of this book 4 is contested; whether the passage was written by Aquinas or not, the motto was popular through the late Middle Ages.

29. Donald R. Howard, *The Idea of the* Canterbury Tales (Berkeley: Univ. of California Press, 1976), 344. Recall, too, Beryl Rowland's infamous diagnosis of that pilgrim as "a testicular pseudo-hermaphrodite of the feminine type": "Animal Imagery and the Pardoner's Abnormality," *Neophilologus* 48 (1964): 56–60.

30. Karras and Boyd, " 'Ut cum muliere,' " 103.

31. At this point it is not enough, in analyzing the sexual history recorded here, to recall Bray's and Goldberg's warnings that not all male-male sex is recognized and understood to be sodomy. This sex act is not explicitly called sodomy in the deposition, but more to the point it may not have even been understood at the time it was performed as *male-male sex* at all. See Alan Bray, *Homosexuality in Renaissance England* (London: Gay Men's Press, 1982), and Jonathan Goldberg, *Sodometries: Renaissance Texts, Modern Sexualities* (Stanford, Calif.: Stanford Univ. Press, 1992).

32. Karras and Boyd, " 'Ut cum muliere,' " argue that a prostitute could be seen as a certain type of person and prostitution as a sexual orientation

and not simply the act of selling sex (103–5). My point about prostitution doesn't assume or refute this, but simply maintains that in an act of prostitution John/Eleanor takes on the feminine role that s/he sheds in other sexual contexts, so the prostitution is an occasion to perform a gender-crossing.

33. See Joan Cadden, *Meanings of Sex Difference in the Middle Ages: Medicine, Science, and Culture* (Cambridge: Cambridge Univ. Press, 1993), 225, for a related discussion of the ways in which the legal system (recording in a French royal register of 1405 a case of female same-sex sexual relations) both strengthens gender distinctions and at the same time at least partially disaggregates socially construed gender norms.

34. Chaucer was most likely living in Kent in the early to mid-1390s. See Pearsall's biography for details of date and place of composition of the *Tales*. I presented some of the material in the next sections in an early form in "Chaucer's Queer Touches/A Queer Touches Chaucer," *Exemplaria* 7 (1995): 76–92.

35. "[T]here is an explosive shock," writes Roland Barthes in *S/Z* about the contact between yet another queer—a eunuch—and a woman in Balzac's *Sarrasine*, "a paradigmatic conflagration, a headlong flight of the two bodies brought together in so unseemly a manner." Roland Barthes, *S/Z*, trans. Richard Miller (New York: Hill and Wang, 1974), 65; *S/Z* (Paris: Seuil, 1970), 72: "[I]l y a choc explosif, conflagration paradigmatique, fuite éperdue des deux corps indûment rapprochés."

36. *Troilus and Criseyde* 4.183. See my *Chaucer's Sexual Poetics* (Madison: Univ. of Wisconsin Press, 1989), chap. 1, "Reading Like a Man," 28–64, for this argument about homosociality in the poem.

37. David Wallace's major and wide-ranging study, *Chaucerian Polity: Absolutist Lineages and Associational Forms in England and Italy* (Stanford: Stanford Univ. Press, 1997), takes as one of its many concerns the processes of group formation that characterize Chaucer's *Canterbury Tales*. In its emphasis on the unifying operations of a *felaweshipe* and the resistances to it in the General Prologue, and particularly the unassimilability of the Pardoner and the Wife of Bath within it, Wallace's generously imagined study shares some basic preoccupations with mine here. He sees that "*Felaweshipe*, a political term, brings a gender politics (more or less visible) to each instance of deployment" (73); one important point of difference, however, concerns the status of a more or less visible politics of sexuality in our respective analyses. In particular, Wallace focuses on Chaucer's creation of the Wife of Bath as central to the Canterbury project: hers is the body that provides Chaucer "everything that he needs to fulfill his particular function as *auctor*" (81–82); while I appreciate the central analytic role that gender is accorded here, and while I grasp the historical bases of the specific analyses of Chaucer's "social totality" (82), I nonetheless resist the "invitation to view Chaucer as, potentially, the Wife of Bath's sixth husband" (82) because

of the virtual inevitability that heterosexual coupling will be naturalized in its elevation to controlling analytical principle here. See note 59, below.

38. Howard, *The Idea of the* Canterbury Tales, 333–87. Howard's discussion of the Pardoner as a grotesque ("it parades before us the other side of things" [372]) and as a Sartrean Other ("He exists to reveal to the society its own evil and to the 'good citizen' the evil in himself" [374]), "throw[ing] into relief" all cultural institutions and "remind[ing] us that every one of us has a secret" (375), astutely presages the kinds of effects now often marked as queer. His comment that "the Pardoner's asexuality throws into relief that whole stratum of the work which touches upon domestic life and sexuality," followed by a list of the sexual situations and behaviors of the pilgrims, most clearly demonstrates what I call the queering effect of this pilgrim; I agree with Steven F. Kruger in his fine article, "Claiming the Pardoner" (*Exemplaria* 6 [1994]: 115–39, esp. 123 and n. 26) that Howard argued so vehemently against sexual typing of the Pardoner (thus the "asexuality" in the above quotation) in order to counteract homophobia in articles which discuss the Pardoner. For treatments of the Pardoner as an ideological or hermeneutic key to the *Tales,* see my "Eunuch Hermeneutics" in *Chaucer's Sexual Poetics,* 156–84; Peggy Knapp, *Chaucer and the Social Contest* (New York: Routledge, 1990), 77–84; and Glenn Burger, "Kissing the Pardoner," *PMLA* 107 (1992): 1143–56; for the Pardoner as complex gay "ancestor," see Kruger, "Claiming the Pardoner," esp. 120.

39. H. Marshall Leicester notes the Pardoner's "deliberately shamming exaggerated virility" at this point in a hypermasculine campiness that strategically calls attention to his "sexual oddity" while it denaturalizes the Host's manliness (*The Disenchanted Self: Representing the Subject in the* Canterbury Tales [Berkeley: Univ. of California Press, 1990], 39).

40. Pearsall, *The Life of Geoffrey Chaucer,* 232. "Ribaudye" (1.3866) is the word the Reeve uses to describe the content of the kind of tale that could quite (i.e., repay, compete with) the *Miller's Tale;* it seems appropriate for a young, vigorous man to tell such a tale, he says, but not for an "oold" one like the Reeve (1.3867)—or a strange one, I might add, like the Pardoner.

41. See Alan J. Fletcher's article, "The Topical Hypocrisy of Chaucer's Pardoner," *Chaucer Review* 25 (1990): 110–26. And for a related argument focused on the Pardoner's sermonizing and its potentially polemical force, see Alan J. Fletcher, "The Preaching of the Pardoner," *Studies in the Age of Chaucer* 11 (1989): 15–35.

42. See Paul Strohm's "Chaucer's Lollard Joke," *Studies in the Age of Chaucer* 17 (1995): 23–42; quotations from pp. 33, 29, 31. I am indebted to Strohm's superb article for my reading of the instability of the historical moment of this text, an instability that ended with the burning of William Sautre in 1401.

43. Caution regarding the evidential status of the Man of Law's endlink

must be taken, as Alcuin Blamires remarks (in making a similar point to Strohm's, in note 42 above) about the timeliness of Chaucer's works ("The Wife of Bath and Lollardy," *Medium Ævum* 58 ([1989]: 224–42, at 224–25): "Since it appears neither in the Hengwrt nor in the Ellesmere MS, it is conceivably spurious. Among more plausible possibilities, it may represent a draft link which Chaucer abandoned—perhaps because, with the passage of time, outright jests concerning Lollardy no longer seemed to him amusing or prudent." See the less cautious article suggesting not only that the Parson, as depicted in the General Prologue, is a Lollard but that he is John Wyclif: Doris V. Ives, " 'A Man of Religion,' " *Modern Language Review* 27 (1932): 144–48.

44. See Fletcher, "Topical Hypocrisy," esp. 116–17 and notes: he points to Wyclif's *Opus evangelicum* (hypocrites as heretics); an interpolation on heresy as simony in the *Fasciculus morum;* a Latin sermon by Wyclif and a Middle English sermon (on preaching and on avarice both as heresy). For another standard digest of these tropes, see the Lollard "Of Prelates," in *The English Works of Wyclif*, ed. F. D. Matthew, EETS 74 (London: Trübner, 1880), esp. chap. 5, 64–69.

45. On "kaityf," see Peggy Knapp, *Chaucer and the Social Contest,* 83.

46. See Paul Strohm, *Social Chaucer* (Cambridge, Mass.: Harvard Univ. Press, 1989), esp. 24–46, for a delineation of the "constantly shifting group" that was "Chaucer's most intimate circle"; see also Fletcher, "Topical Hypocrisy," 116, for Chaucer's anti-Lollard acquaintances.

47. Fletcher, "Topical Hypocrisy," 114, 120.

48. The narrator's usage is deftly outlined by Jill Mann in *Chaucer and Medieval Estates Satire* (Cambridge: Cambridge Univ. Press, 1973), 187–202.

49. The literature on the Pardoner and sexuality grows apace; Monica McAlpine's 1980 article, "The Pardoner's Homosexuality and How It Matters," *PMLA* 95 (1980): 8–22, has proved consistently useful and inspiring. See also the materials in note 38 and, for a sampling of more work, Michael A. Calabrese, " 'Make a Mark That Shows': Orphean Song, Orphean Sexuality, and the Exile of Chaucer's Pardoner," *Viator* 24 (1993): 269–86; Allen J. Frantzen, "*The Pardoner's Tale*, the Pervert, and the Price of Order in Chaucer's World," in *Class and Gender in Early English Literature: Intersections,* ed. Britton J. Harwood and Gillian R. Overing (Bloomington: Indiana Univ. Press, 1994), 131–47; Robert S. Sturges, "The Pardoner, Veiled and Unveiled," 261–78; Glenn Burger, "Doing What Comes Naturally: The *Physician's Tale* and the Pardoner," in *Masculinities in Chaucer: Approaches to Maleness in the* Canterbury Tales *and* Troilus and Criseyde, ed. Peter G. Beidler (Cambridge: D. S. Brewer, 1998), 117–30.

50. See Karras and Boyd, " 'Ut cum muliere,' " 108, where gender transgression is claimed as the main feature of the Pardoner's representation;

see also Burger, "Kissing the Pardoner," who argues that the Pardoner is not absolutely other, but in being proximate reveals the constructedness of identity (esp. 1147).

51. Rosemond Tuve, *Seasons and Months: Studies in a Tradition of Middle English Poetry* (1933; rpt. Cambridge: D. S. Brewer; Totowa, N.J.: Rowman and Littlefield, 1974); Tuve, "Spring in Chaucer and before Him," *Modern Language Notes* 52 (1937): 9–16; James A. Hart, " 'The Droghte of March': A Common Misunderstanding," *Texas Studies in Literature and Language* 4 (1963): 525–29; A. Stuart Daley, "Chaucer's 'Droghte of March' in Medieval Farm Lore," *Chaucer Review* 4 (1970): 171–79.

52. On Chaucer's detailed knowledge of Guido, see *The Complete Works of Geoffrey Chaucer*, ed. W. W. Skeat (Oxford: Oxford Univ. Press, 1894), 5: 1–2, Introduction to Explanatory Notes to *Troilus;* see also the notes on these lines in *The Riverside Chaucer*, 798–99. For "the drought of March" as the time before which manure should be gathered for dressing the arable fields, see the *Husbandry* by Walter of Henley, c. 65: "And if any strawe, or litter, remayne of the feeding of your cattayle, cause that to be strewed within thy yarde or without in muckhylles [dunghills] . . . and before the drought of March cause also alle that is scattered within youre yarde or without to be gotten together" (1577 translation of the late-thirteenth-century text by William Lambarde [*Walter of Henley and Other Treatises on Estate Management and Accounting*, ed. Dorothea Oschinsky (Oxford: Clarendon, 1971), 327]; see A. Stuart Daley (previous note) for discussion.

53. For an analysis of binary oppositions in the General Prologue that focuses on linguistic and textual phenomena, see Joel Fineman, "The Structure of Allegorical Desire," in *Allegory and Representation*, ed. Stephen J. Greenblatt, Selected Papers from the English Institute n.s. 5 (Baltimore: Johns Hopkins Univ. Press, 1981), 26–60. David Lawton finds duality to be an organizing principle in the General Prologue (and links that piece to the *Parson's Prologue* and *Tale*), remarking on the place of Lollard ideas in the framing of the *Tales:* see his "Chaucer's Two Ways: The Pilgrimage Frame of *The Canterbury Tales*," *Studies in the Age of Chaucer* 9 (1987): 3–40.

My analysis here is indebted to Eve Kosofsky Sedgwick, *Epistemology of the Closet* (Berkeley: Univ. of California Press, 1990). Early versions of this analysis were presented in "Chaucer's Queer Touches/A Queer Touches Chaucer," and in "A Kiss Is Just a Kiss: Heterosexuality and Its Consolations in *Sir Gawain and the Green Knight*," *diacritics* 24.2–3 (Summer–Fall 1994): 205–26. The present analysis has been strengthened by the provocations of Allen J. Frantzen's critique in "Between the Lines: Queer Theory, the History of Homosexuality, and Anglo-Saxon Penitentials," *Journal of Medieval and Early Modern Studies* 26 (1996): 255–96.

54. See Jane Chance's intricate reading of these General Prologue lines in "Zephirus, Rape, and Saint Thomas à Becket: The Political Vernacu-

lar," chap. 5 of *The Mythographic Chaucer: The Fabulation of Sexual Politics* (Minneapolis: Univ. of Minnesota Press, 1995), 171–83.

55. Anne Laskaya, *Chaucer's Approach to Gender in the* Canterbury Tales, Chaucer Studies 23 (Cambridge: D. S. Brewer, 1995), 196–97; Jane Chance, *The Mythographic Chaucer*, 171–83.

56. Lucretius, *De rerum natura*, ed. and trans. H. A. J. Munro, 4th ed. (Cambridge: Deighton Bell, 1886), 1: 250–53:

> postremo pereunt imbres, ubi eos pater aether
> in gremium matris terrai praecipitavit;
> at nitidae surgunt fruges ramique virescunt
> arboribus, crescunt ipsae fetuque gravantur.

> Lastly rains die, when father ether has tumbled them into the lap of mother earth; but then goodly crops spring up and boughs are green with leaves upon the trees, trees themselves grow and are laden with fruit.

See Hart, " 'The Droghte of March,' " 526 n. 5; *Secretum secretorum*, from *Three Prose Versions of the Secreta secretorum*, ed. Robert Steele, EETS e.s. 74 (London: Kegan Paul, Trench, Trübner, 1898), 73; quoted by Tuve, *Seasons and Months*, 66. Cf. the "Ashmole" version of the *Secretum secretorum*, entitled *The Secrete of Secretes*, a "[f]ifteenth-century version (written perhaps soon after 1445) of the augmented Latin recension represented by Bodleian MS. Rawlinson C.274 and B.L. MS. Royal 12 E.xv" (*Secretum secretorum: Nine English Versions*, ed. M. A. Manzalaoui, EETS 276 [Oxford: Oxford University Press, 1977], 18): "The erth all fully resceyve[th] his garnementis and fairenesse, and is as a faire spouse and a full specious [beautiful] damysell arraied with broches, and clad with many-fold coloures that she may appere to me [*sic*] in the day of hir mariage" (56). And note, with Ann W. Astell, that Wyclif drew repeatedly on the *Secretum secretorum* in his *De officio regis* (1379) in his discussion of the proper rule of the realm (*Chaucer and the Universe of Learning* [Ithaca: Cornell Univ. Press, 1996], 37).

57. This personification in seasonal discourse is evidenced elsewhere in the *Canterbury Tales:* e.g., the *Knight's Tale* (1.1043–45); for personification of the sun, see the *Squire's Tale* (5.48–51). See Tuve, *Seasons and Months*, passim, for these and other references.

58. See the *Secretum secretorum* on spring's changes in the landscape: "þe snow resoluys [melts], waters rynnen among hilles, wellys ouerfluen, moistures styen vp [ascend] to þe croppys [tops] of trees and to þe heuedys [heads] of braunches, cornys [crops of grain] bygynnes to grewe" (72–73). See Tuve, *Seasons and Months*, 53.

59. Sedgwick, *Epistemology of the Closet*, 11–12. See Wallace's analysis of these opening lines in *Chaucerian Polity*, esp. 66–67: he points out that since a sense of obligation is unique to humans, the last lines of the eighteen-

line sentence about the pilgrims' obligation to Thomas à Becket reveal "the discovery of a uniquely human act" — an act which, I would argue, is also typified in this context as humanly *heterosexual.*

60. For the *De planctu,* see Larry Scanlon, "Unspeakable Pleasures: Alain de Lille, Sexual Regulation and the Priesthood of Genius," *Romantic Review* 86 (1996): 213–42, esp. 218–27; for the *Roman de la rose,* see Simon Gaunt, "Bel Acueil and the Improper Allegory of the *Romance of the Rose,*" *New Medieval Literatures* 2 (1998): 65–93.

61. See Burger, "Doing What Comes Naturally," for an analysis of the workings of the "natural" order in the *Physician's Tale* and the residue of the perverse that animates the performance that follows, the *Pardoner's Prologue* and *Tale.*

62. Pearsall, *The Life of Geoffrey Chaucer,* 228, quotes from J. S. P. Tatlock's *Development and Chronology of Chaucer's Works,* Chaucer Society 2nd ser., 37 (London: K. Paul, Trench, Trübner, 1907), 189: the *Tales* are "a kind of foundling asylum for the waifs and strays of [Chaucer's] earlier begetting."

63. See my *Chaucer's Sexual Poetics* for Chaucer's use of sexualized figures of literary production.

64. For the classic statement of literary history as a heterosexual family romance, see Harold Bloom, *The Anxiety of Influence: A Theory of Poetry* (New York: Oxford Univ. Press, 1973), esp. 36–37.

65. See my "Rivalry, Rape and Manhood: Gower and Chaucer," in *Chaucer and Gower: Difference, Mutuality, Exchange,* ed. Robert F. Yeager, Univ. of Victoria English Literary Studies Monograph Series 51 (Victoria, B.C.: Univ. of Victoria Press, 1991), 130–52.

66. Eleanor Prescott Hammond, *Chaucer: A Bibliographical Manual* (New York: Macmillan, 1908), 256–57; George Lyman Kittredge, "Chaucer's Discussion of Marriage," *Modern Philology* 9 (1911–12): 435–67, rpt. in *Chaucer Criticism,* ed. Richard Schoeck and Jerome Taylor (Notre Dame: Univ. of Notre Dame Press, 1960), 1:130–59; the argument is adapted in Kittredge, *Chaucer and His Poetry,* Fifty-fifth Anniversary Edition with intro. by B. J. Whiting (Cambridge, Mass.: Harvard Univ. Press, 1970), 185–86. Clyde Kenneth Hyder, *George Lyman Kittredge: Teacher and Scholar* (Lawrence: Univ. of Kansas Press, 1962), 200 n. 8, remarks that "Though it has been proposed, for instance, to place the Nun's Priest's Tale and the Tale of Melibeus in the group, neither mentions sovereignty in marriage. The connection seems remote." For a recent use of the concept of the Marriage Group, see Astell, *Chaucer and the Universe of Learning,* esp. 145–78.

67. Kittredge, *Chaucer and His Poetry,* 170.

68. Kittredge, *Chaucer and His Poetry,* 186, 188, 189.

69. Kittredge, *Chaucer and His Poetry,* 189. It's noteworthy that major studies of Chaucer to appear in the last decade of the twentieth century

(Pearsall's *Life of Geoffrey Chaucer*, for example, and Wallace's *Chaucerian Polity*) revalue the Wife of Bath, making her the central figure of Chaucer's last work; this is a welcome critical development that reflects the impact of feminist studies, but it nonetheless does not displace the heterosexual presumptions that underwrote the critical formation of the Marriage Group in 1911.

70. Kittredge, *Chaucer and His Poetry*, 211, 180. In his 1893 essay, "Chaucer's Pardoner" (*Atlantic* 92 [December 1893]: 829–33), Kittredge obliquely gestures toward the Pardoner's body: "His debasement seems to be utter, for one must not forget the picture in the general prologue" (833). This is the closest Kittredge gets—and it is not very close—to a description of this pilgrim's person. I thank Larry Scanlon for this and other references to Kittredge's early writings.

71. Kittredge, *Chaucer and His Poetry*, 217, 216.

72. On the break in the narrative frame at this point, see Ann Astell, "The *Translatio* of Chaucer's Pardoner," *Exemplaria* 4 (1992): 411–28, esp. 413–14. And see also Burger, "Doing What Comes Naturally," 122–24, for ideas about naturalization and narrative framing.

73. Kittredge, *Chaucer and His Poetry*, 217.

74. Kittredge, *Chaucer and His Poetry*, 214. Or, as Donald Howard so clearly saw, the Pardoner is constitutively an actor, and his Canterbury performance is a performance of a performance. Howard, *The Idea of the* Canterbury Tales, 339–76.

75. On 20 March 1997, the U.S. National Public Radio call-in show, *Talk of the Nation*, held a discussion of the *Canterbury Tales* in which the dramatic persona interpretive model, as well as various specific Kittredgean readings, were the bases of many of the comments.

76. "George served on the *Advocate* Board from February of 1880 to February of 1882, being elected president for the last year of this term. The president was managing editor, presided at meetings, and made assignments—in short, bore the chief editorial responsibility for the magazine" (Hyder, *George Lyman Kittredge*, 18). According to Hyder, Kittredge many years later, in 1929, wrote of the ongoing *Advocate:* "I should emphasize the importance of keeping such a paper as remote as possible from professional journalism in its ideals and methods, so that it can be truly representative of that stage of life and culture which is characteristic of the best undergraduate spirit in the best colleges" (20).

77. Hyder, *George Lyman Kittredge*, 20. See Richard Ellmann, *Oscar Wilde* (New York: Knopf, 1988), 173–79, for an account of Wilde's disastrous American reception in early 1882.

78. Kittredge, "Chaucer's Pardoner," 830.

79. See Ellmann, *Oscar Wilde*, 175–76. Ellmann speculates further about Wilde's meeting with Henry James (179): "We must imagine Henry James

revolted by Wilde's knee-breeches, contemptuous of the self-advertising and pointless nomadism, and nervous about the sensuality. . . . For the tolerance of deviation, or ignorance of it, were alike in jeopardy because of Wilde's flouting and flaunting."

80. Hyder, *George Lyman Kittredge*, 33.

81. Pearsall, *The Life of Geoffrey Chaucer*, 253.

82. In addition, nonnormative sex acts are suggested by the allusion to Zephirus, who, according to mythographers, raped Flora, as Jane Chance points out. Chance argues that "Chaucer's deployment of Zephirus in the *General Prologue* also warns against heresy and tyranny, through a series of mythological and literary associations chiefly drawn from Dante's *Paradiso*," and heresy brings with it associations with unnatural sexuality. Chance, *Mythographic Chaucer*, 171–83, at 173.

83. John Ganim, *Chaucerian Theatricality* (Princeton: Princeton Univ. Press, 1990), 14.

84. Alcuin Blamires, in his fine article, "The Wife of Bath and Lollardy," 224–42, at 230.

85. Guillaume de Lorris and Jean de Meun, *Le Roman de la rose*, ed. Félix Lecoy, Classiques français du Moyen Age 92, 95, 98, 3 vols. (Paris: Champion, 1965–70); trans. Charles Dahlberg, *The Romance of the Rose* (Princeton: Princeton Univ. Press, 1971), in which the line numbering corresponds not to the Lecoy edition but to the Ernest Langlois edition (1914–24).

86. See James A. Brundage, *Law, Sex, and Christian Society in Medieval Europe* (Chicago: Univ. of Chicago Press, 1987), 533–34, and Allen J. Frantzen, "The Disclosure of Sodomy in *Cleanness*," PMLA 111 (1996): 451–64, who quotes Brundage at 456 (but note Elizabeth B. Keiser's reservations in her *Courtly Desire and Medieval Homophobia: The Legitimation of Sexual Pleasure in* Cleanness *and Its Contexts* [New Haven: Yale Univ. Press, 1997], 241 n. 38). I owe the observation of this tradition's possible applicability here to Jennifer Graves.

87. Hiding defects: *Rose*, tr. Dahlberg, 230; *Rose*, ed. Lecoy, 13313–14: "Briefment, s'el set seur lui nul vice, / couvrir le doit, se mout n'est nice" (2.155); faking orgasm: *Rose*, tr. Dahlberg, 244; *Rose*, ed. Lecoy, 14275–80. For the Prioress's acting like a woman, see Priscilla Martin, *Chaucer's Women: Nuns, Wives, and Amazons* (Iowa City: Univ. of Iowa Press, 1990), 31–34.

88. On "discursive consciousness" in the Canterbury context, see H. Marshall Leicester, *The Disenchanted Self*, esp. 14–28.

89. If interpretation of the words *crescite et multiplicamini* was an orthodox test of Lollardy (since the suspicion was that Lollards used that text to justify promiscuity), the Wife enthusiastically avers that "That gentil text kan I wel understonde" without really clarifying her "attitude to procreation itself": see Blamires, "The Wife of Bath," 233. For the opinion that the

biblical text is used by Lollards against vows of continence, see Roger Dymmok, *Liber contra duodecim errores et hereses Lollardorum,* ed. H. S. Cronin (London: Wyclif Society, 1922), 274–76; see Ruth Nissé Shklar, "Cobham's Daughter: *The Book of Margery Kempe* and the Power of Heterodox Thinking," *Modern Language Quarterly* 56 (1995): 277–304, at 299.

90. See my *Chaucer's Sexual Poetics,* 113–31.

91. Thomas Laqueur, *Making Sex: Body and Gender from the Greeks to Freud* (Cambridge, Mass.: Harvard Univ. Press, 1990).

92. "Monster!" is Sarrasine's response to that denaturalizer of femininity, La Zambinella—a castrated man who plays a woman on the Italian stage. Sarrasine has fallen in love with "her," and suddenly recognizes that the woman whom he has adored is a "nothing," no woman at all and no man either. When disabused, he screams: "Monster! . . . you have wiped women from the earth" (*S/Z,* 252; see discussion and notes above, in the introduction).

93. For Gower's Tale of Florent, see *The English Works of John Gower,* ed. G. C. Macaulay, EETS e.s. 81–2, 2 vols. (London: Oxford Univ. Press, 1900), 1: 74–86, and the convenient reprint of this text with *The Marriage* and *The Weddynge* in W. F. Bryan and Germaine Dempster, eds., *Sources and Analogues of Chaucer's* Canterbury Tales (1941; Atlantic Highlands, N.J.: Humanities Press, 1958), 224–64.

94. In *The Weddynge,* marriage produces a lovely wife out of a disgusting "sowe" (597) with tusks (one pointing up, one pointing down). And yet a bit of queerness, a destabilization of the sought-after normative heterosexual relations, might linger in this mid-fifteenth-century romance, as Gawain gives up jousting and lies around with his beautiful new wife "[a]s a coward" (808). Such queerness is adumbrated by the explicit homosocial emphases of this rendition (Gawain marries Ragnell for love of Arthur [369–71], and Arthur, in turn, hastens to find out on the morning after the wedding, "Why slepyst thou so long in bed?" [732]), emphases that finally conflict with its ostensible heterosexual imperative. Edward Vasta, "Chaucer, Gower, and the Unknown Minstrel: The Literary Liberation of the Loathly Lady," *Exemplaria* 7 (1995): 395–418, argues for a genuinely culturally liberatory impulse (focused on the Loathly Lady) in this romance, as opposed to the official culture representations by Chaucer and Gower.

95. Howard, *The Idea of the* Canterbury Tales, 376.

96. Kruger, "Claiming the Pardoner," 131. See also Frantzen, "*The Pardoner's Tale,*" esp. 142, on the function of waste, and its linkage to sex, in the *Tale.*

97. Paul Strohm discusses the Lollard context of these lines in "Chaucer's Lollard Joke," passim.

98. *The Two Ways,* 577–86, ed. V. J. Scattergood, *The Works of Sir John Clanvowe* (Totowa, N.J.: Rowman and Littlefield; Cambridge: D. S. Brewer,

1975), 72: "ffor þei þat woln waaste þe goodis þat God hath sent hem, in pruyde of the world, and in lustes of here flessh, and goon to þe tauerne and to þe bordel, and pleyen at þe dees, waaken loonge anyȝtes, and sweren faste [loudly], and drynken, and ianglen to muche, scoornen, bakbiten, iaapen, gloosen, boosten, lyen, fiȝten, and been baudes for here felawes, and lyuen al in synne, and in vanitee, þei been hoolde 'goode felawes.' And moore harme is þere is [*sic*] now in this world muche swich curside felashipe." Note David Lawton's comment on this text: it is not a Lollard document, but it testifies to "real historical conflict within the lived experience of Chaucer's circle" ("Chaucer's Two Ways," 40).

99. Howard, *The Idea of the* Canterbury Tales, 338.

100. Glenn Burger, "Kissing the Pardoner," 1146; see also Kruger, "Claiming the Pardoner," 136–37.

101. Kruger, "Claiming the Pardoner," 137.

102. "The Life of Infamous Men," 77; "La Vie des hommes infâmes," 3: 237–38: "Jean Antoine Touzard, mis au château de Bicêtre le 21 Avril 1701: 'Récollet apostat, séditieux, capable des plus grands crimes, sodomite, athée si l'on peut l'être; c'est un véritable monstre d'abomination qu'il y aurait moins d'inconvénient d'étouffer que de laisser libre.' "

103. Foucault, "Theatrum Philosophicum," in *Language, Counter-Memory, Practice*, ed. Donald F. Bouchard, trans. Donald F. Bouchard and Sherry Simon (Ithaca: Cornell Univ. Press, 1977), 165–96, at 183; *Critique* 282 (1970): 885–908, rpt. *Dits et écrits*, 2: 75–99, at 89: "[L]'intensité . . . est en elle-même une pure différence: différence qui se déplace et se répète, différence qui se contracte ou s'épanouit, point singulier qui resserre ou desserre, en son événement aigu, d'indéfinies répétitions. Il faut penser la pensée comme irrégularité intensive. Dissolution du moi." For Deleuzian intensity as distinct from phenomenology (with its "unified subject" and "originary experience"), see Brian Massumi, *A User's Guide to* Capitalism and Schizophrenia: *Deviations from Deleuze and Guattari* (Cambridge, Mass.: MIT Press, 1992), 47 and n.

104. Massumi, *A User's Guide*, 47.

105. Foucault, "Theatrum Philosophicum," 185; "une pensée du multiple—de la multiplicité dispersée et nomade que ne limite et ne regroupe aucune des contraintes du même" (2: 90).

106. Eribon, *Michel Foucault et ses contemporains*, 265, quoting the book cover describing *Les Vies parallèles:* "Les Anciens aimaient à mettre en parallèle les vies des hommes illustres; on écoutait parler à travers les siècles ces ombres exemplaires. Les parallèles, je sais, sont faites pour se rejoindre à l'infini. Imaginons-en d'autres qui, indéfiniment, divergent. . . . Ce serait comme l'envers de Plutarque: des vies à ce point parallèles que nul ne peut plus les rejoindre." Michael Lucey quotes this passage (and notes Judith Butler's use of it as well) in his exploration of queer relations in Balzac,

"Balzac's Queer Cousins and Their Friends," in Eve Kosofsky Sedgwick, ed., *Novel Gazing: Queer Readings in Fiction* (Durham, N.C.: Duke Univ. Press, 1997), 167–98, at 169. I am indebted to Michael Lucey for discussions about "La Vie des hommes infâmes" and other prefaces by Foucault, in the course of team-teaching a graduate seminar, "Dissymmetries: Lesbian Theory, Gay Theory," at Berkeley in the fall of 1995.

107. Judith Butler, *Gender Trouble: Feminism and the Subversion of Identity* (New York: Routledge, 1989), 102. Note, too, that Foucault himself in his 1980 Introduction to the American edition of *Herculine Barbin* (published with additions as "Le Vrai sexe") practices the kind of queer history I am describing by drawing together not only the two texts—Alexina/Herculine's memoirs and psychiatrist Oscar Panizza's story based on them, *A Scandal at the Convent*—but the very lives of the writers themselves. Of Panizza's reading Alexina's text, Foucault writes: "[T]here is something surprising about this imaginary encounter between the little provincial French girl of indeterminate sex and the frenzied psychiatrist who was later to die in the asylum at Bayreuth," and goes on to dilate on the psychic and social dynamics that end up linking the two. See his introduction to *Herculine Barbin, Being the Recently Discovered Memoirs of a Nineteenth-Century French Hermaphrodite*, trans. Richard McDougall (New York: Pantheon, 1980) at xv–xvii; "Le Vrai sexe," *Arcadie* 323 (November 1980): 617–25, rpt. *Dits et écrits*, 4: 115–23, at 122.

108. See Didier Eribon's short article for this interpretation of Foucault's later work: "S'acharner à être gay," *Ex Aequo*, no. 5, May 1997.

109. Boyd and Karras, "Interrogation," 460.

110. Foucault expresses forcefully the importance of "discursive practices" and "the events produced therein" beyond textuality in "My Body, This Paper, This Fire" ("Mon corps, ce papier, ce feu"), his reply to Derrida's 1963 review of *Madness and Civilization:* "Derrida is doing no more than revive an old old tradition . . . the reduction of discursive practices to textual traces; the elision of the events produced therein and the retention only of marks for a reading . . . what can be seen here so visibly is a historically well-determined little pedagogy. A pedagogy which teaches the pupil that there is nothing outside the text." See introduction, n. 40, for this reference. Foucault varied in his estimation of the status and value of literature: in *The Order of Things*, for example, he asserts literature's break with language: "At the moment when language, as spoken and scattered words, becomes an object of knowledge, we see it reappearing in a strictly opposite modality: a silent, cautious deposition of the word upon the whiteness of a piece of paper, where it can possess neither sound nor interlocutor, where it has nothing to say but itself, nothing to do but shine in the brightness of its being." *The Order of Things: An Archaeology of the Human Sciences* (New York: Random House, 1970), 300; originally *Les Mots et les choses* (Paris:

Gallimard, 1966), 313. See also his *Death and the Labyrinth: The World of Raymond Roussel*, trans. Charles Ruas (Garden City, New York: Doubleday, 1986); originally *Raymond Roussel* (Paris: Gallimard, 1963), where Roussel's works are seen to elude modern disciplinarity. See also "A Preface to Transgression" ("Préface à la transgression," 1963) and "Language to Infinity" ("Le Langage à l'infini," 1963) in *Language, Countermemory, Practice*, ed. Bouchard, 29–52, 53–67; *Dits et écrits*, 1: 233–50, 250–61. In contrast, for a view reinforcing the one explicitly expressed here in "The Life of Infamous Men," see "What Is an Author?" (1969) (*Language, Countermemory, Practice*, 113–38, esp. 126; "Qu'est-ce qu'un auteur?" *Dits et écrits*, 1: 789–821). For a discussion of the issues and these references, see Geoff Bennington and Robert Young, "Introduction: Posing the Question," *Post-Structuralism and the Question of History*, ed. Derek Attridge, Geoff Bennington, and Robert Young (Cambridge: Cambridge Univ. Press, 1987), 1–11, at 7.

111. Michael Lucey, "Balzac's Queer Cousins and Their Friends," 169.

112. *I, Pierre Rivière, Having Slaughtered My Mother, My Sister, and My Brother . . .*, ed. Michel Foucault, trans. Frank Jellinek (1975; Lincoln: Univ. of Nebraska Press, 1982), x, xi, xiii; *Moi, Pierre Rivière, ayant égorgé ma mère, ma soeur et mon frère . . .* (Paris: Gallimard, 1973), 11, 12, 14.

113. As I shall examine more fully in the next chapter, Robert Glück takes up such a double position as well. In "Fame," an essay that cites Foucault, Glück carefully discusses and defends the use of "real" people in his narratives, describing a host of differences such a practice makes to a work's effects on its readers, and at the same time he remains committed to the exploration of the "already-known," the "fiction of personality" ("Fame," *Poetics Journal* 10 [1998]: 218–22).

114. Scott Bravmann, in *Queer Fictions of the Past: History, Culture, and Difference* (Cambridge: Cambridge Univ. Press, 1997), considers the roles of "history" and "literature" in relation to queer historical imaginations, and proposes different kinds of truths: "[H]istorical truths—the strategic lessons to be drawn from history—might well be approached through a literary historiography that draws on the dissolution of the distinction between realistic and fictional representations as proposed by recent theories of discourse and locates 'factual' as well as 'subjective' truths in the ways we understand, interpret, and write about the past" (29). See also Michael Camille, *Master of Death: The Lifeless Art of Pierre Remiet, Illustrator* (New Haven: Yale Univ. Press, 1996), for discussion of "what can be learned" from a conventionally objective and from a "more subjective, embodied and imagined" historical account (8–9).

115. "The Life of Infamous Men," 80; "La Vie des hommes infâmes," 3: 241: "Le point le plus intense des vies, celui où se concentre leur énergie, est bien là où elles se heurtent au pouvoir, se débattent avec lui, tentent d'utiliser ses forces ou d'échapper à ses pièges."

116. Allen Barnett, "Philostorgy, Now Obscure," in *The Body and Its Dangers and Other Stories* (New York: St. Martin's, 1990), 34–61, at 47.

117. Robert Glück, *Margery Kempe* (New York: Serpent's Tail, 1994), 82. His comment about "disorganizing" a self was made in a conversation with the graduate seminar "Dissymmetries" (see note 106) on 25 October 1995.

118. That the Pardoner flashes fake relics is in itself not quite as unusual as was once thought (by me, among other critics): correcting earlier scholarly opinion, Siegfried Wenzel notes in "Chaucer's Pardoner and His Relics," *Studies in the Age of Chaucer* 11 (1989): 37–41, that a simile based on the association of pardoners with false relics appears in the fourteenth-century English *Fasciculus morum.*

3 Margery Kempe Answers Back

1. Middle English text from *The Book of Margery Kempe,* ed. Sanford Brown Meech and Hope Emily Allen, EETS 212 (1940; rpt. Oxford: Oxford Univ. Press, 1982), 112, 116; modern English translation from *The Book of Margery Kempe,* trans. B. A. Windeatt (Harmondsworth, U.K.: Penguin, 1985), 153. All parenthetical references in my text refer to these editions in that order.

2. Important articles engaging the issue of Margery's clothes include Dyan Elliott, "Dress as Mediator between Inner and Outer Self: The Pious Matron of the High and Later Middle Ages," *Mediaeval Studies* 53 (1991): 279–308; Mary Erler, "Margery Kempe's White Clothes," *Medium Ævum* 62 (1993): 78–83; and Gunnel Cleve, "Semantic Dimensions in Margery Kempe's 'Whyght Clothys,'" *Mystics Quarterly* 12 (1986): 162–70.

3. *The Liber Celestis of St. Bridget of Sweden,* ed. Roger Ellis, EETS 291 (Oxford: Oxford Univ. Press, 1987), 14; qtd. in Gunnel Cleve, "Margery Kempe: A Scandinavian Influence in Medieval England?," in *The Medieval Mystical Tradition in England,* ed. Marion Glasscoe (Cambridge: D. S. Brewer, 1992), 163–78, at 176.

4. Erler, "Margery Kempe's White Clothes," 79. Cf. Elliott, "Dress as Mediator," on Margery's "anomalous" state as represented in her clothes (294–95).

5. Allen in *The Book of Margery Kempe,* ed. Meech and Allen, 314–315; cf. 311; *The Chastising of God's Children,* ed. Joyce Bazire and Eric Colledge (Oxford: Basil Blackwell, 1957), 51. In a Lollard case that links procreation with desire, an accusation against William Ramsbury stresses procreation so strongly that (in conjunction with other accusations) we might hear the ideas of the Brethren of the Free Spirit, that contemporary sect "whose more extreme adherents used their asserted freedom from the possibility of

sin to justify all forms of immorality," as Anne Hudson puts it in "A Lollard Mass," *Journal of Theological Studies* n.s. 23, pt. 2 (1972): 407–19, at 409.

The idea, reputed to circulate among Lollards, that all women should be common, is scorned by Roger Dymmok as antisacramental and heretical. It is heard in the Norwich heresy trials later, for example in William Colyn's accusation and confession (Norman P. Tanner, ed., *Heresy Trials in the Diocese of Norwich, 1428–31*, Camden 4th ser. 20 [London: Royal Historical Society, 1977], 91).

The Chastising of God's Children, written between c. 1382 and 1408, is a devotional treatise drawing on various Continental treatises, heavily on Ruysbroek's *Spiritual Espousals;* in chap. 11, for example, Ruysbroek's denunciations of the Brethren of the Free Spirit are linked to some English Lollards (ed. Bazire and Colledge, 53–54, 141–42). For further suggestion of a link between Norwich, hotbed of Lollardy, and the Low Countries, see Norman P. Tanner, *The Church in Late Medieval Norwich, 1370–1532* (Toronto: Pontifical Institute of Mediaeval Studies, 1984), 65–66; note that the Norwich lay beguinage-like communities of which Tanner speaks were never associated with heresy.

6. See Nancy F. Partner, "Reading *The Book of Margery Kempe,*" *Exemplaria* 3 (1991): 29–66, esp. 33, 39–40: Margery's clothes mark her as different; she worries that her ostentation at this time in her life might remind people of her earlier vain habits, when she tried to attract attention and signify her high social status as the daughter of the former mayor of Lynn instead of as the wife of her lower status husband.

7. Ruth Nissé Shklar, "Cobham's Daughter: *The Book of Margery Kempe* and the Power of Heterodox Thinking," *Modern Language Quarterly* 56 (1995): 277–304.

8. Compare the "Fayr whyte clothys & whyte kerchys" (18; "fair white clothing and white kerchiefs" [52–53]) which she provided for the child Mary in an early vision: as I argue below, Margery enacts an *imitatio Mariae* as well as an *imitatio Christi.*

9. Hope Phyllis Weissman, "Margery Kempe in Jerusalem: *Hysterica Compassio* in the Late Middle Ages," in *Acts of Interpretation: The Text in Its Contexts, 700–1600*, ed. Mary J. Carruthers and Elizabeth D. Kirk (Norman, Okla.: Pilgrim Books, 1982), 201–17, esp. 215.

10. For the Hieronymian tradition, see, for starters, Jerome's *Adversus Jovinianum* 1.26, trans. W. H. Fremantle in *The Principal Works of Saint Jerome,* Nicene and Post-Nicene Fathers, 2nd ser. (New York: Christian Literature Co., 1893), 6: 366: "If, however, Jovinianus should obstinately contend that [the Apostle] John was not a virgin (whereas we have maintained that his virginity was the cause of the special love our Lord bore to him), let him explain, if he was not a virgin, why it was that he was loved more than

the other Apostles." ("Si autem obnixe contenderit, Joannem virginem non fuisse, et nos amoris praecipui causam virginitatem diximus, exponat ille, si virgo non fuit, cur caeteris Apostolis plus amatus sit?" *Patrologia latina*, 23:205–338, ed. J.-P. Migne [Paris, 1845], at 247). For the Brigittine version, see Susan Dickman, "Margery Kempe and the Continental Tradition of the Pious Woman," in *The Medieval Mystical Tradition in England*, ed. Marion Glasscoe (Cambridge: D. S. Brewer, 1984), 150–68, at 159: Christ says to Bridget, "Ordinary, honorable matrimony [*communis laudabilis status*] is pleasing to Me. Moses, who led My people out of the thraldom of Egypt, was married, Peter was called to be an apostle while his wife was still living. Judith found grace in My eyes by her widowhood. But John, who was a virgin, pleased Me most, and I gave My mother into his care."

For the question of how it feels to be "less perfect," compare the *Wife of Bath's Prologue*, 99–101, referring to 2 Timothy 2.20. (And also compare David Aers, "The Making of Margery Kempe: Individual and Community," in *Community, Gender, and Individual Identity: English Writing, 1360–1430* [London: Routledge, 1988], 73–116, at 91: Margery's *Book* "discloses at least something of the experiential reality, the human costs of such ideology and sexual arrangements, ones which theological abstractions occlude"). The Wife of Bath, of course, makes it sound like fun to play the role of the wooden vessel. Such an attitude attends her project of mimesis, her taking up and occupying a derogated social position and turning it to her own benefit. Margery's mimetic projects operate in different registers—her "answering back" and saintly *imitatio*—but in both the Wife's and Margery's cases, such projects are of very limited subversive effectiveness.

11. Dickman, "Margery Kempe," 157, quoting Johannes Jørgensen, *Saint Bridget of Sweden*, trans. I. Lund, 2 vols. (New York: Longmans Green, 1954), 1: 45. See also Aron Andersson, *Saint Bridget of Sweden* (London: Catholic Truth Society, 1980), 15.

12. Nancy Partner is straightforward in arguing that Margery's form of worship is sexual; she maintains that Margery redirects her desire away from husband John (experiencing a vast repulsion from sex with him) toward Christ (who invites her to share a bed, as it is appropriate for a husband to be "homly," familiar, with his wife). But as Partner argues, "Not even the Jesus who assured her that he 'loves wives also' could exorcise and relieve her of a complex of unconscious guilt-stricken desire for which no penance was ever enough" ("Reading *The Book*," 54).

13. Jean Gerson, *Regulae mandatorum* (1400–15), 99, in *Oeuvres complètes*, ed. P. Glorieux (Paris: Desclée, 1960–73), 9: 118; trans. Thomas Tentler, *Sin and Confession on the Eve of the Reformation* (Princeton: Princeton Univ. Press, 1977), 231, cited by Aers, "The Making of Margery Kempe," 93; Jean Gerson, *De probatione spirituum* (1415), 11, in *Oeuvres complètes*, 9: 184. For brief discussion and translation of the latter passage, see Barbara Obrist,

"The Swedish Visionary: Saint Bridget," in *Medieval Women Writers,* ed. Katharina M. Wilson (Athens: Univ. of Georgia Press, 1984), 227–39, at 236.

14. Marjorie Garber, *Vested Interests: Cross-Dressing and Cultural Anxiety* (New York: Routledge, 1992), 17 and passim. See the methodological caveat in my chapter 2, above.

15. Margery's *Book* breaks down distinctions other than virgin/mother, heretic/orthodox: see Wendy Harding, "Body into Text: *The Book of Margery Kempe,*" in *Feminist Approaches to the Body in Medieval Literature,* ed. Linda Lomperis and Sarah Stanbury (Philadelphia: Univ. of Pennsylvania Press, 1993), 168–87, esp. 170: "The exchange recorded in *The Book of Margery Kempe* is at times a conjunction, at times a confrontation, between various dichotomous elements in late medieval society: the dominant and the marginalized, masculine and feminine, mind and body, clergy and laity, and written and oral modes of expression. Shaped in part by an unequal struggle for control of channels of communication, the resultant work destabilizes and subverts these historically hierarchical binary oppositions."

16. Lynn Staley, *Margery Kempe's Dissenting Fictions* (University Park: Pennsylvania State Univ. Press, 1994), esp. 59.

17. Aers, "The Making of Margery Kempe," 99, emphasis original.

18. Dickman, "Margery Kempe," 161.

19. Sarah Beckwith, *Christ's Body: Identity, Culture, and Society in Medieval Writing* (New York: Routledge, 1993), 84. Note that Barrie Ruth Strauss disagrees, taking Margery's relations to Christ "as her lover, father, and Lord" as yet another part of her disempowerment, indicating her "reinscription within heterosexuality": "Freedom through Renunciation? Women's Voices, Women's Bodies, and the Phallic Order," in *Desire and Discipline: Sex and Sexuality in the Premodern West,* ed. Jacqueline Murray and Konrad Eisenbichler (Toronto: Univ. of Toronto Press, 1996), 245–64.

20. Sheila Delany, *Writing Woman: Women Writers and Women in Literature, Medieval to Modern* (New York: Schocken, 1983), 90; Aers, "The Making of Margery Kempe," 93.

21. See *On the Properties of Things: John Trevisa's Translation of Bartholomaeus Anglicus,* De proprietatibus rerum, gen. ed. M. C. Seymour, 3 vols. (Oxford: Clarendon, 1975), 1: 118, "De sensu tactus": "Þeiȝ [though] his wit [i.e., touch] be in alle þe parties of þe body he is principalliche in þe palmes of þe hondes and in þe soles of þe feet."

22. For this description of queerness in an analysis of the Pardoner, see my "Chaucer's Queer Touches/A Queer Touches Chaucer," *Exemplaria* 7 (1995): 75–92.

23. Staley, *Margery Kempe's Dissenting Fictions,* writes of "Kempe's primary focus on the social discomfort Margery's behavior occasions" (65).

24. Shklar, "Cobham's Daughter," 297.

25. Staley, *Margery Kempe's Dissenting Fictions,* 65.

26. See Ruth Nissé Shklar's Ph.D. dissertation, "Spectacles of Dissent: Heresy, Mysticism and Drama in Late Medieval England," University of California at Berkeley, 1995, esp. 143–45, and "Cobham's Daughter," esp. 296–97.

27. See H. Ansgar Kelly, "The Right to Remain Silent: Before and after Joan of Arc," *Speculum* 68 (1993): 992–1026, esp. 995, and my discussion above, in chapter 1.

28. See Shklar, "Cobham's Daughter," 296–97, for a correlation of this passage with the *Twelve Conclusions* and further incisive comments on the interchange between the mayor and Margery. For an analysis of female same-sex homoeroticism in the *Book* that notes this passage, see Kathryn Lavezzo, "Sobs and Sighs between Women: The Homoerotics of Compassion in *The Book of Margery Kempe*," in *Premodern Sexualities*, ed. Louise Fradenburg and Carla Freccero (New York: Routledge, 1996), 175–98.

29. Harding, "Body into Text," 175.

30. *The Cloud of Unknowing* 52, ed. Phyllis Hodgson, EETS o.s. 218 (London: Oxford Univ. Press, 1944), 96–97; trans. James Walsh, *The Cloud of Unknowing* (New York: Paulist Press, 1981), 220. See, further, chap. 53:

> For som men aren so kumbred in nice corious contenaunces in bodily beryng, þat whan þei schal ouȝt here, þei wriþen here hedes onside queyntely, & up wiþ þe chin; þei gape wiþ þeire mouþes as þei schuld here wiþ hem, & not wiþ here eres. Som, when þei schulen speke, poynten wiþ here fyngres, or on þeire fyngres, or on þeire owne brestes, or on þeires þat þei speke to. (99)

> For some people are so burdened with quaint and unseemly posturing in their behaviour, that when they have to listen to anything, they waggle their heads from side to side and up and down most oddly. They gape with open mouths, as though they are listening with them and not with their ears. Others, when they have to speak, use their fingers, either poking on their own fingers or their chests, or the chests of those to whom they are speaking. (223)

And this list of "vnordeynde & vnsemely contenaunces" (98) goes on. Thanks to Martha Rust for this reference.

31. Elliott, "Dress as Mediator," traces the late medieval matron's development of a model of spirituality different from twelfth-century *imitatio*, "a model that, indeed, abandoned any *direct* correspondence between outer and inner selves" by focusing on the inner self and bypassing direct *imitatio* of an external model (303, emphasis in original). While this development makes excellent sense of Margery's preoccupation with her inner life—and explains deftly the complexity of the "rebellion" her clothing and other behaviors offer—it tends to downplay the prominence of saintly role

models and reenactments in Margery's narrative. Perhaps we might say that Margery's story registers the pain and frustration of being barred (by gender hierarchy) from "the strict imitation of an external *exemplum*" (Elliott, 303).

32. On Margery as a "merowr" for others so that they should "takyn exampil" of her, see 186. This discussion of Margery's *imitatio* does not deny the usefulness of Susan Dickman's approach ("The critical question which needs answering is not who inspired Margery Kempe, for her inspiration must have been in the air much as feminism is in the air today, but where does Margery fit into the complex mosaic of late medieval pious women[?]" ["Margery Kempe," 152]); this is an apt corrective to overly positivistic scholarly accounts. But my discussion seeks to respond to the *Book*'s narrative interests in naming Margery's saintly models.

33. For Bynum's treatment of Margery, see *Holy Feast, Holy Fast: The Religious Significance of Food to Medieval Women* (Berkeley: Univ. of California Press, 1987), passim, and *Fragmentation and Redemption: Essays on Gender and the Human Body in Medieval Religion* (New York: Zone Books, 1991), esp. 167–69, 179. Despite Bynum's use of the term "queer" at one point to describe Margery's white clothes, my view of Margery's life and relation to saintly behaviors differs markedly from her emphasis: Bynum seems to absorb Margery's experiences into a general framework of devout women's beliefs and understandings in which gender finally drops out as a category (the crucial difference was not finally between male and female, Bynum argues, but between humanity and divinity [179]). But I am concerned about the sometimes very drastic effects of gendered and sexualized power dynamics on Margery's life; these social phenomena Bynum of course recognizes but her concern lies more in analyzing women's and men's beliefs. In my reading, gender and sexuality always weigh heavily, always make a difference in Margery's life in her community: Margery goes crazy (she says in the first chapter of her *Book*) because she fears damnation and is reproved by her (male) confessor before she finishes her full confession at a moment of great physical danger that is unique to women (childbirth). It may well be that Margery's experience in her flesh contributes to her desire to identify with Christ, the divine Word made flesh, as Bynum might argue, but this episode also highlights the ways in which women are particularly subjected to the harshness of institutional practices on which they are nonetheless completely dependent. For a mention of gender dynamics of this episode, see Strauss, "Freedom through Redemption?" 256–57. And for a general account of the shifting power relations between Margery and her confessors, see Janette Dillon, "Holy Women and Their Confessors or Confessors and Their Holy Woman? Margery Kempe and Continental Tradition," in *Prophets Abroad: The Reception of Continental Holy Women in Late-Medieval England*, ed. Rosalynn Voaden (Cambridge: D. S. Brewer, 1996), 115–40.

34. I am using the term to specify a *relation*—as David M. Halperin has explained, " 'queer' does not name some natural kind or refer to some determinate object." See his clear and sharp discussion in *Saint Foucault: Towards a Gay Hagiography* (New York: Oxford, 1995), 61–67, at 62.

35. Dickman, "Margery Kempe," 166, argues compellingly that Margery's "singularity, isolation and individuality" represent a particularly English style of late-medieval female piety. Tanner, in *The Church in Late Medieval Norwich*, 64, provides material in support: "As a form of religious life outside the priesthood and the established religious orders, the solitary life of a hermit or anchorite was much more popular in late medieval England than life in a community." My interest in looking at Margery as queer, as singular, is to analyze the effects of her being separated from others and disjunct within her own life as well: her narrative registers her sense of her own difference from others more than it does her similarity to, say, the anchoress Julian.

36. Sarah Beckwith, "A Very Material Mysticism: The Medieval Mysticism of Margery Kempe," in *Medieval Literature: Criticism, Ideology, and History*, ed. David Aers (New York: Saint Martin's, 1986), 34–57, has analyzed the alienating phenomenon of positive mysticism, with its use of imagery and analogy, and its deployment of a desired but ever-only-approximated mimesis of the incarnated Christ. This ideology finally perpetuates the mystic's (usually, the woman's) social subjection. Beckwith highlights the ideological effects of ideals of wholeness and unity that cannot be imitated, but which the mystic will nonetheless ever desire to imitate. In its structural disjunctiveness, then, such mysticism could well be seen as a self-queering process, as it sets up a model for approximation that will never be reached. I add my analysis to Beckwith's finely tuned study of the social implications of this supposedly transcendent practice of mysticism.

37. Elliott, "Dress as Mediator," 279.

38. Cleve, "Margery Kempe: A Scandinavian Influence in Medieval England?" 171, notes this narrative shift.

39. Staley, *Margery Kempe's Dissenting Fictions*.

40. This example was pointed out to me by Frank Ordiway.

41. For a fairly current judgment about the relationship between the spiritual and the bodily in the *Book of Margery Kempe*, see Wolfgang Riehle, who blames Margery for not "separating the sensual from the spiritual" (*The Middle English Mystics*, trans. Bernard Standring [London; Routledge and Kegan Paul, 1981], 11; qtd. by Harding, "Body into Text," 184).

42. Tertullian, *Adversus Praxean* sec. 25, in vol. 2 of *Opera*, Corpus christianorum, series latina (Turnhout: Brepols, 1954), 2: 1195–96; Saint Augustine, *De trinitate* 1.8–9, ed. W. J. Mountain and Fr. Glorie, 2 vols., Corpus christianorum, series latina 50–50A (Turnhout: Brepols, 1968), vol. 1, pp. 52–55.

43. Saint Jerome, Homily on John 1.1–14, in *Opera*, Corpus christiano-

rum, series latina 72–80 (Turnhout: Brepols, 1958), 78.2: 520–23; Saint Bernard, Sermon 28.8–9 in *Sermones super cantica canticorum,* ed. J. Leclercq, C. H. Talbot, and H. M. Rochais (Rome: Cistercian Editions, 1957), 1: 197–98.

44. See Marguerite Waller on this and the many appropriable significances of *noli me tangere:* "Academic Tootsie: The Denial of Difference and the Difference It Makes," *diacritics* 17 (1987): 2–20.

45. Nicholas Love, *Nicholas Love's* Mirror of the Blessed Life of Jesus Christ, ed. Michael G. Sargent (New York: Garland, 1992), 200–201. Note that Love's translation was approved and commended by Arundel in about 1410 "for the edification of the faithful and the confutation of heretics or lollards"; in his work Love made major additions against Lollard beliefs (see Sargent's introduction, xliv–lviii). See also *Meditations on the Life of Christ: An Illustrated Manuscript of the Fourteenth Century,* ed. Isa Ragusa and Rosalie B. Green, trans. Isa Ragusa (Princeton: Princeton Univ. Press, 1961), 363.

46. *The Trinity,* trans. Stephen McKenna (Washington, D.C.: Catholic University of America Press, 1963), 27–28; *De trinitate,* 1.9 (Mountain and Glorie, ed., vol. 1, p. 54).

47. *Life and Works of Saint Bernard,* ed. John Mabillon, trans. Samuel J. Eales (London: John Hodges, 1896), 4: 182; *Sermones super cantica canticorum,* Sermon 28.9 (ed. Leclercq, Talbot, and Rochais, 1: 198).

48. The tension is neatly expressed in the manuscript of the *Book:* toward the end of bk. 1, when Christ is thanking Margery for her solicitude, he says, "I thanke þe for as many tymys as þu hast bathyd me in þi sowle at hom in þi chambre as þow I had be þer present in my Manhod, for I knowe wel, dowtyr, alle þe holy thowtys þat þu hast schewyd to me in þi mende" (214) ("I thank you for as many times as you have bathed me, in your soul, at home in your chamber, as though I had been present there in my manhood, for I well know, daughter, all the holy thoughts that you have shown me in your mind" [255]). Her spiritual care of his spiritual body is clear enough in this statement. But he then goes on: "And also, dowtyr, I thank þe for alle þe tymys þat þu hast herberwyd me & my blissyd Modyr in þi bed" (214) ("And also, daughter, I thank you for all the times that you have harboured me and my blessed mother in your bed" [255]). In the Meech and Allen edition a note on this line remarks that the word "gostly" has been added "*in red in outer margin with red caret after* bed" (214). It can't be insignificant that "gostly" was an afterthought.

49. The term is Biddy Martin's, in "Sexualities without Genders and Other Queer Utopias," *diacritics* 24.2–3: 104–21, at 119.

50. For a current perspective on queerness and traditional kinship relations, see Eve Kosofsky Sedgwick, *Tendencies* (Durham, N.C.: Duke Univ. Press, 1993), on the violence of the very term "family": "Tales of the Avun-

culate," esp. 71–72; see chap. 8, "The Politics of Gay Families," 195–213, of Kath Weston, *Families We Choose: Lesbians, Gays, Kinship* (New York: Columbia Univ. Press, 1991), for discussion of the politics of contemporary gay families.

51. Leo Bersani's discussion of the difference between recognizing the hypocrisies of hierarchical social structures and actually undermining them (a discussion developed in the context of his analysis of s/m), might be useful to recall here: *Homos* (Cambridge, Mass.: Harvard Univ. Press, 1995), 77–112.

52. Robert Glück, *Margery Kempe* (New York: Serpent's Tail, 1994). Page numbers in my text refer to this edition.

53. Earl Jackson Jr., *Strategies of Deviance: Studies in Gay Male Representation* (Bloomington: Indiana Univ. Press, 1995), 208.

54. I owe this observation to Jennifer Kao.

55. For Glück's observation about "disorganizing" a self, see chapter 2, above, note 117.

56. *Archaeology of Knowledge*, trans. A. M. Sheridan Smith (New York: Pantheon, 1972), 17; *L'Archéologie du savoir* (Paris: Gallimard, 1969), 28.

57. The lack of the literary criterion of originality, in fact, is one thing (in addition to social tumult and wars) Glück finds that we postmoderns have in common with people living in the fifteenth century. See "Interview with Robert Glück," by Earl Jackson Jr., *Red Wheelbarrow* 1.1 (Spring 1995): 24–40, esp. 39. Cf. Glück, *Margery Kempe*, 31.

58. "Interview with Robert Glück," 40.

59. Glück, "Fame," *Poetics Journal* 10 (1998): 218–22, at 220.

60. From the cover description of the Gallimard series "Les Vies parallèles," in which Foucault published *Herculine Barbin, dite Alexina B.*: "Ce serait comme l'envers de Plutarque: des vies à ce point parallèles que nul ne peut plus les rejoindre." See my discussion in the previous chapter.

61. "Fame," 220–21.

62. Jackson, *Strategies of Deviance*, 207.

63. Eve Kosofsky Sedgwick, "Across Gender, across Sexuality: Willa Cather and Others," *South Atlantic Quarterly* 88 (1989): 53–72, at 61.

64. "Fame," 218–19.

65. "Dismissal over AIDS Fear," *New York Times*, 25 July 1995, A8.

66. This discourse of contamination was loudly voiced during the national arts controversies of 1989–90 (especially about Robert Mapplethorpe) and reiterated more recently—July 1995—in Congress in a senator's denunciation of queer performance art and his claim that both Endowments sponsor projects that "infect" American culture. See the documents collected in Richard Bolton, ed., *Culture Wars: Documents from the Recent Controversies in the Arts* (New York: New Press, 1992) for examples of this discourse of poison, pollution, and contamination in the debates over the

NEA in 1989–90. A 1995 memo by Sen. Spencer Abraham (R-Michigan) outlines his proposal to privatize the Endowments; he claims that "the NEH's projects may well have a longer lasting impact than the NEA's, because they infect American education rather than only its art museums and theaters." See the *Congressional Record,* 17 July 1995, S10150–53.

67. *Congressional Record,* 17 July 1995, H7055–104.

68. *Congressional Record,* 20 June 1996, H6643–44; *Congressional Record,* 11 July 1997, H5157.

69. See *Creative America: A Report to the President;* for Rep. Conyers's remarks, *Congressional Record,* 12 March 1997, H945; for the letters by college presidents and lawmakers, see *Chronicle of Higher Education,* 20 June 1997, A29.

70. For coverage of Dick Armey's letter, see the *San Francisco Chronicle,* 26 March 1997, A4; for Trueman's testimony, see *Congressional Record,* 15 April 1997, E667; Trueman argued that the NEA, by funding what he calls pornographic works and calling them art, "poses serious problems in the prosecution of child pornography cases" as well as obscenity cases.

71. Paulette Walker Campbell, "New NEH Chairman Hopes to Revive Some Grant Programs That Have Been Cut," *Chronicle of Higher Education,* 12 December 1997, A34. William R. Ferris made the point about recovering some programs in his remarks to the House Appropriations Subcommittee on Interior and Related Agencies in March 1998.

72. Michael Bérubé, "The NEA Has Outlived Its Purpose, and I Want My 40 Cents Back," *Chronicle of Higher Education,* 1 August 1997, B6. On increased oversight and regulation of the NEA: the National Council on the Arts (which advises the NEA on projects to fund) must now include three senators and three representatives; and an amendment in the debates over fiscal 1998 by Senators Ted Stevens (R-Arkansas) and Chris Dodd (D-Connecticut), passed by voice vote, expressed the sense of the Senate that hearings should be held on the proper mechanism for federal funding for the arts and the role of the private sector, and that legislation should be brought before the full Senate for debate and passage during the 105th Congress. Further, the late June 1998 ruling by the United States Supreme Court in *NEA v. Karen Finley* establishes that "general standards of decency" must be considered in granting Federal arts monies. On "extending the reach" of NEH programs, see Paulette Walker Campbell, "Humanities Endowment's Fund-Raising Effort Starts Small," *Chronicle of Higher Education,* 9 October 1998, A42–43, at A42; of NEA programs, "Senate Refuses to Cut Off Arts Agency," *San Francisco Chronicle,* 16 September 1998, A8. On the fiscal 1996 budgets: the Senate and House agreed to slash the NEH's budget by 38 percent, the NEA's by about 41 percent; see Paulette V. Walker, "Facing Cuts, Arts and Humanities Agencies Seek Private Funds," *Chronicle of Higher Education,* 16 February 1996, A31.

73. The Appropriations Committee had recommended instead shaving the 1996 NEH budget by 40 percent. The House Economic and Educational Opportunities Committee, in reauthorizing the Endowment, had planned a three-year phaseout (*Congressional Record*, 17 July 1995, H7056).

74. *Congressional Record*, 17 July 1995, H7055.

75. H7055. Compare the similar view of Rep. Doolittle, *Congressional Record*, 17 July 1995, H7058: "Regardless of what one thinks about the record of the National Endowment for the Humanities and the controversial programs, the fact of the matter is, with a $4.7 trillion national debt, we cannot afford as a country to be borrowing money for the purpose of entertainment."

76. *Congressional Record*, 20 June 1996, H6643.

77. *Congressional Record*, 20 June 1996, H6644.

78. *Congressional Record*, 11 July 1997, H5158.

79. Lynne Cheney, resignation letter to her staff after the 1992 elections: the NEH should be emphasizing "traditional scholarship, and traditional approaches to traditional scholarship" (qtd. by John K. Wilson in *The Myth of Political Correctness: The Conservative Attack on Higher Education* [Durham, N.C.: Duke Univ. Press, 1995], 62).

80. Another project that imaginatively traces queer relations across time was derided by Rep. Peter Hoekstra (R-Michigan) in comments about his own 1996 amendment to reduce funding for the fiscal 1997 NEA budget. This project was *The Watermelon Woman*, an NEA-sponsored 1996 film by Cheryl Dunye (*Congressional Record*, 20 June 1996, H6637) that depicts a black lesbian filmmaker's search for a mysterious actress from the 1930s known as "The Watermelon Woman." Rep. Hoekstra's amendment (which he subsequently withdrew) would have reduced funding by $31,500, the amount granted to this film. The film was vociferously defended by Rep. Jackson-Lee of Texas in terms of its representation of a black woman's struggle in the entertainment industry; Jackson-Lee minimized the impact of its sexual content (*Congressional Record*, 20 June 1996, H6637, 6645).

Rep. Sawyer (D-Ohio) in the July 1997 debate over 1998 NEH funding spoke eloquently about the importance of relations with the past:

> The Bradley Commission on History, a decade ago, articulated the same kinds of things when they suggested, as we need to derive [*sic*] from the National Endowment for the Humanities, the importance of developing a shared sense of humanity, to understand ourselves and others, to understand how we resemble and differ from one another, to question stereotypes of ourselves and others, to discern the difference between fact and conjecture, to grasp the complexity of historical cause, to distrust the simple answer and the dismissive explanation, to respect particularity and avoid false analogy, to recognize the abuse of historical lessons, and to understand that ignorance of the past may make us prisoners of it, to recognize

that not all problems have solutions, to be prepared for the irrational, the accidental, in human affairs, and to grasp the power of ideas and character in history. (*Congressional Record,* 11 July 1997, H5167).

81. Several representatives made precisely these points in the discussion of the proposed 1995 amendment that followed. Rep. Pat Williams (D-Montana): "[T]he Nation's memory matters; . . . identity matters; . . . history matters" (*Congressional Record,* 17 July 1995, H7056). Rep. Nancy L. Johnson (R-Connecticut): "How can a great nation shape its future if it does not have the information through which it must understand its past?" (H7057). Rep. William J. Martini (R-New Jersey): "Through NEH, we have also preserved history—both good and bad. Some Members of Congress oppose the NEH because of this. Those Members believe that painful history is best forgotten. . . . It has been said time and again, and I hestitate to repeat it—but history does repeat itself and societies can learn from their mistakes" (H7059).

82. "The National History (Sub)Standards," *Wall Street Journal,* 23 October 1995, A16.

83. John K. Wilson, "Razing the National History Standards," *Democratic Culture* 4.1 (Spring 1995): 5–9, at 5. Frank Rich, "Cheney Dumbs Down," *New York Times,* 26 February 1995, E15, notes Cheney's about-face on the standards, from "favorite grant" to condemnation.

84. *Congressional Record,* 18 January 1995, S1026, quoted in Wilson, "Razing," 5. Charles Krauthammer, "History Hijacked," *Washington Post,* 4 November 1994, A25: "two malignant tendencies of the new historiography" are "its obsession with counting by race and gender and its refusal to exercise any faculties of discrimination for fear of, well, discriminating."

85. According to Wilson, Cheney went on to decry the lack of mention of "the things that have happened in this country that should make us proud to be American." "Erasing the negative side of our history," writes Wilson, "is the first step for Cheney and the Republicans toward ignoring the problems we face today" ("Razing," 9). Rep. Martini's statement about such painful history is in *Congressional Record,* H7059.

86. John Fonte, "We the Peoples," *National Review,* 25 March 1996, 47–49; for Clinton's and Appleby's responses, see Elaine Woo, "Standards for Teaching History Unveiled—Again," *Los Angeles Times,* 13 April 1996, A1, A16.

87. MIT historian John W. Dower, quoted in Anthony Flint, "What of Our Past? Historians Disagree," *Boston Globe,* 25 July 1995, A1, 14 (qtd. in "Academic Freedom: A TDC Special Report," *Democratic Culture* 4.2 [Fall 1995]: 8–11, at 9). Flint summarizes the controversy: "The curators were accused of blame-America-first revisionism; the critics were charged with trying to sanitize history, and scolded for being 'patriotically correct' " (A1). Sean Wilentz's review of *History on Trial,* an account of the standards contro-

versy by several of the historians responsible for developing the standards (Gary B. Nash, Charlotte Crabtree, and Ross E. Dunn, *History on Trial: Culture Wars and the Teaching of the Past* [New York: Knopf, 1997]), makes the point that "[c]ollege and university historians perhaps have the most to learn from 'History on Trial.' Unless they work closely with schoolteachers and education officials, history teaching is likely to suffer enormously. At best, schoolteachers will proceed oblivious of current historical research and at worst, in the words of one California educator, 'history will soon be as dead as Latin in the schools.' " *New York Times Book Review*, 30 November 1997, 28, 31, at 31. Note that new NEH chairman William R. Ferris's initiative for 1999 includes a program, "My History Is America's History," more safely concentrating attention on individual families and their relations to larger historical currents in the United States.

88. John K. Wilson, "The Academy Speaks Back," rev. of *PC Wars: Politics and Theory in the Academy*, ed. Jeffrey Williams; *Higher Education under Fire: Politics, Economics, and the Crisis of the Humanities*, ed. Michael Bérubé and Cary Nelson; and *After Political Correctness: The Humanities and Society in the 1990s*, ed. Christopher Newfield and Ronald Strickland, *Democratic Culture* 4.1 (Spring 1995): 29; Jeffrey Williams, *PC Wars: Politics and Theory in the Academy*, ed. J. Williams, as quoted by Wilson, "The Academy," 29.

89. Rep. Louise Slaughter (D-New York) pointed this out in discussion of Rep. Chabot's 1995 amendment and, a year later, of Rep. Shadegg's amendment (*Congressional Record*, 17 July 1995, H7059; 20 June 1996, H6646); the point was made again in 1997 and again in spring 1998 (in Ferris's comments to the House Appropriations Subcommittee on Interior and Related Agencies).

90. Robert V. Hanle and W. Robert Connor, quoted by Paulette Walker Campbell, "Humanities Endowment's Fund-Raising Effort Starts Small," A43.

91. See above, note 72.

92. Campbell, "Humanities Endowment's Fund-Raising Effort Starts Small," A43.

93. The Chabot amendment to defund in 1996 was defeated 148–277, with 9 not voting. The Shadegg amendment to increase the NEH 1997 budget reduction (to achieve the allegedly agreed-on three-year phase-out of the Endowment) was defeated (*Congressional Record*, 20 June 1996, H6647). Rep. Sidney Yates (D-Illinois), arguing against it, maintained that there was in fact no agreement within the Republican party or between the two parties regarding "precisely how we would phase out" the NEH (H6642). The Chabot amendment to defund in fiscal 1998 was defeated 96–328, with 10 not voting. Similarly, a Senate amendment (Jesse Helms [R-North Carolina] and John Ashcroft [R-Missouri]) to defund the NEA in

fiscal 1998 was defeated in a 23–77 vote. For fiscal 1999, both the House and the Senate turned aside efforts to defund the NEA.

94. Tim Miller and David Román, " 'Preaching to the Converted,' " *Theatre Journal* 47 (1995): 169–88. Note that the NEA Four ultimately lost in *NEA v. Karen Finley.* See above, note 72.

95. Letter to the editor, "The MLA and Conservatives," by Elizabeth Powers, *MLA Newsletter,* 29.2 (Summer 1997): 18.

96. Heather Findlay, "Queer Dora: Hysteria, Sexual Politics, and Lacan's 'Intervention on Transference,' " *GLQ: A Journal of Lesbian and Gay Studies* 1 (1994): 323–47, esp. 337, adapts Laclau and Mouffe in her invigorating discussion of queer coalition politics. See Ernesto Laclau and Chantal Mouffe, *Hegemony and Socialist Strategy: Towards a Radical Democratic Politics,* trans. Winston Moore and Paul Cammack (London: Verso, 1985), esp. 104–5. On overdetermination of a social field, see 98: "The symbolic—i.e., overdetermined—character of social relations therefore implies that they lack an ultimate literality which would reduce them to necessary moments of an immanent law." "Articulation" is "any practice establishing a relation among elements such that their identity is modified as a result of the articulatory practice" (105). See also Joshua Gamson, "Must Identity Movements Self-Destruct? A Queer Dilemma," *Social Problems* 42 (1995): 390–407, for a discussion of the innovations in understanding social movements that queer activism and theory can suggest.

Coda: Getting Medieval

1. From *Pulp Fiction: A Quentin Tarantino Screenplay.* Copyright © 1994, Quentin Tarantino. Reprinted with permission by Hyperion. Page 108. All references to *Pulp Fiction* are to this screenplay ("scr." before a page reference in my text indicates nondialogue material); it should be noted that there are some differences between this published screenplay and the wide-release movie.

The late Erskine Peters, in a personal communication, suggested that the line really sounds like "get me evil on your ass," an expression from African American vernacular, and that Tarantino, "in casting the vernacular from the streets onto the page misheard the original and subsequently misrepresented it." The screenplay does say "Medieval"; Peters's suggestion is an interesting one, though, in that it points not to Tarantino's appropriation of black vernacular but his *mis*appropriation of it, a point that supports a fuller critique of the film's racism (see, for an example of such critique, Sharon Willis, "The Fathers Watch the Boys' Room," *Camera Obscura* 32 [1993–94]: 40–73).

2. Todd McCarthy, "*Pulp Fiction*," *Variety*, 23 May 1994, 9; Courtney Love, interview with Kevin Sessums, "Love Child," *Vanity Fair*, June 1995, 106–15, 169–71; quotation on 108 (emphasis original):

> Across the living room is the Buddhist altar on which most of Cobain's ashes are kept in an open urn. . . . "I *wanted* his heart. I wanted his heart to put an oak in it. I was going fucking medieval."
>
> "An oak?" I ask.
>
> "Yeah. I wanted to plant an oak in it and have it grow. It's an old Saxon tradition."

Tarantino's earlier work in *Reservoir Dogs* "spoke to Kurt Cobain" (according to another *Vanity Fair* article quoted by J. Hoberman in "Pulp and Glory," *Village Voice*, 11 October 1994, 61, 75 [at 61]). Cobain thanked Tarantino in the liner notes to Nirvana's *In Utero*.

3. "Idol Threats: Bastards!" *Film Threat* 20 (February 1995): 20.

4. My own place of employment at the time was implicated, as *Time* magazine reported, "Berkeley, long thought of as a peacenik kind of place, got medieval last week as the BIG GAME, the yearly clash with Stanford, got ugly" (*Time*, 8 December 1997, 112).

5. One reason—obvious enough that I take it for granted in this discussion—is that its use in the film fits into an existing range of connotations in the United States and in Europe of "medieval." See Fred C. Robinson's intentionally humorous yet nonetheless troubled presidential address to the Medieval Academy in 1984, "Medieval, the Middle Ages," *Speculum* 59 (1984): 745–56, for a delineation of the term's pejorative meanings, among them "outmoded," "hopelessly antiquated," "tyrannical," and simply "evil," especially when torture and warfare are concerned. For excellent discussion of the development of "the ideological function of 'middle ages,' " explicitly taking up and filling in Robinson's account, see Pat Rogers, "Thomas Warton and the Waxing of the Middle Ages," in *Medieval Literature and Antiquities: Studies in Honour of Basil Cottle*, ed. Myra Stokes and T. L. Burton (Cambridge: D. S. Brewer, 1987), 175–86.

6. The Arthurian chivalric romance is a genre that has a lot in common with the gangster crime genre for which Tarantino has become famous. After all, what is more Arthurian than *Pulp Fiction*'s gangsters, dressed in their black suits of "armor," performing tasks for a central lord, bonding as brothers, going off alone on adventures, splattering blood and gore, facing death? What is more Arthurian than a watch-amulet, symbol of fierce filial loyalty? Than a mistress from a far-off land? Than riding off on a superbly looked-after animal, a "hog"? Than names that are full of descriptive significance? What is more Arthurian than being seduced by the lord's wife while he is away? Than a solitary debate of issues of loyalty to one's lord? Than having a character central to the narrative with a nick on his neck?

If that last is pure coincidence with *Sir Gawain and the Green Knight,* as I am certain it is, the other thematic similarities I have just enumerated are far from happenstance: they are part and parcel of romance plotting, the conventions of which are familiar to anyone steeped in American or European pop culture. The romance narrative genre, as I mentioned in chapter 2, has a big ostensible task: to promote some version of heterosexuality against all odds. For an elaboration of this analysis of *Gawain* in relation to *Pulp Fiction,* see my "Getting Medieval: *Pulp Fiction,* Gawain, Foucault," in *The Book and the Body,* ed. Dolores W. Frese and Katherine O'Brien O'Keeffe (Notre Dame: Univ. of Notre Dame Press, 1997), 116–63.

7. Richard Corliss, "Saturday Night Fever," *Time,* 6 June 1994, 73.

8. *Li Livres de jostice et de plet,* 18.24.22, specifies this law from the legal school of Orléans, c. 1270: see reference above, chapter 1, n. 117, and n. 41 for discussion of secular punishments for sodomy in late medieval England. For discussion of sodomy and other sexual legislation throughout the Western medieval period, see Louis Crompton, "The Myth of Lesbian Impunity: Capital Laws from 1270 to 1791," *Historical Perspectives on Homosexuality,* spec. issue of *Journal of Homosexuality* 6.1–2 (1980–81): 11–25, esp. 13; John Boswell, *Christianity, Social Tolerance, and Homosexuality* (Chicago: Univ. of Chicago Press, 1980); James Brundage, *Law, Sex, and Christian Society in Medieval Europe* (Chicago: Univ. of Chicago Press, 1987). Death by sword had been recommended by Justinian in his 533 CE *Institutions,* and death in his two later constitutions on the subject, while literary sources of the period state that castration was the punishment; burning was recommended by Valentinian, Arcadius, and Theodosius (390 CE) and the Theodosian Code of 438, which was picked up in the West by Alaric II in 506; see Eva Cantarella, *Bisexuality in the Ancient World* (New Haven: Yale Univ. Press, 1992), 173–86. These laws suggest punishments that endured through at least the high Middle Ages in the West. Thanks to David Greenberg on the MEDGAY Internet list for these references.

9. Dir. Don Siegel, Universal Pictures, 1973. I thank Alfred Arteaga for this bit of cinematic lore.

10. Janet Maslin, "Quentin Tarantino's Wild Ride on Life's Dangerous Road," *New York Times,* 23 September 1994, C1, C34, at C34.

11. Anthony Lane, "Degrees of Cool," *New Yorker,* 10 October 1994, 95–97, at 96. Note that Roger Avary contributed the story of "The Gold Watch" sequence, though Tarantino adapted the Avary script and wrote the monologues; see Jeff Dawson, *Quentin Tarantino: The Cinema of Cool* (New York: Applause, 1995), 143–46.

12. Note, too, that another intertextual reference—to *Air Force,* a 1943 Howard Hawks film—underlines the anal theme in this monologue. (A Howard Hawks film festival was playing in Amsterdam while Tarantino was there writing the *Pulp Fiction* screenplay.) Captain Koons recalls here

that the watch was given by Butch's granddad on Wake Island to "a gunner on an Air Force transport named Winocki"—John Garfield, that is, in the 1943 movie, who rigs a machine gun in the tail of the B-17 they call the *Mary Jane*. Thanks to Frank Grady, who pointed this reference out to me; as he put it, "Boy, are the Japanese Zeros surprised."

See Willis, "The Fathers Watch the Boys' Room," for an analysis of the thematics of shit in three of Tarantino's screenplays (*Reservoir Dogs, True Romance,* and *Pulp Fiction*), particularly its relation to anal sex, race, and history. Willis seems, however, to be somewhat taken in by the films' assimilation of sodomy to shit: concerned to analyze what she sees as the infantile fantasies of *Pulp Fiction,* she does not call homophobia homophobia. On the rape scene, furthermore, she assumes that "we" laugh as Bruce Willis "unaccountabl[y]" changes his mind and "goes to seek a weapon with which to rescue Marcellus" [*sic*]; she thus seems already to have assumed what she is ostensibly arguing: that the audience itself participates, according to Tarantino's intention, in "anal aggressivity" (50–51).

Michael Rogin, too, suggests that the audience participates in the rape of Marsellus: "We, the audience, as well as the Bruce Willis character, are not supposed to be on the side of the sodomizers; but in fact the sodomizers are doing *our work* for us" (quoted in Cecil Brown, "Doing that Ol' Oscar Soft-Shoe," *San Francisco Examiner Magazine,* 26 March 1995, 24–27, 37–41, at 40). It is notable that both Willis and Rogin, ultimately occupied with racism in *Pulp Fiction,* downplay the power of the homophobic address of the film and assume an audience that accedes to a homophobic identification. See bell hooks, "Cool Tool," in the March 1995 *Artforum* discussion of the film, "Pulp the Hype: On the Q.T." (62–67, 108–110), for an analysis that takes into consideration both racism and homophobia.

13. *Sleep with Me,* dir. Rory Kelly, August Entertainment, 1994; *Reservoir Dogs,* dir. Quentin Tarantino, Miramax, 1992. Note that Tarantino's *Top Gun* riff (in *Sleep with Me*) was, according to some, Roger Avary's idea, which the two had rehearsed for years (Jami Bernard, *Quentin Tarantino: The Man and His Movies* [New York: HarperPerennial, 1995], 173; see also the section "The Gay Thing"). Discussing his friend and former employee, Lance Lawson recalls Tarantino while he worked at Video Archives in southern California's Manhattan Beach and wrote *True Romance* and *Natural Born Killers:* "You know back then, Quentin was a bit of a homophobe. He was really a kid who'd never been out of LA county. Being able to travel the world was such a broadening experience and so good for him[;] . . . it's really made him a better person." Lawson is remembering conversations they had—about sleeping with Elvis, for example—that eventually ended up in *True Romance* (Dawson, *Quentin Tarantino,* 37). Tarantino himself, in an interview with the gay press, "agrees with the suggestion that he's able to throw gay and gay-ish references into his work because his generation is

cool with the subject: 'I really think so, actually.' " Steve Warren, "Gay 'Top Gun'? A Talk with Tarantino," San Francisco *Sentinel,* 12 October 1994, 33. In Lisa Kennedy's "Natural Born Filmmaker: Quentin Tarantino Versus the Film Geeks" (*Village Voice,* 25 October 1994, 29–32), her pal "the Girl Pup" puts another hypothesis more baldly: " 'What he wants is a big black man to fuck him up the ass!' Well, she's frank if nothing else, and for her a guy wanting it up the ass by a brother is not necessarily a bad thing" (32).

14. See bell hooks, "Cool Tool," and Robin Wood, "Slick Shtick," in the March 1995 *Artforum* discussion of the film, "Pulp the Hype: On the Q.T." (62–67, 108–10), for observations on *Pulp Fiction*'s relation to *Reservoir Dogs.* Tarantino himself, always ready to court a market, when asked about the Australian *Metro* article on homosociality and homosexuality in *Reservoir Dogs,* laughs: "but what was really funny was Jerry Martinez and I were saying, you know what? If he's really going to go down this road, he left out a lot of things" (qtd. in Bernard, *Quentin Tarantino,* 185).

15. John J. Winkler, *The Constraints of Desire: The Anthropology of Sex and Gender in Ancient Greece* (New York: Routledge, 1990), 54–64. I was alerted to this phrase by Will Roscoe, "Strange Craft, Strange History, Strange Folks: Cultural Amnesia and the Case for Lesbian and Gay Studies," *American Anthropologist* 97 (1995): 448–53.

16. See Marc Steyn in *The Spectator,* 22 October 1994, 60–61, at 61.

17. This questionably masculine sexual behavior (Willis's giving his girlfriend "oral pleasure") has a racial component in *True Romance.* In a scene early in the movie, a bunch of men have been debating cunnilingus, and a professed difference between two black men seems to be fomented by the white man in the group. "Any nigger say he don't be eating pussy is lyin' his ass off," says one, while another insists, "If I ever did eat some pussy—*I* would never eat any pussy, right—but *if I did* eat some pussy, I sure as hell wouldn't tell no goddamn body about it. I'd be ashamed as a motherfucker, man." To which the other replies that if he smoked enough dope, "you'd be in there suckin' niggers' dicks."

18. See Willis, "The Fathers Watch the Boys' Room"; Lee Edelman, in "Tearooms and Sympathy or, The Epistemology of the Water Closet," *The Lesbian and Gay Studies Reader,* ed. Henry Abelove, Michèle Aina Barale, and David M. Halperin (New York: Routledge, 1993), 553–74, discusses the problematics of elimination in the context of 1960s national security in the United States.

19. The film represents one other major character's violation in an episode that further demonstrates this preoccupation: Uma Thurman's OD-ing Mia is hysterically, hyperdramatically punctured by Vince with a gigantic needle full of adrenaline. (Recall, too, the penetrated state of Lance's wife Jody [Rosanna Arquette]: "All of my piercing, sixteen places on my body, every one of 'em done with a needle. Five in each ear. One through the

nipple of my left breast. One through my right nostril. One through my left eyebrow. One through my lip. One in my clit. And I wear a stud in my tongue" [31].) Lance instructs Vincent, as he readies himself to stab Mia: "[S]he's got a breast plate in front of her heart, so you gotta pierce through that" (62). The penetration is horrifying: "Lance demonstrates a stabbing motion, which looks like 'The Shape' killing its victims in HALLOWEEN" (scr. 62). This over-the-top injection does some serious work in the whole project of constructing straight masculinity: it serves to deflect the homoerotics, in an earlier scene in Lance's bedroom, of Vince's shooting Lance's "shit" (32) into his vein. (While Vince shoots up, he and Lance talk about "fuckin with a guy's automobile[.] You don't fuck another man's vehicle" [34A].) That huge horse needle full of adrenaline, *that's* penetration, and it happens to women—whereas Vince's is just a little prick.

20. See "Quentin Tarantino on *Pulp Fiction*, as told to Manohla Dargis," *Sight and Sound*, November 1994, 16–19, at 17.

21. hooks, "Cool Tool," 108.

22. Dennis Cooper, "Minor Magic," in "Pulp the Hype: On the Q.T.," *Artforum* (March 1995), 66. Though heavily ironized, belief in a Christian God—its loss and at least strategic recapture—is a key element of *From Dusk to Dawn* (Dimension Films/Miramax, 1996), written by Tarantino, directed by Robert Rodriguez.

23. Tarantino said to *Rolling Stone:* "*Deliverance* did it. *American Me* did it, too. There's like three butt-fucking scenes in *American Me*. That's definitely the one to beat in that particular category." Qtd. in Bernard, *Quentin Tarantino*, 208.

24. hooks, "Cool Tool," 65–66.

25. Willis, "The Fathers Watch," 62.

26. hooks, "Cool Tool," 66.

27. Willis, "The Fathers Watch," observes the significance of the "flesh" color of Marsellus's Band-Aid (49). The image of the black woman appears for a moment in the movie but not in the published screenplay. See Willis, 56–67.

28. *The History of Sexuality*, vol. 1: *An Introduction*, trans. Robert Hurley (New York: Pantheon, 1978); *La Volonté de savoir* (Paris: Gallimard, 1976). *The Use of Pleasure*, trans. Robert Hurley (New York: Pantheon, 1985); *L'Usage des plaisirs* (Paris: Gallimard, 1984). *The Care of the Self*, trans. Robert Hurley (New York: Pantheon, 1986); *Le Souci de soi* (Paris: Gallimard, 1984).

Karma Lochrie, "Desiring Foucault," *Journal of Medieval and Early Modern Studies* 27 (1997): 3–16, makes many similar points in her essay of admonition to "beware the dangers of deploying Foucault" (13): among these points are her discussions of inconsistencies in Foucault's delineation of the Middle Ages and the fact that Foucault's Middle Ages excludes all women.

29. See "On the Genealogy of Ethics: An Overview of Work in Progress," *The Foucault Reader*, ed. Paul Rabinow (New York: Pantheon, 1984), 340–72, at 347–48: "One of the numerous points where I was wrong in that book was what I said about this *ars erotica*. I should have opposed our science of sex to a contrasting practice in our own culture." Ann Laura Stoler, *Race and the Education of Desire: Foucault's* History of Sexuality *and the Colonial Order of Things* (Durham, N.C.: Duke Univ. Press, 1995), suggests that Foucault's race politics are complex; his work "offers ways to rethink the colonial order of things, ways that challenge—and sometimes derive from—him" (13). My treatment here of Foucault's use of the Middle Ages is provisional and will have to be reconsidered in light of Stoler's question: "What happens to Foucault's chronologies when the technologies of sexuality are refigured in an imperial field?" (6).

30. David M. Halperin, "Forgetting Foucault: Acts, Identities, and the History of Sexuality," *Representations* 63 (Summer 1998): 93–120.

31. David M. Halperin, *One Hundred Years of Homosexuality and Other Essays on Greek Love* (New York: Routledge, 1990), 29.

32. Foucault, *Discipline and Punish: The Birth of the Prison*, trans. Alan Sheridan (New York: Vintage, 1979), 251; *Surveiller et punir: Naissance de la prison* (Paris: Gallimard, 1975), 292.

33. Jonathan Goldberg, *Sodometries: Renaissance Texts, Modern Sexualities* (Stanford: Stanford Univ. Press, 1992), 19.

34. Goldberg, *Sodometries*, 19.

35. At the same time, I would emphasize that such contexts do not necessarily *ensure* the emergence of sodomy into discourse: sometimes sodomy, even as it might be specifically feared, cannot be spoken or is not recognized as such even in those stigmatized contexts, and thus a sense of the differential operations of sexual discourses within specific contexts must be maintained.

36. *Natural Born Killers*, dir. Oliver Stone, story by Quentin Tarantino, Warner Brothers, 1994. On female characters, see Dawson, *Quentin Tarantino*, 154–55. And note a scene cut from the original screenplay of *Reservoir Dogs:* according to Bernard, *Quentin Tarantino*, 141, it was to have occurred "between Joe and Mr. Pink, in which Joe says his girlfriend wants him to read Sylvia Plath's *The Bell Jar* and then discuss it with him. The subtext of the scene is the relationship between Joe and Pink, and how they relate to the women in their lives."

37. Halperin, "Forgetting Foucault," 97–100.

38. "Sexual Choice, Sexual Act: An Interview with Michel Foucault," trans. James O'Higgins, *Salmagundi* 58–59 [1982–83]: 10–24; rpt. in *Foucault Live: Interviews, 1961–84* (New York: Semiotext[e], 1996), 322–34.

39. Halperin, "Forgetting Foucault," note 8.

40. Halperin, "Forgetting Foucault," in note 8, draws attention to a tran-

script of interviews Foucault held with a young gay man, Thierry Voeltzel (published under Voeltzel's name), in the summer of 1976, as he was finishing vol. 1 of the *History of Sexuality.* In response to the young man's narrative that recalls to Foucault an earlier time before homosexual identification, Foucault remarks: "The category of the homosexual was invented lately. It didn't use to exist; what existed was sodomy, that is to say a certain number of sexual practices which, in themselves, were condemned, but the homosexual individual did not exist" ("La catégorie de l'homosexuel a été inventée tardivement. Ça n'existait pas, ce qui existait, c'était la sodomie, c'est-à-dire un certain nombre de pratiques sexuelles qui, elles, étaient condamnées, mais l'individu homosexuel n'existait pas"). However unacademic the setting, and however heuristic the contrast, it is clear that Foucault is depending here on a basic historical analysis—creating the opposition between sodomy and homosexuality which he later abandoned, as Halperin observes. The change in Foucault's thinking seems to have had something to do with Boswell's *Christianity, Social Tolerance, and Homosexuality,* which he discusses approvingly in interviews several times, including "De l'amitié comme mode de vie: Un entretien avec un lecteur quinquagénaire," *Le Gai pied* 25 (April 1981): 38–39, rpt. *Dits et écrits, 1954–88,* ed. Daniel Defert and François Ewald, 4 vols. (Paris: Gallimard, 1994), 4: 163–67 ("Friendship as a Way of Life," trans. John Johnston, *Foucault Live,* 308–12); "Histoire et homosexualité: Entretien avec M. Foucault," *Masques* 13 (Spring 1982): 14–24, rpt. *Dits et écrits,* 4:286–95 (trans. by John Johnston as "History and Homosexuality," *Foucault Live,* 363–70). See my discussion above, in the introduction.

41. Pierre Payer, "Foucault on Penance and the Shaping of Sexuality," *Studies in Religion* 14 (1985): 313–20; Anne Clark Bartlett, "Foucault's 'Medievalism,' " *Mystics Quarterly* 20 (1994): 10–18; Foucault, "Introduction," *The Archaeology of Knowledge,* in *The Archaeology of Knowledge and the Discourse on Language,* trans. A. M. Sheridan Smith and Rupert Sawyer (New York: Pantheon, 1972), 12; *L'Archéologie du savoir* (Paris: Gallimard, 1969), 22, on "le discours du continu." For a useful discussion of the relationship of Foucault's work to conventional historiography (and a discussion of his utopianism), see Allan Megill, *Prophets of Extremity: Nietzsche, Heidegger, Foucault, Derrida* (Berkeley: Univ. of California Press, 1985), 190–98. See also Halperin's distinction between Foucault's "discursive analysis" in *History of Sexuality,* vol. 1, and a "historical assertion" ("Forgetting Foucault," 111).

42. "The History of Sexuality," interview with Lucette Finas, trans. Leo Marshall, in *Power/Knowledge: Selected Interviews and Other Writings, 1972–1977,* ed. Colin Gordon (New York: Pantheon, 1980), 183–93, at 193; "Les Rapports de pouvoir passent à l'intérieur des corps," *La Quinzaine*

littéraire 247 (1–15 January 1977): 4–6, rpt. *Dits et écrits,* 3:228–36, at 236. For a discussion of the intended "political impact" of Foucault's "intellectual activities," see David M. Halperin, "The Queer Politics of Michel Foucault," in *Saint Foucault: Towards a Gay Hagiography* (New York: Oxford Univ. Press, 1995), esp. 24–25.

43. Foucault, *The Archaeology of Knowledge,* 17; *L'Archéologie du savoir,* 27. John Mowitt's unpublished manuscript, "Queer Resistance: Foucault and *The Unnamable,*" comments usefully on Foucault's performativity. See also the section, "Performing Foucault," in Eve Kosofsky Sedgwick, "Gender Criticism," in *Redrawing the Boundaries: The Transformation of English and American Literary Studies,* ed. Stephen Greenblatt and Giles Gunn (New York: MLA, 1992), 271–302, at 285–91.

44. "Nietzsche, Genealogy, History," in *Language, Counter-Memory, Practice: Selected Essays and Interviews,* ed. Donald F. Bouchard, trans. Donald F. Bouchard and Sherry Simon (Ithaca: Cornell Univ. Press, 1977), 139–64, esp. 154–57; originally published as "Nietzsche, la généalogie, l'histoire," *Hommage à Jean Hyppolite* (Paris: Presses Universitaires de France, 1971), 145–72; rpt. in *Dits et écrits,* 2: 136–56.

45. For contrasting analyses of Foucault's claims concerning confession, see Pierre Payer, "Foucault on Penance," and Gregory W. Gross, "Secret Rules: Sex, Confession, and Truth in *Sir Gawain and the Green Knight,*" *Arthuriana* 4 (1994): 146–74.

46. See Bartlett, "Foucault's 'Medievalism,' " 15, for other moments of linguistic nostalgia in Foucault's works. And see chapter 2, note 110, for a discussion of Foucault's shifting attitude toward language in literature.

47. *History of Sexuality,* 1: 3; *La Volonté de savoir,* 9: "Des gestes directs, des discours sans honte, des transgressions visibles, des anatomies montrées et facilement mêlées, des enfants délurés rôdant sans gêne ni scandale parmi les rires des adultes: les corps 'faisaient la roue.' "

48. Bartlett castigates what she sees as "Foucault's view of the Middle Ages as a sort of utopian realm, which offers a cultural space free of the routine and disabling surveillance that, for Foucault, characterizes modern society" ("Foucault's 'Medievalism,' " 15). Eve Kosofsky Sedgwick finds "utopian or elegiac elements," but sees them as "fugitive" ("Gender Criticism," 280).

49. Foucault, "On the Genealogy of Ethics," 343, 347.

50. Judith Butler, for example, makes this focus on the body as imprintable surface clear: *Gender Trouble: Feminism and the Subversion of Identity* [New York: Routledge, 1990], 134–39.

51. *Discipline and Punish,* 253; *Surveiller et punir,* 293.

52. *Herculine Barbin: Being the Recently Discovered Memoirs of a Nineteenth-Century French Hermaphrodite,* trans. Richard McDougall (New

York: Pantheon, 1980), vii–xvii, esp. vii–viii; "Le Vrai sexe," *Dits et écrits,* 4: 116 (for full bibliographic details, see above, chapter 2, n. 107). See Arnold Davidson, "Sex and the Emergence of Sexuality," *Critical Inquiry* 14 (1978): 16–48, esp. 19, on Foucault's simplifications of medieval and early modern legal, religious, and medical treatment of hermaphrodites, and Lorraine Daston and Katharine Park, "Hermaphrodites in Renaissance France," *Critical Matrix: Princeton Working Papers in Women's Studies* 1 (1985): 1–19, esp. 3, 6–7.

53. Bersani, "Is the Rectum a Grave?" in *AIDS: Cultural Analysis, Cultural Activism,* ed. Douglas Crimp (Cambridge, Mass.: MIT Press, 1988), 197–222, at 219. Note that Bersani (in "Is the Rectum a Grave?") takes issue with what he sees as Foucault's turn away from sex acts and with Foucault's description of S/M (such a reinvention or deliberate play) as "not a reproduction . . . of the structure of power" (in Bersani, *Homos* [Cambridge, Mass.: Harvard Univ. Press, 1995], 88). My argument doesn't take up the specific question of the workings of power in, or the subversiveness of, S/M; my focus is on the potential for sex acts to shatter the liberal notion of the individual subject, a potential Bersani readily grants.

54. Butler, *Gender Trouble,* 97.

55. "Sade, sergent du sexe," *Cinématographe* 16 (December 1975–January 1976), 3–5; rpt. in *Dits et écrits,* 2: 821–22: "Il faut inventer avec le corps, avec ses éléments, ses surfaces, ses volumes, ses épaisseurs, un érotisme non disciplinaire: celui du corps à l'état volatil et diffus, avec ses rencontres de hasard et ses plaisirs sans calcul"; English translation modified from James Miller, *The Passion of Michel Foucault* (New York: Simon and Schuster, 1993), 278. (See Halperin, *Saint Foucault,* 143–52, for sharp critique of Miller's project.) Compare Leo Bersani and Ulysse Dutoit in *The Forms of Violence: Narrative in Assyrian Art and Modern Culture* (New York: Schocken, 1985), 72: "The shock of 'castration' can thus have the beneficent result of detaching desire from the phallus, and of promoting the discovery of new surfaces" (qtd. in Teresa de Lauretis, *The Practice of Love: Lesbian Sexuality and Perverse Desire* [Bloomington: Indiana Univ. Press, 1994]: 79).

56. Quoted in Halperin, *Saint Foucault,* 94.

57. "[U]n érotisme . . . du corps à l'état . . . diffus"; "ce grand plaisir du corps en explosion": "Sade, sergent du sexe," 821–22; fragments quoted in translation by Miller, *Passion of Michel Foucault,* 278, 274.

58. "Nous avons donc à nous acharner à devenir homosexuels et non pas à nous obstiner à reconnaître que nous le sommes" ("De l'amitié comme mode de vie," 163; "Friendship as a Way of Life," 308). See also "History and Homosexuality," 369–70; "Histoire et homosexualité," 24. For Foucault's emphasis on becoming, see also "Sex, Power, and the Politics of Identity," an interview with Bob Gallagher and Alexander Wilson, *The Advocate,* 7 August 1984, 26–30, 58, rpt. in *Foucault Live,* 382–90; and Ed Cohen, in

his excellent "Foucauldian Necrologies: 'Gay' 'Politics'? Politically Gay?" *Textual Practice* 2.1 (Spring 1988): 87–101.

59. "S/M is *the use* of a strategic relationship as a source of pleasure (physical pleasure). It is not the first time that people have used strategic relations as a source of pleasure. For instance, in the Middle Ages there was the institution of 'courtly love,' the troubadour, the institutions of the love relationships between the lady and the lover, and so on. That as well was a strategic game. . . . What is interesting is that in this heterosexual life those strategic relations come before sex. It's a strategic relation in order to obtain sex. And in S/M those strategic relations are inside sex, as a convention of pleasure within a particular situation." Gallagher and Wilson, "Sex, Power, and the Politics of Identity," 388; see also 384. According to Miller (*Passion of Michel Foucault*, 262–63) this interview took place in 1982. In the 1982 *Salmagundi* interview, "Sexual Choice, Sexual Act," Foucault linked courtly love with S/M, making the same contrast: "You find emerging in places like San Francisco and New York what might be called laboratories of sexual experimentation. You might look upon this as the counterpart of the medieval courts where strict rules of proprietary courtship were defined" (*Foucault Live*, 330). For a critique of Foucault's "theoretical sleight-of-hand" in separating power structures from pleasure in his discussions of S/M, see Bersani, *Homos*, 77–112, esp. 88–89.

60. See Saint Jerome, Letter 22, to Eustochium, which develops this idea in meticulous detail (sec. 5 and passim, in *Epistulae*, ed. Isidorus Hilberg, 3 vols., CESL 54–56 [Vienna: F. Tempsky, 1910–18], 1: 143–211, esp. 149–50). Judith Butler, uncharacteristically on the side of the exegetes here, analyzes such a deconstruction in her *Bodies That Matter: On the Discursive Limits of "Sex"* (New York: Routledge, 1993), 244 n. 7.

61. Halperin, *Saint Foucault*, 15–16.

62. Sarah Schulman, *My American History: Lesbian and Gay Life During the Reagan/Bush Years* (New York: Routledge, 1994), discusses the dissymmetries of and rifts between men's and women's political commitments in ACT UP and in other activist contexts (e.g., pp. 216–17, 238). Cathy Cohen, "Punks, Bulldaggers, and Welfare Queens: The Radical Potential of Queer Politics?" *GLQ: A Journal of Lesbian and Gay Studies* 3 (1997): 437–65, points to the failure of current queer politics to destabilize systems of domination.

63. "Sade, sergent du sexe" in *Dits et écrits*, 2: 819: "Il y a là anarchisation du corps où les hiérarchies, les localisations et les dénominations, l'organicité, si vous voulez, sont en train de se défaire. . . . C'est une chose 'innommable,' 'inutilisable,' hors de tous les programmes du désir; c'est le corps rendu entièrement plastique par le plaisir: quelque chose qui s'ouvre, qui se tend, qui palpite, qui bat, qui bée." English translation modified from Miller, *Passion of Michel Foucault*, 274.

64. Hayden White, *The Content of the Form: Narrative Discourse and Historical Representation* (Baltimore: Johns Hopkins Univ. Press, 1987), 104–41, at 105; noted in Halperin, *Saint Foucault,* 74.

65. Cohen, "Foucauldian Necrologies," 96.

66. Biddy Martin, "Feminism, Criticism, and Foucault," *New German Critique* 27 (1982): 3–30, at 11.

Bibliography

"Academic Freedom: A TDC [Teachers for a Democratic Culture] Special Report." *Democratic Culture* 4.2 (Fall 1995): 6–35.

Aers, David. "Figuring Forth the Body of Christ: Devotion and Politics." In *Figures of Speech: The Body in Medieval Art, History, and Literature*, ed. Allen J. Frantzen and David A. Robertson, 1–14. Spec. issue of *Essays in Medieval Studies* 11, Proceedings of the Illinois Medieval Association (1994).

———. "The Making of Margery Kempe: Individual and Community." In *Community, Gender, and Individual Identity: English Writing, 1360–1430*, 73–116. London: Routledge, 1988.

———. Preface. In *From Medieval Christianities to the Reformations*, ed. David Aers, 139–43. Spec. issue of *Journal of Medieval and Early Modern Studies* 27 (1997).

———. "A Whisper in the Ear of Early Modernists; or, Reflections on Literary Critics Writing the 'History of the Subject.'" In *Culture and History, 1350–1600: Essays on English Communities, Identities and Writing*, ed. David Aers, 177–202. Detroit: Wayne State Univ. Press, 1992.

Agamben, Giorgio. *The Coming Community*. Trans. Michael Hardt. Minneapolis: Univ. of Minnesota Press, 1993.

Air Force. Dir. Howard Hawks. Warner Brothers, 1943.

Alanus de Insulis. *De planctu Naturae*. Ed. Nikolaus Häring. *Studi medievali*. 3rd ser., no. 19 (1978).

Albertus Magnus. *Quaestiones super De animalibus*. In vol. 12 of *Opera Omnia*, ed. members of the Institutum Alberti Magni Coloniense. Münster, Aschendorff, 1955.

Anderson, Benedict. *Imagined Communities: Reflections on the Origins and Spread of Nationalism*. London: Verso, 1983.

Andersson, Aron. *Saint Bridget of Sweden*. London: Catholic Truth Society, 1980.

An Anglo-Saxon Dictionary. Ed. Joseph Bosworth and T. Northcote Toller. Oxford: Oxford Univ. Press, 1882–98.

Appiah, Kwame Anthony. "Is the 'Post-' in 'Postcolonial' the 'Post-' in 'Postmodern'?" In *Dangerous Liaisons: Gender, Nation, and Postcolonial Perspectives,* ed. Anne McClintock, Aamir Mufti, and Ella Shohat, 420–44. Minneapolis: Univ. of Minnesota Press, 1997.

Appleby, Joyce. "One Good Turn Deserves Another: Moving beyond the Linguistic; A Response to David Harlan." *American Historical Review* 94 (1989): 1326–32.

Aquinas, Saint Thomas. "De regimine principum ad regem Cypri." In vol. 16 of *Opera omnia.* Parma: Pietro Fiaccadori, 1864. Reprint. New York: Musurgia, 1950.

———. *Summa theologica.* 3 vols. Trans. Fathers of the English Dominican Province. London: Burns Oates and Washbourne; New York: Benziger Bros., 1921.

———. *Summa theologica.* Parma, 1852–73. Reprint. New York: Musurgia, 1949.

Arnold, Thomas, ed. *Select English Works of John Wyclif.* 3 vols. Oxford: Clarendon, 1869–71.

Astell, Ann W. *Chaucer and the Universe of Learning.* Ithaca: Cornell Univ. Press, 1996.

———. "The *Translatio* of Chaucer's Pardoner." *Exemplaria* 4 (1992): 411–28.

Aston, Margaret. "William White's Lollard Followers." In *Lollards and Reformers: Images and Literacy in Late Medieval Religion,* 71–100. London: Hambledon Press, 1984.

Augustine, Saint. *De civitate Dei.* Ed. Bernard Dombart and Alphonse Kalb. Corpus christianorum, 47–48. Turnhout: Brepols, 1955.

———. *The City of God.* Trans. Henry Bettenson. 1972. Reprint. Harmondsworth, U.K.: Penguin, 1984.

———. *De trinitate.* Ed. W. J. Mountain and Fr. Glorie. Corpus christianorum, series latina 50–50A. Turnhout: Brepols, 1968.

———. *The Trinity.* Trans. Stephen McKenna. Washington, D.C.: Catholic University of America Press, 1963.

———. *Epistvlae.* 5 vols. Ed. A. Goldbacher. Vienna: F. Tempsky; Leipzig: G. Freytag, 1911.

———. *The Confessions and Letters of St. Augustin.* Trans. Philip Schaff. Nicene and Post-Nicene Fathers first series, 1. Reprint. Grand Rapids, Mich.: Eerdmans, 1956.

Ayenbite of Inwit. Ed. Richard Morris, trans. Dan Michel. EETS o.s. 23. London: Kegan Paul, Trench, Trübner, 1866.

Bale, John. *A Brefe Chronycle concernynge the Examinacyon and death of the blessed martyr of Christ Syr Johan Oldecastell.* [Antwerp?]: 1544.

Barnett, Allen. "Philostorgy, Now Obscure." In *The Body and Its Dangers and Other Stories,* 34–61. New York: St. Martin's, 1990.

Barthes, Roland. *Camera Lucida: Reflections on Photography.* Trans. Richard Howard. New York: Hill and Wang, 1981. Originally published as *La Chambre claire.* Paris: Seuil, 1980.

———. *Empire of Signs.* Trans. Richard Howard. New York: Hill and Wang, 1982. Originally published as *L'Empire des signes.* Geneva: Albert Skira, 1970.

———. "The Grain of the Voice." In *Image, Music, Text,* trans. Stephen Heath, 179–89. New York: Hill and Wang, 1977. Originally published as "Le Grain de la voix." *Musique en jeu* 9 (1972): 57–63.

———. "Historical Discourse." Trans. Peter Wexler. Reprint. In *Structuralism: A Reader,* ed. Michael Lane, 145–55. London: Jonathan Cape, 1970.

———. *Incidents.* Trans. Richard Howard. Berkeley: Univ. of California Press, 1992. Originally published as *Incidents.* Paris: Seuil, 1987.

———. "Michelet, l'Histoire et la Mort." *Esprit* 178 (April 1951): 497–511.

———. *Michelet.* Trans. Richard Howard. New York: Hill and Wang, 1987. Originally published as *Michelet par lui-même.* Paris: Seuil, 1954.

———. *The Pleasure of the Text.* Trans. Richard Miller. New York: Farrar, Straus and Giroux, 1975. Originally published as *Le Plaisir du texte.* Paris: Seuil, 1973.

———. "Reflections on a Manual." Trans. Sandy Petrey. *PMLA* 112 (1997): 69–75.

———. *Roland Barthes by Roland Barthes.* Trans. Richard Howard. New York: Hill and Wang, 1977. Originally published as *Roland Barthes par Roland Barthes.* Paris: Seuil, 1975.

———. *The Rustle of Language.* Trans. Richard Howard. New York: Hill and Wang, 1986. Originally published as *Le Bruissement de la langue.* Paris: Seuil, 1984.

———. *S/Z.* Trans. Richard Miller. New York: Hill and Wang, 1974. Originally published as *S/Z.* Paris: Seuil, 1970.

———. *Sade, Fourier, Loyola.* Trans. Richard Miller. New York: Hill and Wang, 1976. Originally published as *Sade, Fourier, Loyola.* Paris: Seuil, 1971.

———. *Writer Sollers.* Trans. Philip Thody. Minneapolis: Univ. of Minnesota Press, 1987. Originally published as *Sollers écrivain.* Paris: Seuil, 1979.

———. "The Surrealists Overlooked the Body." In *The Grain of the Voice: Interviews, 1962–1980,* trans. Linda Coverdale, 243–45. New York: Hill and Wang, 1985. Originally published as "Les Surréalistes ont manqué le corps." In *Le Grain de la voix,* 230–32. Paris: Seuil, 1981.

Bartholomaeus Anglicus. *De proprietatibus rerum.* Trans. John Trevisa under the title *On the Properties of Things,* gen. ed. M. C. Seymour. 3 vols. Oxford: Clarendon, 1975–88.

Bartlett, Anne Clark. "Foucault's 'Medievalism.'" *Mystics Quarterly* 20 (1994): 10–18.

Baudrillard, Jean. *Cool Memories, 1980–85*. Paris: Editions Galilée, 1987.

———. *Oublier Foucault*. Paris: Editions Galilée, 1977.

———. *Simulations*. Trans. Paul Foss, Paul Patton, and Philip Beitchman. New York: Semiotext(e), 1983.

Beckwith, Sarah. *Christ's Body: Identity, Culture, and Society in Medieval Writing*. New York: Routledge, 1993.

———. "Ritual, Church and Theater: Medieval Dramas of the Sacramental Body." In *Culture and History, 1350–1600: Essays on English Communities, Identities and Writing*, ed. David Aers. Detroit: Wayne State Univ. Press, 1992.

———. "A Very Material Mysticism: The Medieval Mysticism of Margery Kempe." In *Medieval Literature: Criticism, Ideology, and History*, ed. David Aers, 34–57. New York: Saint Martin's, 1986.

Benjamin, Walter. "A Small History of Photography." 1931. Reprint. In *One-Way Street and Other Writings*, trans. Edmund Jephcott and Kingsley Shorter, 240–57. London: NLB, 1979.

———. "Theses on the Philosophy of History." In *Illuminations*, ed. Hannah Arendt, trans. Harry Zohn, 253–64. New York: Schocken, 1969.

Bennett, Judith M. "Our Colleagues, Ourselves." In *The Past and Future of Medieval Studies*, ed. John Van Engen, 245–58. Notre Dame: Univ. of Notre Dame Press, 1994.

Bennington, Geoff, and Robert Young. "Introduction: Posing the Question." In *Post-Structuralism and the Question of History*, ed. Derek Attridge, Geoff Bennington, and Robert Young, 1–11. Cambridge: Cambridge Univ. Press, 1987.

Bernard of Clairvaux, Saint. *Life and Works of Saint Bernard*. Ed. John Mabillon, trans. Samuel J. Eales. London: John Hodges, 1896.

———. *Sermones super cantica canticorum*. Ed. J. Leclercq, C. H. Talbot, and H. M. Rochais. Rome: Cistercian Editions, 1957.

Bernard, Jami. *Quentin Tarantino: The Man and His Movies*. New York: HarperPerennial, 1995.

Bernardino of Siena, Saint. *Opera omnia*. 9 vols. Florence: Ad Claras Aquas, 1950–65.

Bersani, Leo. *Homos*. Cambridge, Mass.: Harvard Univ. Press, 1995.

———. "Is the Rectum a Grave?" In *AIDS: Cultural Analysis, Cultural Activism*, ed. Douglas Crimp, 197–222. Cambridge, Mass.: MIT Press, 1988.

Bersani, Leo, and Ulysse Dutoit. *The Forms of Violence: Narrative in Assyrian Art and Modern Culture*. New York: Schocken, 1985.

Bérubé, Michael. "The NEA Has Outlived Its Purpose, and I Want My 40 Cents Back." *Chronicle of Higher Education*, 1 August 1997, B6.

Betteridge, Thomas. "Anne Askewe, John Bale, and Protestant History." *From Medieval Christianities to the Reformations,* ed. David Aers. Spec. issue of *Journal of Medieval and Early Modern Studies* 27 (1997): 265–84.

Bhabha, Homi K. "DissemiNation: Time, Narrative, and the Margins of the Modern Nation." In *Nation and Narration,* ed. Homi K. Bhabha, 291–322. London: Routledge, 1990.

———. "Postcolonial Authority and Postmodern Guilt." In *Cultural Studies,* ed. Lawrence Grossberg, Cary Nelson, and Paula A. Treichler, 56–68. New York: Routledge, 1992.

———. "Postcolonial Criticism." In *Redrawing the Boundaries: The Transformation of English and American Literary Studies,* ed. Stephen Greenblatt and Giles Gunn, 437–65. New York: MLA, 1992.

———. "Signs Taken for Wonders: Questions of Ambivalence and Authority under a Tree outside Delhi, May 1817." In *The Location of Culture,* 102–22. New York: Routledge, 1994.

Biddick, Kathleen. "A Response to David Aers's 'Figuring Forth the Body of Christ.'" In *Figures of Speech: The Body in Medieval Art, History, and Literature,* ed. Allen J. Frantzen and David A. Robertson. Spec. issue of *Essays in Medieval Studies* 11, *Proceedings of the Illinois Medieval Association* (1994).

———. *The Shock of Medievalism.* Durham, N.C.: Duke Univ. Press, 1998.

Biller, P. P. A. "Birth-Control in the West in the Thirteenth and Early Fourteenth Centuries." *Past and Present* 94 (February 1982): 3–26.

Bjørnerud, Andreas. "Outing Barthes: Barthes and the Quest(ion) of (a Gay) Identity Politics." *New Formations* 18 (Winter 1992): 122–41.

Blackmore, Josiah, and Gregory S. Hutcheson, eds. *Queer Iberia.* Durham, N.C.: Duke Univ. Press, 1999.

Blamires, Alcuin. "The Wife of Bath and Lollardy." *Medium Ævum* 58 (1989): 224–42.

Bloch, Marc. *The Historian's Craft.* Trans. Peter Putnam. New York, Knopf, 1953.

Bloom, Harold. *The Anxiety of Influence: A Theory of Poetry.* New York: Oxford Univ. Press, 1973.

Bolton, Richard, ed. *Culture Wars: Documents from the Recent Controversies in the Arts.* New York: New Press, 1992.

The Book of Margery Kempe. Ed. Sanford Brown Meech and Hope Emily Allen. EETS 212. 1940. Reprint. Oxford: Oxford Univ. Press, 1982.

The Book of Margery Kempe. Trans. B. A. Windeatt. Harmondsworth, U.K.: Penguin, 1985.

The Book of Vices and Virtues. Ed. W. Nelson Francis. EETS 217. London: Oxford Univ. Press, 1942.

Boswell, John. *Christianity, Social Tolerance, and Homosexuality: Gay People in Western Europe from the Beginning of the Christian Era to the Fourteenth Century*. Chicago: Univ. of Chicago Press, 1980.

———. Correspondence. The Boswell Archives. Clayton, California.

———. "Eros, Ethos, and Going to College: An Interview with John Boswell." *Yale Daily News Magazine* (December 1983): 6–9.

———. "Gay History." Review of David F. Greenberg, *The Construction of Homosexuality. Atlantic* (February 1989): 74–78.

———. "Historian John Boswell on Gay [*sic*], Tolerance and the Christian Tradition." Interview by Richard Hall. *The Advocate*, 28 May 1981, 20–23, 26–27.

———. "Revolutions, Universals, and Sexual Categories." In *Hidden from History: Reclaiming the Gay and Lesbian Past*, ed. Martin Duberman, Martha Vicinus, and George Chauncey Jr., 17–36. New York: Meridian, 1990.

———. *Same-Sex Unions in Premodern Europe*. New York: Villard Books, 1994.

Bowden, Muriel. *A Commentary on the General Prologue to the* Canterbury Tales. 1967. Reprint. London: Souvenir Press, 1975.

Bowers, Margaretta K. *Conflicts of the Clergy: A Psychodynamic Study with Case Histories*. New York: Thomas Nelson, 1963.

Boyarin, Daniel. "Are There Any Jews in 'The History of Sexuality'?" *Journal of the History of Sexuality* 5 (1995): 333–55.

Boyd, David Lorenzo, and Ruth Mazo Karras. "The Interrogation of a Male Transvestite Prostitute in Fourteenth-Century London." *GLQ: A Journal of Lesbian and Gay Studies* 1 (1995): 459–65. See also Karras, Ruth Mazo, and David Lorenzo Boyd.

Boyle, L. E. "The *Oculus Sacerdotis* and Some Other Works of William of Pagula." *Transactions of the Royal Historical Society*, 5th ser., no. 5 (1955): 81–110.

Bravmann, Scott. *Queer Fictions of the Past: History, Culture, and Difference*. Cambridge: Cambridge Univ. Press, 1997.

Bray, Alan. "Homosexuality and the Signs of Male Friendship in Elizabethan England." In *Queering the Renaissance*, ed. Jonathan Goldberg, 40–61. Durham, N.C.: Duke Univ. Press, 1994.

———. *Homosexuality in Renaissance England*. London: Gay Men's Press, 1982.

Bridget of Sweden, Saint. See *The Liber Celestis of Saint Bridget of Sweden*.

Brinton, Bishop Thomas. *The Sermons of Thomas Brinton, Bishop of Rochester (1373–1389)*. 2 vols. Ed. Mary Aquinas Devlin, O.P. Camden Society 86. London: Royal Historical Society, 1954.

Britton. Ed. and trans. Francis Morgan Nichols. 1865. Reprint, 2 vols. Holmes Beach, Fl.: W. W. Gaunt, 1983.

Brooten, Bernadette J. *Love between Women: Early Christian Responses to Female Homoeroticism*. Chicago: Univ. of Chicago Press, 1996.
Browe, Peter. *Die eucharistischen Wunder des Mittelalters*. Breslauer Studien zur historischen Theologie. Breslau: Verlag Müller and Seiffert, 1938.
Brown, Catherine. "Queer Representation in the *Arcipreste de Talavera,* or The *Maldezir de Mugeres* Is a Drag." In *Queer Iberia,* ed. Josiah Blackmore and Gregory S. Hutcheson. Durham, N.C.: Duke Univ. Press, forthcoming 1999.
Brown, Cecil. "Doing That Ol' Oscar Soft-Shoe." *San Francisco Examiner Magazine,* 26 March 1995, 24–27, 37–41.
Brown, Peter. "Augustine and Sexuality." Protocol of the Forty-Sixth Colloquy, Center for Hermeneutical Studies, Berkeley, 22 May 1983, 12.
Brownlee, Marina S., Kevin Brownlee, and Stephen G. Nichols, eds. *The New Medievalism*. Baltimore: Johns Hopkins Univ. Press, 1991.
Brundage, James A. *Law, Sex, and Christian Society in Medieval Europe*. Chicago: Univ. of Chicago Press, 1987.
———. "Playing by the Rules: Sexual Behavior and Legal Norms in Medieval Europe." In *Desire and Discipline: Sex and Sexuality in the Premodern West,* ed. Jacqueline Murray and Konrad Eisenbichler, 23–41. Toronto: Univ. of Toronto Press, 1996.
Bryan, W. F., and Germaine Dempster, eds. *Sources and Analogues of Chaucer's* Canterbury Tales. 1941. Reprint. Atlantic Highlands, N.J.: Humanities Press, 1958.
Bullough, Vern L. "Postscript: Heresy, Witchcraft, and Sexuality." In *Sexual Practices and the Medieval Church,* ed. Vern L. Bullough and James Brundage, 206–17. Buffalo, N.Y.: Prometheus, 1982.
———. "The Sin against Nature and Homosexuality." In *Sexual Practices and the Medieval Church,* ed. Vern L. Bullough and James Brundage, 55–71. Buffalo, N.Y.: Prometheus, 1982.
Burger, Glenn. "Doing What Comes Naturally: The *Physician's Tale* and the Pardoner." In *Masculinities in Chaucer: Approaches to Maleness in the* Canterbury Tales *and* Troilus and Criseyde, ed. Peter G. Beidler, 117–30. Cambridge: D. S. Brewer, 1998.
———. "Erotic Discipline . . . Or 'Tee Hee, I Like My Boys to Be Girls': Inventing with the Body in Chaucer's *Miller's Tale.*" In *Becoming Male in the Middle Ages,* ed. Jeffrey Jerome Cohen and Bonnie Wheeler, 245–60. New York: Garland, 1997.
———. "Kissing the Pardoner." *PMLA* 107 (1992): 1143–56.
Butler, Judith. "Against Proper Objects." *differences* 6.2–3 (Summer–Fall 1994), 1–26.
———. *Bodies That Matter: On the Discursive Limits of "Sex."* New York: Routledge, 1993.

———. "Critically Queer." *GLQ: A Journal of Lesbian and Gay Studies* 1 (1993): 17–32.

———. *Gender Trouble: Feminism and the Subversion of Identity.* New York: Routledge, 1990.

Bynum, Caroline Walker. *Fragmentation and Redemption: Essays on Gender and the Human Body in Medieval Religion.* New York: Zone Books, 1991.

———. *Holy Feast, Holy Fast: The Religious Significance of Food to Medieval Women.* Berkeley: Univ. of California Press, 1987.

Cadden, Joan. *Meanings of Sex Difference in the Middle Ages: Medicine, Science, and Culture.* Cambridge: Cambridge Univ. Press, 1993.

———. Review of *Same-Sex Unions in Premodern Europe,* by John Boswell. *Speculum* 71 (1996): 693–96.

———. "Sciences/Silences: The Natures and Languages of 'Sodomy' in Peter of Abano's *Problemata* Commentary." In *Constructing Medieval Sexuality,* ed. Karma Lochrie, Peggy McCracken, and James A. Schultz, 40–57. Minneapolis: Univ. of Minnesota Press, 1997.

Calabrese, Michael A. " 'Make a Mark That Shows': Orphean Song, Orphean Sexuality, and the Exile of Chaucer's Pardoner." *Viator* 24 (1993): 269–86.

Camille, Michael. "The Book as Flesh and Fetish in Richard de Bury's *Philobiblon.*" In *The Book and the Body,* ed. D. W. Frese and K. O'Brien O'Keeffe, 34–77. Notre Dame: Univ. of Notre Dame Press, 1997.

———. *Master of Death: The Lifeless Art of Pierre Remiet, Illuminator.* New Haven: Yale Univ. Press, 1996.

Campbell, Paulette Walker. "Humanities Endowment's Fund-Raising Effort Starts Small," *Chronicle of Higher Education,* 9 October 1998, A42–43.

———. "New NEH Chairman Hopes to Revive Some Grant Programs That Have Been Cut." *Chronicle of Higher Education,* 12 December 1997, A34.

Cantarella, Eva. *Bisexuality in the Ancient World.* Trans. Cormac Ó Cuilleanáin. New Haven: Yale Univ. Press, 1992.

Cantor, Peter. *Verbum abbreviatum. Patrologia latina,* ed. J.-P. Migne, 205: cols. 21–554. Paris, 1855.

Case, Sue-Ellen. "The Student and the Strap: Authority and Seduction in the Class(room)." In *Professions of Desire: Lesbian and Gay Studies in Literature,* ed. George E. Haggerty and Bonnie Zimmerman, 38–46. New York: MLA, 1995.

Cassian, John. *Cassian on Chastity: Institute 6, Conference 12, Conference 22.* Trans. Terrence G. Kardong. Richardton, N.D.: Assumption Abbey Press, 1993.

A Catalogue of the Manuscripts in the Cottonian Library Deposited in the British Museum. London: L. Hansard, 1802.

Certeau, Michel de. "History: Science and Fiction." In *Heterologies: Dis-*

course on the Other, trans. Brian Massumi, 199–221. Minneapolis: Univ. of Minnesota Press, 1986.
———. *The Writing of History*. Trans. Tom Conley. New York: Columbia Univ. Press, 1988.
Chance, Jane. *The Mythographic Chaucer: The Fabulation of Sexual Politics*. Minneapolis: Univ. of Minnesota Press, 1995.
Charley Varrick. Dir. Don Siegel. Universal Pictures, 1973.
Chartier, Roger. *On the Edge of the Cliff: History, Language, and Practices*. Trans. Lydia G. Cochrane. Baltimore: Johns Hopkins Univ. Press, 1997.
The Chastising of God's Children. Ed. Joyce Bazire and Eric Colledge. Oxford: Basil Blackwell, 1957.
Chaucer, Geoffrey. *The Complete Works of Geoffrey Chaucer*. 6 vols. Ed. W. W. Skeat. Oxford: Oxford Univ. Press, 1894.
———. *The Riverside Chaucer*. 3rd ed. Gen. ed. Larry D. Benson. Boston: Houghton Mifflin, 1987.
Cheney, Lynne V. "The End of History." *Wall Street Journal*, 20 October 1994, A26.
———. "The National History (Sub)Standards." *Wall Street Journal*, 23 October 1995, A16.
Chiffoleau, Jacques. "Dire l'indicible: Remarques sur la catégorie du *nefandum* du XIIe au XVe siècle." *Annales ESC* 45 (1990): 289–324.
Clanvowe, John. *The Two Ways*. In *The Works of Sir John Clanvowe*, ed. V. J. Scattergood, 577–86. Totowa, N.J.: Rowman and Littlefield; Cambridge: D. S. Brewer, 1975.
Cleve, Gunnel. "Margery Kempe: A Scandinavian Influence in Medieval England?" In *The Medieval Mystical Tradition in England*, ed. Marion Glasscoe, 163–78. Cambridge: D. S. Brewer, 1992.
———. "Semantic Dimensions in Margery Kempe's 'Whyght Clothys.'" *Mystics Quarterly* 12 (1986): 162–70.
The Cloud of Unknowing. Ed. Phyllis Hodgson. EETS o.s. 218. London: Oxford Univ. Press, 1944.
Cohen, Cathy. "Punks, Bulldaggers, and Welfare Queens: The Radical Potential of Queer Politics?" *GLQ: A Journal of Lesbian and Gay Studies* 3 (1997): 437–65.
Cohen, Ed. "Foucauldian Necrologies: 'Gay' 'Politics'? Politically Gay?" *Textual Practice* 2.1 (Spring 1988): 87–101.
Cohen, Jeffrey Jerome, and Bonnie Wheeler. "Becoming and Unbecoming." In *Becoming Male in the Middle Ages*, ed. Jeffrey Jerome Cohen and Bonnie Wheeler, vii–xx. New York: Garland, 1997.
Congressional Record. 1995–97. Washington, D.C.
Cooper, Dennis. "Minor Magic." In "Pulp the Hype: On the Q.T." *Artforum* (March 1995): 62–66, 110.

Corliss, Richard. "Saturday Night Fever." *Time*, 6 June 1994, 73.
Crompton, Louis. "The Myth of Lesbian Impunity: Capital Laws from 1270 to 1791." In *Historical Perspectives on Homosexuality*. Spec. issue of *Journal of Homosexuality* 6.1–2 (1980–81): 11–25.
Cross, Claire. " 'Great Reasoners in Scripture': The Activities of Women Lollards, 1380–1530." In *Medieval Women*, ed. Derek Baker, 359–80. Oxford: Blackwell, 1978.
Cutrone, Christopher. "Glenn Ligon: 'A Feast of Scraps' and *Photos and Notes*." http://www.xsite.net/~ccutrone/ligon.html.
The Cyrurgie of Guy de Chauliac. Ed. Margaret S. Ogden. EETS 265. Oxford: Oxford Univ. Press, 1971.
Daley, A. Stuart. "Chaucer's 'Droghte of March' in Medieval Farm Lore." *Chaucer Review* 4 (1970): 171–79.
Damian, Saint Peter. *Liber Gomorrhianus*. Ed. C. Gaetani. *Patrologia latina*, ed. J.-P. Migne, 145: cols. 159–90. Paris, 1853.
Daston, Lorraine, and Katharine Park. "Hermaphrodites in Renaissance France." *Critical Matrix: Princeton Working Papers in Women's Studies* 1 (1985): 1–19.
Davidson, Arnold. "Sex and the Emergence of Sexuality." *Critical Inquiry* 14 (1978): 16–48.
Davis, Kathleen. "Post-Colonial Nationalism Theory and the Medieval English Text." Paper presented at the New Chaucer Society Congress, Los Angeles, 1996.
Davis, Norman, et al. *A Chaucer Glossary*. Oxford: Clarendon, 1979.
Dawson, Jeff. *Quentin Tarantino: The Cinema of Cool*. New York: Applause, 1995.
De Lauretis, Teresa. *The Practice of Love: Lesbian Sexuality and Perverse Desire*. Bloomington: Indiana Univ. Press, 1994.
———. "Sexual Indifference and Lesbian Representation." 1988. Reprint. In *The Lesbian and Gay Studies Reader*, ed. Henry Abelove, Michèle Aina Barale, and David M. Halperin, 141–58. New York: Routledge, 1993.
———, ed. *Feminist Studies/Critical Studies*. Bloomington: Indiana Univ. Press, 1986.
De Lorris, Guillaume, and Jean de Meun. *Le Roman de la rose*, ed. Félix Lecoy. Classiques français du Moyen Age 92, 95, 98. 3 vols. Paris: Champion, 1965–70.
———. *The Romance of the Rose*. Trans. Charles Dahlberg. Princeton: Princeton Univ. Press, 1971.
Deanesly, Margaret. *The Lollard Bible and Other Medieval Biblical Versions*. 1920. Reprint. Cambridge: Cambridge Univ. Press, 1966.
Delany, Sheila. *Writing Woman: Women Writers and Women in Literature, Medieval to Modern*. New York: Schocken, 1983.

Derrida, Jacques. "Cogito and the History of Madness." In *Writing and Difference,* trans. Alan Bass, 31–63. Chicago: Univ. of Chicago Press, 1978.
———. "Women in the Beehive: A Seminar with Jacques Derrida." In *Men in Feminism,* ed. Alice Jardine and Paul Smith, 189–203. New York: Methuen, 1987.
Dickman, Susan. "Margery Kempe and the Continental Tradition of the Pious Woman." In *The Medieval Mystical Tradition in England,* ed. Marion Glasscoe, 150–68. Cambridge: D. S. Brewer, 1984.
Dillon, Janette. "Holy Women and Their Confessors or Confessors and Their Holy Women? Margery Kempe and Continental Tradition." In *Prophets Abroad: The Reception of Continental Holy Women in Late-Medieval England,* ed. Rosalynn Voaden, 115–40. Cambridge: D. S. Brewer, 1996.
Dinshaw, Carolyn. "Chaucer's Queer Touches/A Queer Touches Chaucer." *Exemplaria* 7 (1995): 76–92.
———. *Chaucer's Sexual Poetics.* Madison: Univ. of Wisconsin Press, 1989.
———. "Getting Medieval: *Pulp Fiction,* Gawain, Foucault." In *The Book and the Body,* ed. Dolores W. Frese and Katherine O'Brien O'Keeffe, 116–63. Notre Dame: Univ. of Notre Dame Press, 1997.
———. "A Kiss Is Just a Kiss: Heterosexuality and Its Consolations in *Sir Gawain and the Green Knight.*" *diacritics* 24.2–3 (Summer–Fall 1994): 205–26.
———. "Rivalry, Rape and Manhood: Gower and Chaucer." In *Chaucer and Gower: Difference, Mutuality, Exchange,* ed. Robert F. Yeager, 130–52. Univ. of Victoria English Literary Studies Monograph Series 51. Victoria, B.C.: Univ. of Victoria Press, 1991.
"Dismissal over AIDS Fear." *New York Times,* 25 July 1995, A8.
Dollimore, Jonathan. *Sexual Dissidence: Augustine to Wilde, Freud to Foucault.* Oxford: Clarendon Press, 1991.
Du Plessis, Michael. Review of *Bringing Out Roland Barthes,* by D. A. Miller. *Discourse* 16.1 (Fall 1993): 174–79.
Duggan, Lisa. "The Discipline Problem: Queer Theory Meets Lesbian and Gay History." *GLQ: A Journal of Lesbian and Gay Studies* 2 (1995): 179–91.
———. "The Trials of Alice Mitchell: Sensationalism, Sexology, and the Lesbian Subject in Turn-of-the-Century America." *Signs* 18 (1993): 791–814.
Dunne, Gillian A. *Lesbian Lifestyles: Women's Work and the Politics of Sexuality.* Toronto: Univ. of Toronto Press, 1997.
Dymmok, Roger. *Liber contra duodecim errores et hereses Lollardorum.* Ed. H. S. Cronin. London: Wyclif Society, 1922.
Eco, Umberto. *Travels in Hyperreality.* Trans. William Weaver. San Diego: Harcourt Brace Jovanovich, 1986.

Edelman, Lee. "Tearooms and Sympathy, or, The Epistemology of the Water Closet." In *The Lesbian and Gay Studies Reader*, ed. Henry Abelove, Michèle Aina Barale, and David M. Halperin, 553–74. New York: Routledge, 1993.

Eilberg-Schwartz, Howard. *God's Phallus and Other Problems for Men and Monotheism*. Boston: Beacon, 1994.

Elliott, Dyan. "Dress as Mediator between Inner and Outer Self: The Pious Matron of the High and Later Middle Ages." *Mediaeval Studies* 53 (1991): 279–308.

———. "Pollution, Illusion, and Masculine Disarray: Nocturnal Emissions and the Sexuality of the Clergy." In *Constructing Medieval Sexuality*, ed. Karma Lochrie, Peggy McCracken, and James A. Schulz, 1–23. Minneapolis: Univ. of Minnesota Press, 1997.

Ellmann, Richard. *Oscar Wilde*. New York: Knopf, 1988.

Emden, A. B. *Biographical Register of the University of Oxford to a.d. 1500*. 3 vols. Oxford: Clarendon, 1957–59.

"Ending NEA a Priority, Armey Pledges in Letter." *San Francisco Chronicle*, 26 March 1997, A4.

The English Text of the Ancrene Riwle edited from Magdalene College, Cambridge, MS Pepys 2498. Ed. A. Zettersten. EETS 274. London: Oxford Univ. Press, 1976.

Eribon, Didier. *Michel Foucault*. Trans. Betsy Wing. Cambridge, Mass.: Harvard Univ. Press, 1991.

———. *Michel Foucault et ses contemporains*. Paris: Fayard, 1994.

———. "S'acharner à être gay." *Ex Aequo*, no. 5 (May 1997): n.p.

Erler, Mary. "Margery Kempe's White Clothes." *Medium Ævum* 62 (1993): 78–83.

Escoffier, Jeffrey, Regina Kunzel, and Molly McGarry, eds. *The Queer Issue: New Visions of America's Lesbian and Gay Past*. Spec. issue of *Radical History Review* 62 (Spring 1995).

Evans, Arthur. *Witchcraft and the Gay Counterculture: A Radical View of Western Civilization and Some of the People It Has Tried to Destroy*. Boston: Fag Rag Books, 1978.

Fasciculi zizaniorum. Ed. Walter Waddington Shirley. Rolls Series. London: Longman, Brown, Green, Longmans, and Roberts, 1858.

Fasciculus morum: A Fourteenth-Century Preacher's Handbook. Ed. and trans. Siegfried Wenzel. University Park: Pennsylvania State Univ. Press, 1989.

Findlay, Heather. "Queer Dora: Hysteria, Sexual Politics, and Lacan's 'Intervention on Transference.'" *GLQ: A Journal of Lesbian and Gay Studies* 1 (1994): 323–47.

Fineman, Joel. "The Structure of Allegorical Desire." In *Allegory and Representation*, ed. Stephen J. Greenblatt, 26–60. Selected Papers from the English Institute n.s. 5. Baltimore: Johns Hopkins Univ. Press, 1981.

FitzRalph, Richard. *Defensio curatorum*. Ed. Aaron Jenkins Perry. Trans. John Trevisa. EETS o.s. 167. London: Oxford Univ. Press, 1925.

Fleta. 3 vols. Ed. and trans. H. G. Richardson and G. O. Sayles. Selden Society 72, 89, 99. London: B. Quaritch, 1955–84.

Fletcher, Alan J. "John Mirk and the Lollards." *Medium Ævum* 55 (1987): 217–24.

———. "The Preaching of the Pardoner." *Studies in the Age of Chaucer* 11 (1989): 15–35.

———. "The Topical Hypocrisy of Chaucer's Pardoner." *Chaucer Review* 25 (1990): 110–26.

Flint, Anthony. "What of Our Past? Historians Disagree." *Boston Globe*, 25 July 1995, A1, 14.

Fonte, John. "We the Peoples." *National Review*, 25 March 1996, 47–49.

Foucault, Michel. *The Archaeology of Knowledge*. Trans. A. M. Sheridan Smith. New York: Pantheon, 1972. Reprint. New York: Barnes and Noble Books, 1993. Originally published as *L'Archéologie du savoir*. Paris: Gallimard, 1969.

———. *Death and the Labyrinth: The World of Raymond Roussel*. Trans. Charles Ruas. Garden City, New York: Doubleday, 1986. Originally published as *Raymond Roussel*. Paris: Gallimard, 1963.

———. *Discipline and Punish: The Birth of the Prison*. Trans. Alan Sheridan. New York: Vintage, 1979. Originally published as *Surveiller et punir: Naissance de la prison*. Paris: Gallimard, 1975.

———. *Dits et écrits, 1954–1988*. 4 vols. Ed. Daniel Defert and François Ewald. Paris: Gallimard, 1994.

———. *Foucault Live: Interviews, 1961–84*. Ed. Sylvère Lotringer. Trans. Lysa Hochroth and John Johnston. New York: Semiotext(e), 1996.

———. *Herculine Barbin, Being the Recently Discovered Memoirs of a Nineteenth-Century French Hermaphrodite*. Trans. Richard McDougall. New York: Pantheon, 1980. Originally published as *Herculine Barbin, dite Alexina B*. Paris: Gallimard, 1978.

———. *The History of Sexuality*, vol. 1: *An Introduction*. Trans. Robert Hurley. New York: Pantheon, 1978. Reprint. New York: Vintage, 1990. Originally published as *Histoire de la sexualité* 1: *La Volonté de savoir*. Paris: Gallimard, 1976.

———. *The History of Sexuality*, vol. 2: *The Use of Pleasure*. Trans. Robert Hurley. New York: Pantheon, 1985. Originally published as *Histoire de la sexualité* 2: *L'Usage des plaisirs*. Paris: Gallimard, 1984.

———. *The History of Sexuality*, vol. 3: *The Care of the Self*. Trans. Robert Hurley. New York: Pantheon, 1986. Originally published as *Histoire de la sexualité* 3: *Le Souci de soi*. Paris: Gallimard, 1984.

———. "The History of Sexuality." Interview with Lucette Finas. Trans.

Leo Marshall. In *Power/Knowledge: Selected Interviews and Other Writings, 1972–1977*, ed. Colin Gordon, 183–193. New York: Pantheon, 1980.
———. *Language, Counter-Memory, Practice*. Ed. Donald F. Bouchard. Trans. Donald F. Bouchard and Sherry Simon. Ithaca: Cornell Univ. Press, 1977.
———. "The Life of Infamous Men." Trans. Paul Foss and Meaghan Morris. In *Michel Foucault: Power, Truth, Strategy*, ed. Meaghan Morris and Paul Patton, 76–91. Sydney: Feral Publications, 1979.
———. *Madness and Civilization: A History of Insanity in the Age of Reason*. Trans. Richard Howard. 1965. Reprint. New York: Vintage, 1988. Originally published as *Folie et déraison: Histoire de la folie à l'âge classique*. Paris: Gallimard, 1972.
———. "My Body, This Paper, This Fire." Trans. Geoff Bennington. *Oxford Literary Review* 4.1 (1979): 9–28.
———. "On the Genealogy of Ethics: An Overview of Work in Progress." In *The Foucault Reader*, ed. Paul Rabinow, 340–72. New York: Pantheon, 1984.
———. *The Order of Things: An Archaeology of the Human Sciences*. New York: Random House, 1970. Originally published as *Les Mots et les choses*. Paris: Gallimard, 1966.
Foucault, Michel, ed. *I, Pierre Rivière, Having Slaughtered My Mother, My Sister, and My Brother*. Trans. Frank Jellinek. 1975. Reprint. Lincoln: Univ. of Nebraska Press, 1982. Originally published as *Moi, Pierre Rivière, ayant égorgé ma mère, ma soeur et mon frère . . .* . Paris: Gallimard, 1973.
Foxe, John. *Acts and Monuments*. 8 vols. London, 1853–70. Reprint. New York: AMS Press, 1965.
Fradenburg, Louise O. " 'Be Not Far from Me': Psychoanalysis, Medieval Studies, and the Subject of Religion." *Exemplaria* 7 (1995): 41–54.
———. " 'So That We May Speak of Them': Enjoying the Middle Ages." *New Literary History* 28 (1997): 205–30.
———. " 'Voice Memorial': Loss and Reparation in Chaucer's Poetry." *Exemplaria* 2 (1990): 169–202.
———. "The Wife of Bath's Passing Fancy." *Studies in the Age of Chaucer* 8 (1986): 31–58.
Fradenburg, Louise O., and Carla Freccero. "Introduction: Caxton, Foucault, and the Pleasures of History." In *Premodern Sexualities*, ed. Louise O. Fradenburg and Carla Freccero, xiii–xxiv. New York: Routledge, 1996.
Frantzen, Allen J. "Between the Lines: Queer Theory, the History of Homosexuality, and Anglo-Saxon Penitentials." *Journal of Medieval and Early Modern Studies* 26 (1996): 255–96.
———. "The Disclosure of Sodomy in *Cleanness*." *PMLA* 111 (1996): 451–64.

———. *The Literature of Penance in Anglo-Saxon England.* New Brunswick, N.J.: Rutgers Univ. Press, 1983.

———. "*The Pardoner's Tale,* the Pervert, and the Price of Order in Chaucer's World." In *Class and Gender in Early English Literature: Intersections,* ed. Britton J. Harwood and Gillian R. Overing, 131–47. Bloomington: Indiana Univ. Press, 1994.

French, Katherine L. "Competing for Space: Medieval Religious Conflict in the Monastic-Parochial Church at Dunster." In *From Medieval Christianities to the Reformations,* ed. David Aers, 215–44. Spec. issue of *Journal of Medieval and Early Modern Studies* 27 (1997).

Gaard, Greta. "Anti-Lesbian Intellectual Harassment in the Academy." In *Antifeminism in the Academy,* ed. VèVè Clark, Shirley Nelson Garner, Margaret Higonnet, and Ketu H. Katrak, 115–40. New York: Routledge, 1996.

Galbraith, V. H. "Thomas Walsingham and the Saint Albans Chronicle, 1272–1422." *English Historical Review* 47 (1932): 12–30.

Gallop, Jane. *Feminist Accused of Sexual Harassment.* Durham, N.C.: Duke Univ. Press, 1997.

Gamson, Joshua. "Must Identity Movements Self-Destruct? A Queer Dilemma." *Social Problems* 42 (1995): 390–407.

Ganim, John. *Chaucerian Theatricality.* Princeton: Princeton Univ. Press, 1990.

Garber, Linda, ed. *Tilting the Tower: Lesbians, Teaching, Queer Subjects.* New York: Routledge, 1994.

Garber, Marjorie. *Vested Interests: Cross-Dressing and Cultural Anxiety.* New York: Routledge, 1992.

Gaunt, Simon. "Bel Acueil and the Improper Allegory of the *Romance of the Rose.*" *New Medieval Literatures* 2 (1998): 65–93.

Gerson, Jean. *Oeuvres complètes.* 10 vols. Ed. P. Glorieux. Paris: Desclée, 1960–73.

Gilmour-Bryson, Anne. "Sodomy and the Knights Templar." *Journal of the History of Sexuality* 7 (1996): 151–83.

Ginzburg, Carlo. "Clues: Root of an Evidential Paradigm." In *Clues, Myths, and the Historical Method,* trans. John and Anne Tedeschi, 96–125. Baltimore: Johns Hopkins Univ. Press, 1989.

Glück, Robert. "Fame." *Poetics Journal* 10 (1998): 218–22.

———. *Margery Kempe.* New York: Serpent's Tail, 1994.

Goldberg, Jonathan. *Sodometries: Renaissance Texts, Modern Sexualities.* Stanford: Stanford Univ. Press, 1992.

Goodich, Michael. *The Unmentionable Vice: Homosexuality in the Later Medieval Period.* Santa Barbara, Calif.: ABC-Clio, 1979.

Gower, John. *The English Works of John Gower.* 2 vols. Ed. G. C. Macaulay. EETS e.s. 81–2. Oxford: Oxford Univ. Press, 1900–1.

———. *The Complete Works of John Gower.* 4 vols. Ed. G. C. Macaulay. Oxford: Clarendon, 1899.

———. *The Major Latin Works of John Gower.* Trans. Eric W. Stockton. Seattle: Univ. of Washington Press, 1962.

Green, Monica. "Female Sexuality in the Medieval West." *Trends in History* 4 (1990): 127–58.

Greenberg, David F., and Marcia H. Bystryn. "Christian Intolerance of Homosexuality." *American Journal of Sociology* 88 (1982): 515–48.

Gross, Gregory W. "Secret Rules: Sex, Confession, and Truth in *Sir Gawain and the Green Knight.*" *Arthuriana* 4 (1994): 146–74.

Gurevich, Aaron I. "The Double Responsibility of the Historian." *Diogenes* 42.4, no. 168 (Winter 1994): 65–83.

Gustafson, Kevin. " 'Gostli Sodomites': The Rhetoric of Deviance in Lollard Translation Polemic." Paper delivered at the Columbia Medieval Guild, New York, 1993.

Halley, Janet E. "*Bowers v. Hardwick* in the Renaissance." In *Queering the Renaissance,* ed. Jonathan Goldberg, 15–39. Durham, N.C.: Duke Univ. Press, 1994.

Halperin, David M. "Forgetting Foucault: Acts, Identities, and the History of Sexuality." *Representations* 63 (Summer 1998): 93–120.

———. *One Hundred Years of Homosexuality and Other Essays on Greek Love.* New York: Routledge, 1990.

———. *Saint Foucault: Towards a Gay Hagiography.* New York: Oxford Univ. Press, 1995.

Halsall, Paul. "An Online Guide to Lesbian, Gay, Bisexual and Trans* History." http://www.fordham.edu/halsall/pwh.

Hammond, Eleanor Prescott. *Chaucer: A Bibliographical Manual.* New York: Macmillan, 1908.

Hansen, Elaine Tuttle. *Chaucer and the Fictions of Gender.* Berkeley: Univ. of California Press, 1992.

Haraway, Donna J. "The Promises of Monsters: A Regenerative Politics for Inappropriate/d Others." In *Cultural Studies,* ed. Lawrence Grossberg, Cary Nelson, and Paula A. Treichler, New York: Routledge, 1992.

———. "Situated Knowledges: The Science Question in Feminism and the Privilege of Partial Perspective." In *Simians, Cyborgs, and Women: The Reinvention of Nature,* 83–201. New York: Routledge, 1991.

Harding, Wendy. "Body into Text: *The Book of Margery Kempe.*" In *Feminist Approaches to the Body in Medieval Literature,* ed. Linda Lomperis and Sarah Stanbury, 168–87. Philadelphia: University of Pennsylvania Press, 1993.

Harlan, David. "Intellectual History and the Return of Literature." *American Historical Review* 94 (1989): 581–609.

Hart, James A. " 'The Droghte of March': A Common Misunderstanding." *Texas Studies in Literature and Language* 4 (1963): 525–29.

Hefele, Karl Joseph von, ed., rev. Henri Leclercq. *Histoire des conciles d'après les documents originaux.* 11 vols. Paris: Letouzey et Ané, 1907–52.

Hexter, Ralph. "John Boswell, 1945–1994." In *The Queer Issue: New Visions of America's Lesbian and Gay Past,* ed. Jeffrey Escoffier, Regina Kunzel, and Molly McGarry, 259–61. Spec. issue of *Radical History Review* 62 (Spring 1995).

———. Review of *The Invention of Sodomy in Christian Theology,* by Mark D. Jordan. *Medieval Review.* http://www.hti.umich.edu/b/bmr/tmr.html.

Hill, Leslie. "Barthes's Body." *Paragraph* 11 (1988): 107–26.

Historia vitae et regni Ricardi Secundi. Ed. George B. Stow, Jr. Haney Foundation Publications 21. Philadelphia: Univ. of Pennsylvania Press, 1977.

Hoberman, J. "Pulp and Glory." *Village Voice,* 11 October 1994, 61, 75.

Hobsbawm, Eric W. "The Historian between the Quest for the Universal and the Quest for Identity." *Diogenes* 42.4, no. 168 (Winter 1994): 51–64.

Holland, Michael. "Barthes, Orpheus . . . ." *Paragraph* 11 (1988): 143–174.

Hollinger, David A. "The Return of the Prodigal: The Persistence of Historical Knowing." *American Historical Review* 94 (1989): 610–21.

Holsinger, Bruce W. "Sodomy and Resurrection: The Homoerotic Subject of the *Divine Comedy.*" In *Premodern Sexualities,* ed. Louise O. Fradenburg and Carla Freccero, 243–74. New York: Routledge, 1996.

The Holy Bible . . . Made from the Latin Vulgate by John Wycliffe and His Followers. 4 vols. Ed. Josiah Forshall and Frederic Madden. Oxford: Oxford Univ. Press, 1850.

hooks, bell. "Cool Tool." In "Pulp the Hype: On the *Q.T.*" *Artforum* (March 1995): 62–66, 108.

Howard, Donald R. *The Idea of the* Canterbury Tales. Berkeley: Univ. of California Press, 1976.

Hudson, Anne. "*Hermofodrita or Ambidexter:* Wycliffite Views on Clerks in Secular Office." In *Lollardy and the Gentry in the Later Middle Ages,* ed. Margaret Aston and Colin Richmond, 41–51. New York: St. Martin's; Stroud, U.K.: Sutton, 1997.

———. "A Lollard Mass." *Journal of Theological Studies* n.s. 23, pt. 2 (1972): 407–19.

———. *The Premature Reformation: Wycliffite Texts and Lollard History.* Oxford: Clarendon Press, 1988.

Hudson, Anne, ed. *English Wycliffite Sermons.* Vol. 3. Oxford: Clarendon, 1990.

———. *Selections from English Wycliffite Writings.* Cambridge: Cambridge Univ. Press, 1978.

Hus, John. *M. Jana Husi Korespondence a dokumenty.* Ed. Václav Novotný. Prague: Komise pro vydávání pramenu náboženského hnutí českého, 1920.

———. *The Letters of John Hus.* Trans. Matthew Spinka. Manchester: Manchester Univ. Press; Totowa, N.J.: Rowman and Littlefield, 1972.

Hyder, Clyde Kenneth. *George Lyman Kittredge: Teacher and Scholar.* Lawrence: Univ. Kansas Press, 1962.

"Idol Threats: Bastards!" *Film Threat* 20 (February 1995): 20.

Ives, Doris V. " 'A Man of Religion.' " *Modern Language Review* 27 (1932): 144–48.

Jack Upland. In *Chaucerian and Other Pieces,* ed. Walter W. Skeat, 191–203. Oxford: Clarendon, 1897.

Jack Upland, Friar Daw's Reply, and Upland's Rejoinder. Ed. P. L. Heyworth. Oxford: Oxford Univ. Press, 1968.

Jackson, Earl, Jr. "Interview with Robert Glück." *Red Wheelbarrow* 1.1 (Spring 1995): 24–40.

———. *Strategies of Deviance: Studies in Gay Male Representation.* Bloomington: Indiana Univ. Press, 1995.

Jacobus, de Voragine. *Legenda aurea.* Ed. T. Graesse. 3rd ed. Bratislava: William Koebner, 1890.

Jacquart, Danielle, and Claude Thomasset. *Sexuality and Medicine in the Middle Ages.* Trans. Matthew Adamson. Cambridge: Polity Press, 1988.

Jerome, Saint. *Adversus Jovinianum. Patrologia latina,* 23: cols. 205–338. Ed. J.-P. Migne. Paris, 1910–18.

———. *Epistulae.* 3 vols. Ed. Isidorus Hilberg. CESL 54–56. Vienna: F. Tempsky, 1910–18.

———. *Opera.* 9 vols. Corpus christianorum, series latina 72–80. Turnhout: Brepols, 1958–90.

———. *Principal Works of Saint Jerome.* Trans. W. H. Fremantle. Nicene and Post-Nicene Fathers, 2nd ser., 6. New York: Christian Literature Co., 1893.

Johansson, Warren, Wayne Dynes, and John Lauritsen. *Homosexuality, Intolerance, and Christianity: A Critical Examination of John Boswell's Work.* New York: Scholarship Committee, Gay Academic Union, 1981.

Johnson, Barbara. *A World of Difference.* Baltimore: Johns Hopkins Univ. Press, 1987.

Johnson, E. N. "American Mediaevalists and Today." *Speculum* 28 (1953): 844–54.

Jordan, Mark D. "Homosexuality, *Luxuria,* and Textual Abuse," *Constructing Medieval Sexuality,* ed. Karma Lochrie, Peggy McCracken, and James A. Schultz, 24–39. Minneapolis: Univ. of Minnesota Press, 1997.

———. *The Invention of Sodomy in Christian Theology.* Chicago: Univ. of Chicago Press, 1997.

———. "A Romance of the Gay Couple." Review of *Same-Sex Unions in Premodern Europe,* by John Boswell. *GLQ: A Journal of Lesbian and Gay Studies* 3 (1996): 301–10.

Jørgensen, Johannes. *Saint Bridget of Sweden.* 2 vols. Trans. I. Lund. New York: Longmans Green, 1954.

Justice, Steven. "Inquisition, Speech, and Writing: A Case from Late-Medieval Norwich." *Representations* 48 (Fall 1994): 1–29.

Kampen, Natalie Boymel. Review of *Love between Women: Early Christian Responses to Female Homoeroticism,* by Bernadette J. Brooten. The *GLQ* Forum: "Lesbian Historiography before the Name?" *GLQ: A Journal of Lesbian and Gay Studies* 4 (1998): 595–601.

Kaplan, Caren. *Questions of Travel: Postmodern Discourses of Displacement.* Durham, N.C.: Duke Univ. Press, 1996.

Karlen, Arno. "The Homosexual Heresy." *Chaucer Review* 6 (1971): 44–63.

Karras, Ruth Mazo. *Common Women: Prostitution and Sexuality in Medieval England.* New York: Oxford Univ. Press, 1996.

Karras, Ruth Mazo, and David Lorenzo Boyd. " 'Ut cum muliere': A Male Transvestite Prostitute in Fourteenth-Century London." In *Premodern Sexualities,* ed. Louise O. Fradenburg and Carla Freccero, 101–14. New York: Routledge, 1996.

Katz, Jonathan Ned. *The Invention of Heterosexuality.* New York: Dutton, 1995.

Keiser, Elizabeth B. *Courtly Desire and Medieval Homophobia: The Legitimation of Sexual Pleasure in* Cleanness *and Its Contexts.* New Haven: Yale Univ. Press, 1997.

Kelly, H. Ansgar. "The Right to Remain Silent: Before and after Joan of Arc." *Speculum* 68 (1993): 992–1026.

Kelly, Joan. "Did Women Have a Renaissance?" In *Women, History and Theory,* 19–50. Chicago: Univ. of Chicago Press, 1984.

Kennedy, Lisa. "Natural Born Filmmaker: Quentin Tarantino Versus the Film Geeks." *Village Voice,* 25 October 1994, 29–32.

Ker, N. R., ed. *The Medieval Libraries of Great Britain: A List of All Surviving Books.* 2nd ed. London: Offices of the Royal Historical Society, 1964.

Kittredge, George Lyman. *Chaucer and His Poetry.* 55th anniv. ed. Intro. B. J. Whiting. Cambridge, Mass.: Harvard Univ. Press, 1970.

———. "Chaucer's Discussion of Marriage." *Modern Philology* 9 (1911–12): 435–67. Rpt. *Chaucer Criticism,* ed. Richard Shoeck and Jerome Taylor. Notre Dame: Univ. of Notre Dame Press, 1960.

———. "Chaucer's Pardoner." *Atlantic* 92 (December 1893): 829–33.

Knapp, Peggy. *Chaucer and the Social Contest.* New York: Routledge, 1990.

Knighton, Henry. *Knighton's Chronicle, 1337–1396.* Ed. and trans. G. H. Martin. Oxford: Clarendon Press, 1995.

Kolve, V. A. *Chaucer and the Imagery of Narrative.* Stanford: Stanford Univ. Press, 1984.

———. "Ganymede/*Son of Getron:* Medieval Monasticism and the Drama of Same-Sex Desire." *Speculum* 73 (1998): 1014–67.

Königshofen, Jacob Twinger von. *Chronik.* In vol. 9 of *Chroniken der deutschen Städte.* Leipzig: S. Hirzel, 1871.

Kramer, Larry. *Reports from the Holocaust: The Making of an AIDS Activist.* New York: St. Martin's, 1989.

Krauthammer, Charles. "History Hijacked." *Washington Post,* 4 November 1994, A25.

Krieger, Susan. *The Family Silver: Essays on Relationships among Women.* Berkeley: Univ. of California Press, 1996.

Kruger, Steven F. "Claiming the Pardoner." *Exemplaria* 6 (1994): 115–39.

———. "Conversion and Medieval Sexual, Religious, and Racial Categories." In *Constructing Medieval Sexuality,* ed. Karma Lochrie, Peggy McCracken, and James A. Schultz, 158–79. Minneapolis: Univ. of Minnesota Press, 1997.

Lacan, Jacques. "God and the *Jouissance* of Woman." In *Feminine Sexuality: Jacques Lacan and the école freudienne,* ed. Juliet Mitchell and Jacqueline Rose, trans. Jacqueline Rose, 137–48. New York: W. W. Norton, 1985.

LaCapra, Dominick. *History and Criticism.* Ithaca: Cornell Univ. Press, 1985.

Laclau, Ernesto, and Chantal Mouffe. *Hegemony and Socialist Strategy: Towards a Radical Democratic Politics.* Trans. Winston Moore and Paul Cammack. London: Verso, 1985.

Lane, Anthony. "Degrees of Cool." *New Yorker,* 10 October 1994, 95–97.

Langland, William. *Piers Plowman by William Langland: An Edition of the C-Text.* Ed. Derek Pearsall. York Medieval Texts, 2nd ser. London: E. Arnold, 1978. Reprint. Berkeley: Univ. of California Press, 1982.

———. *Piers Plowman: The B Version.* Ed. George Kane and E. Talbot Donaldson. Rev. ed. London: Athlone, 1988.

The Lanterne of Liȝt. Ed. Lilian M. Swinburn. EETS 151. London: Kegan Paul, Trench, Trübner; Oxford: Oxford Univ. Press, 1917.

Laqueur, Thomas. *Making Sex: Body and Gender from the Greeks to Freud.* Cambridge, Mass.: Harvard Univ. Press, 1990.

Laskaya, Anne. *Chaucer's Approach to Gender in the* Canterbury Tales. Chaucer Studies 23. Cambridge: D. S. Brewer, 1995.

Lauritsen, John. "Religious Roots of the Taboo on Homosexuality." *GALA [Gay Atheist League of America] Review* 1.2–5 (1978).

———. Review of *Christianity, Social Tolerance, and Homosexuality,* by John Boswell. *GALA [Gay Atheist League of America] Review* 3.12 (1980): 9–18.

Lavers, Annette. *Roland Barthes: Structuralism and After.* London: Methuen, 1982.

Lavezzo, Kathryn. "Sobs and Sighs between Women: The Homoerotics of Compassion in *The Book of Margery Kempe*." In *Premodern Sexualities*, ed. Louise O. Fradenburg and Carla Freccero, 175–98. New York: Routledge, 1996.

Lawton, David. "Chaucer's Two Ways: The Pilgrimage Frame of *The Canterbury Tales*." *Studies in the Age of Chaucer* 9 (1987): 3–40.

Laȝamon: Brut. 2 vols. Ed. G. L. Brook and R. F. Leslie. EETS 250, 277. Oxford: Oxford Univ. Press, 1963, 1978.

Leff, Gordon. *Heresy in the Later Middle Ages: The Relation of Heterodoxy to Dissent c. 1250–c. 1450*. 2 vols. Manchester: Manchester Univ. Press; New York: Barnes and Noble, 1967.

———. "Wyclif and Hus: A Doctrinal Comparison." In *Wyclif in His Times*, ed. Anthony Kenny, 105–25. Oxford: Clarendon Press, 1986.

Leicester, H. Marshall, Jr. *The Disenchanted Self: Representing the Subject in the* Canterbury Tales. Berkeley: Univ. of California Press, 1990.

Lemay, Helen Rodnite. "William of Saliceto on Human Sexuality." *Viator* 12 (1981): 165–81.

Lerner, Robert E. *The Heresy of the Free Spirit in the Later Middle Ages*. Berkeley: Univ. of California Press, 1972.

Lewis, C. S. *The Allegory of Love*. 1936. Reprint. New York: Oxford Univ. Press, 1958.

The Liber Celestis of St. Bridget of Sweden. Ed. Roger Ellis. EETS 291. Oxford: Oxford Univ. Press, 1987.

Livingstone, E. A., ed. *The Concise Oxford Dictionary of the Christian Church*. Oxford: Oxford Univ. Press, 1977.

Li Livres de jostice et de plet. Ed. Pierre Rapetti. Paris: Didot Frères, 1850.

Lochrie, Karma. "Desiring Foucault." *Journal of Medieval and Early Modern Studies* 27 (1997): 3–16.

———. *Covert Operations: The Medieval Uses of Secrecy*. Philadelphia: Univ. of Pennsylvania Press, 1998.

———. "Women's 'Pryvetees' and Fabliau Politics in the Miller's Tale." *Exemplaria* 6 (1994): 287–304.

Lombardo, Patrizia. *The Three Paradoxes of Roland Barthes*. Athens: Univ. of Georgia Press, 1989.

Lorde, Audre. *Sister Outsider*. Freedom, Calif.: Crossing Press, 1984.

Loserth, Johann. *Johann von Wiclif und Guilelmus Peraldus: Studien zur Geschichte der Entstehung von Wiclifs Summa Theologiae*. Vienna: Alfred Hölder, 1916.

Love, Courtney. "Love Child." Interview with Kevin Sessums. *Vanity Fair* (June 1995): 106–15, 169–71.

Love, Nicholas. *Nicholas Love's* Mirror of the Blessed Life of Jesus Christ. Ed. Michael G. Sargent. New York: Garland, 1992.

Lucey, Michael. "Balzac's Queer Cousins and Their Friends." In *Novel Gaz-*

ing: Queer Readings in Fiction, ed. Eve Kosofsky Sedgwick, 167–98. Durham, N.C.: Duke Univ. Press, 1997.

Lucian of Samosata. *Lucian*. 7 vols. Ed. and trans. M. D. Macleod. Loeb Classical Library. Cambridge, Mass.: Harvard Univ. Press, 1961.

Lucretius. *De rerum natura*. 3 vols. 4th ed. Ed. and trans. H. A. J. Munro. Cambridge: Deighton Bell, 1886.

Lyon, Earl D. "Roger de Ware, Cook." *Modern Language Notes* 52 (1937): 491–94.

McAlpine, Monica. "The Pardoner's Homosexuality and How It Matters." *PMLA* 95 (1980): 8–22.

McCarthy, Todd. "*Pulp Fiction*." *Variety*, 23 May 1994, 9.

McFarlane, K. B. *The Origins of Religious Dissent in England*. 1952. Reprint. New York: Collier Books, 1966.

McHardy, A. K. "*De heretico comburendo*, 1401." In *Lollardy and the Gentry in the Later Middle Ages*, ed. Margaret Aston and Colin Richmond, 112–26. New York: St. Martin's; Stroud, U.K.: Sutton, 1997.

McNamara, Jo Ann, and Suzanne Wemple. "The Power of Women through the Family in Medieval Europe: 500–1100." *Feminist Studies* 1 (1973): 126–41.

McNaron, Toni A. H. *Poisoned Ivy: Lesbian and Gay Academics Confronting Homophobia*. Philadelphia: Temple Univ. Press, 1997.

McSheffrey, Shannon. *Gender and Heresy: Women and Men in Lollard Communities, 1420–1530*. Philadelphia: Univ. of Pennsylvania Press, 1995.

Mann, Jill. *Chaucer and Medieval Estates Satire*. Cambridge: Cambridge Univ. Press, 1973.

Mannyng, Robert. *Handlyng Synne*. Ed. Idelle Sullens. Binghamton, N.Y.: MRTS, 1983.

Map, Walter. *De nugis curialium: Courtiers' Trifles*. Ed. and trans. M. R. James. Rev. C. N. L. Brooke and R. A. B. Mynors. Oxford: Clarendon, 1983.

Martin, Biddy. "Feminism, Criticism, and Foucault." *New German Critique* 27 (1982): 3–30.

———. "Sexualities without Genders and Other Queer Utopias." *diacritics* 24.2–3 (Summer–Fall 1994): 104–21.

Martin, Geoffrey. "Knighton's Lollards." In *Lollardy and the Gentry in the Later Middle Ages*, ed. Margaret Aston and Colin Richmond, 28–40. New York: St. Martin's; Stroud, U.K.: Sutton, 1997.

Martin, Hervé. *Le Métier de prédicateur en France septentrionale à la fin du Moyen Age (1350–1520)*. Paris: Cerf, 1988.

Martin, Priscilla. *Chaucer's Women: Nuns, Wives, and Amazons*. Iowa City: Univ. of Iowa Press, 1990.

Maslin, Janet. "Quentin Tarantino's Wild Ride on Life's Dangerous Road." *New York Times*, 23 September 1994, C1, C34.

Mass, Lawrence. "Sexual Categories, Sexual Universals: A Conversation with John Boswell." In *Homosexuality as Behavior and Identity: Dialogues of the Sexual Revolution*, 2: 202–33. 2 vols. New York: Harrington Park, 1990.

Massumi, Brian. *A User's Guide to* Capitalism and Schizophrenia: *Deviations from Deleuze and Guattari*. Cambridge, Mass.: MIT Press, 1992.

Matter, E. Ann. "My Sister, My Spouse: Woman-Identified Women in Medieval Christianity." *Journal of Feminist Studies in Religion* 2 (1986): 81–93.

———. Review of *Christianity, Social Tolerance, and Homosexuality*, by John Boswell. *Journal of Interdisciplinary History* 13 (1982): 115–17.

Matthew, F. D., ed. *The English Works of Wyclif Hitherto Unprinted*. EETS 74. 2nd rev. ed. London: Kegan Paul, Trench, Trübner, 1902.

Medieval Handbooks of Penance. Trans. John T. McNeill and Helena M. Gamer. 1938. Reprint. New York: Columbia Univ. Press, 1990.

Medieval Latin Word List from British and Irish Sources. Ed. J. H. Baxter and Charles Johnson. Oxford: Oxford Univ. Press; London: Humphrey Milford, 1934.

Meditations on the Life of Christ: An Illustrated Manuscript of the Fourteenth Century. Ed. Isa Ragusa and Rosalie B. Green. Trans. Isa Ragusa. Princeton: Princeton Univ. Press, 1961.

Middle English Dictionary. Ed. Hans Kurath (1952–1987). Gen. ed. Robert E. Lewis (1987–). Ann Arbor: Univ. of Michigan Press, 1952–.

Miller, B. D. H. " 'She Who Hath Drunk Any Potion' . . . ." *Medium Ævum* 31 (1962): 188–93.

Miller, D. A. *Bringing Out Roland Barthes*. Berkeley: Univ. of California Press, 1992.

Miller, James. *The Passion of Michel Foucault*. New York: Simon and Schuster, 1993.

Miller, Tim and David Román. " 'Preaching to the Converted.' " *Theatre Journal* 47 (1995): 169–88.

Mintz, Beth, and Esther D. Rothblum, eds. *Lesbians in Academia: Degrees of Freedom*. New York: Routledge, 1997.

Mirk, John. *Instructions for Parish Priests*. Ed. Edward Peacock, 1868. Rev. F. J. Furnivall, 1902. EETS o.s. 31. London: Kegan Paul, Trench, Trübner, 1902.

———. *John Mirk's Instructions for Parish Priests*. Ed. Gillis Kristensson. Lund: Gleerup, 1974.

———. *Mirk's Festial*. Ed. Theodor Erbe. EETS e.s. 96. London: Kegan Paul, Trench, Trübner, 1905.

Moore, R. I. *The Formation of a Persecuting Society: Power and Deviance in Western Europe, 950–1250*. New York: Basil Blackwell, 1987.

Moore, Stephen D. *God's Gym: Divine Male Bodies of the Bible*. New York: Routledge, 1996.

Mowitt, John. "Queer Resistance: Foucault and *The Unnamable.*" Unpublished manuscript.

Murray, Stephen O. *American Gay.* Chicago: Univ. of Chicago Press, 1996.

Nancy, Jean-Luc. *The Inoperative Community.* Ed. Peter Connor. Trans. Peter Connor et al. Minneapolis: Univ. of Minnesota Press, 1991.

Netter, Thomas. *Doctrinale antiquitatum fidei catholicae ecclesiae.* 3 vols. Ed. B. Blanciotti. Venice, 1759. Reprint. Farnborough, U.K.: Gregg Press, 1967.

Nichols, Stephen G. "The New Medievalism: Tradition and Discontinuity in Medieval Culture." In *The New Medievalism,* ed. Marina S. Brownlee, Kevin Brownlee, and Stephen G. Nichols, 1–26. Baltimore: Johns Hopkins Univ. Press, 1991.

Nirenberg, David. *Communities of Violence: Persecution of Minorities in the Middle Ages.* Princeton: Princeton Univ. Press, 1996.

Noonan, John T., Jr. *Contraception: A History of Its Treatment by the Catholic Theologians and Canonists.* Cambridge, Mass.: Harvard Univ. Press, 1966.

Obrist, Barbara. "The Swedish Visionary: Saint Bridget." In *Medieval Women Writers,* ed. Katharina M. Wilson, 227–39. Athens: Univ. of Georgia Press, 1984.

Olsen, Glenn W. "The Gay Middle Ages: A Response to Professor Boswell." *Communio: International Catholic Review* 8 (1981): 119–38.

Olsson, Kurt. "Natural Law and John Gower's *Confessio Amantis.*" *Medievalia et Humanistica* n.s. 11 (1982): 229–61.

Otterspeer, Willem. "Huizinga before the Abyss: The von Leers Incident at the University of Leiden, April 1933." Trans. Lionel Gossman and Reinier Leushuis. In *European Medieval Studies under Fire,* ed. Helen Solterer, 385–444. Spec. issue of *Journal of Medieval and Early Modern Studies* 27 (Fall 1997).

Owst, G. R. *Preaching in Medieval England: An Introduction to Sermon Manuscripts of the Period c. 1350–1450.* 1926. Reprint. New York: Russell and Russell, 1965.

Pantin, W. A. *The English Church in the Fourteenth Century.* Cambridge: Cambridge Univ. Press, 1955.

Partner, Nancy F. "Did Mystics Have Sex?" In *Desire and Discipline: Sex and Sexuality in the Premodern West,* ed. Jacqueline Murray and Konrad Eisenbichler, 296–311. Toronto: University of Toronto Press, 1996.

———. "Making Up Lost Time: Writing on the Writing of History." *Speculum* 61 (1986): 90–117.

———. "Reading *The Book of Margery Kempe.*" *Exemplaria* 3 (1991): 29–66.

Patel, Geeta. "Home, Homo, Hybrid: Translating Gender." *College Literature* 24 (1997): 133–50.

Patterson, Lee. "On the Margin: Postmodernism, Ironic History, and Medieval Studies." *Speculum* 65 (1990): 87–108.

———. "The Place of the Modern in the Late Middle Ages." In *The Challenge of Periodization: Old Paradigms and New Perspectives*, ed. Lawrence Besserman, 51–66. New York: Garland, 1996.

Patton, Cindy. *Inventing AIDS*. New York: Routledge, 1990.

Payer, Pierre. "Foucault on Penance and the Shaping of Sexuality." *Studies in Religion* 14 (1985): 313–20.

Pearsall, Derek. *The Life of Geoffrey Chaucer: A Critical Biography*. Oxford: Blackwell, 1992.

Pecock, Reginald. *The Repressor of Over Much Blaming of the Clergy*. Ed. Churchill Babington. Rolls Series. London: Longman, Green, Longman, and Roberts, 1860.

Peikola, Matti. " 'Whom clepist þou trewe pilgrimes?': Lollard Discourse on Pilgrimages in *The Testimony of William Thorpe*." In *Essayes and Explorations: A 'Freundschrift' for Liisa Dahl*, ed. M. Gustafsson, 73–84. Anglicana Turkuensia 15. Turku, Finland: Univ. of Turku, 1996.

Peraldus, William. *Summa aurea de virtutibus et vitiis*. Venice, 1497.

Pfander, H. G. "Some Medieval Manuals of Religious Instruction in England and Observations on Chaucer's Parson's Tale." *Journal of English and Germanic Philology* 35 (1936): 243–58.

Piedra, José. "In Search of the Black Stud." In *Premodern Sexualities*, ed. Louise Fradenburg and Carla Freccero, 23–43. New York: Routledge, 1996.

Poenitentiale Theodori. Ed. Arthur West Haddan and William Stubbs. In *Councils and Ecclesiastical Documents Relating to Great Britain and Ireland*. Oxford: Clarendon, 1871.

Powers, Elizabeth. "The MLA and Conservatives: Letter to the Editor." *MLA Newsletter* 29.2 (Summer 1997): 18.

President's Committee on the Arts and the Humanities. *Creative America: A Report to the President*. Washington, D.C.: Government Printing Office, 1997.

Purity [*Cleanness*]. Ed. Robert J. Menner. Yale Studies in English 61. 1920. Reprint. Hamden, Conn.: Archon, 1970.

Purvey, John. *Remonstrance against Romish Corruptions in the Church*. Ed. J. Forshall. London: Longman, Brown, Green, and Longmans, 1851.

Rich, Frank. "Cheney Dumbs Down." *New York Times*, 26 February 1995, E15.

Richardson, Diane, ed. *Theorizing Heterosexuality: Telling It Straight*. Buckingham, U.K.: Open Univ. Press, 1996.

Richardson, H. G. "Heresy and the Lay Power under Richard II." *English Historical Review* 51 (1936): 1–28.

Rickert, Edith. Letter. *Times Literary Supplement*, 20 October 1932, 761.
Riehle, Wolfgang. *The Middle English Mystics*. Trans. Bernard Standring. London: Routledge and Kegan Paul, 1981.
Riley, Henry Thomas. *Memorials of London and London Life*. London: Longmans, Green, 1868.
Robert of Flamborough. *Liber poenitentialis*. Ed. J. J. Francis Firth. Toronto: Pontifical Institute of Mediaeval Studies, 1971.
Robertson, D. W., Jr. "Some Observations on Method in Literary Studies." 1969. Reprint. In *Essays in Medieval Culture*, 73–84. Princeton: Princeton Univ. Press, 1980.
Robinson, Fred C. "Medieval, the Middle Ages." *Speculum* 59 (1984): 745–56.
Rocke, Michael. *Forbidden Friendships: Homosexuality and Male Culture in Renaissance Florence*. New York: Oxford Univ. Press, 1996.
Rogers, Pat. "Thomas Warton and the Waxing of the Middle Ages." In *Medieval Literature and Antiquities: Studies in Honour of Basil Cottle*, ed. Myra Stokes and T. L. Burton, 175–86. Cambridge: D. S. Brewer, 1987.
Roscoe, Will. "Strange Craft, Strange History, Strange Folks: Cultural Amnesia and the Case for Lesbian and Gay Studies." *American Anthropologist* 97 (1995): 448–53.
Rowland, Beryl. "Animal Imagery and the Pardoner's Abnormality." *Neophilologus* 48 (1964): 56–60.
Rubin, Miri. *Corpus Christi: The Eucharist in Late Medieval Culture*. Cambridge: Cambridge Univ. Press, 1991.
———. "The Eucharist and the Construction of Medieval Identities." In *Culture and History, 1350–1600: Essays on English Communities, Identities, and Writing*, ed. David Aers, 65–90. Detroit: Wayne State University Press, 1992.
Ruggiero, Guido. *The Boundaries of Eros: Sex, Crime and Sexuality in Renaissance Venice*. New York: Oxford Univ. Press, 1985.
Russell, Henry G. "Lollard Opposition to Oaths by Creatures." *American Historical Review* 51 (1946): 668–84.
Russell, Jeffrey Burton. *Satan: The Early Christian Tradition*. Ithaca: Cornell Univ. Press, 1981.
Said, Edward W. "The Problem of Textuality: Two Exemplary Positions." *Critical Inquiry* 4 (1978): 673–714.
Saint Bride and Her Book: Birgitta of Sweden's Revelations. Ed. and trans. Julia Bolton Holloway. Focus Library of Medieval Women. Newburyport, Mass.: Focus, 1992.
Sargent, Michael G. "The Transmission by the English Carthusians of Some Late Medieval Spiritual Writings." *Journal of Ecclesiastical History* 27 (1976): 225–40.

Scanlon, Larry. "Unspeakable Pleasures: Alain de Lille, Sexual Regulation and the Priesthood of Genius." *Romantic Review* 86 (1996): 213–42.

Scase, Wendy. Piers Plowman *and the New Anticlericalism.* Cambridge: Cambridge Univ. Press, 1989.

Scattergood, V. J. "Perkyn Revelour and the *Cook's Tale.*" In *Reading the Past: Essays on Medieval and Renaissance Literature,* 183–91. Portland, Or.: Four Courts Press, 1996.

Schofield, John. *Medieval London Houses.* New Haven: Yale Univ. Press, 1994.

Schor, Naomi. "Dreaming Dissymmetry: Barthes, Foucault, and Sexual Difference." In *Men in Feminism,* ed. Alice Jardine and Paul Smith, 98–110. New York: Methuen, 1987.

Schulman, Sarah. *My American History: Lesbian and Gay Life During the Reagan/Bush Years.* New York: Routledge, 1994.

Scott, Joan W. "The Evidence of Experience." *Critical Inquiry* 17 (1991): 773–97.

Secretum secretorum. Three Prose Versions of the Secreta secretorum. Ed. Robert Steele. EETS e.s. 74. London: Kegan Paul, Trench, Trübner, 1898.

Secretum secretorum: Nine English Versions. Ed. M. A. Manzalaoui. EETS 276. Oxford: Oxford University Press, 1977.

Sedgwick, Eve Kosofsky. "Across Gender, across Sexuality: Willa Cather and Others." *South Atlantic Quarterly* 88 (1989): 53–72.

———. *Epistemology of the Closet.* Berkeley: Univ. of California Press, 1990.

———. "Gender Criticism." *Redrawing the Boundaries: The Transformation of English and American Literary Studies,* ed. Stephen Greenblatt and Giles Gunn, 271–302. New York: MLA, 1992.

———. *Tendencies.* Durham, N.C.: Duke Univ. Press, 1993.

Seneca the Elder. *Declamations:* vol. 1, *Controversiae.* Ed. and trans. M. Winterbottom. Loeb Classical Library. Cambridge, Mass.: Harvard Univ. Press, 1974.

Seven Sages of Rome. Ed. Karl Brunner. EETS 191. London: Oxford Univ. Press, 1933.

Shklar, Ruth Nissé. "Cobham's Daughter: *The Book of Margery Kempe* and the Power of Heterodox Thinking." *Modern Language Quarterly* 56 (1995): 277–304.

———. "Spectacles of Dissent: Heresy, Mysticism and Drama in Late Medieval England." Ph.D. diss., University of California at Berkeley, 1995.

———. "Widows Deliciously Fed: Appetite and Economy in the 1395 *Conclusions* of the Lollards and the *Wife of Bath's Tale.*" Paper presented at the MLA Convention, Chicago, 1995.

Sleep with Me. Dir. Rory Kelly. August Entertainment, 1994.

Solterer, Helen. "Performing Pasts: A Dialogue with Paul Zumthor." In *European Medieval Studies under Fire*, ed. Helen Solterer, 595–640.

———, ed. *European Medieval Studies under Fire, 1919–1945.* Spec. issue of *Journal of Medieval and Early Modern Studies* 27 (1997).

Somerset, Fiona. " 'Mark him wel for he is on of þo': Training the Lay Gaze in the Conclusions, Dymmok's Reply, and Chaucer." Paper presented at the International Congress on Medieval Studies at Kalamazoo, Michigan, 1996.

Spiegel, Gabrielle M. *The Past as Text: The Theory and Practice of Medieval Historiography.* Baltimore: Johns Hopkins Univ. Press, 1997.

Spillers, Hortense. "Interstices: A Small Drama of Words." In *Pleasure and Danger: Exploring Female Sexuality*, ed. Carole S. Vance, 73–100. Boston: Routledge and Kegan Paul, 1984.

Spivak, Gayatri Chakravorty. "Subaltern Studies: Deconstructing Historiography." In *In Other Worlds: Essays in Cultural Politics*, 197–221. New York: Routledge, 1988.

Staley, Lynn. *Margery Kempe's Dissenting Fictions.* University Park: Pennsylvania State Univ. Press, 1994.

Stein, Joel. "The First Frosh." *Time*, 8 December 1997, 112.

Steyn, Marc. "Passing Motions." *The Spectator*, 22 October 1994, 60–61.

Stock, Brian. *Listening for the Text: On the Uses of the Past.* Baltimore: Johns Hopkins Univ. Press, 1990.

Stoler, Ann Laura. *Race and the Education of Desire: Foucault's* History of Sexuality *and the Colonial Order of Things.* Durham, N.C.: Duke Univ. Press, 1995.

Strauss, Barrie Ruth. "Freedom through Renunciation? Women's Voices, Women's Bodies, and the Phallic Order." In *Desire and Discipline: Sex and Sexuality in the Premodern West*, ed. Jacqueline Murray and Konrad Eisenbichler, 245–64. Toronto: University of Toronto Press, 1996.

Strohm, Paul. "Chaucer's Lollard Joke." *Studies in the Age of Chaucer* 17 (1995): 23–42.

———. *Social Chaucer.* Cambridge, Mass.: Harvard Univ. Press, 1989.

———. Summary remarks. "Cultural Frictions" conference, Georgetown Univ., Washington, D.C., October 1995.

Strouse, Jean. "Homosexuality since Rome." *Newsweek*, 29 September 1980, 79–81.

Stryker, Susan. "Introduction." In *The Transgender Issue.* Spec. issue of *GLQ: A Journal of Lesbian and Gay Studies* 4 (1998): 145–58.

Sturges, Robert S. "The Pardoner, Veiled and Unveiled." In *Becoming Male in the Middle Ages*, ed. Jeffrey Jerome Cohen and Bonnie Wheeler, 261–78. New York: Garland, 1997.

Szittya, Penn R. *The Antifraternal Tradition in Medieval Literature.* Princeton: Princeton Univ. Press, 1986.

Talk of the Nation. National Public Radio. 20 March 1997.

Tanner, Norman P. *The Church in Late Medieval Norwich, 1370–1532.* Toronto: Pontifical Institute of Mediaeval Studies, 1984.

———, ed. *Heresy Trials in the Diocese of Norwich, 1428–31.* Camden 4th ser. 20. London: Royal Historical Society, 1977.

Tarantino, Quentin. *From Dusk to Dawn.* Written by Quentin Tarantino. Dir. Robert Rodriguez. Dimension Films/Miramax, 1996.

———. *Natural Born Killers.* Story by Quentin Tarantino. Dir. Oliver Stone. Warner Brothers, 1994.

———. *Pulp Fiction.* Stories by Quentin Tarantino and Roger Avary. Written and dir. Quentin Tarantino. Miramax, 1994.

———. *Pulp Fiction: A Quentin Tarantino Screenplay.* New York: Hyperion, 1994.

———. "Quentin Tarantino on *Pulp Fiction*, as told to Manohla Dargis." *Sight and Sound* (November 1994): 16–19.

———. *Reservoir Dogs.* Written and dir. Quentin Tarantino. Miramax, 1992.

———. *True Romance.* Written by Quentin Tarantino. Dir. Tony Scott. Warner Brothers, 1993.

Tatlock, J. S. P. *Development and Chronology of Chaucer's Works.* Chaucer Society 2nd ser., 37. London: K. Paul, Trench, Trübner, 1907.

Tentler, Thomas. *Sin and Confession on the Eve of the Reformation.* Princeton: Princeton Univ. Press, 1977.

Tertullian. *Adversus Praxean.* In vol. 2 of *Opera.* Corpus christianorum, series latina. Turnhout: Brepols, 1954.

Thomas, A. H., and Philip E. Jones, eds. *Calendar of Plea and Memoranda Rolls Preserved among the Archives of the Corporation of the City of London at the Guildhall.* 6v. Cambridge: Cambridge Univ. Press, 1926–61.

Thomson, Williell R. *The Latin Writings of John Wyclyf: An Annotated Catalog.* Toronto: Pontifical Institute of Mediaeval Studies, 1983.

Todd, James Henthorn, ed. *Apology for Lollard Doctrines.* 1842. Reprint. London: Johnson Reprint, 1968.

Toews, John E. "Intellectual History after the Linguistic Turn: The Autonomy of Meaning and the Irreducibility of Experience." *American Historical Review* 92 (1987): 879–907.

Traub, Valerie. "The (In)Significance of 'Lesbian' Desire in Early Modern England." In *Queering the Renaissance,* ed. Jonathan Goldberg, 62–83. Durham, N.C.: Duke Univ. Press, 1994.

———. "The Psychomorphology of the Clitoris." *GLQ: A Journal of Lesbian and Gay Studies* 2 (1995): 81–113.

Trumbach, Randolph. Review of *Same-Sex Unions in Premodern Europe*, by John Boswell. *Journal of Homosexuality* 30.2 (1995): 111–17.

Tuck, J. Anthony. "Carthusian Monks and Lollard Knights: Religious Attitude at the Court of Richard II." In "Reconstructing Chaucer," *Studies in the Age of Chaucer*, Proceedings, no. 1 (1984), ed. Paul Strohm and Thomas J. Heffernan, 149–61. Knoxville, Tenn.: New Chaucer Society, 1985.

Tuve, Rosemond. *Seasons and Months: Studies in a Tradition of Middle English Poetry*. 1933. Reprint. Cambridge: D. S. Brewer; Totowa, N.J.: Rowman and Littlefield, 1974.

———. "Spring in Chaucer and before Him." *Modern Language Notes* 52 (1937): 9–16.

Vance, Carole S. "Social Construction Theory: Problems in the History of Sexuality." In *Homosexuality, Which Homosexuality? International Conference on Gay and Lesbian Studies*, by Dennis Altman, Carole Vance, Martha Vicinus, Jeffrey Weeks, et al., 13–34. Amsterdam: Uitgeverij An Dekker/Schorer, 1989; London: GMP, 1989.

———, ed. *Pleasure and Danger: Exploring Female Sexuality*. Boston: Routledge and Kegan Paul, 1984.

Vasta, Edward. "Chaucer, Gower, and the Unknown Minstrel: The Literary Liberation of the Loathly Lady." *Exemplaria* 7 (1995): 395–418.

Walker, Paulette V. "Facing Cuts, Arts and Humanities Agencies Seek Private Funds." *Chronicle of Higher Education*, 16 February 1996, A31.

Wallace, David. *Chaucerian Polity: Absolutist Lineages and Associational Forms in England and Italy*. Stanford: Stanford Univ. Press, 1997.

Waller, James C. "'A Man in a Cassock Is Wearing a Skirt': Margaretta Bowers and the Psychoanalytic Treatment of Gay Clergy." *GLQ: A Journal of Lesbian and Gay Studies* 4 (1998): 1–15.

Waller, Marguerite. "Academic Tootsie: The Denial of Difference and the Difference It Makes." *diacritics* 17 (1987): 2–20.

Walsingham, Thomas. *Annales Ricardi Secundi*. Ed. Henry Thomas Riley. Rolls Series. London: Longmans, Green, Reader, and Dyer, 1866.

———. *Historia anglicana*. 2 vols. Ed. Henry Thomas Riley. Rolls Series. London, 1864. Reprint. New York: Kraus Reprint, 1965.

Walter of Henley and Other Treatises on Estate Management and Accounting. Ed. Dorothea Oschinsky. Oxford: Clarendon, 1971.

Warner, Michael. "Normal and Normaller: Beyond Gay Marriage." *GLQ: A Journal of Lesbian and Gay Studies* 5 (1999): 119–71.

Warren, Steve. "Gay 'Top Gun'? A Talk with Tarantino." San Francisco *Sentinel*, 12 October 1994, 33.

Watson, Nicholas. "Desire for the Past: Reflections on the Study of Medieval Religion." *Studies in the Age of Chaucer* 21 (forthcoming 1999).

Weeks, Jeffrey. *Invented Moralities: Sexual Values in an Age of Uncertainty.* New York: Columbia Univ. Press, 1995.

Weissman, Hope Phyllis. "Margery Kempe in Jerusalem: *Hysterica Compassio* in the Late Middle Ages." In *Acts of Interpretation: The Text in Its Contexts, 700–1600,* ed. Mary J. Carruthers and Elizabeth D. Kirk, 201–17. Norman, Okla.: Pilgrim Books, 1982.

Wenzel, Siegfried. "Chaucer's Pardoner and His Relics." *Studies in the Age of Chaucer* 11 (1989): 37–41.

Weston, Kath. *Families We Choose: Lesbians, Gays, Kinship.* New York: Columbia Univ. Press, 1991.

White, Hayden. *The Content of the Form: Narrative Discourse and Historical Representation.* Baltimore: Johns Hopkins Univ. Press, 1987.

Wilentz, Sean. Review of *History on Trial: Culture Wars and the Teaching of the Past,* by Gary B. Nash, Charlotte Crabtree, and Ross E. Dunn. *New York Times Book Review,* 30 November 1997, 28, 31.

Willis, Sharon. "The Fathers Watch the Boys' Room." *Camera Obscura* 32 (1993–94): 40–73.

Wilson, John K. "The Academy Speaks Back." Rev. of *PC Wars: Politics and Theory in the Academy,* ed. by Jeffrey Williams; *Higher Education under Fire: Politics, Economics, and the Crisis of the Humanities,* ed. by Michael Bérubé and Cary Nelson; and *After Political Correctness: The Humanities and Society in the 1990s,* ed. by Christopher Newfield and Ronald Strickland. *Democratic Culture* 4.1 (Spring 1995): 29.

———. *The Myth of Political Correctness: The Conservative Attack on Higher Education.* Durham, N.C.: Duke Univ. Press, 1995.

———. "Razing the National History Standards." *Democratic Culture* 4.1 (Spring 1995): 5–9.

Winkler, John J. *The Constraints of Desire: The Anthropology of Sex and Gender in Ancient Greece.* New York: Routledge, 1990.

Woo, Elaine. "Standards for Teaching History Unveiled—Again." *Los Angeles Times,* 13 April 1996, A1, A16.

Wood, Robin. "Slick Shtick." In "Pulp the Hype: On the Q.T." *Artforum* (March 1995): 62–66, 110.

Woodford, William. *Responsiones contra Wiclevum et Lollardos.* Ed. Eric Doyle. *Franciscan Studies* 43 (1983): 17–187.

Wordsworth, Ann. "Derrida and Foucault: Writing the History of Historicity." In *Post-Structuralism and the Question of History,* ed. Derek Attridge, Geoff Bennington, and Robert Young, 116–25. Cambridge: Cambridge Univ. Press, 1987.

Wright, Thomas. *Political Poems and Songs.* 2 vols. Rolls Series. London: Longman, Green, Longman, and Roberts, 1859–61.

Wunderli, Richard M. *London Church Courts and Society on the Eve of the Reformation.* Cambridge, Mass.: Medieval Academy of America, 1981.

Wyclif, John. [*see also* Arnold, Thomas, and Matthew, F. D.] *De simonia*. Ed. Sigmund Herzberg-Fränkel and Michael Henry Dziewicki. Wyclif Society. London: Trübner, 1898.

———. *On Simony*. Trans. Terrence A. McVeigh. New York: Fordham Univ. Press, 1992.

———. *Opus evangelicum*. 4 vols. Ed. Johann Loserth. Wyclif Society. London: Trübner, 1896.

Zimmerman, Bonnie, and Toni A. H. McNaron, eds. *The New Lesbian Studies: Into the Twentieth Century*. New York: Feminist Press of CUNY, 1996.

Žižek, Slavoj. *The Sublime Object of Ideology*. New York: Verso, 1989.

Zumthor, Paul. *Speaking of the Middle Ages*. Trans. Sarah White. Lincoln: Univ. of Nebraska Press, 1986.

Index

Carolyn Dinshaw is Professor of English and Director of the Center for the Study of Gender and Sexuality at New York University. She previously taught at the University of California, Berkeley. She is the author of *Chaucer's Sexual Poetics* and is editor (with David M. Halperin) of *GLQ: A Journal of Lesbian and Gay Studies.*

Library of Congress Cataloging-in-Publication Data

Dinshaw, Carolyn.
Getting medieval : sexualities and communities,
pre- and postmodern / Carolyn Dinshaw.
p. cm. — (Series Q)
Includes bibliographical references and index.
ISBN 0-8223-2330-3 (cloth : alk. paper). — ISBN 0-8223-2365-6
(pbk. : alk. paper)
1. Sex—History. 2. Homosexuality—History. 3. Gay communities—History. 4. Sex in literature. 5. Homosexuality in literature. 6. Literature, Medieval. 7. Civilization, Medieval. I. Title. II. Series.
HQ14.D56 1999
306.7'09—dc21 98-32015